D0152804

BIOGRAPHICAL DICTIONARY OF CONTEMPORARY CATHOLIC AMERICAN WRITING

BIOGRAPHICAL DICTIONARY
OF CONTEMPORARY
CATHOLIC AMERICAN WRITING

Edited by
Daniel J. Tynan

GREENWOOD PRESS
New York • Westport, Connecticut • London

Library of Congress Cataloging-in-Publication Data

Biographical dictionary of contemporary Catholic American writing /
edited by Daniel J. Tynan.
   p. cm.
   Bibliography: p.
   Includes index.
   ISBN 0–313–24585–1 (lib. bdg. : alk. paper)
   1. American literature—Catholic authors—Bio-bibliography.
2. American literature—Catholic authors—Dictionaries. 3. American
literature—20th century—Bio-bibliography. 4. American
literature—20th century—Dictionaries. 5. Authors, American—20th
century—Biography—Dictionaries. 6. Catholic authors—Biography—
Dictionaries. 7. Catholic literature—Bio-bibliography.
8. Catholic literature—Dictionaries. I. Tynan, Daniel J.
PS153.C3B5   1989
016.81′09′9222—dc19   88–38488

British Library Cataloguing in Publication Data is available.

Copyright © 1989 by Daniel J. Tynan

All rights reserved. No portion of this book may be
reproduced, by any process or technique, without the
express written consent of the publisher.

Library of Congress Catalog Card Number: 88–38488
ISBN: 0–313–24585–1

First published in 1989

Greenwood Press, Inc.
88 Post Road West, Westport, Connecticut   06881

Printed in the United States of America

The paper used in this book complies with the
Permanent Paper Standard issued by the National
Information Standards Organization (Z39.48–1984).

10 9 8 7 6 5 4 3 2 1

For my parents, Martha Murphy Tynan (1903–1983) and Joseph Francis Tynan (1900–1987): they knew the trials and consolations of keeping the Faith.

CONTENTS

PREFACE

This volume contains 135 biographical-critical essays on a representative group of contemporary Catholic American poets, dramatists, and fiction writers. Not since the publication of Matthew Hoehn's *Catholic Authors: Contemporary Biographical Sketches, 1930–1947* (New York: J. J. Little and Ives, Co., 1948; reprint, Detroit: Gale Research, 1981) has such an inventory of Catholic American writers appeared.

Although I had originally intended to make this volume an all-inclusive survey, I soon made three important discoveries: first, there are a lot of Catholic writers out there, both well-known and undiscovered; second, these writers write a lot; and third, remarkably, there aren't yet enough scholars around to evaluate the large resource of unexamined texts. Consequently, this volume does not pretend to inclusiveness, but rather to representativeness. I apologize at the start to any writers who feel, perhaps justly, that they too have earned a place in the dictionary.

Notably unrepresented in the text are Hispanic American writers. Greenwood Press published *Chicano Literature: A Reference Guide* in 1985 and has underway a biographical dictionary of other Hispanic writers in the United States. Rather than duplicate the research and materials contained in these two volumes, I have included an essay by Professor Genaro Padilla which examines the place of Catholicism in the work of these important writers.

Overall, then, I see this biographical dictionary as a starting point; first, for more research on the authors contained in this volume; second, for continued reflection on the many forms of contemporary Catholic American writing; third, for the unearthing of still more Catholic American writers; and, finally, for renewed scholarly interest in some excellent and often neglected literary texts.

A note on the bibliographies: while the "Works By" bibliographies contain virtually all fiction, poetry, drama, and, in some cases, non-fiction works by the authors, the "Works About" bibliographies are limited to five critical essays or, where none exists, book reviews plus references to other biographical sources. The general biographical sources are indicated by the codes noted below; numbers following these abbreviations refer to volume numbers, with the exception of *Catholic Authors* in which case the number in parentheses refers to the date of publication.

AW	*American Writers: A Collection of Literary Biographies*. Ed. Leonard Ungar. New York: Scribner's, 1959–1974.
AWS	*American Writers: A Collection of Literary Biographies: Supplement II*. Ed. Leonard Ungar. New York: Scribner's, 1974–1981.
AWW	*American Women Writers*. Ed. Lina Mainiero. New York: St. Martin's Press, 1979–1981.
CA	*Contemporary Authors*. Detroit: Gale Research, 1962–Present.
CANR	*Contemporary Authors. New Revision Series*. Detroit: Gale Research, 1981–Present.
Cat A (1947)	*Catholic Authors: Contemporary Biographical Sketches, 1930–1947*. Ed. Matthew Hoehn. Newark, N.J.: St. Mary's Abbey, 1948.
Cat A (1952)	*Catholic Authors: Contemporary Biographical Sketches, 1930–1947*. Ed. Matthew Hoehn. Newark, N.J.: St. Mary's Abbey, 1952.
CD	*Contemporary Dramatists*. Fourth Edition. Ed. D. L. Kirkpatrick. London: St. James Press; New York: St. Martin's Press, 1987.
CN	*Contemporary Novelists*. Second Edition. Ed. James Vinson and D. L. Kirkpatrick. New York: St. Martin's Press, 1986.
DLB	*Dictionary of Literary Biography*. Detroit: Gale Research, 1978–Present.
TCA	*Twentieth Century Authors: A Biographical Dictionary of Modern Literature. First Supplement*. Ed. Stanley J. Kunitz and Howard Haycraft. New York: The H. W. Wilson Co., 1955.

ACKNOWLEDGMENTS

Many people have helped nurse this project toward its birth. I would like to thank especially Dean Glenn Brooks and the Research and Development Board at Colorado College for providing time free of all teaching duties to carry out portions of the research, writing, and editing. The Paul Sheffer Memorial Fund for Roman Catholic Studies administered by the Religion Department at Colorado College supported a month's continuing work once the project was launched. For various kinds of encouragement, I would like to thank Professor George Butte, Chairperson of the English Department at Colorado College; for insightful comments on my writing, my colleagues Professors John Longo and Thomas Mauch; and for good judgment and good leads, Professor Victor Nelson-Cisneros.

The Reference Librarians at Tutt Library of Colorado College searched for sources and answered my questions, no matter how naive; Diane Brodersen patiently sorted through a myriad of interlibrary loan requests, and Head Librarian John Sheridan told good, funny stories on many a dreary day among the stacks.

Finally, unique thanks to my wife, Nancy, whose infinite patience and mild disposition tolerated the many moods of this sometimes cranky writer and editor.

INTRODUCTION

In some ways, it is difficult to say how all of the writers represented in this volume can be called Catholic writers. Some of them were born and raised Catholics and continue to call themselves practicing Catholics, and, like David Plante, they may even write autobiographical novels about their Roman Catholic upbringing; others, like Christopher Durang, were born and raised Catholics but left the Church at some point; still others, like Mary Gordon, consider themselves practicing Catholics but express criticism of certain Church rules and make exceptions in their own lives to the application of those rules; others, like John Gregory Dunne, left the Church but still refer to themselves as cultural Catholics—or at least they could be called such whether they like it or not. Then there are those who, like Caroline Gordon and Allen Tate, converted to Catholicism and remained Catholics until their deaths; still others, like Robert Lowell, who converted to Catholicism but subsequently left the Church. As writers, some, like J. F. Powers and Brother Jonathan Ringkamp, deal almost exclusively with Catholic experiences or with issues like celibacy and birth control as they affect the lives of Catholics. On the other hand, Robert Olen Butler writes about subjects that do not seem to be directly linked to Catholicism, whereas Eugene O'Neill wrote about experiences both Catholic and secular. And each writer may express one or a multitude of attitudes toward Catholicism, ranging, even within one work, from reverence to revulsion. In any case, it is safe to say that the writers represented in this volume constitute a wide spectrum of contemporary Catholic American experience.

What do they have in common? Put simply, at some time in their lives— whether at birth, near death, or in between—they were all baptized Catholics. This means that whether or not they have accepted Catholicism as the permanent organizing value and belief system in their lives and in their imaginations, they all are likely to at least share a concern for the impact of a Catholic vision of the world upon them. They all professed belief, if only for a brief period in their lives, in the central dogmas of Roman Catholicism: that God sent down His Son to redeem humanity and that Jesus was crucified, died, was buried, and on the third day rose again from the dead. His Church continues into the present day and celebrates the central reality of Catholicism: the mystery of Christ's presence in the Eucharist. The perpetuation of the Church in this world also relies on an acceptance of the supreme authority of the Pope as the direct descendant of St. Peter.

Beyond a belief in these basic tenets, there may be little else that holds these writers together as a coherent group. In fact, it is easier to say what they share as American writers than what they share as Catholic writers. For example, in their tendency to express dissatisfaction with the ideals and practices of the Roman Catholic Church, many of these writers tap into a traditionally American stream of dissent which goes back to seventeenth-century Puritan writing.

But for the moment, let us try to narrow the definition of Catholic writing. For example, is there a uniquely Catholic view of contemporary experience? Does it have something to do with the primary force which shapes the imagination? If so, how do we talk about that? Critic Albert Sonnenfeld in *Crossroads: Essays on the Catholic Novelists* (York, South Carolina: French Literature Publications Co., 1982) argues that there really is something called the Catholic novel: it is, he says, "a novel written by a Catholic, using Catholicism as his informing mythopoeic structure or generative symbolic system and where the principal and decisive issue is the salvation or damnation of the hero or heroine" (p. vii). Flannery O'Connor also proves helpful in this regard. In *Mystery and Manners: Occasional Prose* (selected and edited by Sally and Robert Fitzgerald, New York: Farrar, Straus and Giroux, 1969), O'Connor insists over and over again that any writer, especially the fiction writer, must be true to the concrete realities of the visible world, "to the truth of what can happen in life. . . . If I had to say what a 'Catholic novel' is, I could only say that it is one that represents reality adequately as we see it manifested in this world of things and human relationships" (p. 172).

At the same time, O'Connor insists that "I see from the standpoint of Christian orthodoxy. This means that for me the meaning of life is centered in our Redemption by Christ and what I see in the world I see in its relation to that" (p. 32). According to O'Connor, the Catholic writer must acknowledge that the sacrament of the Eucharist relives the mystery of Christ's incarnation and death for humanity's sins. This proves that natural reality itself can be sacramental. Says O'Connor: "the natural world contains the supernatural. And this doesn't mean that [the Christian novelist's] obligation to portray the natural is less; it means it is greater" (p. 175). Thus the Catholic writer will usually see reality with two perspectives—one focusing on the supernatural and the other on the natural—and these two ways of viewing remain always in conflict. Indeed, for O'Connor, they must remain in conflict if the writer is to remain true to his or her calling. That is, it is too tempting for the devout writer to turn his or her writing over to the service of theology or dogma, sacrificing fidelity to the realities of the natural world.

O'Connor's injunction that the writer view reality with two sets of eyes holds implications for the writers represented in this volume in at least two ways: First, the writer may find that the doctrines of the Church in their eternal dimensions come into conflict with the personal beliefs of the writer and certainly with the world of nature—meaning not simply the world of trees and animals, but the world of human institutions. Second, the writer may find not only that his or her own beliefs conflict with Church teaching, but also that aesthetic choices may conflict with the earthly authority of the Church, especially when the writer's methods involve the creation of sexually explicit scenes or with the symbolic embodiment of the supernatural within the natural.

O'Connor's formulation of the dilemma of the Catholic writer provides some terms in which to consider the variety of Catholic experiences represented in these writers. For example, certain Catholic writers believe in the central mystery of Christ's Incarnation and the ritual reenactment of the Incarnation within the Sacrament of the Eucharist, but they refuse to accept unequivocally Papal infallibility or canon law. To put it another way, Catholic writers may insist on the freedom to explore with one eye the conflict among the abstractions, the laws, the traditions of the church, and the concrete reality of flawed human beings struggling to do their best in a fallen world.

The reluctance or the willingness to accept the authority of Rome takes many forms, but it is probably no more striking than in questions involving sexual behavior. Whether the issue is birth control, abortion, surrogate parenting, celibacy, sexual relationships outside or within marriage, masturbation, or homosexuality, the Church's attempts to impose limitations on sexual behavior stir intense feelings on all sides. The former priest James Kavanaugh shows in both his novels—one of which is entitled *The Celibates*—that sexual feelings constitute a normal part of human relationships, whether in the laity or in the clergy, male or female. Kavanaugh insists that sexual feelings and actions among nuns and priests will not interfere with the responsibilities of a religious vocation; furthermore, in at least one instance, Kavanaugh suggests that emotional relationships between priests—whether sexual or not—and intensely emotional, asexual relationships between priests and women can actually augment the priest's power by helping him to understand more profoundly the dilemmas faced by most of his parishioners.

The well-known and controversial novelist Father Andrew Greeley strongly defends the explicit portrayal of sexual relationships in his own works. In "Fiction and the Religious Imagination" (*America*, April 6, 1985), Greeley argues that fiction writing extends his ministry to spread Church teachings and to carry forward the Church's heritage into the modern world. Applying his professional skills as a sociologist to examine reader reaction to his own novels, Greeley demonstrates that readers who accept and even approve of his sexually explicit writing also tend to hold a more beneficent image of God—as mother, lover, or friend. Perhaps even more importantly, Greeley argues that religion originates in experiences that renew our hope and that these experiences find expression in narratives that help others to understand the same experiences. Thus, telling a story with sexually explicit scenes may actually excite in readers not so much a sensual response to forbidden acts as a religious response to the sacramental nature of God's love.

Even though Greeley's position troubles some Church leaders, it does help accommodate the conflict between the spiritual and the earthly which troubles a writer like James Kavanaugh. In a sense, Greeley shares Flannery O'Connor's sentiments about Catholic writing, for O'Connor holds that in a secular world which has turned a deaf ear to spirituality, it becomes necessary to shock dulled sensibilities into recognizing anew the efficacy of salvific manifestations of the supernatural in our lives. In other words, what O'Connor achieves through the use of violence and the grotesque, Greeley achieves in his novels through the use of sex.

Furthermore, Greeley's finding makes it clear that the rights of individual Catholics to express themselves sexually in a variety of ways, both inside and outside of marriage, raises more than the moral question of the Church's right to invade the privacy of Catholic bedrooms. The question ultimately comes down to the relationship between theological and psychological values. By refusing to accept human frailty, the Church's theological rigidity drives characters to choose suicide in Kavanaugh's novels. However, the theological and psychological need not always conflict. As Greeley's fiction shows, emotional expression brings self-realization without violating sacramental theology. In fact, sexual expression teaches, by analogy, of God's loving choice to express Himself, as it were, in natural creation, through the sacraments.

Fascinated by sacramental mysteries, Catholic writers sometimes explore the power of sacraments to impart grace. For example, Harry Sylvester in his novel *Dayspring* creates as his main character professor of anthropology Robert Bain who converts to Catholicism in order to study the cultural patterns of New Mexican Penitentes. He views his own baptism with the detachment appropriate to a scientist but finds himself—in spite of himself—succumbing to a genuine belief in Catholicism. As Sylvester would see it, the surprising strength of Bain's unwanted faith attests to the efficacy of baptism to mark an errant soul as belonging to the Mystical Body of Christ.

On the other hand, sacramental manifestations need not always fall within Church definitions. In Flannery O'Connor's "Good Country People," the divinity manifests itself in Hulga's life through the perverted attentions of Manly Pointer, the demented Bible salesman. It hardly seems appropriate to call the action of his taking Hulga's leg a sacramental act in the same way that Bain's baptism is, but it nonetheless reveals the workings of the supernatural within the natural, and it opens for Hulga, as baptism does for Bain, at least the possibility of eternal salvation.

If O'Connor and Greeley agree about the sacramental revelation of divine mystery in the natural world, she would differ most from him in her insistence on the trials and adversities which faith must endure. It is painful to be gracefull in O'Connor's fictional world, as the Grandmother discovers in "A Good Man Is Hard to Find." O'Connor believes that it is too easy to mollycoddle the spiritual sensibility, and it would be misleading to conclude that all of the writers represented here believe that Rome should have no authority over even the most intimate behaviors of the faithful. While Kavanaugh and others might argue that the authoritarianism of Rome crushes the human capacity for compassion, O'Connor points out that compassion can sometimes mean nothing more than a kind of psychological "Instant Uplift," although she herself accepts the meaning of compassion as "a suffering-with . . . which blunts no edges and makes no excuses" (*Mystery and Manners*, p. 166). Moreover, many of the writers do not seem to be concerned with Rome's power in their lives; they may have decided, like Eugene O'Neill, who resolved the question at the age of fifteen, that it is not worth expending any creative energies on the issue, or, like Walker Percy or Caroline Gordon, that to be Catholic includes accepting—not challenging—the traditional and infallible role played by popes throughout history.

However, the conflict between the psychological and the theological surfaces in less than explicit ways. For example, what characters could be more guilt-ridden than those of Eugene O'Neill, who said that unless we understood that he was Irish, we could not understand his work? In this case, to be Irish means to be Irish-Catholic. The psychological effects of guilt as a consequence of sin characteristically come under close and painful scrutiny in writers like Christopher Durang, John Gregory Dunne, Mary Gordon, and others. Often it is useful for these writers to see that sin is a willful offense not necessarily against God, but against a set of abstract rules embodied in canon law.

One of the best representatives of those writers who remain staunchly Catholic but faithful to representing life in the real world—as O'Connor demands of the Catholic novelist—is Walker Percy. With close attention to detail, to the observed fact and event, Percy keeps his worldly eye fixed on the life around him. At the same time, he creates characters—usually male—who find in the sameness of their everyday lives the crisis which can lead them to resist the emptiness of the modern world and to search for another way to salvation. In *Love Among the Ruins*, Dr. Thomas More resists the pragmatists who would use his lapsometer to improve the human condition. Turning away from the seductiveness of pride and of facile technological humanistic answers to complex dilemmas deeply rooted in human nature, Percy confronts instead the ancient questions of self-identity and the meaning of life. As Alfred Kazin has said, Percy is a "pilgrim of faith who believes that there is a true way, a lost tradition, that he will yet discover" ("The Pilgrimage of Walker Percy," *Harpers*, June, 1971, p. 84). This, in spite of the fact that Percy acknowledges, through his character Dr. Thomas More—descendant of Saint Thomas More—that all utopian visions ultimately collapse into ruin.

Humanity is fallen, but individuals must also take responsibility for their moral choices. Percy's characters drift toward a moment in their lives when they are suddenly struck with an acute sense of who they are, of how they are engaged in the world. Still, they are journeyers, always searching, observing, questioning, resisting the suction into the abyss at the very core of Western man.

If Walker Percy represents those Catholics who can find in their faith and its traditions hard answers to the problems of modern life, Christopher Durang exemplifies the rebellious Catholics who have written their anger into their works. His controversial play *Sister Mary Ignatius Explains It All for You* bitterly attacks Church authority in the figure of Sr. Mary Ignatius. Although the play starts off as a humorous satire on the easy catechetical answers which Sr. Mary Ignatius offers to complex moral problems, it ends up grimly in fatal violence when Sr. Mary Ignatius appears to shoot her former students who have returned to tell her that her answers have not brought meaning into their lives.

Not only does the content of the play attack the Church, but so does its structure. The first part of the play relies largely on the catechetical forms which organize moral teachings for grade-school and high-school aged students in Catholic schools, and which embody and foster a certain mentality: neat, arbitrary, absolute, self-contained, simplistic. When Sr. Mary Ignatius finally resorts to violence as the only way of handling skeptical and rebellious, but well-meaning Catholics, she reveals the failure of catechetical structures to reconcile life in the religion class with life in the real world. For Durang, the Church has no humane response to feelings of doubt and despair, and so the play reveals and attacks the institutional insensitivity of the Church to the humanity of the faithful. Beyond the secure constraints of the catechism, there is only violence. If you cannot accept my teachings, or worse yet, if you challenge them, Sr. Mary Ignatius seems to say, then die.

Even though Durang may have rejected Roman Catholicism, he relies, like James Joyce in the "Ithaca" section of *Ulysses*, on the definitions, the issues, and even the structures of Church teaching in order to shape his work—at least *Sister Mary Ignatius*. Durang is like other Catholic writers including John Gregory Dunne who have also left the Church but who consider themselves to be cultural Catholics; in this sense, they remain Catholic writers. Dunne finds in his Catholic background—especially in its memorable characters and moral ambiguities—the stuff from which to make his imaginative world.

Like Durang and Dunne, Mary Gordon has mined the unsettled terrain of modern Catholicism for her three novels. *Final Payments* and *The Company of Women* might be called Catholic novels because, if nothing else, their action follows the familiar Catholic pattern of sin-repentance-redemption in which only good works can bring salvation. *Men and Angels*, however, seems more a feminist novel which probes the conflict between roles for Anne Foster who struggles to realize herself both within and outside of her marriage. At the same time, the novel takes on a theological dimension as Anne, like Isabel in *Final Payments*, tries to love an unlovable woman, in this case, Laura Post, her housekeeper and babysitter. And when the unlovable Laura commits suicide, Anne tortures herself with guilt, wondering if she might have done something more, if Laura's death were not a result of Anne's failure of charity. Her real understanding of Laura's pain and its causes, however, comes when she learns that Laura's own mother had never loved her daughter. Anne is shocked and terrified at this violation of a mother's contract. Hate replaces love, and this explains why Laura could never be lovable: because she had never been loved by her own mother, she would never know how to love anyone. Ironically, Laura, the religious fanatic, cannot take comfort from the Biblical message that all people are beloved of God. Indeed, for most human beings, love of God provides inadequate sustenance for life in the world, since, as Anne's friend Jane tells her, "The love of God means nothing to a heart that is starved for human love."

Anne's life will never be the same because of her contact with Laura Post. Anne has learned that she is incapable of loving an unlovable person; she has learned what the failure of parental love leads to; she has learned that the worst can always happen in life—no one is ever really safe in the world, nothing is ever really assured, especially not the life of a child. But the main lesson of the novel seems to be that Anne must nurture and express her own maternal feelings, that she must truly love her own children. As crucial as this message is and as much as it conforms to the message of John's Gospel, it may not have as much to do with a Catholic vision of existence as it does with sound psychological principles of child development. It is as though Gordon has turned her back on Catholicism, though she is really only facing away from Catholicism and meeting the secular world, moving beyond the environment and people who nurtured and inspired her earlier novels.

In his relationship to the world as a Catholic novelist, Robert Olen Butler picks up, in a sense, where Mary Gordon leaves off. Butler turns his eyes away from any peculiarly Catholic material into the psychological and political realities of contemporary America. Three of his novels deal with the lives of Vietnam veterans and a fourth fictionalizes the relationships between characters involved in the development of the atomic bomb in 1944. The third work in the Vietnam trilogy, *On Distant Ground*, may be his best work. It traces several weeks in the life of David Fleming as he is court-martialed for aiding the enemy. Even though it is true that David freed Tuyen, a Viet Cong intelligence operative and prisoner of war, his offense is not what it appears to be, even though his actions may be defined within the terms of the army's criminal code. Outside of that code, however, David's action saved the life of a fellow human being and so, in a sense, brought out the best in David.

But that is only half the story. When David sees the television news accounts of the children of American soldiers and Vietnamese women returning to the states, he becomes convinced that he has a child by a Vietnamese woman with whom he has had a two-month-long affair. Although now married and a father, David decides that he must return to Vietnam as Saigon is falling and rescue

his son. His failure to go would constitute David's real crime, a kind of Hawthornian violation of the human heart through abandonment. David achieves his
goal, but only with the aid of Tuyen who is now director of security for the
Communist government in Saigon. The title of the novel refers to the land David
must travel in order to find his son. But even more significantly, it refers to the
stance David has always taken in his relationships: somewhat aloof, always on
distant ground. When David goes to Saigon, he takes responsibility for his
Vietnamese son and feels for the first time in his life real human connection. In
the end, he finds a set of values to replace those of the battlefield. Commitment
to wife and family not only brings comfort but becomes for David a moral act.

In this way, Butler explores the nature of morality in the modern world.
David's journey to Saigon in the closing days of the war becomes a psychological
journey in which he explores his motivations for freeing the prisoner, as well
as his feeling of spiritual and emotional emptiness. When David finds his son
in Saigon and learns that the boy's mother is dead, he decides to bring the boy
back to the United States. But, to his horror, David responds without feeling to
the first sight of his boy who bears the Oriental features of his mother and looks
nothing like David. It is only through an act of moral will that David can take
responsibility for the boy's well-being.

The point of this discussion of Butler's novel is that there is nothing particularly
Catholic about it, either explicitly or implicitly. This is especially ironic because
Butler has said that the older he gets, the more religious he becomes. In a larger
sense, Butler shares the same concerns as other Catholic American writers in
that he wants to find out what is really important about life: he wants to understand
himself, the world, and God. He wants to know if God could actually become
manifest in the vicious, ugly, spiritual hell of the Vietnam War.

And so the writers represented in this volume speak in a wide range of Catholic
voices from the self-consciously Catholic like Flannery O'Connor, Walker Percy,
and Andrew Greeley, to the embittered cultural Catholic like Christopher Durang,
to the silently Catholic like Robert Olen Butler. But they are all in some ways
both Catholic and American, and it is worth spending a little time examining
the ways in which these writers fit into the large landscape of contemporary
American writing. In particular, their conflicts and compulsions originate in the
chasm between dream and reality, ideal and real, in a familiarly American way.

The American Dream may be hard to define, but it is possible to recognize
some of its elements by looking at writers who lived centuries apart: Benjamin
Franklin and F. Scott Fitzgerald. The Dream involves characters in the sweep
of changing circumstances, usually moving them upward—at least for a while—
like Ben Franklin and Jay Gat[z]sby from rags to riches. The move is possible,
the conditions improve because the United States system of democratic politics
and capitalist economics supposedly opens up the corridors of power and money
for all people, regardless of color, religion, or country of origin. Whether on
the frontier with Natty Bumppo, on the plantation with Frederick Douglass, or

on the stump with Frank Skeffington, American men and women (in literature and in life) apparently expect to make happy and successful lives for themselves.

Unfortunately, this dream fails to come true for many Americans who struggle in their jobs for a fulfillment which their material purchases can never provide. For all the glitz of his parties, the lavishness of his mansion and clothes, Jay Gatsby finds a moment of peace only when he believes he has recaptured through his love for Daisy a sense of wholeness which occurred, ironically, *before* he bought his way into the high society of West Egg. Gatsby's elusive American Dream turns ashen when Daisy kills Myrtle Wilson in the Ash Heaps between Long Island and Manhattan; the dream turns deadly as Gatsby's blood warms the autumn waters of his perfect swimming pool.

No American dramatist portrays the world of the shattered American Dream better than Eugene O'Neill in *The Iceman Cometh*. Taking comfort in their booze and the proximity of other warm bodies, the defeated characters in Harry Hope's Bar epitomize the price paid for investing in ephemeral realities. Americans believe they can accomplish whatever they want, achieve both a modicum of material comfort from jobs and also a degree of emotional sustenance from their family life. But for O'Neill's characters, there is little difference between dreams and delusions. The glad-handing, optimistic drummer Hickey tries to convert the others to his gospel of success, but he pays the ultimate price for his self-delusion. It is only after the boozers in the bar recognize that Hickey's message of self-realization is in itself another delusion of happiness that they can return to the relative peace and predictability of their sodden lives. Although the solution of alcohol and pipe dreams will probably lead to self-destruction rather than to self-realization, it nevertheless offers these men their only comfort in a setting which has become an American nightmare.

Anglo-American writers have always needed to confront this gap between the ideal and the real. Puritans came to this land because they believed that their ideals of religious faith needed purifying from the corruption of a worldly church. The framers of the Constitution knew that even though all people might have been created with a right to the fulfillment of an American Dream, these same people needed a system of government which would maintain order in the nation. In other words, we must account for the gap between the ideal of a perfect system of government and the reality of a fallen human community. Hawthorne understood what the failure to live up to the ideals of religious life could do to a soul; Dimmesdale's guilt saps his vigor and marks his breast indelibly—or so report those in Salem who supposedly saw the mark.

Disillusionment with old ideals characterizes many American writers during the first half of the twentieth century. In the face of the waste wrought by World War I, Ernest Hemingway turned his pen to the concrete sensuous world because the world of metaphysical abstractions like love, courage, and patriotism was rendered absurd by the muck and cold and gas of the trenches. T. S. Eliot's waste land has become a cliché for the meaningless, barren environment in which spiritually hollow travellers, alienated from themselves, other people and their surroundings, search for some sense of connection and value. Eliot's poem decries the values which Jake Barnes and his merry pranksters seem to hold, but it also bemoans the loss of traditional values and the value of tradition.

In the years since World War II, a central image for the human condition comes from Thomas Pynchon's story "Entropy." All individuating energy will ultimately dissipate into a kind of universal broth at which point all life will cease. Pynchon's Oedipa Maas finds herself trapped within a system of semiotic clues which seem to lead ultimately to nowhere. Where is there a place of spiritual recourse, a rock to offer shadow from the relentless sun? It seems a long way that the nation has come from the paradigm of Franklin's life of worldly accomplishment. But we sense the despair of the moment only because we can remember the promise of putting into harbor on Cape Cod or struggling to find the right words for a declaration of independence in Philadelphia, or staking a claim for gold in Cripple Creek. American writers have always in some sense been writers of dissent because they have read the space between our culturally expressed values of religious freedom, equality, and happiness for all, and the reality of witch-hunting, racism, and the misery of the homeless. Walt Whitman could create the embodiment of a new American spirit in the language of the people because he knew that the ideal of the American self was expressed not only in the Declaration of Independence but also in the daily activities of the farmers, prostitutes, and mechanics. Like so many American authors, he wanted to put the nation back on track, and so, like so many American authors, he was a writer of dissent.

In this way at least, contemporary Catholic American writers of all stripes and colors flow into the mainstream of American writing. Flannery O'Connor and Walker Percy dissent from the consensus of worldliness which they see as defining the age; Christopher Durang dissents from the simplistic rules of canon law which guide the Church on her daily rounds. In all three cases, criticism of and dissent from the status quo impels the pen to act like Whitman's or Fitzgerald's or O'Neill's and to get things back on track. Catholic writers want to reestablish confidence in the crucial rather than the peripheral Catholic teachings, to sort out the difference between essential supernatural truths and accidental canon law. But like Whitman, they have a sense of an ideal system and they want to reshape, revitalize, and live within that system.

Whitman believed in the spiritual nature of the flesh and so he exalted the body and all materiality. Although some Catholic American writers might not see with Whitman's vision, they might envy Whitman's poetic sacramental marriage of natural and supernatural—a marriage which confuses Catholic writers who cannot accept the Church's intrusions into their worldly lives but who will accept the teachings of Christ's gospel of eternal love. Like Laura Post in Mary Gordon's *Men and Angels*, most of us need more than only the warm comforts of human love and less than only the cold consolation of Divine Love.

The conflict between the worldly and the spiritual which characterizes so much contemporary Catholic American writing cannot be resolved. The history of the Catholic Church and its commitment to both spiritual power and worldly authority attests to the results of the conflict: bloody wars, insensitive clergy, martyrdom, the peace of Christ, compassion, the affirmation of life. The contradictory nature of the Catholic experience finds expression in the wide range of voices represented in this volume. Their Catholicism sometimes defines their creative work, sometimes enriches and expands it, sometimes even limits it; but idealistic and hopeful at its core, their Catholicism always makes their work a part of American literature, often at its best.

BIOGRAPHICAL DICTIONARY
OF CONTEMPORARY
CATHOLIC AMERICAN WRITING

THE CATHOLIC CHURCH IN CHICANO LITERATURE

Genaro M. Padilla

It has been a commonplace to think of Chicanos and Catholicism in the same breath. Indeed, there are Hispanics who practice other faiths, but of the 52 million Catholics in the United States some 20 million are Hispanic, and most of these—about 12 million—are Mexican Americans.* The rituals, beliefs, and ideology of Catholicism itself are deeply embedded in Mexican culture; they may even be said to reside at the center of much cultural practice. Yet, Catholic doctrine and especially the Church itself occupy a shaky place in nearly all Chicano literature written during the last thirty years. This apparent incongruity between literary and cultural practice raises pressing questions about literary representation and religious affiliation. How can it be that the devotion to the Catholic faith discovered again and again in Hispano-Mexicano literary practice—whether oral or textual—during the four centuries preceding the twentieth should so abruptly undergo the kind of transformation it has in the contemporary period? Why is it that recent Chicano writers as a group have set themselves into an oppositional literary camp against the Catholic Church and its doctrine? Where are the sources of this literary renunciation? The situation of course is historically complex.

It would be reductive, first of all, and not a little idealized to imagine that before the middle of this century, Hispanos were a simple, devoted people who accepted the doctrines and policies of the Catholic Church with unquestioned obeisance. Chronicle accounts and legends of the Spanish exploration and settlement of the Americas include numerous tales of confrontation between the clergy and soldiers, but also between the priests and the lay community. In his autobiographical narrative, "Recuerdos históricos y personales tocante a la Alta California" (1875), Mariano G. Vallejo remembers being excommunicated along

*The terms Mexican American, Chicano, Hispano, and even Mexicano are used in this chapter to refer to that group of people of Mexican descent. Such is done in everyday discourse.

with two friends for three days in 1831 by Padre Estenga for reading "Rousseau, Voltaire, and several other books of anti-Catholic feeling." Vallejo records the event in comic tone, but from other narrative references to his relations with the Church it is apparent that he remained a recalcitrant "free thinker."

Yet, notwithstanding the example of Vallejo's flirtation with schism and historical evidence of other more serious tensions between the Church and the community, Mexican Americans have remained devout practitioners of the faith, as their literature and daily ritual have proven. The sacraments of baptism, communion, and marriage, Sunday and Holy Day mass, Christmas and Lenten devotions, as well as the solemn rituals attending death have all occupied a central place in cultural practice for centuries. The ceremony surrounding these religious events often provided the occasion for dramatic productions, as well as for composing and transmitting sacred ballads, allegorical tales, and religious verse, phrases, and sayings. These practices pervaded everyday life and settled into a pattern of religious literary consciousness that was manifested in both oral and textual forms.

Folk drama in the Mexican Southwest has traditionally had religious content and purpose. *Adán y Eva*, a dramatization of Genesis, was performed as early as 1598 in New Mexico, and together with *Los Pastores* (*The Shepherds*) and *Los Tres Magos* (*The Three Wise Men*) during Christmas, and Passion plays during the Lenten season have all continued to be staged for the last 400 years. This liturgical drama depicting the creation of man and the fall, the birth of Christ, and the redemption was performed in churches, in homes, or on village streets by members of the community. In fact, since it was the case that many villages had no priest, religious performances often took the place of Midnight Mass or Easter services.

Such attention to the spiritual life of the community displayed itself in numerous devotional semiliterary practices that pervaded the entire life experience as well. Baptism, for example, the occasion for simultaneous induction into the Church and the community, provided the occasion for verse exchange. Upon completion of baptism, a child's godparents returned the child to her or his parents with the words:

> Recíba esta prenda amada, (Receive this lovely jewel),
> Que de la iglesia salio (Who has just left the Church)
> Con lós sántos sacramentos (Blessed with the holy sacraments)
> Y él agua que recibío. (And the holy water bestowed.)

At other points in the life cycle, similarly appropriate ritual verse bound individuals to the Church and its community. Coextensive with wedding vows repeated in Church, young couples, in New Mexico at least, often knelt before a *poeta* to hear and take to heart "*La entriega*," a long and formal "Wedding Song," in which the solemnity and indissolubility of the marriage were enjoined upon them:

En el medio de la iglesia, (At the altar in the Church)
el sacerdote decía, (the priest said to both,)
que se case estos dos ("Let these two be married)
como San José y María. (Just like Mary and St. Joseph.")

El padre le preguntó (The father then asked them,)
si quieren casarse, dí ("If you wish to marry, say")
y la iglesia los oyó (Whereupon all in the church)
que los dos dijieron, sí. (heard them both answer, "Yes.")

At the end of life, the deceased was sent off to his or her heavenly home (presumably) accompanied by the singing of *alabados*, or sacred hymns. In fact, it would have been extremely rare for anyone from adolescence to old age not to carry a full repertoire of *alabados* and scores of prayer verse in his or her memory for instant recitation, not only for wakes but during the Lenten season and for daily meditation.

Such devotional habits of mind found expression in more textual ways as well. Although the staging of folk plays, the singing of *alabados*, and the relating of *cuentos morales*, or morality tales, have often been considered evidence of an enduring and even singular oral tradition in Mexican culture, the fact is that poetry and fiction were published extensively in newspapers throughout the nineteenth and early twentieth centuries. Much of this literature was devotional. Along with political verse, satire, love lyrics, and encomiums, newspapers in Los Angeles, San Francisco, and Santa Barbara in California, as well as those in San Antonio, Texas, and Las Vegas, New Mexico, to name only a few, regularly published well-sustained religious poetry with such titles as "*A la Religion*" (in *El Clamor Publico*, Los Angeles, August 7, 1855), "*La Madre de Dios*" (in *La Gaceta*, Santa Barbara, January 10, 1880), "*Adios: A la Santisima Virgen de Guadalupe*" (in *La Voz del Pueblo*, Las Vegas, New Mexico, 1897).

One of these early poems, "*Las hermanas de caridad*" (in *El Clamor Publico*, 1857) praises the selfless work of the "Sisters of Charity" in a manner that priests and nuns are hardly likely to receive in recent Chicano literature. Here one of the nuns, imaged as "*un angel humano*," appears to a suffering beggar:

Nadie tiene quien alivie (He has no one to alleviate)
Males que va padeciendo (The evils he is suffering)
Y en la muerte está creyendo (And so wonders if in death)
Terminara tanto mal. (He can end, at last his torment.)

Mas, sus ojos de repente (But, suddenly his eyes brighten)
Toman señales de agrado: (Reflecting a new joy)
. . .
Veamos; un angel humano (See! A human angel)
Se le acerca con ternura, (Approaches him tenderly,)
Y cuidados sin mensura (And compassionately offers)
Le ofrece su compasion. (To care for him ceaselessly.)

These sisters, who give their lives to the poor and destitute, are, the poet declares, "Muy propriamente llamadas/'Hermanas de Caridad' " (So appropriately named/'The Sisters of Charity').

In this century, as we shall see, the literary representation of the clergy has shifted from general respect to disdain. Moreover, the literature itself has almost entirely become secularized, and in the work of many of the best known Chicano writers has assumed a tenor of religious skepticism that alienates it from Church and doctrine both. It is in the period just before World War II and thereafter that we discover a writer whose own ideological evolution may be regarded as a prefiguration of, and participation in, a discourse that questions the Church's historical relations with the Mexican American.

Fray Angélico Chavez (b. 1910), a Franciscan priest, is the best, and perhaps the last, exemplar of devotional poetry written by a Hispano. Most of Chavez's poetry is steeped in a meditative tradition that praises God, Christ, the Blessed Mother, and the angels and saints in Heaven, all the while rejoicing in his desire to shun the world and yet questioning his capacity to sing with a throat "Filled up with sand," as he writes in "Carmen Deo Nostro," a poem that appears in his first collection of verse, *Clothed with the Sun* (Santa Fe: Writers Editions, 1939). Subsequent verse collections—*Eleven Lady Lyrics and Other Poems* (Paterson, N.J.: St. Anthony Guild Press, 1945), *The Single Rose* (Santa Fe: Los Santos Bookshop, 1948), *The Virgin of Port Lligat* (Fresno, Calif.: Academy Literary Guild, 1959), and his *Selected Poems with an Apologia* (Santa Fe: Press of the Territorian, 1969)—each reaffirmed Chavez's steadfast Catholic sensibility. *The Single Rose* and *The Virgin of Port Lligat* are both long, meditative reflections on the problem of man's relationship to God in the modern scientific world, and especially, as in the case of *The Virgin of Port Lligat*, a world in which the metaphysical seems confounded by nuclear physics, but only until the poet discovers a religious metaphor in molecular fission that undergirds rather than disrupts faith.

Fray Angélico's historical studies, published prodigiously over a span of four decades, focus squarely upon the institutional formation of the Catholic Church in New Mexico. *Our Lady of the Conquest* (Albuquerque: University of New Mexico Press, 1948), *Missions of New Mexico* (Albuquerque: University of New Mexico Press, 1956), *Archives of the Archdiocese of Santa Fe, 1678–1900* (Washington, D.C.: Academy of American Franciscan History, 1957), *Coronado's Friars* (Washington, D.C.: Academy of American Franciscan History, 1968), *The Oroz Codex* (Washington, D.C.: Academy of American Franciscan History, 1972) established Chavez's reputation as a consummate Church archivist and regional historian. More recently, however, his church-related historical writing has taken on a culturally and politically revisionist turn. In *But Time and Chance: The Story of Padre Martínez of Taos* (Santa Fe: William Gannon, 1981) and *Trés Macho He Said: Padre Gallegos of Albuquerque* (1985), Fray Angélico has argued forcefully for the vindication of two New Mexican priests who were excommunicated for political rather than ecclesiastical reasons by Archbishop Jean-Baptiste Lamy in the late 1850s. Chavez's misgivings about the Americanization of the Mexican-Catholic Church in the Southwest, however, did not develop only in the last decade. Although Chavez has sustained a faithful Christian vision in his writing, much of his short fiction stories collected in *New Mexico Triptych* (Paterson, N.J.: St. Anthony Guild Press, 1940) and *From an Altar Screen: El Retablo* (New York: Farrar, Straus, Cudahy, 1957) contain subtle denunciations of the French and Irish clerical disdain for Mexican religious customs and folkart—wood-carved statues called "santos" and paintings called "retablos" that adorned village church altars.

Chavez's critique of ethnocentrically motivated Church policies against the Mexican clergy and the suppression of distinct Mexican-Catholic religious practices during the century after the American conquest (1846–1848) was so assiduously uncompromising and opposed to certain Anglo historiographers, the likes of Paul Horgan whose *Lamy of Santa Fe* (1975) had won the Pulitzer Prize, that neither was accepted by any of the presses that had earlier welcomed his work. His last two books were published with the help of Fray Angélico Chavez's supporters who believed that his work is meritorious no matter how much it disrupts the normal ethnocentric flow of cultural or Church history.

Fray Angélico Chavez's ideological evolution from the meditative poetry of his early career to his more recent interrogatory and revisionist writing marks a significant turn toward a sensibility no longer satisfied to accept Church fiat. If such oppositional voicing emerges in a Franciscan, one can imagine the voice non-clerical writers will assume in questioning the Church, the clergy, and the social consequences of Church doctrine. There is just no getting around the fact that in the contemporary period—roughly from 1960 to the present—Chicano writers have openly lashed out against the clergy, have attacked the institutional policies of the Church for disregarding the community's material needs, and have vigorously challenged such Catholic doctrine as a soul-withering force that has expedited the social suppression of Chicanos. José Antonio Villarreal, Tomás Rivera, Rudolfo Anaya, Rolando Hinojosa, and Oscar Zeta Acosta, among the prose writers; Ricardo Sánchez, Bernice Zamora, Alma Villanueva, and Alurista, among the poets; and Luis Valdez, Estella Portillo-Trambley, and Denise Chavez in the theater, are all Chicano authors whose work has been regarded seriously during the last three decades. In the work of nearly all, the Catholic Church in the Chicano experience has been severely scrutinized.

The alienation from the Church and the deep skepticism that mark recent Chicano literature have their basis in the unreconciled tensions between an authoritarian Church and the community it should serve. Material history, as it were, has caught up with the Church in Chicano literature. The Church's alignment with the dominant class has been found out and exposed. The conflict between the landless poor and the Church in Mexico, for instance, that peaked during the Revolution of 1910 and that became a major theme in much post-Revolution literature is also embedded in much Chicano narrative that discovers a doctrine of complicity with social suppression in the spiritual teachings of the Church.

Moreover, it seems to me the same modernist sensibility appears in other American, and, I might add, Irish and French literary texts—another major source of religious skepticism. One might say that the modern period has made it all but impossible for philosophically and ideologically sensitive writers from any culture to affirm doctrinal faith with much, if any, conviction. Hence, schooled in European, North American, and Latin American intellectual movements, contemporary Chicano writers work within a discursive formation that has hardened against traditional Church teaching.

These two influences, one largely textual, the other socio-historically particular, intersect with recurrent Church/community antagonisms to produce a discourse of religious skepticism, alienation, and anti-clericism. Although it may be said that most Mexican Americans still identify themselves as practicing Catholics who sustain a filiopious relationship with the Church, Chicano writers reject any part of such filiopiety and, I would argue, now participate in a wider discourse of religious skepticism that coincides with that in other modern and post-modern literary texts.

Fifty-six years after Father Arnall blasted the fear of God's eternal vengeance into Stephen Dedalus and his fellow catechumens in *A Portrait of the Artist as a Young Man*, Father Byrnes, an Irish priest posted in a village in central New Mexico, repeats the performance in Rudolfo Anaya's *Bless Me, Ultima* (Berkeley, Calif.: Quinto Sol, 1972). This time the protagonist is Antonio Marez, a sensitive boy of eight years who wants to "learn the mysteries of God" and whose mother, like Stephen's, imagines him becoming a priest. Voicing the same metaphor of the sparrow carrying one grain of sand across a wide ocean, Father Byrnes forces a shudder from the village children as he images eternity and damnation:

"It would never finish," June shook her head sadly. "Just in a bucket of sand there must be a million grains, and to move that would take thousands of years. But to move the whole mountain of sand—." She ended her sentence in despair. . . .

"Is that how long eternity is?" Agnes asked bravely. "Is that how long the souls have to burn?"

"No," Father Byrnes said softly and we looked to him for help, but instead he finished by saying, "when the little bird has moved that mountain of sand across the ocean, this is only the first day of eternity."

We gasped and fell back in our seats, shuddering at the thought of spending eternity in hell. (Anaya 193–94)

Such priests and their minions, the various and usually nameless nuns and lay do-gooders who make life miserable for young Chicano characters, have provided a rich, if predictable, comic field for satirizing harsh doctrine and clerical myopia. Most of the clergy who inhabit Chicano novels are of a type. Whether priests or nuns, they are almost always caricatured as creatures whose sexual repression results in severe frustration which in turn evinces cranky behavior, contorted facial expressions, meanness, spiritual threats, and confessional excesses.

In José Antonio Villarreal's *Pocho* (Garden City, N.Y.: Doubleday, 1959), the priest who hears the young Richard's first and subsequent confessions is quite literally an aural voyeur. When we first see Richard, he is nine years old, has just made his first Holy Confession, and is filled with questions about God's attributes, His mysterious presence in the universe, and especially about the nature of sin. But, as he relates his initiatory experience to his mother, Richard is confounded by the priest's questions: "He asked me if I like to play with myself, and I said yes, and he was angry. . . . He asked also if I sometimes play with Luz. You yourself make me play with her, so I answered yes. Then he wanted to know if I ever touch her, and I said I do, and he was angrier" (Villareal 35). This early realization is crucial to his inexorable movement away from the Church. In fact, when he is a teenager, Richard knowingly taunts the priest during confession with his lurid masturbatory images, the gravest of which is imagining what "Sister Mary Joseph looked like if she took off all those clothes— even if she only changed to a regular dress" (Villarreal 115).

Villarreal's mock tone in such episodes, however, is balanced by a more serious examination of doctrinal uncertainty in Richard's developing conscious-ness. The clergy is criticized for their reluctance, or perhaps their inability, to engage Richard's theological curiosity. Richard, for instance, discovers that no one, least of all the clergy, is willing to answer his brooding questions: "I asked the sister in Catechism, and she looked stern and . . . the priest told me there are some things we are not to ask, but just believe" (Villarreal 85). It is just such clerical disdain that serves Villarreal's narrative disclosure, in *Pocho* and much more extensively in his novel of the Mexican Revolution, *The Fifth Horseman* (Garden City, N.Y.: Doubleday, 1972), of the socially inimical role played by the Church in Mexican culture. Richard's father, Juan Rubio, one day responds to the boy's questions about his antipathy for the clergy by telling him that in pre-Revolutionary Mexico it was common for priests to betray the sanctity of the confessional:

When someone broke into one of the [hacienda] warehouses to steal some corn or beans to feed his family, the priest would arrive, hear confession, and hold Mass. Then the landowner had a fiesta for him, and he would leave. The next morning, the man who had taken the food would be found hanging from a mesquite. (Villarreal 100)

By the time he is eighteen, Richard is convinced that priests are little more than self-serving hypocrites, that the Church is historically aligned with the rich, and that the candles his mother lights to Heaven are useless.

Much like Richard, the unnamed boy in Tomás Rivera's novela " *. . . y no se lo trago la tierra*" [" *. . . and the earth did not part*"] (Berkeley, Calif.: Quinto Sol, 1971) steadily moves away from intimidating doctrine to outright rejection of a God who does nothing to ameliorate his family's wretched socioeconomic condition. The boy's doubts, like those of Antonio and Richard, begin when he is preparing for his first communion. The catechism lessons he recites conjure absurd notions of sin, especially the "number and kinds of sins and the circum-stances which change their nature." And like the priest in *Pocho*, the catechetical nun seems most interested in ferreting out sins of the flesh. Such hazing achieves its desired result; the boy decides to confess hundreds of sins: "I'd better confess

200, and that way no matter how many I forget I won't commit sacrilege . . . and the Commandments . . . against all Ten Commandments . . . the more sins I confess to, the purer my soul will be" (Rivera 61).

In the title chapter, the boy, older, less intimidable, and increasingly angry with the privation his family is made to endure as migrant workers, openly questions a God "who doesn't give a damn about us poor people." One day his father suffers sunstroke that nearly kills him. His mother lights candles and prays, and the boy wonders:

"What does Mother gain by doing that? Why is it we are here on earth as though buried alive? Either the germs eat us from the inside or the sun from the outside . . . one day unexpectedly he is felled by the sun. And powerless to do anything. And to top it off, praying to God. God doesn't even remember us. . . . There must not be a God. . . . No, better not say it, what if father should worsen?" (Rivera 50–51)

But when his little brother is also felled by sunstroke, there is no retraction when he cries out in despair and rage:

. . . he said what he had been wanting to say for a long time. He cursed God. For a split second he saw the earth open up to devour him. But, although he didn't look down, he then felt himself walking on very solid ground; *it was harder than he had ever felt it.* (Rivera 55)

This moment of recognition that the social conditions endured by his family are not ordained, that God is either absent from human affairs or at least absent from doctrinal metaphors promising heavenly rewards to those who are exploited, poor, displaced here on earth, signifies the turn toward a form of self-empowerment that leads to social change.

For contemporary Chicano writers, then, any affirmation of doctrine that seems inextricably linked to the historical suppression of the community is anathema. This oppositional strategy is at its best in the literature that fully explores the socio-ideological underpinnings of doctrine and Church policy, and, I would suggest, less thoughtful when the clergy is summarily caricatured as in Oscar Acosta's lampoon of Cardinal McIntyre in *The Revolt of the Cockroach People* (New York: Bantam, 1973), Luis Valdez's buffoonish Church fathers in El Teatro Campesino productions, or Rudolfo Anaya's Father Cayo in *Heart of Aztlan* (Berkeley, Calif.: Editorial Justa, 1976), who nearly chokes on his own bile when he hysterically lashes out at members of the community who try to enlist his support for a strike.

The Church and especially the clergy provide an easy literary target, but a people's questions about faith itself are more difficult to dismiss. The failed candles and silent churches in which the only answer to one's prayers is "the whistling of the wind filling the empty space" (Anaya, *Bless Me, Ultima*) that accrue in Chicano literature provide a resounding metaphor of spiritual desire and frustration that best signifies the Chicano writer's ontological uncertainty. Even when faith seems intact, when the sacraments of the Church are administered by sympathetic clergy, uncertainty and despair often prevail. In Estella

Portillo-Trambley's play *The Day of the Swallows* (1971), for example, the parish priest, Father Prado, proves to be sensitive and caring, even after he has heard Josefa, the main character, confess her long lesbian relationship with Alysea. Josefa, however, guilt ridden and disconsolate, commits suicide by drowning. The Church, the sacraments, a caring priest simply fail. It is too late for the ministrations of "un angel humano."

To be fair, and honest, one would have to say that the great majority of Mexican Americans—mostly working class—remain self-identifiably Catholic, while the influential, but still small intellectual class, which includes our best writers, participate in a discourse of skepticism and renunciation that generally characterizes modern literature and thought. The result, it seems, is that no one can any longer be solaced or saved by the Church in contemporary Chicano literature.

THE WRITERS

B

MARGARET BANNING (1891–1982). Margaret (Culkin) Banning was born in Minnesota, often the setting for her novels and stories. She was educated in Duluth schools and at Vassar College. She entered social work upon graduation and traveled extensively, including trips to Russia and to London as a delegate to the Atlantic Congress in 1959. Banning wrote over thirty volumes, predominately novels, and contributed hundreds of articles and stories to leading popular magazines. In addition, she lectured throughout the country on American life, her travels, and international problems.

Banning's novels can be divided roughly into two types: those with theological themes and those with social themes. The theological novels present the characters in terms of their responses to such issues as abortion, religious conversion, religiously mixed marriages, and loss of religious faith. Representative of these novels are *Fallen Away* (loss of religious faith, 1951); *The Convert* (conversion to Catholicism, 1957); *The Vine and the Olive* (abortion, 1964); and *Lifeboat Number Two* (priestly vows, 1971). The social novels present the impact of social issues on the characters, particularly women: *The Dowry* (a woman combines marriage and a career, 1954); *The Iron Will* (a woman's resolute stand against a legal ruling, 1936); *The Will of Magda Townsend* (a late middle-aged writer's efforts to retain independence and integrity, 1974); and *The Splendid Torments* (corruption in Washington, D.C. politics, 1976). The theological novels are superficial. The characters, confronted with serious theological issues, are never deeply touched though they quote Catholic teaching as though they had memorized but never quite understood the Church fathers. The social novels are no more penetrating than the theological though Banning had been a social worker and had traveled extensively throughout the United States.

Though she wrote extensively and found a wide reading audience, Banning rarely exhibited a mastery of techniques in fiction. From the earliest novels to the last, the characters remain the same. The admirable male characters are invariably tall, lean, often tanned, intelligent in a placid way, educated in the "right" schools. The admirable female characters are just as invariably slender, beautiful, vibrant, and poised. Even when they pass into and beyond middle age they retain these characteristics, mellowed but unmistakable. Further, Banning rendered little attention to the fine techniques of narrative literature: character development, narrative points of view, patterns of imagery, syntactic style, climaxes, and convincing resolutions. Often, as in *Lifeboat Number Two*, she tried to balance multiple plots without a firm grip on the function of the omniscient narrator.

Banning wrote about a world of elegant people who dined at their clubs; ate grapes and cheese for dessert; worried about stocks and bonds; sustained romantic, candlelight marriages in big, expensive, old houses with servants; and carried on torpid, meaningless love affairs. If she ever saw poverty and pain, she relentlessly prevented their entrance to her pages. Her journal of a trip through South America (*Salud! A South American Journal*, 1941) is devoid of any significant reference to the poor, the uneducated, the laboring class. If she ever witnessed earthy humor, perceived the irony of existence, or realized the degree to which people both endured and enjoyed their lives, she ignored them when she wrote. If she is to be remembered it will be because she tirelessly simplified ideas for readers of the slick magazines and achieved popularity through characters and plots which were invariably romantic.

SELECTED BIBLIOGRAPHY

Works by Banning: *The Iron Will*. New York: Harper, 1936; *Salud. A South American Journal*. New York: Harper, 1941; *Fallen Away*. New York: Harper, 1951; *The Dowry*. New York: Harper, 1954; *The Convert*. New York: Harper, 1957; *The Vine and the Olive*. New York: Harper, 1964; *Lifeboat Number Two*. New York: Harper, 1971; *The Will of Magda Townsend*. New York: Harper, 1974; *The Splendid Torments*. New York: Harper, 1976.

Works about Banning: CA 1; CANR 4.

Frank L. Ryan

MARION ELVERA BENASUTTI (1908–). A versatile writer of short stories, magazine features, book reviews, and newspaper articles, Benasutti is the author of a widely acclaimed book, *No SteadyJob for Papa*, her story of growing up in an Italian immigrant family. In this novel, she endows her lively narrative skills with a "smiling-through-the-tears" nostalgia.

Mrs. Benasutti was born in Philadelphia, and after living some six years in a small western Pennsylvania mining town, her family moved back to Philadelphia, where she attended public schools and Temple University. She was married to Frank Benasutti (deceased) and bore him two children, Noel and Frank. She has been the editor of various publications, the recipient of numerous awards for literary excellence, and a member of many writers', women's, and religious organizations. Mrs. Benasutti is perhaps best known for *No SteadyJob for Papa*, published in 1966, with subsequent multiple U.S. and foreign printings, including a German paperback in 1973. She brings to her work a disarming innocence, which is enhanced by her shrewd powers of observation and a depth of religious feeling. The book was recorded by the American Association for the Blind and has been used in ethnic studies in Philadelphia schools.

SELECTED BIBLIOGRAPHY

Works by Benasutti: *No Steady Job for Papa.* New York: The Vanguard Press, 1966.
Works about Benasutti: "Review of *No Steady Job for Papa.*" *Kirkus Reviews* (1 October 1966), p. 1067. CA 21–22.

Robert M. Sebastian

DANIEL BERRIGAN, SJ (1921–). Poet, playwright, and author of many prose works, Daniel Berrigan is also a radical priest who has served time in prison because of his anti-war activism. His literary honors include the Lamont Poetry Award for *Time without Number* (1957) and the Frederick Melcher Award for his prose work *The Dark Night of Resistance*, which also received the Thomas More Medal for the most distinguished work of Catholic literature of 1971. *False Gods, Real Men* (1969), a collection of poems (some written during Berrigan's 1968 peace mission to Hanoi), was nominated for a National Book Award. Both Berrigan's literary works and his political activism spring from a profoundly religious nature that seeks the voice of Jesus in history.

Daniel Berrigan, born on May 9, 1921, in Virginia, Minnesota, is the fifth of the six children of Thomas and Frieda Berrigan. After socialist activities cost Thomas Berrigan his job as a railroad engineer, the family moved to a farm in Syracuse, New York. In 1939 Daniel Berrigan began to study for the priesthood with the Society of Jesus. Sent to France in 1953, he was, as he put it, "radicalized" by worker priests he met there. Upon his return to the United States, he taught at the Jesuits' Brooklyn Preparatory School and then from 1957 to 1963 at Le Moyne College in Syracuse. In addition to teaching, he was writing and working among the poor.

In the mid–1960s, Berrigan was teaching at Cornell University and playing a leading role in the opposition to the war in Vietnam. With his younger brother, Philip, and seven other protestors, he destroyed draft records in Catonsville, Maryland in May 1968. This act and its consequences became the subject of Berrigan's play entitled *The Trial of the Catonsville Nine* (1970), which has been performed around the United States and abroad. When it opened in 1971, Berrigan was in the federal prison at Danbury, Connecticut. After serving eighteen months of his three-year sentence, he was released on parole.

Since the end of the Vietnam War, Berrigan's political activism has been directed against U.S. involvement in Central America and the nuclear arms race. In 1981 he and others were convicted of breaking into the General Electric Company in King of Prussia, Pennsylvania. To protest the manufacture of nuclear weapons there, they damaged missile nose cones and poured blood on equipment and documents. For these acts, Berrigan was sentenced to from three to ten years in prison. He is currently appealing.

In prison and out, Berrigan has been a prolific writer. Major themes in his poetry and prose are the attempt to create the kingdom of God on earth, the divinity in man that should make it possible, and guilt over humanity's short-comings and the imperfect condition of the world. "The Face of Christ," for example, begins: "The tragic beauty of the face of Christ" will shine in the face of all humans, especially those abandoned without comfort (from *The World for Wedding Ring*, 1962). In *Lights on in the House of the Dead* (1974), his prison diary, he writes, "I believe with all my crooked heart that we are guilty as a nation of unutterable crimes against humanity." Sometimes he uses the term "innocence" ironically to express moral blindness to one's guilt. In his poem "The Pilots Released," which appears in both *Night Flight to Hanoi* (1968) and *False Gods, Real Men*, Berrigan describes the mental and spiritual state of the Americans who flew bombers over North Vietnam. Berrigan saw the effects of American bombs and napalm: "We saw a picture of the pitiful, crisped remains of a woman, burned to a twisted black remnant . . . ." He describes the captured American airmen as innocent instruments of atrocity.

Berrigan's poetry is free verse, unrhymed and without a fixed poetic rhythm. He often puts content before form, but in his best work, he fits one to the other admirably. He takes his images from his faith, from scripture, and from the world around him. In *Encounters* (1960), he presents a series of monologues by Biblical characters. One of the best of these is "Abraham," which explores the mystery and terror of the Biblical story.

The main flaw in Berrigan's poetry is that it is sometimes too propagandistic, too shrill, such as one of his *Prison Poems*, "You Could Make a Song of It A Dirge of It A Heartbreaker of It." Nevertheless, there are many poems that express Berrigan's anger and despair with a controlled passion and a sure sense of imagery. His most purely political work, the verse play *The Trial of the Catonsville Nine*, may be his most enduring—as a record of a dark time in American history, as a work of art, and as an affirmation of the duty to follow conscience when it clashes with established law.

SELECTED BIBLIOGRAPHY

Works by Berrigan: *Time Without Number.* New York: Macmillan, 1957; *Encounters.* Cleveland: World, 1960; *The World for Wedding Ring: Poems.* New York: Macmillan, 1962; *No One Walks Waters: New Poems.* New York: Macmillan, 1966; *Love, Love at the End: Parables, Prayers, and Meditations.* New York: Macmillan, 1968; *Night Flight to Hanoi.* New York: Macmillan, 1968; *False Gods, Real Men.* New York: Macmillan, 1969; *No Bars to Manhood.* Garden City, N.Y.: Doubleday, 1970; *The Trial of the Catonsville Nine.* Boston: Beacon, 1970; *The Dark Night of Resistance.* Garden City, N.Y.: Doubleday, 1971; *America Is Hard to Find.* Garden City, N.Y.: Doubleday, 1972; *Jesus Christ.* Garden City, N.Y.: Doubleday, 1973; *Prison Poems.* Greensboro, N.C.: Unicorn Press, 1973; *Selected and New Poems.* Garden City, N.Y.: Doubleday, 1973; *Lights on in the House of the Dead: A Prison Diary.* Garden City, N.Y.: Doubleday, 1974; *Uncommon Prayer: A Book of Psalms.* Seabury Press, 1978; *The Discipline of the Mountain: Dante's Purgatorio in a Nuclear World* [a translation with commentary]. San Francisco, CA.: Seabury Press, 1979; *We Die before We Live: Talking with the Very Ill.*

San Francisco, CA.: Seabury Press, 1980; *Steadfastness of the Saints: A Journal of Peace and War in Central and North America*. Maryknoll, N.Y.: Orbis Books, 1985; *The Mission: A Film Journal*. New York: Harper & Row, 1986; *To Dwell in Peace*. New York: Harper & Row, 1987.

Works about Berrigan: Casey, William Van Etten, and Philip Nobile (eds). *The Berrigans*. New York: Avon, 1971 [articles from the January 1971 issue of *Holy Cross Quarterly*]; Gray, Francine Du Plessix. *Divine Disobedience: Profiles in Catholic Radicalism*. New York: Alfred Knopf, 1970 [the article on the Berrigans is an expansion of one that appeared in the *New Yorker*, 9 April 1970]; Kiefer, Rita Brady. "The 'Fragile Unkillable Flower' of Daniel Berrigan's Poetry." *Christian Century* 93 (24 November 1976), pp. 1038–42, 1047. CA 33–36. DLB 5. CANR 11.

Laraine R. Fergenson

TED BERRIGAN (1934–1983). Twelve years younger than Jack Kerouac,* Ted Berrigan could be called a camp follower of the Beat Generation. To do so, however, would be to link him by implication with Walt Whitman, Allen Ginsberg, and the open road, whereas the most commonly acknowledged influences in Berrigan's work are Apollinaire, Thomas Wolfe, Frank O'Hara,* John Ashbery, Paul Blackburn, and Kenneth Koch. In a poem like "Tambourine Life" there are echoes of Ezra Pound's *Cantos* and Charles Olson's *Maximus*. Typical of Berrigan's poetry is the playful typography, the sense that semichaotic form attempts to do justice to immensely chaotic life. Berrigan's poetry has little in it that is memorable or distinct—it seems to dismiss these criteria for art in favor of spontaneity and process—yet he is also not to be entirely ignored. If his experiments in form produce few successful poems, they nevertheless remain, a kind of vigor at one of literature's outposts.

Born Edmund Joseph Michael Berrigan, Jr., in Providence, Rhode Island, a town and a life he escaped by joining the army in 1954, he received his B.A. at the University of Tulsa in 1959, took an M.A. there in 1962, and then moved to New York City. There Berrigan edited an influential small magazine, *C*, and used the press to put out his most significant volume of poems, *The Sonnets*, in 1964. Berrigan made his living by teaching, first at the St. Marks Art Project, then at the University of Iowa and Northwestern University. He was married to and divorced from Sandra Alper; with his second wife, Alice Notley, he had three children. Before his death at the age of thirty-eight, Berrigan saw the publication of his collected poems, *So Going Around Cities* (1980), the title of which comes from John Ashbery, and a novel, *Clear the Range* (1977).

Although his career was to some extent fostered by the academy, Berrigan would have preferred a more bohemian label. He greatly admired painters, wrote criticism for *Art News*, and compared his poetic methods to the paintings of William de Kooning. Equations of poetry with painting are, however, specious, as Frank O'Hara admitted in his poem, "Why I Am Not A Painter." Berrigan's art is verbal; it can partake of the community through syntax, or attempt an individual expressiveness via the asyntactic. For the most part, Berrigan's poetry is syntactic and comprehensible; in fact, it is too often marred by cliché or otherwise unexceptional diction. Critics have had a difficult time coming to grips with an output that ranges from viable experiment (*The Sonnets*) to generic Beat sentiment ("Under The Southern Cross"). Gilbert Sorrentino called *The Sonnets* "a notable book" and *Living with Chris* unreviewable "puff" ("Ten Pamphlets", 60). In the same mainstream poetry publication *Poetry* a few years earlier, Marvin Bell was noncommittal or respectfully baffled. Hayden Carruth was one of the first and best mainstream critics to confront Berrigan's work. Four years after their publication, Carruth found in *The Sonnets* a knowledgeable hermeticism. Carruth ingeniously worked out Berrigan's complicated method of line arrangement, and he gave it Apollinaire's appellation "collage." By rereading these poems with Carruth's guidance, one can discover the resuscitated voices of youthful modernism.

In fact, Berrigan did nothing new. Virtually every experiment he attempted had been done twenty years before his birth, and he seems to have known that this was true. His novel, *Clear the Range*, is of a genre perfected by Tom Robbins, though Berrigan's book is darker and never quite comes alive.

In the Summer 1968 issue of *The Paris Review*, Berrigan (along with Aram Saroyan and Duncan McNaughton) interviewed a dissolute and monomaniacal Jack Kerouac. The subject's performance was pathetic, yet Berrigan and his friends remained worshipful in their questioning: "You've written about Buddha. Wasn't Jesus a great guy too?" This is almost as close as Berrigan ever gets to religion in his work. Instead, the spirituality that inhabits it is ideological and countercultural. In Berrigan's work there is no wrestling over scripture and authority; there is only the formal process of composition and the general referent of the life lived, the friends encountered and lost. Finally, his work is not fully engaged with anything but its own process. There is too little effort to make strangers share in his feelings about the world; his independence is self-defeating.

SELECTED BIBLIOGRAPHY

Works by Berrigan: BOOKS AND PAMPHLETS: A Lily for My Love. Providence, R.I.: Oxford Press, 1959; *The Sonnets*. New York: "C" Press, 1964; *Living with Chris*. New York: Boke Press, 1965; *Bean Spasms: Collaborations by Ted Berrigan and Ron Padgett*. New York: Kulcher Press, 1967; *Many Happy Returns to Dick Gallup*. New York: Angel Hair Books, 1967; *Many Happy Returns*. New York: Corinth Books, 1969; *Doubletalk*. With Anselm Hollo. Iowa City: T. G. Miller, 1969; *In The Morning Rain*. London: Cape Goliard Press, 1970 and New York: Grossman, 1971; *The Drunken Boat*. New York: Adventures in Poetry, 1974; *A Feeling for Leaving*. New York: Frontward Books, 1975; *Red Wagon: Poems*. Chicago: Yellow Press, 1976; *Clear the Range*. New York: Adventures in Poetry/Coach House South, 1977; *So Going around Cities: New and Selected Poems 1958–1979*. Berkeley, Calif.: Blue Wind Press, 1980. Interview: "The Art of Fiction XLI: Interview with Jack Kerouac." *The Paris Review* Summer 1968, pp. 61–105.

Works about Berrigan: Bell, Marvin. "Four Young Poets." *Poetry* (August 1965); pp. 371–72; Carruth, Hayden. "Making It New." *The Hudson Review* (Summer 1968);

pp. 399–412; Martz, Louis L. "Recent Poetry." *Yale Review* (June 1969); pp. 592–605; Sorrentino, Gilbert. "Ten Pamphlets." *Poetry* (April 1968); p. 60. CANR 14. DLB 5.

David Mason

JOHN BERRYMAN (1914–1982). Although his poetry was often linked to the works of such "confessional poets" as Robert Lowell,* Sylvia Plath, and Anne Sexton, John Berryman never felt at home with that kind of excruciating, at times limiting, autobiographical writing. While his poems are profoundly personal, they nevertheless reflect at the same time Berryman's abiding concern for poetic form and with the creation of a literary persona who expresses, through the mirroring distance of art, not just the special concerns of Berryman the man, but also the psychic life of an entire age.

Born John Smith—he was named after his father—in Macalester, Oklahoma, on October 25, 1914, Berryman grew up in a staunchly Roman Catholic family. He abandoned his Catholicism in college, only to return to a more generalized form of Christian faith near the end of his life (see his "Eleven Addresses to the Lord" in *Love & Fame*). But the central event of Berryman's existence, one tied to his eventually leaving the church, occurred on June 26, 1926, in Tampa, Florida. After threatening to walk into the sea with one of his two sons, John Smith Sr., fearing that his wife was about to leave him, killed himself, "shot his [the father's as well as, figuratively, the son's] heart out" beneath his son John's bedroom window, thereby initiating a lifetime of grief, guilt, and suffering for the twelve-year-old boy.

Berryman's mother soon remarried, and John took his new father's surname, but he disliked, even feared the man, and they were never close. Berryman attended an Episcopalian prep school, then Columbia College where he began to write seriously poetry, essays, and some fiction. But it was as a poet that he discovered his distinctive voice. He was later to marry three times, father children, become an alcoholic, and teach English and creative writing at a number of universities, chief among them the University of Minnesota. But he never got over, never could find any substitute for his sense of self-ravagement as well as betrayal for his father's suicide.

John Berryman's poetry consists chiefly of an elaborate working out of something he called, in one of his early lyrics, "The Ball Poem," "the epistemology of loss," or what in a later description of his major work, *The Dream Songs* (1969), he described as an "irreversible loss," centering on the tragi-comic protagonist of the songs, Berryman's literary doppelgänger, Henry Pussycat. Mixing an Elizabethan sonneteer's high formalism with a raucous Grouchoian sense of low humor and linguistic exuberance, Berryman creates a darker American version of Leopold Bloom, a "weary-daring" man, moving half in dream, half in reality, the image of whose lost father hovers over him and "hangs heavy in the land." The picture we achieve of Henry "moving in the world"—for the *Dream Songs* seem to contain no single unifying structural principle—is that of a man exposed from birth to senseless pain and suffering, a self turned inside out for all the world to see.

For John Berryman the birth trauma is a reality felt throughout one's life: it is our first loss, and it is followed by countless others. "All the world like a woolen lover" once comforted Henry, writes Berryman in his important first "Dream Song." Then came a separation: afterwards nothing followed as it should have. Thus Henry, now motherless, later fatherless (through that brutal suicide) is layed open, exposed like a sacrificial victim to the world's (felt as personal and public) cruel assaults.

In his attempts to escape the fatality which shadows him, Henry dons the disguises and the false voices of many different "characters," all of them manifestations of his own victim—and at times victimizing—self. Sometimes he allied himself with the plight of the American black, and, using dialect, calls himself "Mr. Bones," a name borrowed from minstrel show sidemen, but also used to express once again the poet's feeling of being exposed to the bone. The voice who calls Henry "Bones" (a Tambo figure) offers him solace, through comedy and ironic self-mockery, for the things he wants but cannot have. On other occasions, and in other poems, Henry identifies with Humphrey Bogart's brave but doomed screen heroes (in such movies as *High Sierra*), with Paul Muni (*Prisoner of Shark Island*), or with Frank Capra's Mr. Deeds, all men who acted, performed "deeds" against their sense of loss or entrapment. Poets figure prominently as well, such as the damned souls, Dylan Thomas and Delmore Schwartz, but it is the luminous ghost of a man who made it through, William Butler Yeats, whom young John Berryman met on a pilgrimage to Ireland, which offers a beacon of light to Henry in his struggle to find some kind of redemptive form for his agonizing personal life.

The Dream Songs, then, compose the fragmentary inner biography of a fragmented self, a self moving like an indigenous alien, a part of and yet apart from, the world he inhabits. What gives Henry's character its representativeness is not simply that he reflects a culture gone mad, but rather that Henry absorbs, takes upon himself, indeed enacts—with a profound sense of self-reproach—the failings of the age. Berryman once described his purpose, close to tragedy, in *The Dream Songs* as being both to "terrify and comfort," and it is through Henry's heroic (and anti-heroic) resistance to and acceptance of his condition that these dual emotions are aroused.

It should go without saying that from his earliest poems through his final works Berryman's preoccupation with his father's suicide dominated his work. Even his acceptance of a "God of rescue" in the "Eleven Addresses to the Lord" turns on substituting one Father, God, for another, the dead John Smith. It is questionable whether Berryman truly believed he could replace his father with God, for he seems throughout all of the rest of his writing, and in the poems which follow "Eleven Addresses," to be more poetically—and personally—at home with homelessness, a lost soul searching for a center in which he does not believe.

In one of Berryman's final poems, "Henry's Understanding," the poet/ Henry is reading late at night in Maine by the same sea into which his father once threatened to take him (*Henry's Fate and Other Poems*). As a sudden pre-dawn chill comes over him, he imagines himself "Suddenly, unlike Bach," and awfully unlike Bach, stripping down, crossing the cold lawn to the cliff at the edge of the sea, and there entering "into the terrible water [to] walk forever" beneath it out toward an island—home, peace, the mother's womb, the father's lap—which he knows he will never reach. John Berryman's life was every child's bad dream from which he or she can never wake. When, finally, the sick alcoholic Berryman took his own life at the age of fifty-nine, jumping into the frozen Mississippi off a Minneapolis bridge in January 1982, he carried with him a lifetime of pain, but he left behind him a literary legacy of books and poems whose power to "terrify and comfort" testify to their author's capacity to make enduring art out of the brutal truths of his own life.

SELECTED BIBLIOGRAPHY

Works by Berryman: POETRY: *Poems*. Norfolk, Conn.: New Directions, 1942; *The Dispossessed*. New York: William Sloan Associates, 1948; *Homage to Mistress Bradstreet*. New York: Farrar, Straus & Giroux, 1956; *The Dream Songs*. New York: Farrar, Straus & Giroux, 1969 (contains *77 Dream Songs*, 1964, and *His Toy, His Dream, His Rest*, 1968); *Love & Fame*. New York: Farrar, Straus & Giroux, 1972; *Henry's Fate and Other Poems, 1967–1972*. New York: Farrar, Straus & Giroux, 1977. PROSE: *Stephen Crane*. New York: William Sloan Associates, 1950; *Recovery*. New York: Farrar, Straus & Giroux, 1973; *The Freedom of the Poet*. New York: Farrar, Straus & Giroux, 1976 (contains essays and fiction).

Works about Berryman: Arpin, Gary Q. *The Poetry of John Berryman*. New York: Kennikat Press, 1978; Conarroe, Joel. *John Berryman: An Introduction to the Poetry*. New York: Columbia University Press, 1977; Haffenden, John. *John Berryman: A Critical Commentary*. New York: New York University Press, 1980; Haffenden, John. *The Life of John Berryman*. London: Routledge, Kegan Paul, 1972; Linebarger, J. M. *John Berryman*. New York: Twayne Publishers, 1974. AW, CANR 33, DLB 48. TCA 83.

John L. Simons

WILLIAM PETER BLATTY (1938–). *The Exorcist* (1971), William Peter Blatty's hugely successful story of demonic possession, remains the work he is most noted for, despite its publication more than fifteen years ago. Equally popular as a novel and a film, *The Exorcist* sold more than twelve million copies, and the film was nominated for ten Academy Awards. The film, one of the modern cinema's biggest money-makers, created substantial publicity for Blatty, whom some viewed as a critic of Catholicism by revealing the Church's uneasy relationship with the rite of exorcism though he called the movie "an apostolic work." The film generated a flurry of controversy among clergy, journalists, psychologists, and sociologists, some of whom sought to discredit *The Exorcist*; many simply offered explanations for its tremendous impact. Most of the critical attention Blatty received was restricted to comments on his sensational subject matter, although many critics have noted the exciting pace he maintains in this work, calling it hair-raising entertainment.

Born in New York City on January 7, 1928, to Lebanese immigrants, William Peter Blatty was raised by his illiterate mother. This enterprising and indomitable woman hawked homemade jelly on the streets of New York to help Blatty attend Brooklyn Prep, a Jesuit school for wealthy boys. After graduation he studied at Georgetown University in Washington, D.C., where he read the *Washington Post* story of an alleged exorcism of a fourteen-year-old boy by a Jesuit priest. Diabolism continued to fascinate Blatty, a doubting Catholic who saw possession as a corroboration, though not proof, of the life of the spirit. After completing a B.A., Blatty enlisted in the Air Force in 1951 where he directed psychological warfare policy. After the Korean War he earned an M.A. in English Literature, and later a Ph.D. from George Washington University. Blatty did not teach but went to work for the United States Information Agency (USIA) and was stationed in Beirut. He began writing humorous articles for *The Saturday Evening Post* and collaborated with James J. Cullen to write *Ulysses and the Cyclops; A Tale From Homer's Odyssey* (1956). His second book, *Which Way to Mecca, Jack?* (1960), humorously dealt with his experiences as a USIA official. Aided by appearances on *The Tonight Show*, news of Blatty's story-telling ability spread, and he was hired to write a screenplay, *The Man from the Diner's Club* (1961) starring Danny Kaye. His other film credits include *A Shot in the Dark* (1964), *What Did You Do in The War Daddy?* (1965), *Gunn* (1967), and *Darling Lili* (1968). *John Goldfarb, Please Come Home!* (1963) was Blatty's third book, which became a much-criticized film said to be gimmicky and weakly plotted. *I, Billy Shakespeare!* (1965) and *Twinkle, Twinkle, Killer Kane* (1967) were his next books, both commercial failures. *The Exorcist* (1971) and *I'll Tell Them I Remember You* (1973), his reminiscence of his mother, followed. Blatty then wrote a non-fictional account, *The Exorcist: From Novel to Film* (1974); a novel, *The Ninth Configuration* (1978); and his latest novel, *Legion* (1983).

Because of his early books and screenplays, William Peter Blatty has a small reputation as a humorist and a satirist, but the works that have caused Blatty both to be taken seriously and censured by the literary community are those that deal with the devil and his works: *The Exorcist* and *Legion*. Blatty's copious research of supernatural topics has been noted by the critics, who comment that the books, though fictional accounts, read like actual case histories. Regarding *The Exorcist*, Blatty revealed in an interview for the *Washington Post* (17 December 1972) "I had no plot when I sat down to write it; I had mountains of research, but no plot whatsoever. I was just pleased simply to write a book that was not a humorous novel for a change." None of *The Exorcist*'s many reviewers disputed its commercialism, though many roundly criticized its style and, in general, deplored its lack of literary merit. "It is a pretentious, tasteless, abominably written, redundant pastiche of superficial theology, comic-book psychology, Grade C movie dialogue and Grade Z scatology," according to *Time* reviewer R. Z. Sheppard (7 June 1971). Despite comments like these, Blatty's diabolistic novels are not *National Enquirer* fare, but neither are they intellectual exercises of any high order. They mix fact and fantasy in gripping detail, drawing us into the possessed's agony and exploring how possession occurs outside the awareness of the victim; perhaps it is connected to guilt or mental instability, but it is more likely the result of demonic forces. Regan, the twelve-year-old girl possessed by Satan in *The Exorcist*, fails to respond to medical and psychiatric treatment, and she is cured only after two Catholic priests exorcise her. The reluctance of Fr. Karras (the younger of the two and a trained psychiatrist) to perform the medieval rite represents the modern clergyman's dilemma when faced with such ancient horrors.

Most religious critics rightfully commented that Blatty's occult books effectively raise the problem of good and evil, but fail to resolve it. *Legion*, with a convoluted plot and style that some have called overwritten, is *The Exorcist*'s horrific and less successful sequel. It explores the nature of evil through the character of Lt. Kinderman (the officer who investigated Regan MacNeil's case in *The Exorcist*). His monologues on life and death, the enigma of God, and the existence of evil are scattered throughout the book, which tells the story of a demonically possessed California mass murderer, long dead, whose spirit has resurfaced in Washington, D.C., and has committed several terrible murders.

In the best possible light, these books may be viewed as moralistic tales, urging that a belief in God is manifested in sacrifice and affection; no real solace or joy is found in religion—only, perhaps, in the next world.

SELECTED BIBLIOGRAPHY

Works by Blatty: NOVELS: *Ulysses and the Cyclops: A Tale from Homer's Odyssey*, with James J. Cullen. New York: Microclassics Press, 1956; *Which Way to Mecca, Jack?* New York: Bernard Geis, 1960; *John Goldfarb, Please Come Home!* New York: Doubleday, 1963; *I, Billy Shakespeare!* New York: Doubleday, 1965; *Twinkle, Twinkle, Killer Kane.* New York: Doubleday, 1967; *The Exorcist.* New York: Harper and Row, 1971; *I'll Tell Them I Remember You.* New York: Norton, 1973; *The Ninth Configuration.* New York: Harper and Row, 1978; *Legion.* S and S Publishing, Inc., 1983. NON-FICTION: *The Exorcist: From Novel to Film.* New York: Bantam, 1974. SCREENPLAYS: *The Man from The Diner's Club*, 1961; *Promise Her Anything*, 1962; *John Goldfarb, Please Come Home*, 1963; *A Shot in the Dark*, 1964; *What Did You Do in the War Daddy?*, 1965; *Gunn*, 1967; *The Great Bank Robbery*, 1967; *Darling Lili*, 1968; *The Exorcist*, 1973; *Twinkle, Twinkle, Killer Kane*, 1981.

Works about Blatty: Moss, Robert F. "Suffering, Sinful Catholics." *Antioch Review* 36 (1978), pp. 170–81; Review of *The Exorcist. America* (20 November 1971), p. 432; Review of *I, Billy Shakespeare! Best Sellers* (1 December 1965), p. 349. CANR 9. CA 7–8.

Linda Bannister

CHARLES ANDREW BRADY (1912–). When his first novel, *Stage of Fools*, appeared in 1953, readers were introduced to an historical novelist whose work has now been favorably compared with that of the best in this genre. While the word "serious" has often been used to describe his work, his work has also been praised for the quality of its characterization, its verisimilitude, and its historicity. The backgrounds which he has chosen reflect his religious and historical interests: two books are based on Viking materials (*This Land Fulfilled*, 1958, and *Viking Summer*, 1956); one is based on Renaissance England (*Stage of Fools*, 1953); and one is based on the France of Chateaubriand (*Crown of Grass*, 1964).

Born on April 15, 1912, in Buffalo, New York, Charles Brady was educated in that city where he completed his undergraduate studies at Canisius College in 1933. Subsequently, he earned an M.A. at Harvard University in 1935. His interest in teaching brought him back to Canisius where he taught for forty years in the English Department. He married Eileen Larson in 1937, and they have six children. In addition to his four novels he has also published a volume of poems, *Wings over Patmos: Poems 1937–1951* (1952), a large number of individual poems, and many critical pieces and reviews.

The themes of Brady's major novels bear out the truth of his assertion that history was very important to him. Closely coupled with his interest in historical matters is his deeply rooted humanistic outlook on life. These can be seen as interwoven in his selection of Sir Thomas More as the subject of the most popular of his novels, *Stage of Fools*. Throughout this book the blend of Brady's abiding interest in truth and humility is apparent. And what better subject to use for an illustration than the life and times of More?

Brady limns More against the background of intrigues at the court, in Parliament, and in the Church to demonstrate how More's unassailable integrity and his love for Christ combined to precipitate his simultaneous failure and success. Using his knowledge of the period to advantage, Brady vivifies a time long past with a passion that makes for excellent reading. One can only speculate about the reasons which caused Brady to cease writing in the novel form. Surely, a greater output might have caused him to be ranked among the foremost American novelists of his time.

Wings over Patmos: Poems 1937–1951 provides ample testimony of the versatility and competence of this award-winning poet. Displaying a deft touch, he strikes the exact tone whether writing of a meditative subject or offering a lesser theme for the delight of a child. Reading this volume is like listening to a musical virtuoso display the range of his instrument.

SELECTED BIBLIOGRAPHY

Works by Brady: NOVELS: *Stage of Fools*. New York: Dutton, 1953; *Viking Summer*. Milwaukee, Wis.: Bruce, 1956; *This Land Fulfilled*. New York: Dutton, 1958; *Sword of Clontarf*. New York: Doubleday, 1960; *Crown of Grass*. New York: Doubleday, 1964. POEMS: *Wings over Patmos: Poems 1937–1951*. New York: Monastine Press, 1952. SHORT STORIES: "Incident on Beaufort Street." *America* (4 April 1953), pp. 16–18; "Jerusalem: the Fifteenth Nisan." *America* (2 April 1955), pp. 16–17.

Works about Brady: Review of *Stage of Fools. Booklist* (1 March 1953), pp. 213, 252; Review of *Sword of Clontarf. Library Journal* (15 April 1960), p. 1704; Review of *This Land Fulfilled. Booklist* (1 November 1958), p. 125. Cat A (1952). CA 5–6.

Leo E. Keenan, Jr.

JAMES WINSTON BRADY (1928–). At twenty-four, this Irishman from Brooklyn, a graduate of Manhattan College (A.B. 1950) with service as a Marine lieutenant in Korea, went to work for the trade-paper empire of Fairchild Publications. His eighteen years with Fairchild in New York, Washington, London, and Paris, finally as the publisher of *Women's Wear Daily* (1964–1971), provided the momentum for his employment as an editor, columnist, and broadcaster over the next fifteen years. More important, Brady's career with Fairchild and the jobs that followed supplied him with most of the settings and characters for the five fat novels he published between 1977 and 1986.

Brady's approach to his novels is consistent. The time is the present: a protagonist in his (more often than her) thirties is plunged into a struggle for success in Paris fashion, television network news, New York daily newspapers, the Catholic Church, or the New York garment district. Brady provides authentic color: how people work from day to day, what they wear, what they eat (and where), who they sleep with (and how). The hero (or heroine) challenges entrenched institutions, emerging sadder but wiser at the hands of pervasive, ruthless adversaries. The characters are drawn from people Brady has known publicly and privately, thinly masked with the usual disclaimers, distortion, and disguise.

In *Superchic* (1974), a non-fiction autobiographical account of his years with Fairchild and *Harper's Bazaar*, Brady furnishes keys to three of these romans à clef. His experiences in France anticipate the events and personalities of *Paris One* (1977), which extends beyond the salons of the couturiers to the fields of perfume flowers in the south. A young American struggles with an Iranian playboy and brutal French agents for control of a fashion house with a lucrative perfume trade. *The Press Lord* (1982), which echoes Brady's seven years as publisher of *Women's Wear Daily*, revolves around the fevered but futile attempt of the owner of a chain of sensational papers to succeed in New York. (The author appears as a hard-driving but humane Irish columnist and editor from Brooklyn.) *Designs* (1986) records the rise and fall of a rich, beautiful, WASP, Colorado-heiress designer and her Seventh Avenue lover in the fashion industry of New York and Paris; the tutelary spirit of Coco Chanel is accompanied by a roll call of New York celebrities.

Brady's two other novels have different sources. *Nielsen's Children* (1978) depicts the triumphs and frustrations of a television interviewer who becomes a network anchorwoman. (Brady worked for CBS.) The roots of *Holy Wars* (1983), dedicated to "my brother Tom, a good priest, and a good man," lie deeper. A young Jesuit is called to Rome to answer for a book based on his role as a revolutionist-priest in Central America. He earns the respect of a Polish Pope who assigns to the young American the reform of the Jesuits; the Pope's plans crumble when he dies in an airplane crash. The priest, who has already renounced the love of a beautiful sculptress, burns his second book (itself entitled *Holy Wars*) and returns to the struggle in the republic of Mirador.

As a rule, Brady submerges his vision of the snares and perils of the contemporary world beneath the accoutrements of a best-seller, although he does seem genuinely fascinated by the glitter around him. His plots unravel in pointless violence (a chase, a shooting, a crash); his characters have no visible motives for succeeding or failing, for falling in or out of bed. The graphic encounters—sadistic or sexual, hetero and homo, plain or kinky, dual or multiple—are seldom related to the character of the participants. A remarkable ability to portray setting can be frittered away in endless name-dropping of the habitués at La Grenouille and Le Périgord, P. J. Clarke's, and Elaine's. Brady's sometimes incisive prose slips into shapeless commonplaces ("both of them . . . were being drawn inexorably into something larger than their love"). Only in *Holy Wars*, with its moral core of the young priest's search for earthly justice and a definition of his relationship to God, do the plot, the character, and the writing remain unspoiled by the jingling of silverware and the squeaking of bedsprings.

SELECTED BIBLIOGRAPHY

Works by Brady: *Superchic*. Boston: Little, Brown, 1974; *Paris One*. New York: Delacorte, 1977; *Nielsen's Children*. New York: Putnam, 1978; *The Press Lord*. New York: Delacorte, 1982; *Holy Wars*. New York: Simon and Schuster, 1983; *Designs*. New York: Crown, 1986.

Works about Brady: CA 101.

Neale R. Reinitz

JIMMY BRESLIN (1930–). Jimmy Breslin has been a sportswriter, a reporter, a columnist, a novelist, and a running mate of Norman Mailer in his unsuccessful bid for the New York mayoralty. Despite these varied roles, Breslin has maintained a consistent voice throughout his career, that of spokesperson for and analyst of the immigrant minorities who have struggled for position in New York in the nineteenth and twentieth centuries. It is no surprise that Breslin can speak eloquently of his own ethnic heritage, but what is remarkable about his journalism and his fiction is that it treats with sympathetic humor and irony the hopes and defeats of peoples often in conflict with the New York Irish: the Italians, the Jews, the blacks, and the Puerto Ricans. *Forsaking All Others* (1982), for example, vividly captures the experiences of two Puerto Ricans in New York, one a confirmed gangster, the other a would-be lawyer trying hard to escape his roots; *Table Money* (1986) depicts the life of a New York sandhog, an Irish worker cutting water tunnels under the city. The center of gravity of Breslin's writing is the Irish of the borough of Queens, but he ranges easily into Brooklyn to make fun of the Mafia and into the Bronx to draw parallels between the nineteenth-century immigrant experiences of the Irish and Jews and the current problems of the blacks and Hispanics, while Manhattan's pretensions are always a useful foil for Breslin's blue collar sympathies. In *The Gang That Couldn't Shoot Straight* (1969), a hilarious spoof of all the serious Mafia exposés, Breslin depicts hoodlums who, although as murderous and cruel as any muckraker could wish, are incompetent at mayhem; his point is that evil lies in all men's hearts, but it is distributed evenly across society—it is not the exclusive property of one ethnic group.

Breslin was born in Jamaica, New York, on October 17, 1930. His mother, a welfare administrator and substitute English teacher, taught Breslin a sympathy for the underdog, especially poor blacks and Hispanics, and a horror of bad grammar, especially the pretentious misuse of the nominative in place of the accusative as in "between you and I." Thus Breslin's persona as street-tough, hard-boiled, and self-educated, is somewhat misleading. A five-year Catholic high school graduate, he also attended Long Island University for two years, and still, in middle age, reputedly reads Montaigne as well as the daily racing form. He married Rosemary Dattolico and had six children; his wife and offspring appeared frequently as characters in his columns, and her death was a major blow. He later married Ronnie Eldridge, a political activist with three children. The mixing of Breslin's Irish-Italian Catholic children bred in Queens with Eldridge's Manhattan-raised Jewish family has occasioned many columns.

Sunny Jim (1962) and *Can't Anybody Here Play This Game?* (1963) attest to Breslin's lifelong interest in sports. The first is an elegiac biography of "America's most beloved horseman," James Fitzsimmons, the trainer of horses such as Nashua and Gallant Fox and a fixture in New York racing for over eighty years. Although the biography's anecdotes about Fitzsimmons and horse racing provide one main interest, Breslin is equally concerned with how a poverty-stricken child of Irish immigrant heritage reached the top of an aristocratic profession while living a saint-like life. Biography becomes hagiography as Breslin investigates how the American dream can be accomplished without selling out. The second book quotes Casey Stengel's line for its title, a plaintive query about the 1962 Mets. Breslin is aware that the answer was in the negative, but he wants to understand the phenomenal appeal of a hopeless loser. Beyond pointing out the obvious, that most Mets fans were also losers in the game of life, the book simply tells stories about that terrible year.

Breslin's contrasts of ethnic groups and boroughs have been conveyed by most of the forms available to twentieth-century prose writers. His sports and feature columns sometimes read like closet dramas, for, by "reinventing" the past styles of writers like Damon Runyon, Breslin relies heavily on dialogue to capture the flavor of New York street life. Breslin's biography, reporting, and fiction sometimes blur into one another. *44* (1978), a roman à clef about David Berkowitz, the "Son of Sam" killer, is a perfect example, for it changes names but keeps the central incidents intact, analyzing the mentalities of killer and cops, citizens and victims. Breslin, who, along with Tom Wolfe, is usually given credit for inventing the "New Journalism" of the 1960s and 1970s, modestly insists he is simply working in the tradition of Runyon and others. His *The World According to Breslin* (1984) and *The World of Jimmy Breslin* (1976) are collections of past columns with commentary by colleagues; *How The Good Guys Finally Won* (1975), "Notes from an Impeachment Summer," examines the torturous impeachment process, contrasting Nixon (described as character-less in every sense of the term) with Tip O'Neill to demonstrate how a blue collar Irish hero can reach the top of his field without betraying his honest working-class values. *World Without End, Amen* (1973) follows a burnt-out New York cop on a trip to Belfast to uncover his heritage.

At its best Breslin's fiction and expository prose offer a fine analysis of the melting pot at work, as immigrants adjust to America and America in turn is changed by immigrant values. He is definitely an American original, a big-city newspaperman who relies on fictive technique to convey blunt sociological and philosophical truths to a mass audience.

SELECTED BIBLIOGRAPHY

Works by Breslin: *Sunny Jim.* New York: Doubleday, 1962; *Can't Anybody Here Play This Game?* New York: Viking, 1963; *The Gang That Couldn't Shoot Straight.* New York: Viking, 1969; *World Without End, Amen.* New York: Viking, 1973; *How the Good Guys Finally Won.* New York: Viking, 1975; *The World of Jimmy Breslin.* New York: Viking, 1976; *44.* New York: Viking, 1978; *Forsaking All Others.* New York: Simon & Schuster, 1982; *The World According to Breslin.* New York: Tichnor and Fields, 1984; *Table Money.* New York: Houghton Mifflin, 1986; *He Got Hungry and Forgot His Manners: A Fable.* New York: Tichnor and Fields, 1987.

Works about Breslin: Casey, Daniel J. "Heresy in the Diocese of Brooklyn: An Unholy Trinity." *Irish-American Fiction: Essays in Criticism.* Edited by Casey, Daniel J., and Robert E. Rhodes. New York: AMS, 1979, pp. 153–72; Eckley, Grace. "Two Irish-American Novelists: J. P. Donleavy and Jimmy Breslin." *Illinois School of Journalism* 55 (1975), pp. 28–33; Lounsberry, Barbara. "Jimmy Breslin's Old America." *Lamar Journal of the Humanities* 10 (1984), pp. 27–32. CA 73–76.

Andrew F. Macdonald

WILLIAM F. BUCKLEY, JR. (1925–). A national celebrity, William F. Buckley, Jr., is one of the most prolific and ubiquitous American writers of our time. His most impressive and influential work has been non-fiction: political tracts, journalism, and several urbane (an adjective that approaches understatement when applied to Buckley), critically acclaimed memoirs which qualify him as the Right's resident New Journalist. Yet since 1976, with the publication of *Saving the Queen*, his series of espionage thrillers featuring Blackford Oakes, CIA agent par excellence, has kept Buckley on top of the best seller list and has established his fame outside conservative circles as much as or more than his television series, *Firing Line*, or his widely syndicated newspaper column.

The spy novel naturally appeals to writers interested in contemporary international relations, so it is hardly surprising that, since the first Oakes novel, Buckley has published, in book form, more fiction than anything else. Buckley's novels are consistently entertaining, stylish, and generously spiced with the famous Buckley drollery which has always made his polemics palatable—even enjoyable—to those who do not share his ideology. As a thriller writer, Buckley also has a way with plots, which are structured intricately and interwoven with satisfying subplots. Despite their virtues, however, the Oakes novels remain only middle-brow entertainments. Judged by the standards of our greatest thriller writers, Graham Greene or John Le Carré, for example, Buckley's novels are lacking. The narrowly polemical content of the novels effectively excludes the moral strenuousness expected of good fiction and the best thrillers.

Buckley was born on November 24, 1925, one of ten children of a wealthy Irish-Catholic family. His remarkable career as a public figure includes so many stellar achievements that only the most significant can be noted here: he founded the *National Review* in 1955, helped organize the Young Americans for Freedom in 1960, ran for mayor of New York on the Conservative Party ticket in 1965, and served two appointments in the Nixon administration. More apposite to a study of his novels are the oft noted biographical similarities between Buckley and his fictional hero, Blackford Oakes: both attended exclusive British prep schools, graduated from Yale, and served in World War II. From 1951 to 1952, Buckley even worked briefly for the CIA in Mexico.

Thus, as James Bond served Ian Fleming, Oakes serves as Buckley's rather playful ego-ideal: he is fiercely handsome, worldly yet buoyant, witty, charming, athletic, and altogether irresistible to women. Oakes even beds the fictitious Queen Caroline of England in *Saving the Queen*. Fittingly, Buckley's hero also is a great fan of William F. Buckley, Jr.: in *Saving the Queen* Oakes mentions his admiration for Buckley's notorious *God and Man at Yale* (1951), and he is an avid reader of *National Review*; he even recommends one of Buckley's editorials to his omniscient superior Ruffus in *The Story of Henri Tod* (1983).

Obviously, the tone of the Oakes novels often borders on the farcical. One of the most deliciously comic moments in the series occurs in *Stained Glass* (1978), where Oakes hears of a "widely caricatured" writer by the name of Razzia (razz ya?) who commands a "depressing ubiquity" as "a syndicated columnist, a television host, an author, editor of his own magazine" and who has just "announced he would also write novels!" One of the characters then proceeds to imitate the "tiresome archness of Razzia and his euphuistic style" by delivering a paragraph from "Razzia" that is one of the most amusing examples of self-satire in recent American letters. Knowing Buckley, one suspects that the passage may in fact be drawn from one of his articles.

However, despite the widely praised sly wit and broad humor which permeate Buckley's espionage novels, they remain earnest thematizations of the primary impetus of contemporary conservatism: anti-communism. Buckley usually portrays Communists as ruthless, humorless, treacherous Party hacks; even the portrait of Fidel Castro in *See You Later Alligator* (1985) conforms to this stereotype. In *Who's On First* (1980) Oakes witnesses the cruel hanging of a heroic young rebel in the Hungarian revolution whose Communist captors refuse to allow him to make the Sign of the Cross. Subplots in both *The Story of Henri Tod* and *See You Later Alligator* feature pairs of passionate young lovers destroyed in cold-blooded fashion by the Communists, proving that they are not only godless, but also the sworn enemies of romance.

On the other hand, as might be expected, when Buckley loads the dice for the West, his anti-communist activists are virtually always high-minded, selfless, and above reproach. Henri Tod's attempt to destroy the Berlin Wall before it can be built is thematically linked to his attempt to save his little sister who has been raped and psychologically maimed by not only the Communists, but also the Nazis. Cecilio Velasco in *Alligator*, an idealistic former Communist and veteran of the Spanish Civil War, who sees the light to become a courageous operative for the West, dies valiantly in an effort to inform Washington of Castro's missile plans in 1962. Most revealing of all is the character of Axel Wintergrin of *Stained Glass*, a charismatic German political hero who has it within his power to bluff the Russians out of East Germany and unite Germany under the aegis of the West. He is, as one critic has pointed out, a secular saint of absolute virtue whose death in a gothic chapel is saturated in blatant Christ associations. Oakes layes it out squarely: "An Axel Wintergrin *could not be permitted to live* in this world."

This is not to say that Buckley paints white hats on everyone on our side and black hats on everyone on theirs. Most fascinating in this regard is the well-researched, often flattering, portrait of Che Guevara in *See You Later Alligator*. In addition, Oakes is often called upon to perform some very unsavory duties as a Cold War warrior. He is, for example, ordered to execute Axel Wintergrin because a successful election of Wintergrin as chancellor, Washington feels, could precipitate a Russian attack on Western Europe. In *Who's On First* Oakes is again called upon to decide between his organizational loyalty and the betrayal of a man (an anti-Communist, of course) he admires.

Yet there is never any question in any of the novels of Western villainy or aggression. Buckley subscribes to a kind of Rambo-esque version of foreign policy, wherein the West's only fault is timidity, which is the real reason the Cold War has not already been won. On a structural level, this vision of Communist perfidy and Western virtue condemns the novels to the formulas of melodrama. And if, as Ralph Harper notes in his study of the thriller (*The World of the Thriller*, Baltimore: The Johns Hopkins U. Press, 1969), the thriller at its best takes evil seriously enough to force us to see the truth about ourselves, then on the moral level Buckley's thrillers are simply not serious. In Buckley's fictional world, as in Fleming's, evil is always projected on the Other, a curious strategy for a Catholic writer.

This occurs not only on the geopolitical level, but also on the psychological level in the heroic figure of Blackford Oakes, more kin to James Bond than George Smiley. Oakes, like all secret agents, lives in a world of high tension and constant peril. Yet the high-spirited, even comic, tone of Buckley's novels makes it difficult to believe that Oakes is ever in serious danger. As in Fleming's novels, suspense exists more because of plot conventions than because of our belief that the hero's fate is uncertain. It is thus very significant that Oakes has never served as a double agent. He has a cover of course—he is a qualified civil engineer—but even when, in *See You Later Alligator*, Oakes must operate inside Castro's Cuba, he is sent as a presidential emissary, and is therefore quite immune to the perils of being "in the cold." These perils, as Harper notes, are very much existential: they are associated with the problems of disguise and identity as the agent must enter into the psychological as well as the physical world of the enemy.

In other words, although Oakes must sometimes confront difficult decisions, his motives are never ambivalent. He remains, as does the nation for which he stands, one-dimensionally virtuous. Thus, even so sympathetic a Buckley critic as Mark Royden Mitchell finds that the lack of ethical ambiguity in the novels lends them an air of smugness. Instead of exploring the dialectics of self-examination, they are structured around the dialectics of debate as when, for example, Oakes and Che exchange witty ripostes in several arguments in *Alligator*. International events in the novels tend to be mediated by the scholastic gamesmanship for which *Firing Line* is famous.

Yet Oakes' character is not without interest. His personal life, rather than his career as an operative, reveals some fascinating traits. Although he is engaged to Sally Partridge, a liberal academic who is a Jane Austen scholar, Oakes is consistently unfaithful, enjoying a succession of torrid affairs with enemy agents as well as queens and anti-Communist rebels. Sally, however, despite some feminist credentials, remains the ideal woman of male fantasy: she waits patiently at home, content with her hero's infrequent visits. In addition, although Buckley portrays Oakes as independent, even rebellious, his father-figure superior, Ruffus, is always available to quell Oakes' doubts and to put events in the proper perspective. Perhaps these contradictions embody Buckley's own wish fulfillments: as both conservative and iconoclast, he must reconcile the need for authority and stability with his proclivities toward skepticism and even irreverence. In the boyish fantasy world of Blackford Oakes, all such dilemmas melt away.

SELECTED BIBLIOGRAPHY

Works by Buckley: NOVELS: *Saving the Queen*. New York: Doubleday, 1976; *Stained Glass*. New York: Doubleday, 1978; *Who's On First*. New York: Doubleday, 1980; *Marco Polo, If You Can*. New York: Doubleday, 1982; *The Story of Henri Tod*. New York: Doubleday, 1983, 1984; *See You Later Alligator*. New York: Doubleday, 1985; *Mongoose, R.I.P.* New York, Random House, 1988. MEMOIRS: *The Unmaking of a Mayor*. New York: Viking, 1966; *Cruising Speed*. New York: Putnam, 1971; *Airborne: A Sentimental Journey*. New York: Macmillan, 1976; *Overdrive: A Personal Documentary*. New York: Doubleday, 1983. POLITICAL TRACTS: *God and Man at Yale*. Chicago: H. Regnary: 1951; *McCarthy and His Enemies*, with L. Brent Bozell. Chicago: H. Regnary: 1954; *Up from Liberalism*. New York: Obolensky/McDowell, 1959; *Four Reforms*. New York: Putnam, 1973; *Racing through Paradise: A Pacific Passage*. New York: Random House, 1987.

Works about Buckley: Ross, Mitchell S. *The Literary Politicians*. New York: Doubleday, 1978, pp. 15–55; Winchell, Mark Royden. *William F. Buckley, Jr.* Boston:
Twayne, 1984. CANR 1. CA 4.

Barry Sarchett

ROBERT OLEN BUTLER, JR. (1945–). Butler writes about, in his own
words, "man's search for love, kinship, connection, God; man's capacity for
desertion, violence, and self-betrayal" (*CA*, 90) Three of his four published
novels set these themes within the framework of the Vietnam War; the fourth,
Countrymen of Bones (1983), imagines a moment toward the end of World War
II as testing begins on the first atomic bomb near Los Alamos, New Mexico.
Butler's great story-telling abilities, his sensitivity to the flickers of emotion
which can alter lives, his understanding of those events which have shaped a
national consciousness, his psychological and moral insights—all combine to
make him an outstanding novelist.

Born on January 20, 1945, in Granite City, Illinois, Butler is the son of a
college professor, Robert Olen, Sr., and Lucille Hall, an executive secretary.
Butler was educated at Northwestern where he earned a B.S. in 1967 and at
the University of Iowa where he received an M.A. in 1969. After three years
(1969–1972) in the U.S. Army—including service in Vietnam as intelligence
agent and as an interpreter to the U.S. adviser to the mayor of Saigon—Butler
worked as a reporter and editor of *Electronic News* (1972–1973). From 1973
to 1974, Butler taught high school in Granite City, Illinois, and then took a
job at *Energy User News* in New York City, where he has served as editor in
chief since 1975.

The Alleys of Eden (1981), Butler's first novel, explores the effects of the
Vietnam War on Clifford Wilkes. Because of his involvement in the unintentional
death of a prisoner of war, Cliff deserts the army and hides out in Saigon where
he meets and falls in love with a Vietnamese prostitute named Lanh. With Lanh,
Cliff finds sexual passion, intimacy, and a reason to live. Cliff's desperate link
to Lanh, profound as it is, is disrupted by the end of the war.

Cliff and Lanh escape to the United States, but once there, instead of enjoying
new freedoms, they feel more trapped than when hiding in Saigon. Since Cliff
is stalked as a deserter and Lanh cannot speak English, both realize that they
can never find a home in the United States. Eventually Cliff flees to Canada and
Lanh moves in with a Vietnamese refugee family in Iowa.

Cliff's loss of identity, isolation, and helplessness become a metaphor for
U.S. involvement in Vietnam: Clifford risks his life to be with Lanh and to
save her life, but he loses not only Lanh, but also his homeland and his sense
of self.

Butler's second novel, *Sun Dogs* (1982), follows the life of one of Cliff's
Vietnam War buddies, Wilson Hand, now a private investigator in New York.
Hand takes a job with an oil drilling company in Alaska to find the thief of the

documents that contain vital statistics about oil reserves on the North Slope. Hand discovers not only that the documents reveal that there is no oil under the North Slope, but also that his lover, Marta, has been feeding these facts to a *New York Times* reporter who plans to reveal the scandalous truth to the American public.

Hand's real quest in Alaska is for a release from the material clutter of modern life. In the end, Hand finds himself at the extremity—on the ledge of a forsaken Alaskan mountain after his plane crashes in a storm. As he lies freezing in his sleeping bag, he feels a strange joy—a feeling he has not experienced since he faced what he thought was certain death in a prison camp in Vietnam. Thus, escape from the clutter means facing death with a pure sense of self, and so Hand, in deep joy, climbs out of his sleeping bag to embrace the fatal cold, offering his life for his pilot who will need the flesh of Hand's body to survive.

In *Countrymen of Bones*, Butler turns from the psychological traumas of Vietnam War veterans to the obsessions of scientific minds, pitting against each other Lloyd Coulter and Darrell Reeves, two scientists in a race against the first atomic explosion near Los Alamos, New Mexico, in 1944. Coulter is obsessed with detonating the bomb; Reeves is obsessed with protecting the bones and artifacts in his archaeological excavation which is located near ground zero. Reeves—whose name means steward of the land—believes in the innocence of his research to help humanity learn from the lives of the dead. Coulter—whose name suggests a blade used to cut the earth—believes in applying modern scientific knowledge to the cause of preserving the nation's future. Although they are bitter rivals, in the end both men come to understand the futility of their obsessions. From the weapons and broken skulls of his excavation, Reeves learns what Coulter learns from the atomic laboratory: the violent heart of humanity seems always to defeat the benevolence of nature and the love between man and woman.

The third work in the Vietnam trilogy, *On Distant Ground* (1985), may be Butler's best work. David Fleming, who served in Vietnam with Clifford Wilkes and Wilson Hand, is court-martialed for aiding the enemy. During the war, David freed Tuyen, a Viet Cong intelligence operative and prisoner of war, thereby violating the army's criminal code. Outside of that code, however, David's action saved the life of a fellow human being and so, in a sense, brought out the best in David.

During a break in the trial, David sees the television news accounts of the children of American soldiers and Vietnamese women returning to the United States, and he becomes convinced that he has had a child by a Vietnamese women with whom he had a two-month-long affair. Although now married and a father by his American wife, David decides that he must return to Saigon and rescue his son. Failure to go would constitute a greater crime than aiding the enemy: a kind of Hawthornian violation of the human heart through abandonment—a common theme in Butler's work. Convicted of aiding the enemy, David sneaks into Saigon amidst its collapse and saves his son but only with the aid of Tuyen who is now the director of security for the Communist government in Saigon.

The title of the novel refers to Vietnam where David must travel to find his son. But it also refers to David's emotional locus: somewhat aloof, always on distant ground. This changes when David goes to Saigon and takes responsibility for his Vietnamese son. David's journey becomes a psychological journey in which he explores his motivations for freeing Tuyen, as well as his feeling of spiritual and emotional emptiness. What David discovers from his exploration—which in many ways recalls Marlowe's search in *Heart of Darkness*—is that emotional responses must also be accompanied by acts of will. When David first sees his Vietnamese son, he responds without anticipated fatherly feelings because his boy bears the Oriental features of his mother and looks nothing like David. It is only through an act of will that David can take charge of his moral responsibility for the boy's well-being. The lesson of morality becomes, too, a lesson in compassion which frees David to love his wife, his children, and himself and brings him for the first time a feeling of human intimacy.

In his search for self-understanding, for love, and for God, Butler—who has said that he is becoming more and more religious—recalls Walker Percy; in his courage to probe psychological and moral dilemmas within symbolic landscapes, Butler recalls Joseph Conrad. In this good company, Butler should develop into one of America's finest contemporary novelists.

SELECTED BIBLIOGRAPHY

Works by Butler: *The Alleys of Eden*. New York: Horizon Press, 1981; *Sun Dogs*. New York: Horizon Press, 1982; *Countrymen of Bones*. New York: Horizon Press, 1983; *On Distant Ground*. New York: Knopf, 1985; *Wabash*. New York: Knopf, 1987.

Works about Butler: CA 112.

Daniel J. Tynan

C

CHARLES CANTALUPO (1951–). For poet and scholar Charles Cantalupo, poetry is a "verbal resurrection" of all that has died or at least disappeared. He was born on October 17, 1951, in West Orange, New Jersey. As an undergraduate, he attended Washington University in St. Louis and the University of Kent at Canterbury; doctoral studies in English were completed at Rutgers University in 1980. He teaches Shakespeare, poetry, and the Bible and literature at the Schuylkill campus of Penn State.

The title of his first volume of poetry, *The Art of Hope* (1983), was inspired by Paul's line from Romans 8:24, "but hope that is seen is not hope." His poetry is a testament to his struggle to live in dark hope. The art of writing is his art of faith, a restatement of the original language of Genesis in its first two chapters. When the loveliness of nature disappears, he suffers, yet he sees the way to praise God, especially in the seasons of nature.

Religious poetics grasp Cantalupo's attention in the long preface to his second collection of poems, *St. Orpheus*. The mood is elegiac, a reminder that for the poet the death of his young, talented wife is an opening into a darker, richer vision.

SELECTED BIBLIOGRAPHY

Works by Cantalupo: *The Art of Hope*. Notre Dame, Ind.: Erasmus Books, 1983. Poetry in such magazines as *Journal of New Jersey Poets, Studia Mystica, The Cord, Christianity and Literature*.

Mary E. Giles

PHILIP CAPUTO (1941–). The publication of *Del Corso's Gallery* (1983) has confirmed the distinction of Philip Caputo as a writer of the uncompromising honesty for which he has been acclaimed for *A Rumor of War* (1977) and *Horn of Africa* (1980). Judged as having written timeless testaments to the men who leave their homes to kill and die in strange lands, he narrates with a mastery

and eloquence of style, whether in formal exposition or in unrestrained colloquialism, that involves the reader with the characters who live violently in the
darker corners of the human soul. From a soldier's account of the war we lost
in Vietnam, to the pictorial record of the maimed and massacred in desert sands,
and eventually to the graphic visualization of the brutal violence in Beirut,
Caputo's works will remain an authentic and striking revelation of America's
involvement in worldwide militarism. The greatest power of his style lies in his
determination to tell the truth.

The son of Joseph and Marie Ylanda (Napolitan), Philip Caputo was born on
June 10, 1944, in Chicago, Illinois, where he spent his childhood and pursued
his education. He received his B.A. in English at Loyola University in 1964.
Once wedded to Jill Esther Ongemach, but divorced in 1982, with two sons, he
is now married to Marcelle Lynn Bass with whom he lives in Key West, Florida.
As a member of the staff of the *Chicago Tribune*, he was a foreign correspondent
in Rome (1972–1974), Beirut (1974–1976), and Moscow (1976–1977).

In his novels, Caputo identifies with his characters as men who depict the
human capacity for evil as they veer into violent confrontations. In *A Rumor of
War*, Caputo states that the one true god of modern war is blind chance and that
death is not to be feared because it is an end to pain. In self-examination, after
he has had to kill, he defines the act as a direct result of war; but when he is
interviewed, he admits that the line between legitimate and illegitimate killing
is blurred. Caputo concludes that his friends had died for no reason and that the
survivors had no longer any purpose or idealism in a lost war. Beyond politics,
strategy, and national interests, and beyond blame and sorrow, his story is about
the best and worst in ordinary men who experience in war camaraderie, courage,
fear, death, ideals, and lost convictions.

Horn of Africa, in which three mercenaries smuggle arms to the rebellious
Moslem tribe on the barren terrain of Africa's Horn, develops the theme of
human evil. With graphic and sometimes shocking detail, he presses the symbolic
journey to the inner recesses of the mind. Combining philosophy of reason,
exciting narration, and a mastery of style, the author involves the reader within
the boundaries of conscience shared by bronze-age warriors and the soldiers of
a modern army.

In *Del Corso's Gallery*, Caputo evolves into an extraordinary writer. The
uncompromising honesty of his other two books combines with his sharp artistry
of developing characters, his mental reflection, and his unrestricted realism. The
reader recognizes the author in Del Corso, the journalist whose only enemy is
the ordinary and whose only aim is the visibility of the truth in this portrayal of
war as life. From Saigon to war-ravaged Beirut, he has learned that war wanders
around the city with capricious insanity. Essentially, Caputo concocts a coherence
between the moment and the future. He has his characters speak, therefore,
according to their faith in God; in the face of death, they feel obliged to pursue
the truth. Though the reader might prefer the more poetic sounds of Caputo's
philosophical reflections, the dying Del Corso must be consistent with a true-

to-life style. As he had called on Jesus at the time he had been hit, so at the moment of death, Del Corso defends his style of faith and life in profanity. His depiction is Caputo's mastery of the expression of fact in fiction.

SELECTED BIBLIOGRAPHY

Works by Caputo: *A Rumor of War*. New York: Holt, Rinehart and Winston, 1977; *Horn of Africa*. New York: Dell Publishing Co., 1980; *Del Corso's Gallery*. New York: Holt, Rinehart and Winston, 1983; *Indian Country*. New York: Bantam, 1987.

Works about Caputo: Hidesaki, Yasuro. "The Peculiarity and Background of Vietnam War Literature." *Kyushu American Literature* 24 (1983), pp. 60–69; McInerney, Peter. "Straight and 'Secret' History in Vietnam War Literature." *Contemporary Literature* 22 (1981), pp. 187–204. CA 73–76.

Rose Basile Green

JAMES CARROLL (1943–). In the six novels he has published, James Carroll achieved his greatest success in the first-person narrator of his fifth novel, *Prince of Peace* (1984). Frank Durkin is vividly alive from first page to last as he tells a story of betrayal and truth; his distinctive voice recalls Carroll's own in the essays and poetry he published earlier in his career. Carroll's weakness as a novelist is his penchant for melodramatic plots blending historical figures with fictional characters, none of whom is quite believable.

James Carroll was born in Chicago in 1943 and grew up in Washington, D.C. He entered the Missionary Society of St. Paul the Apostle, the Paulists, in 1963, was ordained a priest in 1969, and spent the period between 1969 and 1974 as a chaplain at Boston University. He left the Paulists in 1975 and married Alexandra Marshall in 1978. The Carrolls have two children.

While still a Paulist, Carroll published several books of spirituality, ranging from *Feed My Lambs—A Beginner's Guide for Parents Who Want to Prepare Their Children for the Eucharist and Penance* (1967) to *A Terrible Beauty: Conversions in Prayer, Politics, and Imagination* (1973). After he left the priesthood, he published a journal of his sabbatical experience at a desert monastery in Israel, *The Winter Name of God* (1975). His years as a Paulist have left an indelible mark on James Carroll; trained to serve, he regards his fiction as a form of ministry in which he confronts readers with truths about family, state, and church.

His first novel, *Madonna Red* (1976), reveals strengths and weaknesses that have persisted in later work: Carroll has a gift for language and a vivid sense of place, but his plots strain credulity and his characters are not persuasive. *Madonna Red* also introduced the novelist's continuing preoccupation with actual events and their impact on invented people. In this instance, an IRA terrorist travels to Washington, D.C., to assassinate the British ambassador to the United States during ceremonies held at St. Matthew's Cathedral to invest the ambassador as a Knight of St. Gregory. The plot turns on a ploy that Newgate Callendar in *The New York Times Book Review* found "neat" but that other reviewers found objectionable in a "potboiler" (*Best Sellers*) and "a mish-mash of bad story-telling and worse theology" (*Critic*).

The assassination plot is linked rather crudely to the story of a nun who defies the Church by "saying Mass." The hero, a priest on the cathedral staff who is a Vietnam veteran, is the connection between the two plots. Despite the absurdity of the stories and the woodenness of the characters, Carroll works hard to explore questions of moral purpose and individual responsibility. Yet he does not capitalize on the painful irony that both the terrorist and the ambassador are Catholic.

Although *Madonna Red* fails, there are flashes of brilliance, and succeeding novels have demonstrated improvement in technique. But Carroll's insistence on large-scale plots and historical characters seems to drain him of the energy needed to explore human life in greater depth. *Mortal Friends* (1978) traces the life of Colman Brady over a forty-five-year period from the time of the Black and Tans in Ireland to the months just before the assassination of John Kennedy.

Carroll's third novel, *Fault Lines* (1980), experiments with a shorter time span, focusing on a mere two days in the lives of an intriguing collection of characters, including a famous draft dodger, a writer, and a movie star who becomes deeply involved with his roles (Richard III, at this point). Again the high moral purpose is evident: Carroll challenges his readers to confront vexing contemporary problems. But, shorn of the world-shaking atmosphere of the earlier novels, the weaknesses of Carroll's plotting and characterization are more evident.

The confrontations work better in this fourth novel, *Family Trade* (1982), but the hero, Jake McKay, and his preoccupations are overshadowed by a gripping narrative of his father's experiences in Berlin as the city collapses in the spring of 1945. What we remember of the novel is the thrill of this long flashback rather than the more serious questions about loyalty and patriotism that Carroll presumably wishes to raise.

All of James Carroll's novels ask moral questions and explore themes of defeat, betrayal, and revenge. Humor is notably absent from Carroll's fictional world; the march of history and the clash of titans prevent characters from enjoying themselves. Grim, earnest Frank Durkin in *Prince of Peace* suffers little from the callowness of earlier Carroll heroes, yet his humor never gets beyond sardonic commentary. He does possess something of an ironic sense of himself, a sense missing in earlier heroes. Carroll opens the novel with the death of Fr. Michael Maguire, the anti-war priest who is the titular hero. A series of artfully arranged flashbacks interspersed with the grim present converge on a climactic scene of betrayal. Unfortunately, once Vietnam enters the story the earnestness of the narrative is sometimes stifling. The weakness for the sweeping canvas of the epic distracts the reader—Korea *and* Vietnam figure in the novel, Cardinal Spellman *and* Dorothy Day *and* Robert Moses all play a part. But Frank Durkin's distinctive narrative voice displays Carroll's gift for language, the perceptive image, the telling phrase. The battle scenes are vivid, as are moments like the reunion between Frank and Michael at the Cloisters.

In *Prince of Peace*, Carroll has created a persuasive character in Frank Durkin. Unfortunately, no such character redeems *Supply of Heroes* (1986) from the weaknesses of earlier novels. The plot covers World War I and the 1916 Easter Rising, from the Western Front to the west of Ireland, from Lord Kitchener to Lady Gregory. Typical of the trite style is the description, in the first paragraph, of wives with "welling eyes" bidding farewell to husbands going to war: "tears never overspilled those ruby cheeks" in public places.

From the start, James Carroll has possessed the necessary moral energy to infuse his work with serious consideration of significant human concerns. What remains for the novelist is to escape from the demands of the sweeping epic plot in order to focus on believable people in believable situations.

SELECTED BIBLIOGRAPHY

Works by Carroll: NOVELS: *Madonna Red*. Boston: Little, Brown, 1976; *Mortal Friends*. Boston: Little, Brown, 1978; *Fault Lines*. Boston: Little, Brown, 1980; *Family Trade*. Boston: Little, Brown, 1982; *Prince of Peace*. Boston: Little, Brown, 1984; *Supply of Heroes*. New York: Dutton, 1986. POETRY: *Forbidden Disappointments*. New York: Newman, 1974. SELECTED NON-FICTION: *A Terrible Beauty: Conversions in Prayer, Politics, and Imagination*. New York: Newman Press, 1973; *The Winter Name of God*. New York: Sheed, 1975; "On Not Skipping the Sermon." *Commonweal* (2–16 November 1984), pp. 603–5; "Beyond the Dream." *Boston Globe Magazine*, 17 March 1985.

Works about Carroll: O'Rourke, William. "Hybrid but Hackenyed," a review of *Prince of Peace*. *Commonweal* (14 December 1984), pp. 694–96. CA 81–84.

John W. Mahon

JIM CARROLL (1951–). With his 1980 album *Catholic Boy*, Jim Carroll joined a handful of artists acknowledged as both poets and musicians. From his diary to his recordings, Carroll consistently portrays an ugly world. Accused of striking a chilling pose, Carroll actually presents the world he has experienced, making the pose and the message—"I just want to be pure"—all the more chilling.

Born in New York City on August 1, 1951, Jim Carroll experienced the rough side of life very early. Dominated by sex, drugs, and crime, his teen years held little promise, save a talent in basketball and a need to write. Working briefly at college and workshops, giving readings, and publishing poems in numerous magazines, anthologies, and pamphlets, he attracted considerable attention with his collection *Living at the Movies* (1973). After he moved to California, he kicked his drug addiction and published *The Basketball Diaries* (1978), his teen autobiography, excerpts from which had been appearing periodically for years. Since 1980, his work has been limited to rock recordings. He now lives in New York with his wife, Rosemary, and their two children.

In *The Basketball Diaries*—crisp, clear, brutal—Carroll glories in his basketball expertise but also portrays the rough lower life in New York, where he snatched purses and prostituted himself to obtain drugs, a focal point of the *Diaries*. The visceral prose hides none of the ugliness but rather highlights it; Carroll coldly flaunts his indecent attitudes and actions, as when he and his friends perform diving stunts into the filth of the Harlem River. No aspect of his life free from ugliness, he savagely considers the congratulations offered on a good game:

the whole scene strictly out of "Leave It To Beaver," all the old men Fred MacMurray types . . . and the women, a pack of poodle walkers . . . teased up bleached hair-dos that reminded me exactly of the higher priced 14th St. whores. . . . It's a Friday night and we all wanted to go to the East River Park and get drunk, do reefer and sniff glue. And that's exactly what we did.

Carroll believes in the wrenching visceral power of rock music over the heady appeal of poetry. *Catholic Boy*, his first recording, received fairly good notices from such periodicals as *Rolling Stone*. The most powerful track on the album is "People Who Died," a death-focused song that, coming from the same brutal, chilling world of Carroll's earlier writing, created a certain cult following. The album's title song, in spite of its driving, almost blasphemous tone, shows the power of Catholicism in Carroll's life. He's a man-child convicted of theft at birth and sent directly from the womb to The Tombs. But he's received every sacrament, including Extreme Unction, and is "redeemed in pain," if also in cynicism. Humanity's fall explains the moral logic of all the other songs, especially "City Drops into the Night." But even there, amidst images of whoring, drugs, and darkness, Carroll's voice provides the moral center of faith in a world where lovers betray lovers with their lovers' best friends.

Later albums, *Dry Dreams* (1982) and *I Write Your Name* (1983) show growth and experimentation, while retaining Carroll's characteristic eerieness and sassiness; reviews remain favorable but not enthusiastic.

Carroll has quickly proved a talented writer, with a crisp, expressive voice. One feels, though, that he has not reached his promise and that his musical excursion might not provide the best medium for it.

SELECTED BIBLIOGRAPHY

Works by Carroll: POETRY: *Living at the Movies*. 1973. New York: Penguin, 1980; *The Book of Nods*. New York: Viking, 1986. AUTOBIOGRAPHY: *The Basketball Diaries*. 1978. New York: Bantam, 1980; *Forced Entries: The Downtown Diaries, 1971–1973*. New York: Viking Penguin, 1987. RECORDINGS: The Jim Carroll Band, *Catholic Boy*. ATCO, SD 38–132, 1980; *Day Dreams*. ATCO, SD 38–145, 1982; *I Write Your Name*. Atlantic, 80123–1, 1983.

Works about Carroll: Flippos, Chet. "A Star Is Borning." *New York* (22 January 1981), pp. 32–33; Graustark, Barbara. "Mean Streets." *Newsweek* (8 September 1980), pp. 80–81; James, Jamie. "The Basketball Diaries." *American Book Review* (February 1980), p. 9; Malanga, Gerald. "Traveling and Living." *Poetry* (December 1974), pp. 162–65; Simels, Steve. "Jim Carroll." *Stereo Review* (February 1981), p. 90. CA 45–48.

Robert A. Russ

ARTHUR CAVANAUGH (1926–). Arthur Cavanaugh's first three novels profoundly explore the impact that family life leaves on his characters. Critics have remarked on this interest in home life and have either praised Cavanaugh for his quiet, but rich evocation of Irish-American life or have seen his stories as slight, a mist about to disappear under a door. Despite his overt sentimentality, these novels—*The Children Are Gone* (1966), *Leaving Home* (1970) and *Missed Trains* (1979)—all understand and confront the lasting childhood impressions that can continue to affect us as adults. Unfortunately, although while maintaining an interest in the past and its effects on the present, Cavanaugh, in his latest novel, *The Faithful* (1986), favors the epic-inducing qualities of a television miniseries over his previously astute eye for small and homey, yet penetrating detail. It remains uncertain whether we will see a return to Cavanaugh's past form.

Arthur Cavanaugh was born on April 9, 1926, in Woodhaven, New York as Arthur Fuchs. By the time he turned twenty-one, he had changed his surname to Cavanaugh, his maternal grandmother's name. He received his education at New York schools and at the College of William and Mary in Virginia. Except for his road experiences as a young actor, Cavanaugh has lived most of his life in New York. He toured with the long-running "Life with Father" company and with the USO overseas company of "Junior Miss." While Cavanaugh did not continue acting, he has perpetuated his theatrical interests. In the 1950s he wrote screenplays for national television, and since 1964 he has acted as the drama critic for *Sign*, a New Jersey-based Catholic magazine. Four novels and one autobiography have been published since 1962. Magazines such as *McCall's* and *Redbook* frequently printed his short stories in the 1960s. One of these, "What I Wish (Oh, I Wish) I Had Said," won an O. Henry Prize in 1965. This story (and others about the Connerty family) also appear—in an altered form—in his second novel, *Leaving Home*. Mr. Cavanaugh lives in Manhattan, is married, and is the father of two grown children.

In Arthur Cavanaugh's writing most all concerns return—however wayward—to their central axis: the family. In *The Children Are Gone*, Callie and Philip Hallard's two young children, Mary Fran and Fip, are stolen. This crisis jars both parents into new awarenesses about their families—past and present. Maggie and Christopher, the main characters of *Missed Trains*, contend with the gaps—missing fathers—in their families. Their actions, often subconsciously, reflect that intense desire to make the family complete once more. In *Leaving Home*, most of the action takes place within the home where Robbie Connerty, the narrator, grows up.

Sometimes the Connerty family seems too good to be true. Generally, everyone gets along and shows understanding and respect for one another. And, yet, Cavanaugh underlies this genial atmosphere with Robbie's brooding and ever-present, if often buried, fear that his parents did not want him. Robbie's leave-taking thus becomes a slow, painful process, full of denial (he hides the family snapshots in the basement and then forgets he has done so). He remains at home longer than the other children, waiting for a sign that he really was desired by his parents.

Cavanaugh depicts attitudes developed in childhoods like Robbie's which often inhibit a person's growth into adulthood. Until Robbie faces his mother, Catherine, with his long hidden anxiety about being unwanted, he cannot take his life in his own hands. However, Catherine, the ideal mother, now appears hard and unsympathetic toward her son's long-festering fear. She sees that he has been carrying it inside but denies the crippling power this terror has inflicted upon him. She treats Robbie's pain as if it were outside him and scolds him as if he had received a bad grade in school.

While Robbie accepts his mother's pronouncements, as readers we must wonder about this acquiescence. Throughout his work Cavanaugh clearly wants his characters to transcend their painful pasts. However, in *Leaving Home*, he brings Robbie up to the point of transcendence and then lets him sink back into denial: his mother's denial, which he accepts as his own, that his fears were real and human. Thus he exchanges one form of repression (hidden snapshots) for another (negation of feelings). Cavanaugh has worked diligently and perceptively to allow his characters their feelings—especially those long harbored from childhood—but he will not, or cannot, completely validate these feelings. In the end Robbie accedes to the voice of his mother's authority. This dilemma of affirming childhood feelings *and* letting go of youth in order to grow makes for a frustrating, but fascinating insight into Cavanaugh's theme of maturation.

Many of Cavanaugh's characters exhibit a strong need for the security of family life that should come from parental approval. However, therein lies the difficulty—receiving the attention they need as children. Cavanaugh also indicates that security can easily be taken away (from loss of parents through death, violence, illness, emotional abandonment); therefore, the security attained becomes very precious—and sometimes tenuous. In *Missed Trains* the lovers, Maggie and Christopher, both lose their fathers at an early age. Both try to convince themselves and others that their fathers left them for unreal reasons. To recognize the truth would verify the frozen incompleteness of their families. Instead, the heroine changes her name from Virginia "Janya" Ruth Belton to Maggie Jones and tries to live out her father's dreams by becoming a famous actress. In *The Children Are Gone*, Philip discovers that both he *and* his daughter, Mary Fran, created—out of a desperate need—symbols of security which they used to ward off the loss of their parents.

All these novels show people who think they have already reckoned with, i.e., buried their own pasts. But Cavanaugh assumes these feelings live inside us somewhere and have to be confronted sometime if we want to live. We must also face long-hidden feelings if we want to regain true security in our lives. Because despite his engaging treatment of children, Cavanaugh is ultimately concerned with adults. Therefore, Philip Hallard must remember his own childhood, however painful. He must face his own past, accept it as true, move on to become his own parent, and finally become a true parent to his own children. Otherwise, the cycle of harmed childhood will continue unabated. While Philip has not physically left his children, he has neglected them enough so that Mary

Fran has become an invisible, silent girl (like Callie, her mother) who uses a familiar landmark (the neighborhood candy store) for the security of home and not the feelings within it. However, Philip can now begin to give real warmth to his daughter because he has finally established a relationship with himself. Philip has made some peace with his past and has given himself comfort through this process; now he has comfort to give to his family.

In *The Faithful*, his most overtly Catholic novel, Cavanaugh turns his attention to surrogate families, this time an order of French nuns. Rather than providing emotional support for Sister Louise, the main character, the order exemplifies the rigidity of Catholic institutions. In spite of this rigidity, however, Louise manages to rediscover her faith. Because the characters, including Louise, seem unreal, we hardly care for her spiritual success because we do not care about her person. On the other hand, Cavanaugh has fully given us Christopher, Philip, Callie, and Robbie who, although somewhat triumphant, are left struggling with the frailties of life. Nevertheless, these are the people who have truly confronted their pasts and, therefore, have chosen to live in the present. So that despite his recent foray into an attempted bestseller, Cavanaugh's less ambitious, yet more substantial, work on family life could illuminate many readers' hearts and minds.

SELECTED BIBLIOGRAPHY

Works by Cavanaugh: NOVELS: *The Children Are Gone*. New York: Simon & Schuster, 1966; *Leaving Home*. New York: Simon & Schuster, 1970; *Missed Trains*. New York: Simon & Schuster, 1979; *The Faithful*. New York: William Morrow & Co., 1986. AUTOBIOGRAPHY: *My Own Back Yard*. New York: Doubleday & Co., 1962. SHORT STORIES: "What I Wish (Oh, I Wish) I Had Said." *McCall's* 90 (August 1963) pp. 68–69 (also appears in *Prize Short Stories, 1965: The O. Henry Awards*); "Something Bright." *McCall's* 90 (September 1963) pp. 84–85; "Roseanne of Yesterday." *McCall's* 91 (April 1964) pp. 140–41; "Hannah for Hope." *McCall's* 91 (August 1964) pp. 74–75; "Nights before Christmas." *McCall's* 92 (December 1964) pp. 100–1.

Works about Cavanaugh: Review of *My Own Backyard*. *Booklist* (1 March 1962), p. 435; Review of *The Children Are Gone*. *America* (16 April 1966), p. 558; Review of *Leaving Home*. *The New York Times Book Review* (7 February 1971), p. 30; Review of *The Faithful*. *Best Sellers* (December 1986), p. 325. CA 17–18.

John R. Thelin

PAT CONROY (1945–). Both of South Carolina's laureates are Atlantans. James Dickey, the official poet laureate, lives in Columbia and writes about his boyhood home in Atlanta. Pat Conroy, the unofficial prose laureate of South Carolina, lives in Atlanta and writes about the Low Country, the setting of all five of Conroy's titles. No Southern alma mater has played more of a literary role than Conroy's Citadel in recording a youth's coming of age.

Conroy was born in Atlanta on October 26, 1945, "sired by a gruff-talking Marine from Chicago and a grits-and-gravy honey from Rome, Georgia" (*The Water Is Wide*, 46). His education as a writer began early: "my mother's reading to me each night was a celebration of language and tradition, a world of Mother Goose and lyric poetry. . . . My youth was a glut of words, a circus of ideas

nurtured by parents. . . . My youth sang the glory of books, the psalms of travel,
. . . of parables of war spoken by a flight-jacketed father, of parables of love and
Jesus sung by a blue-eyed mother, a renegade Baptist, a converted Catholic, a
soldier of the Lord'' (*The Water Is Wide*, 158).

Conroy grew up on the "necklace of Marine bases strung through the swamp-
lands of the Carolinas and Virginia'' (*The Great Santini*, 49). He was graduated
from Beaufort High School in South Carolina in 1963, then from The Citadel
in Charleston in 1967. He went back to Beaufort High School as a teacher. The
next year he taught at Daufuskie Island, off the coast of Beaufort. In 1969 he
married Barbara Bolling of Beaufort. They were divorced in 1977. In 1970
Conroy quit teaching and published his first book, *The Boo*, which celebrates
his friendship with Lt. Col. Thomas Nugent Courvoisie, the assistant comman-
dant of cadets at The Citadel when Conroy was a student there. In an ''Introduction'' to a 1981 edition of *The Boo*, Conroy admits that when he wrote the
penultimate chapter, ''Me and the Boo,'' ''I heard the resonant, unmistakable
sound of my voice as a writer for the first time'' (p. 13).

The year Conroy had spent teaching at Daufuskie Island became the source
of his second book, *The Water Is Wide*, a work of non-fiction, published in
1972. It was subsequently made into the movie *Conrack*. His third book, *The
Great Santini*, did not appear until 1976. In it he returns to his own student years
in high school in Beaufort for the story of the Meecham family, including the
gruff Marine father and Georgia belle mother. This book also was filmed, with
Robert Duvall and Blythe Danner. In 1981 Conroy married Lenore Gucewitz;
they live in Rome, Italy.

In his fourth book, *The Lords of Discipline* (1980), Conroy returns to The
Citadel and focuses on his life as a student. His most recent book, *The Prince
of Tides* (1986), marks Conroy's first departure from his South Carolina setting.
The book tells the story of two brothers and a sister and their lives in a shrimping
family on the South Carolina coast, but it is narrated to a psychiatrist in New
York.

Conroy's themes revolve around the initiation of a father-son rivalry, growing
up Catholic, racial tension in the South of his youth, and, like most Southern
writers, the South itself as a character. The most remarkable feature of Conroy's
style is his combination of humor and strength.

Conroy considers that he only narrowly escaped the trap of racism. Under the
influence of teenage peer pressure, ''"nigger-knocking was great fun during the
carnival of blind hatred I participated joyfully in during my first couple of years
in high school'' (*The Water Is Wide*, 15). Then his high school English teacher
Gene Norris introduced him to Pete Seeger's ''We Shall Overcome'': ''I remember that moment with crystal clarity . . . as a turning point in my life: a
moment terrible in its illumination of a toad in my soul'' (*The Water Is Wide*,
99). Some of Conroy's finest writing would grow out of this conviction so intense
that ''a black man could have probably handed me a bucket of cow piss, com-

manded me to drink it in order that I might rid my soul of the stench of racism, and I should have only asked for a straw'' (*The Water Is Wide*, 114).

Conroy's strongest characterization is typically that of a growing, suffering youth in the bittersweet rebellion against his father, a conflict realized most successfully in Conroy's portrait of Colonel Bull Meecham and his son Ben in *The Great Santini*. Two scenes in particular reveal the depths of Conroy's feelings for this aspect of growing up. Father and son play basketball and, for the first time, the son wins. Ben has finally beaten his father, but the father loses as gracelessly as he always has won. The father does not change,

beaten by a son for the first time in his life . . . the lone figure of [a] father standing there under the basket, sweating, red-faced, and mute, watching the celebration of his wife and children with the inchoate, resurrected anger of a man who never quit in his life. (*The Great Santini*, 145)

And for Ben, the real triumph is just not to cry as his still physically superior father bounces the ball off his son's head all the way across the yard, through the house, and up the stairs to Ben's room. Eighty pages later in the novel, Ben celebrates his eighteenth birthday. His father awakens him at four o'clock in the morning to give him a birthday present, his old World War II flight jacket. "The Jacket he wore was a part of his father's history, a fragment of Bull's biography," and "Ben could not have felt more changed if he had put on the silks of Father Pickney, prayed over a piece of unleavened bread, and felt it quiver with the life and light of God" (*The Great Santini*, 227).

Just as Conroy uses the father-son relationship for scenes of intensity, he uses scenes from a Catholic upbringing for some of his best humor. The Meecham children protest that too many Hail Mary's for their father's safe return is "turning this into a Novena" (*The Great Santini*, 13). Bull Meecham warns his son Ben that *Anna Karenina* is probably "a skin book," that "these novels you and Mary Anne read all the time are just so much bullshit. You ought to concentrate on classics like *The Baltimore Catechism*" (*The Great Santini*, 110). "Because poor ol' Protestants don't know any better," Mary Anne reminds Ben of "that time I told Jamie Polk you only spoke Latin and that was the only language Catholic boys were allowed to speak. Every time he would ask Ben a question, Ben would hit him with a line from the Confiteor" (*The Great Santini*, 74). Conroy offers their finest moments at the first meeting of "the Wednesday-night catechism class sponsored by the Confraternity of Christian Doctrine" (*The Great Santini*, 212). At this first session, Sister Loretta Marie discourages them from masticating the Host at Communion. But Mary Anne observes that "Jesus Christ tastes a lot like bread" (*The Great Santini*, 215) and bets "He likes the stomach better than where he goes next" (*The Great Santini*, 215). Conroy has also written that "all ex-Catholics are fugitives from their childhoods" and that "the Catholic school experience is our cultural touchstone," both of these statements in an essay entitled "Confessions of an Ex-Catholic" (*Atlanta Gazette*, 1 June 1977), but in which he also wrote "I am still as Catholic as the Pope." Tom

Wingo, in *The Prince of Tides*, tells his sister's psychiatrist, "you have no idea how weird it is to be raised a Catholic in the Deep South" (p. 51) because "the Catholic soul is Mediterranean and baroque and does not flourish or root easily in this inhospitable soil of the American Deep South" (p. 147).

Finally, as is usually the case in Southern fiction, the South itself plays a central role. En route to Ravenel to take up his new assignment, Bull Meecham objects to singing "Dixie." He insists that "Georgia is the armpit of Dixie. Of course we all is only going to South Carolina, the sphincter of America" (*The Great Santini*, 35). But South Carolina's Low Country has sustained Pat Conroy through five books. He is generally too interested in his characters to write much about landscape, although he has written movingly of Daufuskie Island in *The Water Is Wide* and of the islands near Beaufort in *The Great Santini* and *The Prince of Tides*.

His most descriptive passages are of Charleston in *The Lords of Discipline*. Charleston

is a feast for the human eye . . . a dark city, a melancholy city, whose severe covenants and secrets are as powerful and beguiling as its elegance, whose demons dance their alley dances and compose their malign hymns to the side of the moon I cannot see. (*The Lords of Discipline*, 1)

Still, "Charleston burns like a flame of purest memory" for this unofficial prose laureate of South Carolina, whose work revives memories of an earlier generation of writers native to Charleston whose combined volumes have not done for the Low Country what Pat Conroy has among the writers of the contemporary South.

SELECTED BIBLIOGRAPHY

Works by Conroy: *The Boo*. Verona, Va.: McClure, 1970; *The Water Is Wide*. Boston: Houghton Mifflin, 1972; *The Great Santini*. Boston: Houghton Mifflin, 1976; *Lords of Discipline*. Boston: Houghton Mifflin, 1980; *The Prince of Tides*. Boston: Houghton Mifflin, 1986.

Works about Conroy: Burkholder, Robert E. "The Uses of Myth in Pat Conroy's *The Great Santini*." *Studies in Modern Fiction* 21 (1979), pp. 31–37; York, Lamar. "Pat Conroy's Portrait of the Artist as a Young Southerner." *Southern Literary Journal* 19 (1987), pp. 34–46. CA 85–88. DLB 6.

Lamar York

JOHN COYNE (1939–). Although John Coyne has flourished, and flourished mightily, as a writer of occult fiction, he has never, he later confessed, felt totally at ease in this subgenre. Beginning in 1979 when he wrote *The Legacy* (freely adapted from the scenario for the movie *The Legacy* [Universal Films, 1979] through the appearance of *The Piercing* (1979), *The Searing* (1980), *Hobgoblin* (1981), and *The Shroud* (1983), he has produced one best-seller after another. Despite his millions of readers and his fame as an occult master, however, Coyne remained unfulfilled and unrealized, writing, as he put it, "Gothic soap." He turned then in 1986 to the writing of mainstream fiction with *Brothers* *and Sisters*, a splendidly orchestrated account of an Irish Scarlet O'Hara, whose will and drive created an Irish-American dynasty of her own.

Yet, despite Coyne's disclaimers about the aesthetic and artistic authority of his occult novels, even a hurried glance at his early work will reveal that he is a careful and devoted craftsman, working with taste and finesse. One finds within these works a skilled ringmaster, whose plot developments, characterizations, and finely chiseled and thought-packed sentences provide the reader with the conviction that Coyne is a very fine writer indeed.

Besides devoting himself to writing novels, Coyne has experienced stints with both the academic and the civil service worlds. He taught English and worked as a dean at the State University of New York at Old Westbury for two years, and he served with the Peace Corps for five years, working in Ethiopia and Washington, D.C. He received his B.A. from Saint Louis University in 1959, where he was connected with the M-Circle, the Mississippi Circle of the Saint Louis University group of writers. In 1962, he acquired a master's degree in English from Western Michigan University. Later, he did further graduate work at Haile Selassie I University, Georgetown University, and George Washington University.

The achievement of John Coyne as a novelist might be assessed by the following: he is a skilled creator of suspense (his heightened sense of atmosphere and expectation), a deft contemporary observer and journalist (his lifelike portraits of persons and places), an acute psychologist (his intensely realized interior reactions of women and men, particularly in their sexual anxieties), a sociologist of sorts (the airing of large issues—the plight of the street poor, women's rights, urban blight, the despoiling of the landscape), and finally the dispenser of information (high fashion, Tudor architecture, the rites and rituals of Catholicism).

Moreover, the major influence upon John Coyne's fictive world is not a closet of monsters, or a den of kooks, but his Catholic world view. Of this he has written:

Sex and religion! I am the only "horror" novelist working the "religious" themes. . . . I think to make horror work, it must be balanced against a system of belief. The Catholic faith gives us that. Horror or occult writing is conservative. It assumes that there is a right and a wrong. It assumes that one is responsible for his or her actions. In the Catholic sense, sinning causes hell or evil to descend upon a person.

His belief, therefore, that where there is a ghost, there is a God seems to be the major scaffolding upon which his novels are built. But underbuttressing this element and providing it with redoubtable support is his crisp, professional style, a style earned from a lifetime devoted to his craft and art.

SELECTED BIBLIOGRAPHY

Works by Coyne: HORROR NOVELS: *The Legacy*. New York: Berkley, 1979; *The Piercing*. New York: Putnam's, 1979; *The Searing*. New York: Putnam's, 1980; *Hobgoblin*. New York: Putnam's, 1981; *The Shroud*. New York: Berkley, 1983. *The Hunting Season*. New York: Macmillan, 1987; NOVEL: *Brothers and Sisters*. New York: E. P. Dutton, 1986.

Works about Coyne: Montesi, A. J. "The Craftsman and the Monsters." In *Discovering Modern Horror Fiction*, ed. Darrell Schweitzer. Washington, D.C.: Starmount House, 1985. pp. 106–19. CA 93–96. CANR 12.

A. J. Montesi

MICHAEL CRISTOFER, pseudonym for Michael Procaccino, (1946–). While the American theatre has been routinely criticized for remaining preoccupied with relationships within the nuclear family, Cristofer has consistently taken on larger issues. The structures of his plays have been called "un-dramatic," and it is true that he frequently makes use of narrative devices, assembles events in an episodic manner, and relies on speeches which go beyond realistic dialogue in elaborating characters. Cristofer's work gives the impression of being written in a frenzy of feeling for human beings caught up in ultimate dilemmas.

Michael Procaccino was born on January 22, 1946, in Trenton, New Jersey, and graduated from nearby Notre Dame High School. He attended Catholic University of America in Washington, D.C., but he left before completing his degree to begin acting professionally. While living on the East Coast, three plays were produced under his given name: *Plot Counter Plot*, *The Mandala*, and *Ammericommedia*. In 1972, he moved to Los Angeles and adopted the name Cristofer (pronounced *kris-TOFF-er*) as a stage name. He has had considerable success as an actor and director.

Cristofer is best known for *The Shadow Box* which, in 1977, won the Pulitzer Prize for best drama and the Tony award for best play. A version produced for television in 1980 won the Humanitas Award in 1981. *The Shadow Box* was the first of four plays by Cristofer which premiered at the Mark Taper Forum in Los Angeles under the direction of Gordon Davidson between 1975 and 1980, and went on to be produced on Broadway. The others are *Ice* (1976), *Black Angel* (1978), and *The Lady and the Clarinet* (1980).

In spite of his Catholic education, Cristofer seems more concerned with the worldly problems of characters living in a godless universe. *The Shadow Box* dramatizes the crises of three terminally ill patients and their loved ones. Cristofer unites the three stories throughout the two acts only by theme and common locale: cottages on the grounds of a large hospital complex. In each of the stories, approaching death teaches that the only thing which makes life worthwhile is knowing that someone needs you. Joe and Maggie find that all they have worked for—the home in the suburbs, and so on—means less now than the memories of the fights they had had over making ends meet. Mark grows cynical over losing his lover, Brian, and is reminded by Beverley that her former husband still needs him. Felicity ironically finds hope in knowing that her mother needs her as a surrogate for the other daughter she has lost.

Two of the plays center on characters who conduct agonizing searches for identity through lengthy, narrative reminiscence punctuated by desperate sexual encounters. In *Ice*, Cristofer uses a snowbound cabin in Alaska as a symbol of isolation for an unlikely trio: Murph, a former male model, Ray, an ex-teacher, and Sunshine, a free-spirited young woman. In *The Lady and the Clarinet*, the scene is Luba's apartment where she has hired a musician to create atmosphere for a romantic dinner. Luba recounts her three disastrous love affairs, pausing for remarks to the clarinet player who answers her with melodies provided in the script. As she tells their stories, Paul, Jack, and George show up to play out the remembered scenes. These stories reveal Luba as a pitiable woman, unable finally to love one man because of her fascination with all men.

The title character of *Black Angel* is Martin Engel, a former Nazi SS officer and convicted war criminal, released from prison in the 1970s and building a retirement cottage for himself and his wife in rural France. While the citizens of a nearby town try to drive him away and the mayor tries to protect him, Engel remains passive. In monologues and in flashbacks, he acknowledges his unremitting guilt and so asks whether society is seeking justice or a scapegoat.

SELECTED BIBLIOGRAPHY

Works by Cristofer: *The Shadow Box* is published by Drama Book Specialists, New York. *Black Angel* and *The Lady and the Clarinet* are available from Dramatists Play Service, New York.

Works about Cristofer: CA 110. CD. DLB 7.

Richard L. Homan

ELIZABETH CULLINAN (1933–). In her two novels and two short-story collections, Elizabeth Cullinan has staked out a small but well defined territory, the lives in the New York City area of Irish-American Catholics whose outlooks have been shaped by two powerful and entangled forces: a devout authoritarian mother and the beliefs and practices of the immigrant Church.

Cullinan's narrow field is rich in the telling detail that evokes a whole psychological history and the bit of dialogue that precisely conveys sibling rivalry, thwarted love, marital tensions, domestic politics, or the relentless anxiety of a daughter who fails to fulfill her mother's grandiose expectations. At the same time, Cullinan shows in these relationships what is honest, enduring, and worthwhile, even though painful. If Cullinan is more vertical than horizontal in her vision, no other writer of the Irish-American experience has probed it so closely, so aware of the tenacious network that binds together family and Church.

Although her short stories have been compared to James Joyce's, she has neither the sense of evil nor the Irish writer's power to evoke disturbing, almost incommunicable resonances. More likely, Cullinan's technique has been influenced by the formal experiments of Anton Chekhov and Joyce. Cullinan's achievement is that she has dramatized a segment of Irish-American Catholic life in a style that is controlled, intelligent, sometimes quietly humorous and aphoristic, occasionally satiric and ironic.

Born in New York City to first-generation Irish-American Catholic parents on June 7, 1933, Cullinan was raised in a family full of nuns and priests, and was educated in parochial schools. She received her college degree in 1954 from Marymount College, New York City. After graduation she worked at *The New*

Yorker where she became the secretary of the editor and novelist, William Maxwell, from whom she learned the craft of fiction. Her first story appeared in 1960 in *The New Yorker*. To write her novel *House of Gold* (1969), which won the Houghton-Mifflin Literary Fellowship, she went to Dublin and lived there for several years, an experience which became the basis for her novel, *A Change of Scene* (1982). She has published two collections of short stories, *The Time of Adam* (1971) and *Yellow Roses* (1977) and has taught at various universities. At present she lives in Manhattan, teaches at Fordham University, and contributes regularly to *The New Yorker*.

Cullinan admits to similarities between her fictional women and herself. The autobiographical voice may be heard in the character of Winnie in *House of Gold* for whom a genealogical chart could be drawn showing her appearances—under different names—in the stories and second novel. (Winnie's real name, Edwina Carroll, shares Elizabeth Cullinan's initials.) In *House of Gold*, Winnie is Mrs. Devlin's watchful granddaughter; in the short stories, she is, for example, the serious child who feels the ineradicable tensions in her parents' marriage, the young woman who has failed love affairs with two men in Ireland (material that will be reexamined in *A Change of Scene*) as well as a married man in New York, and the unmarried woman in her late forties who, in "A Good Loser," concludes she is not unhappy with her state. She may be Marjorie in "Only Human" whose priest uncle's death forces her to grapple with the deepest dimensions of Catholicism.

In Cullinan's world the women are much stronger, much more resilient than the men: the model set by old Mrs. Devlin of *House of Gold* has been followed less successfully by her daughter Elizabeth, Winnie's mother, who figures in such stories as "The Reunion." When the mother is not physically present, as in the Irish stories, an older woman becomes the surrogate: a figure echoing the novelist Mary Lavin appears prominently in the story, "Maura's Friends," and in *A Change of Scene* where Oona Ross, a writer, provides a substitute family and home for the narrator, Ann Clarke, who is Winnie in Dublin.

The single male figure who ultimately emerges as admirable is the Jesuit administrator, Father Phil, the suave friend of the rich and Mrs. Devlin's son in *House of Gold*. He becomes Father James Fox in "The Ablutions" where he receives a shock—verbally and spiritually—when he discovers his wealthy friends love the Mass only for its drama and panoply, not for its reenactment of Christ's sacrifice. His response to his moment of grace becomes explicit in a second story, which may be Cullinan's best, "Only Human," where he is the dead Father James Murray. Through the comments of Murray's Jesuit colleagues, the prattle of his sister, and the acerbic observations of the female narrator, Marjorie, who shares many of Winnie's characteristics, the reader slowly learns that the aloof and autocratic administrator has spent his final years answering the insistent calls for help that besieged him. Leaving the wake with the sacristan, Brother Desnoes, Marjorie journeys underground to the tomb-like chapel where her uncle's funeral Mass will be celebrated and sees all the trappings and marble pomp of the pre-Vatican II Church. She sees behind them as well. She realizes that just as Christ gave Himself through the Mass in a superhuman sacrifice for others, so her uncle, in his spiritual evolution, had given his life in a much smaller, altogether human way to others. A priestly vocation rooted in a psychological and sociological commitment to Church and mother had flowered into holiness.

Cullinan's writing probably will continue to follow the formal design that shapes *A Change of Scene*. Instead of opening in medias res, that novel begins with a woman in New York receiving a phone call from a former lover, a man she had known ten years before in Dublin. The voice from the past causes her to recreate and reassess her sojourn in Dublin where she had gone as a woman in her twenties to create and claim an identity distinct from the emotional claims and inherited values of her Irish-American family. Like that narrator, Ann Clarke, Cullinan explores and reexplores her personal experiences and human relationships, unexpectedly finding heightened meanings that suddenly radiate from the past and clarify the present.

SELECTED BIBLIOGRAPHY

Works by Cullinan: NOVELS: *House of Gold*. Boston: Houghton, 1969; *A Change of Scene*. New York: Norton, 1982. SHORT-STORY COLLECTIONS: *The Time of Adam*. Boston: Houghton, 1971; *Yellow Roses*. New York: Viking, 1977. UNCOLLECTED SHORT STORIES: "Idioms." *New Yorker* 31 (January 1977), pp. 31–35; "A Good Loser." *New Yorker* 15 (August 1977), pp. 32–44; "Commuting." *Irish Literary Supplement* 2.1 (1983), pp. 34–35.

Works about Cullinan: Connelly, Maureen. Review of *A Change of Scene*. *Irish Literary Supplement* 2.1 (1983), pp. 36; Kennedy, Eileen. "Bequeathing Tokens: Elizabeth Cullinan's Irish-Americans." *Eire-Ireland* 16.4 (1981), pp. 94–102; Murphy, Maureen. "Elizabeth Cullinan: Yellow and Gold." In *Irish-American Fiction: Essays in Criticism*, ed. Daniel J. Casey and Robert E. Rhodes. New York: AMS, 1979, pp. 139–51. CA 25–28. CANR 11.

Eileen Kennedy

J. V. CUNNINGHAM (1911–1985). Though by no means unrecognized in his lifetime, Cunningham's work is not as widely read as it deserves to be. When he is praised it is usually by calling him "our greatest epigrammatist," as if the epigram could never seriously threaten calcified literary hierarchies. It is remarked that he is abstract, dry, bitter, that his oeuvre is small and, at first glance, insubstantial. What critics too seldom notice is that Cunningham is a poet (he preferred to be called a verse-maker) whose vision is as complex as that of T. S. Eliot and Robert Lowell. Cunningham confronts the modern world—its incongruities, its apparent emptiness, its loss—with directness and a purifying anger. Toward the end of his life he said in an interview, "I have no religious beliefs," yet his vision requires the existence of Catholicism, the logic of its authorities, to be understood. The list of what Cunningham rejected would be longer than what he could hold onto; he had no appetite for cant or the superfluous word, and he ruthlessly edited his work. Because of this, Cunningham can be read as a kind of antidote to the more self-satisfied poets of our age.

He was born on August 23, 1911, in Cumberland, Maryland, and when only a few years old moved with his family to Billings, Montana. Because of this move, he knew little about his mother's Irish Catholic family. His father was a construction worker, also of Irish Catholic descent. In Billings, Cunningham went with his brothers to St. Vincent's Parochial School. He spent summers on a nearby ranch, a period alluded to in his poem, "Montana Fifty Years Ago." When he was twelve his family moved to Denver, where he finished the eighth grade at St. Elizabeth's School on Tennyson Street and the next fall entered a Jesuit high school. Having skipped two grades early on, Cunningham graduated from high school at the age of sixteen and went to work at various Denver newspapers. His father had died suddenly the year before in an industrial accident. Cunningham referred to the Market Crash of 1929 as "the dominant experience of my life." In an important interview with the poet Timothy Steele, he details the years of hard luck, wandering throughout the southwest looking for work while educating himself in modern poetry. His early education had emphasized the classics, yet by the age of eighteen he had encountered all the major modernists and, at what some would call an opposite literary pole, the poems of Jonathan Swift.

There had been abortive attempts at college, and finally Cunningham, with the help of Yvor Winters, went to Stanford University, taking his A.B. in 1934 and his Ph.D. eleven years later. Cunningham had studied both the classics and mathematics—he taught math at a military base in World War II—but he settled on English as his academic discipline. Though in 1957 Winters dedicated his book, *The Function of Criticism*, to Cunningham, his influence on the younger poet's career may be overstressed. Certainly Cunningham expressed gratitude for Winters' help, and for a while the two even shared the same publisher, Alan Swallow. But Winters rightly pointed out that Cunningham possessed his own mind and might have been led to Renaissance studies by W. D. Briggs and the love of Ben Jonson's verse as much as anything else. In addition, Cunningham showed little appetite for the sort of canon-making criticism in which Winters was engaged; for the most part, he divided his attentions between Renaissance scholarship and the revision of his poems. He taught at a number of universities, including Harvard and the University of Virginia, before settling at Brandeis in 1953. There were awards: two Guggenheim Fellowships and others from the National Institute of Arts and Letters and the Academy of American Poets. Cunningham was married three times; by his first marriage to Barbara Gibbs, he fathered one daughter; his second marriage to Dolora Gallagher was childless; in 1950 he married Jessie MacGregor, with whom he lived until his death on March 28, 1985.

Cunningham's scholarship is characterized by astute textual readings and an interest in literary style balanced by careful historical interpretation. Scholarship offered Cunningham a way out of the self, an outlet for affections that do not often surface in his poetry. In the essay "The Quest of the Opal," he writes about himself in the third person, in what he calls "a chastity of diction and a crispness of technique," as if the self were finally nothing more than one of discourse's "devices." (*Collected Essays*, Chicago: Swallow Press, 1976, p. 407.) This is where Cunningham's inability to believe on faith alone is given its most forthright explication. Catholicism suggests less a social identity than a method of argument derived largely from Thomas Aquinas. In Cunningham's work, the relentless logic and consideration of alternative positions create a consciousness of fictions and significations, with a residue of disconnected anger. As he wrote in "The Journal of John Cardan," "a man must live divided against himself: only the selfishly insane can integrate experience to the heart's desire, and only the emotionally sterile would not wish to."

If there is a Cunningham persona, a typical figure who suffers and taunts us in the poems, it would be mistaken to call him emotionally sterile. That he can find "no virtue, except in sinuous exacting speech" by itself suggests that virtue is something he has sought and failed to find in himself and the rest of humanity. In "Timor Dei" he rejects the Catholicism with which he was raised, yet he admits that what he fears most is absolute fear, a God without confidence. Wit, in this context, is a bitter joy, an attempt to compensate for inconsolable loss. Cunningham's reliance upon reason is almost pathological; he mistrusts paradox, yet he seems simultaneously aware that reason's solutions, like the proofs of mathematical theorems, are finally rhetorical. His small poem, "Montana Pastoral," as much as Eliot's *Waste Land*, suggests that the conventions of elegy have failed to demonstrate the actual depletion of meaning from existence. Finally, in a sequence like *Doctor Drink*, man is reduced to his ugliest state, isolate, a sophist drowning in his own bile.

It is usual at such moments to stress the redemption of art, but, enjoyable as his poems are, Cunningham makes no redemptive claim. Perhaps this is why he is at his best when he criticizes our illusions about love and poetry. With regard to poetic form, for example, he easily dismisses the prevalent notion that metrical regularity is meaningless. While most contemporary poets write as though free verse and a sort of watered-down imagism were law, Cunningham is unafraid of the metered line and the pithy abstraction. Yet it is not true that his verse offers no sensuous images and textures. His beautiful sequence *To What Strangers, What Welcome* is full of them.

Cunningham is, among other things, one of our best poets about the western landscape. He sees it as a pared, difficult place where no mirage can solidify— a landscape, as it were, abstracted, yet real and worn by its being. This is the landscape one imagines behind even his most philosophical poems; it is the bony grimace behind his epigrams about love and sex. Cunningham is the kind of poet who disproves our critical categories; working in the rigorous tradition of Martial and stressing the plain style of Cicero, or that of Ben Jonson, he is among the most "modern" of our poets.

SELECTED BIBLIOGRAPHY

Works by Cunningham: POETRY: *The Helmsman*. San Francisco: The Colt Press, 1942; *The Judge Is Fury*. New York: Swallow Press/Morrow, 1947; *Doctor Drink: Poems*. Cummington, Mass.: Cummington Press, 1950; *The Exclusions of a Rhyme: Poems and Epigrams*. Denver: Swallow Press, 1964; *Some Salt: Poems and Epigrams*. Madison, Wis.: Perishable Press, 1967; *The Collected Poems and Epigrams of J. V. Cunningham*. Chicago: Swallow Press, 1971. PROSE AND CRITICISM: *The Quest of the Opal: A Commentary on "The Helmsman."* Denver: Swallow Press, 1950; *Woe or Wonder: The Emotional Effect of Shakespearean Tragedy*. Denver: University of Denver Press, 1951; *The Collected Essays of J. V. Cunningham*. Chicago: Swallow Press, 1976; *Emily Dickinson: Lyric and Legend*. Los Angeles: Sylvester and Orphanos, 1980. EDITED: *The Renaissance in England*. New York: Harcourt, Brace & World, 1966; *The Problem of Style*. Greenwich, Conn.: Fawcett, 1966; *In Shakespeare's Day*. New York: Fawcett, 1970.

Works about Cunningham: Carruth, Hayden. "A Location of J. V. Cunningham." *Michigan Quarterly Review* (Spring 1972), pp. 75–83; Gullans, Charles. *A Bibliography of the Published Writings of J. V. Cunningham*. Los Angeles: University of California Library, 1973; Steele, Timothy. "An Interview with J. V. Cunningham." *The Iowa Review* (Fall 1985), pp. 1–24; Taylor, Henry. "The Example of J. V. Cunningham." *The Hollins Critic* (October 1982), pp. 1–13; Winters, Yvor. *The Poetry of J. V. Cunningham*. Denver: Swallow Press, 1961. CA 2. CANR 2. DLB 5.

David Mason

D

BILL C. DAVIS (1951–). Popular recognition and critical acclaim came to Bill C. Davis in 1980 as a result of his first full-length play produced in New York, *Mass Appeal*. Comparing it to other plays on Catholic themes produced around the same time, such as Christopher Durang's *Sister Mary Ignatius Explains It All For You*, critics praised *Mass Appeal* for its delightful mixture of explosive comedy and human understanding, for evoking laughter that led to sadness and compassion rather than to uneasiness, rage, or insanity. Although some believed that it did not sufficiently resolve its topical conflicts between tradition and innovation, charm and commitment, love and celibacy, most agreed that its two characters were genuine and vulnerable enough to stir empathy.

Bill C. Davis was born on August 25, 1951, and received most of his education at Catholic schools in Poughkeepsie, New York. He attended Holy Trinity grammar school and then Our Lady of Lourdes High School, where he graduated in June 1969. He entered Marist College in January 1971 and graduated in May 1974. He has acted in his plays *Mass Appeal* and *Wrestlers* (1987), and he has written screenplays for the film of *Mass Appeal* and the television drama *Internal Combustion*. From 1975 to 1979 he worked as a housefather at Rhinebeck Country Village, a home for problem children in Rhinebeck, New York; this experience must influence his ideas on family, play, and institutional service. He now resides in New Milford, Connecticut.

In all of his plays Davis explores the effects of institutions on people, and in *Mass Appeal* the institution is the Church. The two meanings of *mass* represent the conflict in the play between a gathering of persons and a ritual act. In his first sermon Mark Dolson, a deacon who is sent to St. Francis Church to prove himself worthy of the priesthood, challenges a congregation to reflect on why they come to church. He wants them to use the ritual act to open their hearts to a higher order of being; he fears that they just go through motions which confirm their vanities and consumerism. Later, when he begins to understand the people more, he is struck by what he calls their silent screams for help, and he blames the Church in part for causing this fearful lack of openness. He expects an institution to hear and answer people's needs, and he does this himself by working with meals-on-wheels and playing the piano at dances for senior citizens. However, he becomes a victim of his own openness when he reveals to the rector of the seminary his past love affairs with both sexes and gets expelled.

Mark's mentor during this training period is Father Tim Farley, the pastor, who is lovable and entertaining, yet easily intimidated by both parishioners and hierarchy. Although he loves the people, he does not seem to notice and serve their deeper needs or challenge them to move forward. He tells them what he knows they want to hear, and he will change the content of a sermon to quiet their coughs of disapproval. In return, they send him bottles of sparkling burgundy. Father Tim illustrates perfectly the attractions and dangers of the Catholic institution, but he is also a vivid character who by his relationship with Mark becomes aware of his failings and reaches a moment of decision between heroic sacrifice and tragic acquiescence.

Dancing in the End Zone (1985) scrutinizes college football as an institution and finds it, like the Church, protective but damaging. James Bernard, a star quarterback with a bad knee, must take injections before every game and hope that his knee pads and offensive line will keep him from further injury. The knee, however, is only a symbol of deeper wounds. James is an adopted child whose parents are separated and whose mother is sick. He is so desperate for affection that he will cling voraciously to any person who shows him sympathy. Humiliated by this tendency, he follows the advice of his coach and his mother and plays football. Its helmets and shoulder pads keep him safe from human contact and distract him from his pain. But then a student who is secretly writing an exposé on gift grades and harmful painkillers for athletes is assigned as his tutor and gradually helps him quit football, experience his emotional pain, and open himself to others in love and dance. This student, whose husband is in jail for anti-nuke activities, realizes that football is a war game based on aggression and defense. It cannot soothe human pain.

Thicker Than Blood, originally called *Family Planning*, is set at a retirement home, and the institution it evaluates is the family, or what the family has become. The retired people who live at the "Accommodation" are treated like children, yet they are not permitted to associate with children in the neighborhood who come to them after being beaten or told to get lost by their parents. When Ralph's daughter comes to visit him, she puts a ham in the oven so that she will have an excuse to leave early. Neville refuses to see his son because his son keeps nagging him to have some kind of heavenly nuptial with his mother, who has died, so he can be legitimized. Jess then tells the tragic story of his family and asks the other retired people to help him paint the porch. Once long ago he could have done a perfect paint job by himself, but he asked his family to help and they did the job sloppily and half jokingly. What is thicker than blood in this play is paint, which signifies self-expression and group activity, things which the family can squelch but which cannot be a substitute for or survive without.

Wrestlers is also a family drama, but the institution that it examines is the rat race—competing, calculating, getting ahead, winning. Two brothers react differently to this institution. Bobby, the elder, has his life planned: college, dean's list, law school, the senate. He is even a planned baby. While he was growing up, he constantly asserted his superiority over his younger brother, Monty, who was a diaphragm baby. Once he put red ants into Monty's black ant farm to watch them fight and see who would win. He ruled Monty like a marine and argued in favor of nuclear missiles for a balance of power. When he flunks out of law school, he is afraid to face his family. He begins to visit Monty, who is now living with Angie in the country and teaching orphans through dance and play. Bobby wants to repair things in the house and build closets for things that are just lying around. Eventually the two brothers find themselves competing for Angie. So the battle goes on, between work and play, fighting and dancing, organization and caprice, until the brothers wonder if they can ever love each other.

The institutions and rituals which Davis proposes and demonstrates in his plays are those which help people express and liberate themselves—dancing, painting, play—and not those which stifle the spirit or foster competition and conformity.

SELECTED BIBLIOGRAPHY

Works by Davis: PLAYS: *Mass Appeal.* New York: Avon Books, 1981; *Dancing in the End Zone.* New York: Samuel French, 1985; *Wrestlers.* New York: Dramatists Play Service, 1987; *Thicker Than Blood.* UNPUBLISHED: property of Sy Fischer Agency, Los Angeles.

Works about Davis: *Theatre World.* New York: Crown, 1980–, pp. 36, 38, 39, 40, 41. CA 110.

Anthony J. Berret, SJ

MARY DEASY (1914–). Mary Deasy was born in 1914 in Cincinnati, Ohio. She graduated from the Cincinnati Conservatory of Music to prepare for a career as a concert pianist but later abandoned that goal to write. She has published stories in *The Atlantic Monthly*, *Mademoiselle*, and other magazines and has twice been awarded the O. Henry prize for short fiction.

The setting for these novels is Cincinnati (called Corioli in the novels) or somewhere close by, and the characters are usually immigrant and first- and second-generation Irish-American. Though her work is "Catholic," involving priests, parishes, and an Irish Catholicism, the major sources for her plots are politics and family. *O'Shaughnessy's Day* (1957), perhaps her best novel, is concerned with the death of a traditional figure in American politics, the ward boss, and the impact of his death on his family. *Devil's Bridge* (1952) stresses the attempt of an idealistic bridge builder to overcome the intricacies and corruption of political commissions. *The Boy Who Made Good* (1955) dramatizes the return to politics of a state official. Family themes are found principally in *The Hour of Spring* (1948), *Ella Gunning* (1950), *Cannon Hill* (1949), and *The Corioli Affair* (1954).

Miss Deasy's writing is characterized by several admirable features: sensitivity to local places like gardens, hidden streets, the life of small towns, life on the banks of the Ohio River, and the complexity of family life, particularly father-son and father-daughter relationships. Her limitations emerge from several sources. Though her political themes are far more penetrating than the religious, they rarely reveal the brutality and greed so much a part of American politics from 1890 to the 1920s, the approximate period covered in the novels. In addition, the major male character is repeated in each novel. He is invariably tall, dark, powerful, idealistically ambitious, rather mysterious, and, above all, "Celtic." Thus, he becomes almost a stock figure rather than a protagonist. There is, too, a predictability in these novels. We know immediately upon their meeting that certain characters will fall in love despite ominous barriers, that others will die so that old romances can be revived, and that the Celtic hero will succeed so that virtuous ambitions can have their day. Perhaps these limitations are inseparable from Deasy's choice of and adherence to a point of view located in young narrators, sometimes first person, whose visions of their world are fresh and idealistic, but not profound.

The world of Deasy's novels is not devoid of sorrow, despair, death, and failure, but it is an orderly world in which triumphs are nicely balanced against failures, virtue is threatened but not vanquished by vice, love often is lost but inevitably restored. It is, in spite of a considerable amount of human wayward-ness, a genteel world which even in the worst of times can afford the haunting memories of fine old gardens and soft, spring rains in which lovers can walk.

SELECTED BIBLIOGRAPHY

Works by Deasy: *The Hour of Spring.* New York: Ayer Co., 1948; *Cannon Hill.* Boston: Atlantic Monthly Press, 1949; *Ella Gunning.* Boston: Atlantic Monthly Press, 1950; *Devil's Bridge.* Boston: Atlantic Monthly Press, 1952; *The Corioli Affair.* Boston: Atlantic Monthly Press, 1954; *The Boy Who Made Good.* Boston: Atlantic Monthly Press, 1955; *O'Shaughnessy's Day.* New York: Doubleday Doran, 1957.

Works about Deasy: Scott, Bonnie Kime. "Women's Perspectives in Irish-American Fiction from Betty Smith to Mary Scott." *Irish-American Fiction: Essays in Criticism.* New York: AMS, 1979, pp. 87–103. CA 5–6.

Frank L. Ryan

MADELINE DEFREES (1919–). While she was Sister Mary Gilbert in the Congregation of the Sisters of the Holy Names of Jesus and Mary, Madeline DeFrees wrote her first volume of poetry and two prose works, in which images of enclosure become metaphors for the rigor of emotional self-definition. In her next collection, *When Sky Lets Go* (1978), the fire and water of the self are loosed in images of worldly freedom which battle toward but do not achieve final resolution. DeFrees' third collection of poems, the chapbook *Imaginary Ancestors* (1978), continues the evolutionary psychic movement of *Sky* in its revelation of the poet's roots, both spiritual and biological. Her most recent collection, *Magpie on the Gallows* (1982), fuses brilliantly the air of intellect with the blood of language: the poems embody both the energy and knowledge divined from ferocity of living, from faith in the elemental word. Compared to John Donne's and Gerard Manley Hopkins' for wit and craft, DeFrees' work is noted for its intellectual strength and its lyrical beauty.

Born on November 18, 1919, in Ontario, Oregon, DeFrees attended private and parochial schools in Portland; she obtained a B.A. from Marylhurst College in 1948 and an M.A. from the University of Oregon in 1951. She also took courses from Karl Shapiro, John Berryman,* and Robert Fitzgerald. DeFrees' ethnic background is uncertain: her mother was adopted and knew nothing of her parentage; her father was either Dutch or French.

DeFrees has listed her most important life events as entering St. Mary's Academy in Portland, entering the convent, leaving the convent, accepting her first nonchurch-related teaching position at the University of Montana, moving to New England in 1979 to direct the Graduate Creative Writing Program at the University of Massachusetts-Amherst, and her retirement in 1985 to Seattle, Washington.

SELECTED BIBLIOGRAPHY

Works by DeFrees: POETRY: *From the Darkroom*. New York: Bobbs-Merrill, 1964; *When Sky Lets Go*. New York: George Braziller, 1978; *Imaginary Ancestors*. Missoula, Mont.: CutBank/SmokeRoot Press, 1978; *Magpie on the Gallows*. Port Townsend, WA: Copper Canyon Press, 1982. SHORT STORIES: "The Model Chapel." *Best American Short Stories of 1962*. Ed. Martha Foley and David Burnett. Boston: Houghton-Mifflin Co., 1962, pp. 167–80; "The Same Old Cracked Tune." *The Lamp* 61, 6 (June 1963), pp. 19–20, 22; "Purple." *Virginia Quarterly Review*, XLI, 1 (Winter 1965), pp. 92–101; "Hedges." *The Portland Review* 24 (1978), pp. 80–90; "*Agave americana*." *Extended Outlooks*. Ed. Jane Cooper et al. New York: Collier Books, 1982, pp. 50–61. CRITICISM: "James Wright's Early Poems: A Study in 'Convulsive' Form." *Modern Poetry Studies* II, 6 (1972), pp. 241–51.

Works about DeFrees: Holland, Robert. "Lost and Found" (omnibus review, including *When Sky Lets Go*). *Poetry* (March 1979), pp. 348–49; Trueblood, Valerie. "Books." *American Poetry Review* (May/June 1979), pp. 17–18. CA 11–12. CANR 4.

CarolAnn Russell

DON DELILLO (1936–). Don DeLillo has written satirically about advertising, the rock music scene, football, mathematics, terrorism, espionage, Americans in Europe, and the threat of toxic poisoning. His works have been called apocalyptic because even if they do not deal directly with last things, they often hint toward the unwritten conclusion of events in a void, or certainly, in a mystery. Critics praise the profundity and brilliance of DeLillo's ideas, condemn the shallowness of his thinking, praise the subtleness of his language, condemn the thinness of his plots and his cool treatment of characters. There is no denying that DeLillo stirs up trouble, if not among the masses, then among a limited number of readers, either enthusiastic and devoted, or irked and frustrated.

DeLillo was born in New York City on November 20, 1936, and spent his childhood and adolescence in Pennsylvania and the South Bronx. After graduating from Fordham University, DeLillo lived in New York and Canada. He seems to spend most of his time either travelling to gather materials for his novels, or writing the novels. He rarely grants interviews and has ever taken to the celebrity trail of talk shows, panel discussions, and visits to universities, even though *White Noise* (1985) won The American Book Award for fiction in 1985. A private man, DeLillo lives with his wife on a modest street in a suburb of New York City.

Like Thomas Pynchon, with whom he is often compared, DeLillo chronicles the chaos, absurdities, boredom, violence, and systems of contemporary American life. *White Noise*, for example, concerns Americans' obsession with technology; Mrs. Gladney secretly takes an experimental pill which supposedly eliminates the fear of death—though not death itself. Meanwhile, advances in chemistry which do not eliminate human bungling create the "airborne toxic event" which forces the Gladney family to evacuate their home, exposing Jack to enough toxicity to begin his slide toward death.

In the form of the noises of the crowds in the supermarket and the mind-dulling drone of the television, among others, the white noise of modern ennui surrounds these characters like entropic forces of destruction; it is the white noise of death, always present but rarely noticed. All sound becomes one sound just as in *Americana* (1971) advertising entices all individuals to become one individual, the manifestation of a limited number of fabricated images: people become images of images. All energy moves toward chaos, abetted by humanity's propensity for violence. DeLillo's attention to detail as a writer counters entropy by affirming the variety and richness of individual beings, whether football jerseys or terrorist assassins.

Individual characters, however, often seem to interest DeLillo less than do ideas. It is difficult to find warm human connection in his work, though there is plenty of the cold, abstract, and violent kind. Gary Harkness and his bumbling roommate in *End Zone* (1972) explore ideas, but their friendship dwindles to silence. Jack Gladney and his wife Babette share moments of closeness, but each harbors a secret which prevents true intimacy, though they probably achieve a level of relationship deeper than any other DeLillo couple. Characters continually drift away from each other as Glen Selvy does from Moll Robbins in *Running Dog* (1978) and David Bell does from everyone in *Americana* and the hero of *The Names* (1982) does from his wife and children. Often enough, people are as detached from themselves as they are from others. David Bell in *Americana* is making an autobiographical film which, he claims, he is not really in.

This detachment opens DeLillo to the charge of coolly discarding his own creations. Characters are metaphysicians of a kind, remote and wooden, like pieces in some board game or props in a drama of ideas. This may result, as one critic has argued, from DeLillo's affinity for Menippean satire in which characters stand for ideas, lacking well-rounded personalities interacting in a logical sequence of events. Ideas disrupt plots and vice versa; in *End Zone*, Gary Harkness tries to make love to his girlfriend in the stacks of the library, but his action is doomed to interruption because plot cannot advance within the universe of ideas.

In discussing DeLillo's posture toward his heroes, Anthony Burgess notes that DeLillo does not really care about people; rather, DeLillo's books are about Americana taken literally: about American things (*CLC*, vol. 13, p. 178). For his part, DeLillo has said that he does not take any attitude toward his characters. "I don't feel sympathetic toward some characters, unsympathetic toward others. I don't love some characters, feel contempt for others. They have attitudes, I don't" (LeClair 22).

What keeps characters from attaching heart to heart is their involvement with systems: football teams, advertising, the CIA, covert operations, the music business, Wall Street; alphabets, language, mathematics, disciplines of studies. Systems play the key role of providing order in place of chaos, and excitement in place of boredom. But at the same time, systems incline to exist for their own sake, squeezing the life out of the human beings struggling to understand their function within the system and impairing their ability to relate to each other and to people in other systems. For DeLillo—like Pynchon—the human tendency to interpret the universe in terms of closed systems will lead to the destruction of humanity.

DeLillo has suggested that, in a way, all his novels are about systems of communication, the making of signs which becomes an infinite process of imposing meaning, of discovering the inadequacy of language to explain, and of beginning over again to test the limitations of language. In *The Names*, James Axton becomes obsessed with finding the mysterious meaning behind the signs that cult members leave as clues to their murders; meanwhile, his anthropologist friend Brademas probes behind the scratchings of alphabets for the origin of all language. The making of images—the language of film—especially lends meaning; in *Running Dog*, Adolf Hitler—his fanatical schemes destroyed—attempts to bring sanity to his last days in the bunker by making home movies. The illusory truth of celluloid images makes fanaticism seem all the more reasonable and even ordinary. In *Americana*, while on assignment to film a documentary about the Navahos in the desert, David Bell ignores his professional duties in order to make a film about his own life. The scenes and characters all arise from memories of David's childhood and recent past, but David must rearrange the material into language and images which bring understanding, thus permitting him to complete his quest for self-knowledge. Ironically, film must inevitably fail to capture the fluidity and mystery of life because, like all closed systems, it must select and choose, leave out and invent.

All systems of ordering signs grow too complicated to communicate the untellable mysteries behind language. At the end of *White Noise*, Jack Gladney meets a Roman Catholic nun who professes no belief in the doctrines of the Catholic Church, but who remains a nun to affirm humanity's need for the pretense of faith. Belief in Catholicism cannot last; but human nature continues, nearly compulsively, to make systems of ritual and signs, chasing fruitlessly to connect sign with signified.

Invent language, reinvent it. This is how DeLillo spends his time, acknowledging that his most satisfying achievement as a writer is "to make interesting, clear, beautiful language . . . " (LeClair 23). For example, DeLillo gives over part two of *End Zone* to describing a football game, reinventing play-by-play descriptions, exposing ordinary cliches for their distance from action and restoring words to a closer relationship with a fast-moving, multilayered event. As Robert Nadeau has pointed out, DeLillo believes that "by detaching ourselves from the word as *Logos*, and placing greater emphasis upon the function of the word as concrete referent, we would be better able to construct an alternate reality more consistent with the metaphysics implied in the new physics" (Nadeau 161). At the same time, DeLillo seems to know that the task is ultimately absurd, but the issue must be engaged, the assumptions questioned. Making a dense difficult book like *Ratner's Star* (1976), for example, challenges the current assumptions of American publishing about the soft food appetite of American readers, even as it plays with the systems of mathematics which DeLillo sees as a kind of pure knowledge, full of mystery and secret codes.

Besides systems, the invention of games provides another antidote to the boredom of contemporary American life. Games lend order by giving shape to unleashed emotions, as football does, or the game of sex, or in *Running Dog*, the game involved with Glen's date with death. His encounters with pursuing assassins approach the grace of fencing or the courtship of basketball. Games bring excitement to life, and beauty to violence and death. DeLillo himself has said that games primarily involve rules and boundaries, the deep and often unexpressed need for some kind of order even for people who would wish to be outside the constraints of daily routine. "Games provide a frame in which we can try to be perfect," says DeLillo, and in which we "can look for perfect moments or perfect structures" (LeClair 22).

What looms behind the need to make games and systems is the mystery of violence, death, and sex. In *The Names*, James Axton finds out that connecting a victim's initials to the initials of the town where he lives justifies murder for the members of a cult. In *Players* (1977), Lyle sees death as the goal of the terrorists who are trying to overthrow a system which they believe to be death-dealing. But the new order of terrorism is in itself as evil as the order it intends to change. With Nathaniel Hawthorne and Herman Melville as unnamed mentors, DeLillo concludes that nothing but ambiguity defines the nature of good and evil. Sowing violence may harvest good: the murderers in *The Names* are not all bad; in *Players*, Lyle functions as a double agent, consorting with terrorists while informing on terrorists for the CIA. Readers may be left wondering who are the good guys and who are the bad, and why DeLillo, unlike most satirists, fails to provide the moral center in his texts to let us know.

In a world of such moral ambiguity, it is no wonder that the characters remain detached, for the alternative to detachment and indifference is obsession and fanaticism. DeLillo uses the image of Hitler in *White Noise* and *Running Dog*, implying that our boring and mundane lives make us attracted to the irresistible, exciting compulsions of great fanatics. It seems impossible within DeLillo's vision to live normal lives with a modicum of emotional fulfillment, though Jack and Babette Gladney may be the exceptions which prove the rule.

Out of boredom with their jobs and out of the emotional tedium of intimate relationship, characters drift into webs of intrigue. In *The Names*, James Axton's professional and marital ennui makes him susceptible to scents of excitement in his environment. Hence, when he reads of the cult murders, he becomes driven to search deeper and deeper into the pattern and meaning of events. Like many of DeLillo's heroes, he finds that the search for meaning becomes equated with the search for death. As DeLillo has said of Glen Selvy in *Running Dog*, "He finds his truth in violence" (LeClair 24). Escaping the boring routines of channel-changing leads inevitably into the unfathomable mysteries of life, beyond systems, into moments of silence and clarity which come in the deserts at the end of *Running Dog* and *The Names*, or in the barren landscapes surrounding Logos College in *End Zone* where characters face "a solitude they have to confront" (LeClair 24).

In his attraction to silences and barren clarity, DeLillo seems at times the frustrated mystic, striving to escape the noise of daily life to find peace in simplicity. All his characters seem entrapped in tangles of complicated action, whether the terrorist intrigues of *Players*, the scientific tapestries of *Ratner's Star*, the underground ties of the pornography and defense industries in *Running Dog*, the fantastic twistings of cult behavior in *The Names*, or the intricate diagrams of offensive plays in *End Zone*. In *Running Dog*, Glen Selvy tries to escape from his assassins by following a straight line across the country to the empty cleanness of the desert. Straight lines lead to death. Ambiguity can resolve into simplicity, but complete simplicity means extinction.

David Bell in *Americana* expresses this theme when he says, "And so purity of intention, simplicity and all its harvests, these were with the mightiest of the visionaries, those strong enough to confront the large madness. For the rest of us, the true sons of the dream, there was only complexity" (p. 138).

If complexity does not resolve into the simplicity of death, escape from complexity—if only partially—can mean the possibility of rebirth. David Bell survives his cross-country quest for self-knowledge and will return to his job among the intrigues of New York's advertising world. *End Zone* ends (more ambiguously) in total silence. *The Names* ends with Axton's son reinventing language. And at the end of *White Noise*, four-year-old Wilder Gladney pedals his bike across four lanes of highway traffic without getting hurt, driven by his child's naive belief that, of course, he will get to the other side safely. That he survives the random conjunction of systems of high-speed roads and technological force remains, like much of life for Don DeLillo, something of a mystery.

SELECTED BIBLIOGRAPHY

Works by DeLillo: *Americana*. Boston: Houghton Mifflin, 1971; *End Zone*. Boston: Houghton Mifflin, 1972; *Great Jones Street*. Boston: Houghton Mifflin, 1973; *Ratner's Star*. New York: Knopf, 1976; *Players*. New York: Knopf, 1977; *Running Dog*. New York: Knopf, 1978; (as Cleo Birdwell) *Amazons*. New York: Knopf, 1980; *The Names*. New York: Knopf, 1982; *White Noise*. New York: Viking, 1985; *Libra*. New York: Viking, 1988.

Works about DeLillo: LeClair, Thomas. "An Interview with Don DeLillo." *Contemporary Literature* 23 (1982), pp. 19–31; Nadeau, Robert. *Readings from the New Book on Nature: Physics and Metaphysics in the Modern Novel*. Amherst: The University of Massachusetts Press, 1981; Stade, George. Review of *Ratner's Star*. *The New York Times Book Review* (20 June 1976), p. 7; Storoff, Gary. "The Failure of Games in Don DeLillo's *End Zone*." In *American Sport Culture: The Humanistic Dimensions*. Lewisburg; London: Bucknell University Press; Associated University Press, 1985. CA 81–84, DLB 6.

Daniel J. Tynan

DAVID DENNY (1938–). Brevity honed in darkness grounds the poetry of David Denny, priest and monk at Nada Hermitage in Crestone, Colorado. He was born in Indiana and moved with his family to Arizona where he attended the University of Arizona. Nourished by the mysticism of Hinduism, Buddhism, and Sufism, he rejoiced to discover through reading Thomas Merton* a mystical, contemplative Christianity.

He traces his contemplative origins to a trip to Afghanistan where, at the age of seventeen, he became convinced that "the struggles of mankind had no merely natural solutions." He joined a contemplative community to participate in the spiritual transformation of human beings and history. He made final vows and was ordained in 1980.

David Denny is not a prolific poet. Perhaps, like John of the Cross—with whom he bears comparison on several levels—his poetry is the outpouring of a love that informs many and varied endeavors at the monastery.

SELECTED BIBLIOGRAPHY

Works by Denny: POETRY: In such magazines as *Studia Mystica*, *Contemplative Review*, and *Desert Call*, "The End of Summer," 22, no. 3 (Fall 1987): 21.

Mary E. Giles

AUGUST DERLETH (1909–1971). August Derleth was a prolific author who, under his own name and under various pseudonyms, published both poetry and prose, both serious fiction and popular short stories and novels. In addition, he was an editor, a reviewer, a biographer, a historian, and an author of juvenile poetry and prose. Although a minor figure in American literature, Derleth received a Guggenheim fellowship in 1938. His work combines readability and charm with a serious purpose. A critical commonplace, however, is that Derleth's work tends to be hackwork and suffers from lack of revision and polishing. Derleth considered such judgment irrelevant because he viewed himself as a storyteller and an entertainer rather than a writer of the contemporary American mainstream. The influence of Catholicism is clear in his work because he often probes questions about what it means to be human, about the relationships between human beings, and about the place of man in the universe.

Derleth was born on February 24, 1909, in Sauk City, Wisconsin, of primarily Bavarian ancestry despite his French name. He was educated at St. Aloysius Parochial School and Sauk City High School, and he received his A.B. from the University of Wisconsin in 1930. He began writing at age thirteen, and his first publication was a story entitled "Bat's Belfry," which appeared in *Weird Tales* in 1926, when Derleth was fifteen. Derleth was the owner and editor of the Wisconsin publishers Arkham House. Derleth was married in 1953 and divorced in 1959. He died in Sauk City of a heart attack on July 4, 1971.

As a poet, Derleth has been compared to Edgar Lee Masters, who praised Derleth as an author whose poetry was uplifting and delightful. Like that of Masters, his poetry does not belong to the high modern tradition which expresses existential angst and is addressed to a small audience; instead, it is characterized by simplicity and homely philosophy, it expresses his love for nature and wild creatures in plain language, and it describes the religious experience that nature can provide.

Derleth's popular fiction encompasses mystery stories, horror stories, fantasy, and science fiction. He is famous as the editor of the works of H. P. Lovecraft. In addition, he edited works by contemporary fantasy and science fiction authors and was one of those responsible for removing the genres from the pulp magazines and presenting them as a serious part of modern fiction. His own work—for example, *The Mask of Cthulu* (1958)—tends to be in the genre exemplified by the title of *Weird Tales* and is heavily influenced by Lovecraft. In 1928, Derleth learned that Arthur Conan Doyle did not intend to write any more Sherlock Holmes mysteries, and he created his own Holmesian detective, Solar Pons, whose name means "Bridge of Light"; his first story about Pons was "The Adventure of the Black Narcissus" (1929). He himself admitted that the stories that he wrote about Pons were literary pastiches, and they are of interest primarily to fans of Sherlock Holmes. He wrote other mysteries, including *Death by Design* (1953) and a study of true crime cases entitled *Wisconsin Murders* (1968). Between 1934 and 1953, he wrote ten Judge Peck mystery novels, which received some critical acclaim when they were published, although now they are considered dated. Derleth borrowed styles and techniques made popular by mystery writers of the 1930s; his plots are intricate, and he researched medical discoveries for innovative ways to commit homicide.

The Judge Peck mysteries are set in Sac Prairie or its vicinity, and so relate to the fiction that Derleth and most readers consider his most important literary achievement: the "Sac Prairie Saga," which established Derleth both as a regional author and as an author concerned with Sac Prairie as a microcosm of modern America. Compromising some 175 works, the saga includes short and long fiction, nonfiction, and poetry, covering the history of Sac Prairie from its beginnings to the twentieth century. In *Walden West* (1961), Derleth calls Sac Prairie "a country to be explored" by those who wish to know "the patterns of the world," and in the only scholarly study to date of the Sac Prairie Saga, Evelyn M. Schroth argues that Derleth is a "Christian gentleman" engaged in a moral quest.

In 1949, Derleth criticized Cardinal Spellman for attacking Eleanor Roosevelt, pointing out that there is a difference between Catholicism as a religious ideal and Catholics who try to practice it. The same distinction might well be made of authors: there is a difference between a Catholic writer and a writer who is a Catholic, and Derleth often seems to be more the latter than the former. Nevertheless, the ethical questions raised in the Sac Prairie Saga and in his poetry and his juvenile work on Father Marquette and Ignatius of Loyola show that Derleth is indeed a writer concerned with issues of interest to American Catholics.

SELECTED BIBLIOGRAPHY

Works by Derleth: FANTASY: "Bat's Belfry." *Weird Tales* 7 (1926), pp. 631–36; *Someone in the Dark*. Sauk City, Wis.: Arkham House, 1941; *Something Near*. Sauk City, Wis.: Arkham House, 1945; *Not Long for This World*. Sauk City, Wis.: Arkham House, 1948; *The Mask of Cthulhu*. Sauk City, Wis.: Arkham House, 1958; *The Trail of Cthulu*. Sauk City, Wis.: Arkham House, 1962; *Dwellers in Darkness*. Sauk City, Wis.: Arkham House, 1976. SOLAR PONS MYSTERIES: "The Adventure of the Black Narcissus." *Dragnet* 2(1929), pp. 69–75. *In Re: Sherlock Holmes—The Adventures of Solar Pons*. Sauk City, Wis.: Mycroft & Moran, 1945; *The Memoirs of Solar Pons*. Sauk City, Wis.: Mycroft & Moran, 1951; *The Return of Solar Pons*. Sauk City, Wis.: Mycroft & Moran, 1958; *The Praed Street Papers*. New York: Candlelight, 1965; *A Praed Street Dossier*. Sauk City, Wis.: Mycroft & Moran, 1968. JUDGE PECK MYSTERIES: *Murder Stalks the Wakely Family*. New York: Loring & Mussey, 1934; *Sentence Deferred*. New York: Scribner, 1939; *The Seven Who Waited*. New York: Scribner, 1943. *Mischief in the Lane*. New York: Scribner, 1944; *Fell Purpose*. New York: Arcadia House, 1953. OTHER MYSTERIES: *Consider Your Verdict: Ten Coroner's Cases for You to Solve*. New York: Stackpole, 1937; *Death by Design*. New York: Arcadia House, 1953; *Wisconsin Murders*. Sauk City, Wis.: Mycroft & Moran, 1968. The Sac Prairie Saga: "The Ertman Sisters." *University of Kansas City Review* 3(1931), pp. 255–59; "Old Ladies." *Midland 19(1932), pp. 5–9;* *Wind over Wisconsin*. New York: Scribner, 1938; *Shadow of Night*. New York: Scribner, 1943; "I Was Walking Helen Home." *Prairie Schooner* 21(1947), pp. 271–75; *The House of Moonlight*. Iowa City: Prairie, 1953; "Camomile." *Dalhousie Review* 36(1959), pp. 453–64; *Walden West*. New York: Duell, Sloan & Pearce, 1961; "The White Stars." *Minnesota Review* 6(1966), pp. 123–28; *Return to Walden West*. New York: Candlelight, 1970. Juvenile works: *Father Marquette and the Great Rivers*. New York: Farrar, Straus & Cudahy, 1955; *St. Ignatius and the Company of Jesus*. New York: Farrar, Straus & Cudahy, 1956; *Wisconsin*. New York: Coward, McCann & Geoghegan, 1967. POETRY: *Collected Poems 1937–1967*. New York: Candlelight, 1967; *The Landscape of the Heart*. Iowa City: Prairie, 1970. *Last Light*. Mt. Horeb, Wis.: Perishable, 1978. NONFICTION PROSE: *The Wisconsin: River of a Thousand Isles*. New York: Farrar & Rinehart, 1942; *H. P. L.: A Memoir*. New York: Ben Abramson, 1945; *Writing Fiction*. Boston: The Writer, 1946; *Sauk County, A Centennial History*. Baraboo, Wis.: Sauk County Centennial Committee, 1948; *Some Notes on H. P. Lovecraft*. Sauk City,

Wis.: Arkham House, 1959; *Concord Rebel: A Life of Henry D. Thoreau.* Philadelphia and New York: Chilton House, 1962; *Three Literary Men: A Memoir of Sinclair Lewis, Sherwood Anderson, Edgar Lee Masters.* New York: Candlelight, 1963; *Vincennes: Portal to the West.* Englewood Cliffs, N.J.: Prentice-Hall, 1968; *Walden Pond: Homage to Thoreau.* Iowa City: Prairie, 1968.

Works about Derleth: Moskowitz, Sam. "I Remember Derleth." *Starship* 18(1981), pp. 7–14; Schroth, Evelyn M. *The Derleth Saga.* Appleton, Wis.: Quintain Press, 1979; Wandrei, Donald. *100 Books by August Derleth.* Sauk City, Wis.: Arkham House, 1962; Wilson, Alison M. *August Derleth: A Bibliography.* The Scarecrow Author Bibliographies, vol. 59. Metuchen, N.J.: The Scarecrow Press, Inc., 1983. CA 2. CANR 4. DLB 9. TCA.

Alexandra Hennessey Olsen

JOSEPH DEVER (1919–1971). Born on September 1, 1919 in Boston, Joseph Dever attended Boston College where he wrote for and edited the college's literary magazine, *The Stylus.* After graduation in 1942, he entered the army, continued writing, and won an award from *Yank* magazine for a short story, "Fifty Missions." After his discharge he was an editor for Bruce Publishing Company in Milwaukee, studied at the Breadloaf Writers' Conference, and contributed to *America, Commonweal, The Critic,* and the *New York Times.*

Each of Dever's major works, three novels and a biography of Richard Cardinal Cushing of Boston, covers the period of approximately 1900 to 1945 in Boston and Chicago. In each, Dever concentrates on problems which helped define the Catholic Irish-American experience in both cities: the attempts to retain religious values, to gain economic security and social respectability, and to extend the Church's influence into social matters. The protagonists of his first, and thoroughly autobiographical, novel, *No Lasting Home* (1947), are members of a Boston Irish-American family who face and conquer at least two of these issues. The older son joins a labor union, serves in World War II, and eventually becomes a Jesuit brother. The younger son graduates from Ignatian College (Boston College) and becomes a writer and editor. A second novel, *A Certain Widow* (1951), also concentrates on a Boston Irish-American family. An older son enters that "other" Boston of Brahmins and Republicans through Harvard Law School and marriage into a Brahmin family. A younger son leaves the seminary, takes over the family's small newspaper, and emerges as the champion of Dever's cherished values: family, Church, and the working class. A third novel, *Three Priests* (1958), traces the careers of three priests from their seminary days to positions of power in the Catholic hierarchy. The Chicago setting removes the tensions betwen Boston's Irish-American Democrats and Brahmin Republicans but more strongly emphasizes through the major character the social responsibilities of the Church. *Cushing of Boston* (1965), an undocumented biography, is anecdotal rather than analytical in its stress on characteristics perceptible in the clerics of the novels: devout family background, unswerving devotion to the working class, and a simple and saintly private life.

These books reveal a Catholicism familiar to every Catholic who grew up between 1900 and 1945, a period of abundant vocations and almost unquestioned acceptance of dogma; of Irish-American neighborhoods and parish cohesiveness; of church attendance and meatless Fridays; of an active sacramental life and fiery Lenten missions. These matters produced a piety which now seems quaint. Regrettably, it encouraged in Dever a tone and a point of view which, at times, almost parody the reality. However, a reading of some of his undergraduate writing and pieces in *America* and *Commonweal* indicates that he regarded himself as a serious Catholic novelist. Unfortunately, the vision, however seriously composed, is limited. It asks alarming questions but offers no ominous answers, hints at the dark side of humans but never probes it, speaks of the extremities of life but expresses neither great anguish nor joy, stresses the priestly life but rarely understands it. Characters live, die, cheat, fall in and out of love, gain and lose faith—in short, they endure existence but only in passing. In its haste to get on with the story, Dever's work has the charm of familiar settings and events but amounts to a recollection—not a literary exploration—of a remarkable period in the history of Irish-American Catholicism.

SELECTED BIBLIOGRAPHY

Works by Dever: NOVELS: *No Lasting Home*. Milwaukee: Bruce Publishers, 1947; *A Certain Widow*. Milwaukee: Bruce Publishers, 1951; *Three Priests*. Milwaukee: Bruce Publishers, 1958. BIOGRAPHY: *Cushing of Boston*. Milwaukee: Bruce Publishers, 1965.

Works about Dever: Review of *Flight from the Dark*. *Times Educational Supplement* (21 September 1984), p. 37. Cat A(1952). CA 19–20.

Frank L. Ryan

JAMES PATRICK DONLEAVY (1926–). What happens when a young and promising writer produces a masterpiece his first time out? *The Ginger Man* (1955), a brilliant novel, has influenced the life style and sensibility of more than one generation, and it is now understood to have been a paradigm for black humorists as diverse as Ken Kesey, Terry Southern, and Joseph Heller. However, the creation of such a distinct literary voice as readers joyfully discover in *Ginger Man* has proven to be a unique burden for its author. In light of the achievement, Donleavy has struggled to equal in other writing the trenchancy and dark lyricism of what has become a modern classic; and, ironically, because of the extraordinary popularity of *Ginger Man*, he has suffered a mixed critical reception in his later career. Whether Donleavy's creative edge is sharper or duller from book to book, he has produced nine novels, five plays (most adapted from the novels), a collection of stories, and two fictional works that virtually defy genre classification. In each instance he has written with the spectre of his initial novel peering down at the page from over his shoulder. Other than to recognize their satire, his critics have viewed all writings since this beginning success with an unavoidable touch of (often unwarranted) skepticism.

In his literary surrealism, Donleavy, a self-described American expatriate living in Ireland, is often compared to fellow Irish writers James Joyce and

Samuel Beckett (Joyce's work is indeed an influence on him as is, however, Franz Kafka's), and less so to Brendan Behan, whom Donleavy knew as early as 1946 when he began three years of study at Trinity College in Dublin. Yet, because of the comic picaresque quality of most of his work, Donleavy may aptly be equated with writers such as Henry Fielding and Laurence Sterne, Henry Miller and Joyce Cary, though it is far gloomier, and perhaps brutal, in his outlook. Donleavy, like no one else, refuses to pull punches in examinations of societies so that readers, while laughing, also often experience a peculiar discomfort, the consequence of incisive savagery.

To one degree or another, Donleavy's books contain fragmentary sentence structure, a shifting point of view, the speaking of one's actions in the third person while thinking in the first—all of this, set in a jagged syntax, creating the sense of a threatened, fragmented consciousness.

Among other themes, a preoccupation with death characterizes Donleavy's work. But universal in the corpus is an all-pervading sense of alienation, and in most instances, specifically, exile. Here readers may see a direct link to the author's actual life. Donleavy was born and raised in New York City in a middle-class home. During World War II he enlisted in the navy, after which he attended Trinity on the GI Bill.

Even in the 1940s Donleavy was beginning to think seriously about living in places other than America, and his Irish Catholic blood lines (his parents were immigrants) may have had more than a passing influence on the eventual decision to take up permanent residence and citizenship in Ireland in 1967. But Donleavy's search for a home results just as much from a yearning to escape his oversized and overly greedy birthplace (according to the author in his "An Expatriate Looks at America") and a general crassness in which writers do not thrive for very long. Returning to the United States during the McCarthy era simply reinforced the disaffection, so that Europe—and eventually Ireland—looked brighter all the time. Donleavy has married twice, in Ireland, and has children from each marriage.

His protagonist in *Ginger Man*, Sebastian Dangerfield, is a bawdy, fictionalized account of himself, an American studying in Dublin, drinking heavily, and living hand to mouth. One of the prevailing criticisms of Donleavy's work is that readers are, essentially, presented with this same character, in various guises, in the protagonists of the other novels. Thus Sebastian becomes a "wealthy man, powerful, lonely, and divorced from grubby enterprise, as Sebastian Dangerfield dreamt of becoming." It is as if Donleavy is stuck on a literary mill; he can only write his same experience in one book after another, with the result that situations—their humor and insights, their very satire—go flat. Such a critical view, however, makes less of what is, from the broader perspective, a huge accomplishment—and Donleavy does enjoy a cadre of faithful readers who find enough pleasure in each book.

Many critics and admirers see the connection between the cruel and the humorous, and they argue that Donleavy's style sustains this vision. He writes novels employing episodic structures, which imbibe the chaotic spirit of the bitter times they describe. Black comedy can often reinvigorate, offering unique insights into the human condition; it may also, though, lead to a madness when the humor disappears. Donleavy pushes his stories, like himself, and the world, to the far limit. Since *Ginger Man* he has been at his best when working with new materials, such as occurs in his most recent book *De Alfonce Tennis* (1984), a subtle and scathing look at manners and mores. This is a good sign, one telling readers that Donleavy's creativity, like Donleavy himself, is alive and well, in Ireland, in self-exile.

SELECTED BIBLIOGRAPHY

Works by Donleavy: NOVELS: *The Ginger Man*. Paris: Olympia, 1955; expurgated, London: Spearman, 1956; New York: McDowell, Oblensky, 1958; unexpurgated, London: Transworld, 1963; New York: Seymour Lawrence/Delacorte, 1965; *A Singular Man*. Boston: Little Brown, 1963. *The Saddest Summer of Samuel S.* New York: Seymour Lawrence/Delacorte, 1966. *The Beastly Beatitudes of Balthazar B.* New York: Seymour Lawrence/Delacorte, 1968. *The Onion Eaters*. New York: Seymour Lawrence/Delacorte, 1971. *A Fairy Tale of New York*. New York: Seymour Lawrence/Delacorte, 1973. *The Destinies of Darcy Dancer, Gentleman*. New York: Seymour Lawrence/Delacorte, 1977. *Schultz*. New York: Seymour Lawrence/Delacorte, 1979. *Leila*. Delacorte/Seymour Lawrence, 1983. GENERAL FICTION: *The Unexpurgated Code: A Complete Manual of Survival and Manners*. New York: Seymour Lawrence/Delacorte, 1975. *De Alfonce Tennis: The Superlative Game of Eccentric Champions, Its History, Accoutrements, Rules, Conduct and Regimen*. New York: E. P. Dutton/Seymour Lawrence, 1984. PLAYS: *The Ginger Man, a Play*. With an Introduction: *What They Did in Dublin*, by the author. New York: Random House, 1961. *Fairy Tales of New York*. New York: Random House, 1961; Harmondsworth, UK: Penguin, 1961; *A Singular Man, The Saddest Summer of Samuel S*, and *The Beastly Beatitudes of Balthazar B* in *The Plays of J. P. Donleavy*. New York: Delacorte, 1972. STORIES: *Meet My Maker the Mad Molecule*. Boston and Toronto: Little, Brown, 1964. ARTICLES: "An Expatriate Looks at America." *Atlantic* 238 (December 1976), pp. 37–46; "The Author and His Image." *Saturday Review* 6 (20 January 1979), pp. 44–46.

Works about Donleavy: Allsop, Kenneth. *The Angry Decade: A Survey of the Cultural Revolt of the Nineteen-Fifties*. London: Owen, 1958; Gilman, Richard. *Common and Uncommon Masks: Writings on Theatre—1961–1970*. New York: Random House, 1971; Hassan, Ihab. *Radical Innocence: Studies in the Contemporary American Novel*. Princeton, N.J.: Princeton University Press, 1961; LeClair, Thomas. "A Case of Death: The Fiction of J. P. Donleavy." In *Contemporary Literature* XII, 3(1971), pp. 329–44; Weales, Gerald. "No Face and No Exit: The Fiction of James Purdy and J. P. Donleavy." In *Contemporary American Novelists*. Ed. Harry T. Moore. Carbondale: Southern Illinois University Press, 1964, pp. 143–54. CA 9–10. CD. CN. TCA.

Burt J. Kimmelman

ANDRE DUBUS (1936–). Unusually acute in observing, understanding, and depicting human behavior, Andre Dubus convincingly portrays the consciousnesses not only of men but also of women and children. He stresses the pained relationships in marriage, divorce, and the family; his approach is realistic, his style understated, and his content frequently sexual, yet his sensibility is deeply religious and his vision moral and compassionate.

Born in Lake Charles, Louisiana, on August 11, 1936, Dubus attended the Christian Brothers' high school in Lafayette (he wrote his first short stories there) and McNeese State College in Lake Charles (B.A., English, 1958). In 1958 he married ("too young," he later said) and joined the Marines; in 1964, leaving the corps after five and a half years of active service, Dubus went to the University of Iowa's Writers' Workshop (M.F.A., 1965). Later he taught at Nichols College in Louisiana (1965–1966) and Bradford College in Massachusetts (1966–1984). He was divorced in 1970, remarried between 1975 and 1977, and married a third time in 1979 the writer Peggy Rambach. In 1984 he resigned from Bradford College, and now lives in Haverhill, in northeastern Massachusetts. He has been a Guggenheim Fellow, a visiting professor at the University of Alabama and Boston University, and, in 1985, the recipient of an NEA fellowship for creative prose. He remains a deeply committed Catholic, and some of his fictions show a respect and affection for Confession and the Eucharist.

Dubus's novels, novellas, and stories have grown out of his experience, and his fictional worlds generally involve Louisiana, the Marine Corps (camps in California and Washington State and an aircraft carrier in the Pacific), and the Merrimack Valley in Massachusetts. Dubus is a typically American writer, in that he concentrates on person, relationship, and psyche while ignoring the political context. His adults, usually from twenty to forty years of age, have problems with marriage, love, and sex; his children, male and from twelve to fifteen years of age, are victims of divorce who must themselves deal with sex and adulthood. Dubus is atypical, however, in his concern for the family and for religion; most of his characters desire fidelity (even their affairs are "monogamous"), and many esteem their God and their Catholicism. While his fictions are sexually explicit and compassionate to all (even to a rapist), his vision is deeply moral and sometimes sacramental.

Dubus' art is fundamentally realistic, though he is selective in his choice of event and detail. His prose is understated, his plotting minimal, his structure informal with a flowing interchange between present and past. He chooses words and metaphors with care, rarely uses humor or irony, and creates a style in which his deeply emotional and moving content is controlled by the restraint of his prose. His best work comes in his Merrimack Valley fiction, especially the interlinked novellas of *We Don't Live Here Anymore* (1984) and the short novel *Voices from the Moon* (1984), which views the same event from six different perspectives.

Dubus' stories have appeared in magazines of quality, including *The New Yorker*, *Sewanee Review*, *The North American Review*, *Ploughshares*, *The Carleton Miscellany*, *Harper's*, and *The Paris Review*. The critics generally have praised him for his craftsmanship, his knowledge of women, his emotional depth, and his honesty. Other critics have commented on his shortcomings: underdeveloped stories, narrowness of vision, obsession with sex and alcohol, and occasional sentimentality. In the *New York Times Book Review* (26 January, 1983, p. 12), Joyce Carol Oates praised the "unhurried precision" of his novella *The Pretty Girl*, his "extraordinary sympathy" with his characters, and his "gift for conveying, with a wonderful sort of clairvoyance, their interior voices." A few months later, in *The New Yorker*, John Updike wrote of *Voices from the Moon*: "How rare it is, these days, to encounter characters with wills, with a sense of choice. . . . For Mr. Dubus, amid the self-seeking tangle of secular America, the Church still functions as a standard of measure, a repository of mysteries that can give scale and structure to our social lives" (4 Feb. 1985, p. 97).

A significant influence on Dubus has been Anton Chekhov; the Russian's story "Peasants," Dubus said, taught him how to cover the passage of a year in a few pages and to find in a single family a microcosm of Russian life. Others have seen some Ernest Hemingway in his style, and I find a bit of Updike in his content. I suggest, finally, one other possibility: in his stories and novellas of the Merrimack Valley, where characters and families reappear and interreact with each other from story to story, Dubus has begun to create a new territory of his own that may someday resemble another fictional county, far to the South, called Yoknapatawpha.

SELECTED BIBLIOGRAPHY

Works by Dubus: NOVELS: *The Lieutenant.* New York: Dial, 1967; *Voices from the Moon.* Boston: Godine, 1984. SHORT STORIES: "Separate Flights." Boston: Godine, 1975; "Adultery and Other Choices." Boston: Godine, 1977; "Finding a Girl in America." Boston: Godine, 1980; "The Times Are Never So Bad." Boston: Godine, 1983; "Land Where My Fathers Died." Winston-Salem, N.C.: Stuart Wright, 1984 ("Land Where My Fathers Died" also appears in *Antaeus* 53 (1984), pp. 190–223). NOVELLAS: *We Don't Live Here Anymore.* New York: Crown, 1984. *The Last Worthless Evening: Four Novellas and Two Short Stories.* New York: Crown, 1987. LITERARY CRITICISM: "Literature." *America* (8 September 1984), pp. 106–9.

Works about Dubus: Holmes, Jon. "With Andre Dubus." *Boston Review* (9 August 1984), pp. 7–8; Kornbluth, Jesse. "The Outrageous Andre Dubus." *Horizon* (April 1985), pp. 16–21; Oates, Joyce Carol. "People to Whom Things Happen." *New York Times Book Review* (16 June 1983), pp. 12, 18; Updike, John. "Books: Ungreat Lives." *The New Yorker* (4 February 1985), pp. 94, 97. CA 21–22. CANR 17.

Joseph J. Feeney, SJ

DOMINICK DUNNE (1926–). Dominick Dunne became famous as a fiction writer with his best-selling *The Two Mrs. Grenvilles* (1985). This roman à clef is based on the killing in 1955 of William Woodward, Jr., the son of a wealthy New York family who was shot to death by his ex-showgirl wife. In Dunne's mix of fact and fiction, the match had been strongly opposed by his family; nonetheless, the family closes ranks to protect her, and she is legally exonerated on her defense that she had mistaken her husband for a burglar. The family's support is superficial, however, and on being ostracized by the society she had determined to enter, the young Mrs. Grenville eventually commits suicide.

Born and raised in Hartford, Connecticut, in a well-to-do Irish Catholic family, Dunne was educated at Williams College. A successful producer of television (*Playhouse 90*) and movies (*Panic in Needle Park*, *The Boys in the Band*, and *Play It As It Lays*, written by Joan Didion, the wife of Dunne's writer brother John), Dunne later turned his back on Hollywood. Undeterred by the lukewarm reception accorded his first novel, *The Winners* (1983), he moved to New York to concentrate on writing. Dunne also became a contributing editor to *Vanity Fair* magazine and the author of a number of celebrity profiles. Interestingly, he has repeatedly dealt with the sensational, whether the murder case of Vickie Morgan (Alfred Bloomingdale's mistress) or the second trial of Claus von Bulow for the attempted murder of his millionaire wife, Sunny. Probably his strongest and most moving *Vanity Fair* piece was the cathartic "Justice: A Father's Account of the Trial of his Daughter's Killer," about the 1982 murder of his own twenty-two-year-old actress daughter, Dominique Dunne.

In both his fiction and non-fiction, Dunne shows little direct interest in Catholicism. Rather, his characters are rich and famous, often ambitious, and, on occasion, are lured to crime to further their cause. He catches the speech and habits of high and low in *The Two Mrs. Grenvilles*: the cigarette holders of the socially elite come from Asprey's of London and the "t" in "often" is not pronounced. Meanwhile, showgirls are given expensive handbags with a hundred-dollar bill neatly tucked inside, and they change their names on the climb up (one goes from Barbara to Baby to Babette). As for the characters, the eponymous ladies are obviously the strongest in the book: Alice Grenville, the matriarch of the family whose upper-class morality leads her to protect her despised daughter-in-law, knowing it binds her family to this upstart forever, and Ann Grenville, beneath whose Mainbocher dress lies "a tiger in heat," yet who had become, as the family admits, "more Grenville than the Grenvilles."

The story is framed by Ann's encounter years after her husband's death with Basil Plant, a figure clearly inspired by the writer Truman Capote, who wrote his own version of the Woodward affair in his scathing "La Côte Basque, 1965" (*Esquire Magazine*, November 1975). Newspaper accounts of the murder and subsequent trial show that much of Dunne's fiction closely follows fact. What he has written, without Capote's acid pen, is a much kinder, obviously fuller, often racy, fast-paced narrative. But for all the detail and the glitz that turned it into one of the best-sellers of the summer in 1985, the novel is thin. It remains all surface.

SELECTED BIBLIOGRAPHY

Works by Dunne: *The Winners: Part II of Joyce Haber's 'The Users'*. New York: Warner Books, 1983; *The Two Mrs. Grenvilles*. New York: Crown, 1985; *People Like Us*. New York: Crown, 1988.

Works about Dunne: Dahlin, Robert. "Interview" in *Publisher's Weekly* (28 June 1985), pp. 76–77; Haden-Guest, Anthony. "Dominick Dunne." *Interview* (September 1985), pp. 104–5; Kessler, Julia Braun. "Dunne Has Last Word on the Elite: Writer Traces Life and Death of an American Socialite." *Los Angeles Times* (12 September

1985), pp. 6–7. REVIEWS: Johnson, Nora. "Hollywood Stories," a review of *The Winners. New York Times* (30 May 1982), p. 9; Langley, Monica. "Designer Fiction: Success First, Sex Second," a review of *The Two Mrs. Grenvilles. The Wall Street Journal* (29 November 1985), p. 11.

Patricia Glossop

JOHN GREGORY DUNNE (1932–). John Gregory Dunne has distinguished himself as a journalist, essayist, screenwriter, and, most recently, novelist. The transition to fiction writer occurred while he was writing his third book *Vegas: A Memoir of a Dark Season* (1974), and he realized that his own Irish-Catholic background was "the mother lode" for a future career as a novelist. He has since written two highly acclaimed novels, *True Confessions* (1977) and *Dutch Shea, Jr.* (1982). As the autobiographical persona in *Vegas* observes: "It is nearly twenty years now since I voluntarily entered a church to celebrate the sacrament of the Mass, yet the Catholicism of my childhood remains the one salient fact of my life." He concludes with the paradoxical observation that although he is "not a practicing Catholic [he remains] an avowed one." Dunne's posture seems even more the "spoiled priest" than F. Scott Fitzgerald who coined this term to describe himself. Although Fitzgerald and Dunne shared the early Catholic experience and an Ivy League education, Dunne chose to reconnect with his primal cultural experience, his Irish-Catholic background, mining it for its quirky folkways, irreverent wit, bizarre characters, and most centrally, its moral outrage against hypocrisy and injustice.

Dunne was born on May 25, 1932, in the upper-middle-class community of West Hartford, Connecticut, to Dr. Richard Edwin and Dorothy Burns Dunne. He attended Portsmouth Priory in Rhode Island, an exclusive Catholic boarding school run by the Benedictine Order. He graduated from Princeton in 1954 with a B.A. in English, and after two years of service in the U.S. Army, he arrived in New York City and became a staff writer at *Time* magazine. For the next twenty years, he worked as a journalist writing occasional columns for *The Saturday Evening Post* (1967–1969) and *Esquire* (1976–1977), but more frequently freelancing for various national periodicals such as *Life*, *Holiday*, *New Republic*, *Harpers*, and *New York Review of Books*. Dunne is married to the writer Joan Didion and they have one child.

In his "Introduction" to the 1985 reissue of his second book *The Studio* (1969), Dunne described his journalistic writing as "essentially donkey work, manual labor of the mind," and he considered *The Studio* no more than an extension of the process in which his " . . . notes were like plans for a bridge." Although Dunne makes a disparaging distinction between his journalistic and subsequent fiction writings, his first book *Delano: The Story of the California Grape Strike* (1967) is a dispassionate yet compelling account of the strike called by Cesar Chavez against produce growers in Coachella Valley south of Delano, California, in the spring of 1965. This event proved to have consequences far beyond the conflict between laborers and farm owners. As Dunne perceptively records: "What Chavez was challenging was a way of life that, to the growers, and indeed to much of California, seemed as God-given and endemic to the valley as the summer sun and the winter floods."

California, and Hollywood in particular, has been central to Dunne's writing both in subject matter and form. *The Studio* was based on his year's observation of the machinations of American filmmaking at Twentieth-Century Fox Studio. It is a primer text on Hollywood creativity which is both hilariously entertaining and technically informative. Curiously, Dunne hated the book, refused to proofread it, leaving that task to his wife, and even requested that his publisher not release it. Years later, his harsh self-evaluation was tempered by time and his subsequent work as a screenwriter probably contributed to his revised opinion of *The Studio*. His screen credits, in collaboration with Joan Didion, include: *Panic in Needle Park* (1971), *Play It As It Lays* (1972), *A Star Is Born* (1976), and *True Confessions* (1981). For Dunne, screenwriting was another journeyman trade plied under the pressures of corporate and market forces. Having worked as a screenwriter, Dunne appreciated the process of filmmaking. In his essay "Gone Hollywood," which appears in the miscellany *Quintana and Friends* (1978), he wrote:

Hustle is a basic ingredient of a screenwriter's life. Writing for the screen is not done in a vacuum but more or less at the whim of agents, stars, directors, producers, studio executives and their wives, husbands, lovers, mistresses and assorted rough trade of all the above.

He further noted that the relationship of a film script to any personal vision is limited by the contractual relationship of screenwriter to film producers. As he observed in his essay "Tinsel," one exchanges independence for the lucrative payoff of screenwriting.

The film writer is first of all *hired*, and as an employee, no matter how gradiose his salary, he must tailor his ideas to his employer. He can wheedle, cajole, or even scream, but if he fails to persuade his employer, he either goes along or gets out.

In spite of his considerable success as a respected journalist and well-paid screenwriter, in the early 1970s, Dunne was on the verge of a breakdown which he details in his third book, the novelistic autobiography *Vegas: A Memoir of a Dark Season*. The particular reason for the crisis is never made explicit, but one assumes his journeyman career as a hired writer had yielded little personal gratification. Clinically, he notes in *Vegas*: "There is a therapeutic aspect to reporting that few like to admit. . . . Reporting anesthetizes one's own problems." In search of some peace in the midst of his "dark season," Dunne reverted to his old habits as voyeur on the demimonde of Las Vegas having as his principal companions a marginal lounge comedian, a prostitute, and a private detective. Eventually, he passed the crisis: "I had arrived in Vegas an emotional paraplegic, obsessed by death, and there I found a kind of peace."

Contributing to the healing process was Dunne's discovery that his own Irish-Catholic background was central to him. "I lost my faith and I lost my Irish and it was years later before I realized that I was the poorer for it." Dunne's subsequent quest in his imaginative writings to retrieve what had been lost brings him back to childhood memories of memories. Dunne's Irish-Catholic novels are not concerned with his own privileged genteel upbringing in West Hartford but rather the world of his grandparents as he describes it in *Dutch Shea, Jr.* "The three P's . . . the Police, politics and the priesthood. That was the only way a mick got out of the Hollow [Irish ghetto in Hartford] in those days. The Yanks wanted to keep us there."

The Spellacy brothers of *True Confessions*, Police Lieutenant Tom and Monsignor Des, represent two of the P's, with the final P being secular and clerical politics. The tale woven around a "Virgin Tramp" murder is little more than a device to explore the brothers' journey out of an Irish ghetto and the subsequent encounter with the palm-laced corruption of Los Angeles in the late 1940s. The vulgar, foul-mouthed, and impetuous Tom brings his brother's clerical ambitions to shambles, but in so doing, he functions as a moralistic savior, rescuing Des from his corrupting ambition to be a bishop. Banished to an obscure desert parish far from the precincts of power in the diocesan office, a dying Des thanks Tom for being his salvation and offers the final observation: "You made me remember something I forgot. Or tried to forget is more like it. You and me, we were always just a couple of harps."

The title character of Dunne's second novel *Dutch Shea, Jr.* is a decent yet flawed person whose blood-drenched memories of his suicide father and bomb-victim daughter are not eased by time. The Evelyn Waugh quote which begins the novel is prophetic " . . . for we possess nothing certainly but the past. . . . " The novel proceeds to its inevitably tragic conclusion (although some scrupulous critics do not agree with the tragic classification), but the character of Dutch Shea, Jr., engages us quite early with his irreverent often vulgar humor which masks his fundamental decency. He acquires heroic stature when his moral sense is outraged by the sham hypocrisies of those in power whether they be conniving attorneys who ply their trade for high-paying clients or monsignors who turn the Catholic Church into a profit-driven bureaucracy. Although Dunne was criticized, once again, for his predilection for obscene, coarse, and scatological language, the novel transcends such criticism on the merits of the extraordinarily haunting character Dutch Shea, Jr.

John Gregory Dunne has enjoyed considerable success in a variety of literary modes, but it is in the imaginative form of the novel that the journeyman builder has evolved into an artist. One can only hope that he will continue to tap the self-described "mother lode" which has thus far yielded *True Confessions*, *Dutch Shea, Jr.*, and his recent novel *The Red, White and Blue*, which focuses on rich Catholics suggesting that the progress of Dunne's subject matter reflects the process of assimilation into the American mainstream experienced by Irish-

Catholics. Dunne appears to be continuing his critical exploration of the personal and cultural costs of assimilation.

SELECTED BIBLIOGRAPHY

Works by Dunne: NOVELS: *True Confessions*. New York: E. P. Dutton, 1977; *Dutch Shea, Jr*. New York: Linden Press/ Simon & Schuster, 1982. *The Red White and Blue*. New York: Simon and Schuster, 1987. NON-FICTION: *Delano: The Story of the California Grape Strike*. New York: Farrar, Straus, & Giroux, 1967; *The Studio*. New York: Farrar, Struas, & Giroux, 1969. AUTOBIOGRAPHY: *Vegas: A Memoir of a Dark Season*. New York: Random House, 1974. ESSAYS: *Quintana and Friends*. New York: E. P. Dutton, 1978. SCREENPLAY CREDITS: *Panic in Needle Park* (1971); *Play It As It Lays* (1972); *A Star is Born* (1976); *True Confessions* (1981).

Works about Dunne: Alig, Tracy., "The Studio: A Review." *America* (5 July 1969), p. 17; Cook, Bruce. "Dark Season." *The New Republic* (9 March 1974), p. 28; Duberman, Martin. "Grapes of Wrath." *The New Republic* (2 December 1967), pp. 23–26; Stade, George. "A Fisherman of Guilt." *New York Times Book Review* (28 March 1982), pp. 1, 24; "Works in Progress: Authors Briefly Discuss Their Books." *New York Times Book Review* (6 June 1982), pp. 11–13; Yardly, Jonathan. "Reportage As Anesthesia." *New York Times Book Review* (3 February 1974), pp. 6–7; Zimmerman, Paul D. "The Internal Regions." *Newsweek* (12 May 1969), pp. 110–14. *CA* 25–28. CANR 14.

Leo F. O'Connor

CHRISTOPHER DURANG (1949–). A much-praised and highly controversial comic playwright, Christopher Durang has written mainly for venues that are more receptive than Broadway to his caustic humor and experimental technique: Off-Broadway and Off-Off Broadway as well as such regional and institutional theatres as the Yale Repertory Theatre. Critics are united in their acclamation of Durang's zany originality and surefire audience appeal, yet they occasionally note that he indulges too frequently in humor for its own sake or otherwise evades inexplicably the stunning thematic points that his comedies often seem to be on the verge of making. Durang's work in the next few years should reveal whether he will write lasting comic plays or simply be known as an active though minor member of the playwrighting generation which followed that of Edward Albee, Arthur Miller, and Tennessee Williams.*

Durang was born on January 2, 1949, in Montclair, New Jersey, and raised as a Catholic. He graduated from Harvard in 1971 and received a Master of Fine Arts from Yale three years later. Though he is primarily known as a playwright, he is also an actor and a song lyricist and has taught both drama and playwrighting. His awards include a Rockefeller Foundation Grant (1976–1977), a Guggenheim Fellowship (1978–1979), a Tony nomination for best book of a musical (*A History of the American Film*, 1978), and an Obie award for *Sister Mary Ignatius Explains It All for You* (1980).

Durang is not afraid to take on weighty themes; the most widely produced of his plays, *Sister Mary Ignatius Explains It All for You*, includes the refrain " 'If God is all powerful, why does He allow evil?' " But it is difficult to ponder such questions except in the highly allusive manner that leads critics to complain of Durang's lack of thematic clarity. Perhaps Durang needs to settle on the genre he wants to specialize in; he has written both parody (*A History of the American Film*, which lampoons movie cliches) and satire (*Sister Mary Ignatius Explains It All for You*, an angry assault on parochial education), but his real strength may lie in such farces as *Beyond Therapy*, a hilarious examination of contemporary relationships between men and women. Because of his anger and his ability to shock, Christopher Durang is sometimes compared to Lenny Bruce, but were he to continue in the farce tradition, where the emphasis is on characters instead of ideas, he could be an American Molière.

SELECTED BIBLIOGRAPHY

Works by Durang: *A History of the American Film*. New York: Avon, 1978; *Christopher Durang Explains It All for You*. New York: Avon, 1983 (contains six plays, including *Sister Mary Ignatius Explains It All for You* and *Beyond Therapy*); *The Marriage of Bette and Boo*. New York: Grave Press, 1987.

Works about Durang: Brustein, Robert. "The Crack in the Chimney: Reflections on Contemporary American Playwriting." *Theater* 9 (1977), pp. 21–29. CA 105. CD.

David Kirby

E

MAURA EICHNER (1915–). "Poetry is the flowering of ordinary possibility," writes Sister Maura, teacher, poet, and essayist. Born in Brooklyn, New York, she learned to love poetry as a child, inspired especially by a semi-invalid uncle who read poems to her and instilled in her a love of words. She received her bachelor's degree from the College of Notre Dame in Baltimore, Maryland, and later joined the School Sisters of Notre Dame, beginning a career in teaching that has taken her from preparatory schools to the college classroom. She earned a master's degree from Catholic University of America and has continued studies at major universities, including the University of London.

Sister Maura is a loved and respected teacher as well as an acclaimed poet. Her contributions to educational and civic life as well as religion have brought her major awards, most recently the 1986 Theodore Hesbergh Award for outstanding contribution to Catholic Higher Education by the Association of Catholic Colleges and Universities.

In *What We Women Know* (1980), the poems evoke the ordinariness of what draws Sister Maura's attentiveness. In "Sunday Morning: Migrant Labor Camp," the divine is in the "Sun and dust" of the altar table, the cat, underneath, surveying the chapel as if it were "a birdcage."

SELECTED BIBLIOGRAPHY

Works by Eichner: POETRY: *Initiate the Heart*. Macmillan, 1946; *The Word Is Love*. New York: Macmillan, 1958; *Bell Sound and Vintage*. Raleigh, N.C.: Contemporary Poetry, 1966; *Walking on Water*. Mahwah, N.J.: Paulist/Newman, 1972; *What We Women Know*. West Lafayette, Ind.: Sparrow Press, 1980; *A Word, A Tree: Christmas Poems*. Pulaski, Wisc.: Franciscan Graphics, 1980; *The Flowering of the Works of God*, 1985. Also in such magazines as *America, Accent, College English, Colorado Quarterly, Contemporary Poetry, Commonweal, Four Quarters, Hopkins Review, Northern Review, Poetry, Sewanee Review, Studia Mystica, Thought, Virginia Quarterly Review*, and *Yale*

Review. ARTICLES AND CRITICAL REVIEWS: In such journals as *The Critic*, *Renascence*, *Spirit*, *Thought*, and *Theology Today*.
  Works about Eichner: CA 37–40. CANR 14.

Mary E. Giles

JOHN ENGELS (1931–). With the 1987 publication of *Cardinals in the Ice Age*, critics have had an opportunity to consider the development of Engels' work. Although Engels has received distinctly favorable reviews from such respected magazines as *Poetry*, *The Hudson Review*, and *The New England Review/Bread Loaf Quarterly*, his work has not yet acquired the readership or critical attention its high quality warrants, a point made repeatedly by his reviewers. However, *Cardinals in the Ice Age*, has recently been elected to the National Poetry Series.

John Engels was born in South Bend, Indiana, on January 19, 1931. He attended the University of Notre Dame for his A.B. degree (1952) and completed military service in the U.S. Navy during 1952–1955, leaving with the rank of lieutenant. After studying in the graduate program at the University of Dublin in 1955, Engels attended the University of Iowa, where he received his M.F.A. in 1957, the year he married Gail Jochimsen. The Engels have had six children; their son Philip, who died in 1965, is the subject of some of Engels' most impressive and moving poems, such as "Nothing Relents" from *Signals from the Safety Coffin* (1978). Engels was an instructor in English at St. Norbert College in West De Pere, Wisconsin from 1957 to 1962. Since 1962 he has been teaching at St. Michael's College in Winooski, Vermont, where he is a professor in the English Department.

Engels' early poetry collections—*The Homer Mitchell Place* (1968) and *Signals from the Safety Coffin*—are dominated by carefully crafted, tightly structured short lyrics focusing on nature and family. These volumes explore the tenuousness of life and the struggles integral to the process of living. Engels often finds meaning applicable to the human condition in the facts and processes of the natural world. In their reliance on densely packed imagery, clotted language, and regular meters and rhyme schemes, many poems of these early collections remind one of the early poetry of Irishman Seamus Heaney, though an Engels poem always communicates a distinctively American voice and a sensibility Catholic in affirming the sacramental power of nature. While Engels' first two collections signalled the arrival of a noteworthy new voice in contemporary American poetry, one can detect in many of the poems echoes of modern American and British poets, most particularly Robert Frost and Dylan Thomas. The final stanza of "The Homer Mitchell Place," the title poem of Engels' first collection, for example, produces a Frost-like persona observing the physical world and posing elegant rhetorical questions in iambic pentameter. Similarly, echoes of Dylan Thomas' lyrical, nostalgic evocations of his boyhood in rural Wales can be heard in the opening stanza of "When in Wisconsin Where I Once Had Time" from *Signals from the Safety Coffin*.

Like his contemporaries Galway Kinnell* and Hayden Carruth, Engels shifted away from reliance on traditional poetic forms in mid-career, writing his later work entirely in organic forms, or free verse, and largely ridding himself of the Frost and Thomas echoes. One of the most striking aspects of his later poetry is Engels' developing interest in extended structures: the long poem and the poetic sequence. *Blood Mountain* (1977), Engels' third volume, is a sequence of linked poems that radically depart from the thematic and formal preoccupations of his earlier work, demonstrating a far greater range of subject and technique. While elements of the natural world are less minutely described in *Blood Mountain* than in Engels' first two collections, they are more mysterious, luminous, and threatening.

Engels' interest in poetic sequences continues in *Vivaldi in Early Fall* (1981), a collection divided into two sequences, "Adam Signing" and "Earth Tremor, the Sky at Night." While rural Vermont again provides the setting for many of the poems in this collection, Engels focuses on the creative impulse and the nature of artistic endeavor, subjects which earlier had been peripheral in his work. Poems drawing from the life and work of Mozart, Van Gogh, Mahler, and Vivaldi show Engels' deepening awareness that art can be a salvific medium and a means of embodying the complexities of human experience.

One persistent criticism of Engels is that he allows the rhetoric of his late poetry occasionally to become forced and overly abstract. At his best, however, Engels keeps his love of expansive rhetoric under control and succeeds in charging intimate, quotidian details of rural life with his extraordinary visionary faculty. The result is a poetry of great resonance, authority, and generosity of spirit.

SELECTED BIBLIOGRAPHY

Works by Engels: *The Homer Mitchell Place.* Pittsburgh: University of Pittsburgh Press, 1968; *Signals from the Safety Coffin.* Pittsburgh: University of Pittsburgh Press, 1975; *Blood Mountain.* Pittsburgh: University of Pittsburgh Press, 1977; *Vivaldi in Early Fall.* Athens: University of Georgia Press, 1981; *Weather-Fear: New and Selected Poems.* Athens: University of Georgia Press, 1983; *Cardinals in the Ice Age.* New York: Graywolf Press, 1987. CRITICAL WORKS EDITED BY ENGELS: *The Merrill Guide to William Carlos Williams.* New York: C. E. Merrill, 1969; *The Merrill Checklist of William Carlos Williams.* New York: C. E. Merrill, 1969; *The Merrill Studies in Paterson.* New York: C. E. Merrill, 1971.

Works about Engels: Review of *Blood Mountain. Sewanee Review* 86 (1978), p. 454; Review of *The Homer Mitchell Place. Virginia Quarterly Review* 45 (1969), p. R21; Review of *Signals from the Safety Coffin. Poetry* 129 (1976), p. 102; Review of *Studies in Paterson. Georgia Review* 27 (1973), p. 291; Review of *Vivaldi in Early Fall. Sewanee Review* 90 (1982), p. R18; Review of *Weather-Fear. New England Review* 6 (1983), p. 342. CA 15–16. CANR 6.

David Lloyd

TISH O'DOWD EZEKIEL (1943–). In her first novel *Floaters* (1984), Ezekiel demonstrates fine control of language, interlacing lyrical passages of self-exploration with bitter vignettes of neighbors, teachers, and friends out of her

Midwestern Catholic childhood. The novel is about death and loss; in it, the protagonist, as child and woman, wrestles with God. Reviewers greeted the novel as "a strong debut," but many criticized its structure, a series of reminiscences interspersed with later experiences. Some felt that the protagonist never emerged as a fully realized character. Almost all commented on the autobiographical nature of the novel, suggesting that it was only nominally fiction and might be more properly classified as memoirs. While working on the novel, Ezekiel received two Avery Hopwood Awards in Creative Writing, two Roy W. Cowden Memorial Fellowships, and the Karl Litzenberg Award in Creative Writing.

Like the narrator of *Floaters*, Tish O'Dowd Ezekiel was born in Michigan into an Irish-American Catholic family. She took her B.A. and M.A. degrees from the University of Michigan, where she now teaches creative writing. She is working on her second novel, *Catbird Court*, to be published by Atheneum. Whereas her first novel was primarily concerned with its protagonist's reaction to her childhood experiences with Catholicism and her later conversion to Judaism, the second novel deals only briefly with Catholicism. Ezekiel and her husband, a social psychologist, have between them three sons and a daughter.

Ezekiel responds to the criticism that *Floaters* is too clearly autobiographical by saying: "It certainly isn't a transcript of my life. No character, including the mother, is strictly representational, but, like most writers, I tried to be true to my experiences. One deals with the things that are troublesome." For Ezekiel, the troublesome things out of her childhood were religion, death, and family relations.

Torn by the love-hate relationships of her Catholic upbringing, the narrator of *Floaters* explores her own being, trying to figure out how she came to be what she is. Although she rejects the "dilapidated hulk my mother had wrapped about her soul," she spends much of her energy merely "defying her insistence that the world is flat and small and mean . . . " (p. 168).

The title of the novel is appropriate because of the double meaning of the word "floaters." As an epigraph informs us, floaters are "the little lights that explode out of the corners of our eyes when we are looking somewhere else" and also the "bodies that bob to the surface, that won't stay buried down there in the muck of the riverbed." The novel is a series of memories, bodies that won't stay buried. When the juxtapositions work, the infolding of present with past and past with other pasts reveals the protagonist's development. Too often, however, the pattern fails to emerge, leaving the memories merely random. "Floaters" as distortion of vision plays too little role in the novel. Although the vision of adult and child differ, the author lets us see no more than the mature narrator understands. With greater experience, Ezekiel might have been able to make more of the floaters as aspects of the narrator's vision which distort reality.

Most of the narrator's quarrel with God is about death and damnation. When she was in the third grade, she asked, "truly in innocence," how "God, omniscient, and infinite in His mercy, can manufacture certain souls, knowing beforehand that they will wind up in hell.'' Father Himmel, ''who holds himself accountable for the state of our souls as well as for our musical education,'' banishes her to the unheated chapel to ''pray for faith.'' As she sits there, associating all of the ''fallen-away Catholics'' with lepers whose flesh falls away, she also considers early Christians soaking up martyr's blood in their handkerchiefs because they knew it would be valuable someday. She knows that she can't pray for faith. She hears ''the first crack in my plaster.''

If her quarrel with God is about death and damnation, her quarrel with Catholicism is more complicated. She never openly blames the Catholic Church for her joyless mother, but the inference is easily drawn. Her mother accepts sex as a cross to be borne but refuses to let her daughter watch Elvis Presley strut like an animal ''around Ed Sullivan's Catholic stage.''

Ezekiel's strengths lie in her range of emotional language and in brilliant character sketches. The limitations, at least in the first novel, lie in developing richly resonant characters and in adequate separation of author from narrator.

SELECTED BIBLIOGRAPHY

Works by Ezekiel: NOVELS: *Floaters*. New York: Atheneum, 1984.

Works about Ezekiel: REVIEWS: Cox, Shelley. *Library Journal* 109, 11 (15 June 1984), p. 125; Koch, Stephen. *New York Times Book Review* (22 July 1984), p. 12; Quinn, Mary Ellen. *Booklist* 80, 20 (15 June 1984), p. 1437.

Ruth Barton

F

JOHN FANTE (1909–1983). When John Fante writes about his father, or the affected trials of his alter-ego, Arturo Bandini, after his father has died, he writes beautifully. In each line of Fante's prose there sings a passion for the drunken, pagan bricklayer, a passion which imbues the author with a gift for seeing and expressing a sense of himself, his family, and his Catholicism. From his first published novel, *Wait until Spring, Bandini* (1938), to several posthumously published novellas, Fante's theme remains in orbit round the influence of a powerfully alive father, a silent, suffering mother, and his own character's artistic desire to break the bonds of family, religion, and his Italian heritage.

John Fante was born April 8, 1911 in Colorado. He attended Catholic school in Boulder, and later Regis High School. He went to the University of Colorado and Long Beach City College. He began to write in 1929, and he published his first short story in 1932 in *The American Mercury*. Other stories appeared in such magazines as *The Atlantic Monthly, Collier's* and *Esquire*. His first published novel, *Wait until Spring, Bandini* appeared in 1938. Fante was also a screenwriter; among his credits are *Full of Life, My Man and I, Something for a Lonely Man*, and *Walk on the Wild Side*. He was stricken with diabetes in 1955; complications brought blindness in 1978. He died on May 8, 1983, at the age of seventy-four.

The bitter, adolescent hatred which powers Fante's "Bandini" novels is often propelled by his Italian heritage and poverty. One of the first glimpses we see of Arturo Bandini, Fante's major protagonist, is one of bitterness:

His name was Arturo Bandini, but he hated it and wanted to be called John. His mother and father were Italians, but he wanted to be an American. His father was a bricklayer, but he wanted to be a pitcher for the Chicago Cubs. . . . He went to a Catholic school, but he wanted to go to a public school. (*Wait until Spring, Bandini*, 34)

The conflict between Arturo's father, Svevo Bandini, and Arturo's mother, Maria Toscana, in *Wait until Spring, Bandini*, is exacerbated by Svevo's work and Maria's persistent Catholicism. Svevo cannot work in the "white prison" of wintertime in Colorado; he remains at home, or he goes out in the evening to drink away his frustrations. Maria, however, prays incessantly and silently, on her rocking chair in the corner of the living room, fingering her beads. As Fante says in *1933 Was a Bad Year* (1985), "She punished us . . . with Our Fathers and Hail Marys, she strangled us with a string of rosary beads" (p. 24). In *The Brotherhood of the Grape* (1977), he describes essentially the same mother as a possessor of a "relentless Catholicism . . . who punished her husband with exasperating tolerance of his selfishness and contempt" (p. 1). Yet the major conflict of Fante's first novel centers upon Svevo's brief and passionate affair with a rich widow. To Arturo's bitter shame, his mother remains silent throughout her husband's absence, whispering prayers and neglecting her familial duties. When Svevo returns home from his two-week-long affair, money jangling in his pocket from the odd jobs the widow supplied him with and squeaking new shoes, Maria acts "with a suddenness that surprised her . . . ten long fingers were at his eyes, tearing down, a singing strength. .that laid streaks of blood running down his face" (p. 161). Svevo, however, becomes triumphant when Arturo goes after him weeks later, in the final scene of the novel, to bring him home, to create a reconciliation between his mother and father. As the widow screams at Arturo and his dog, both wreaking havoc in her yard, she exclaims: " 'You peasants . . . You foreigners! You're all alike, you and your dogs and all of you.' " This strikes Svevo to the heart, and he answers, " 'That's my boy. You can't talk to him like that. That boy's an American' " (p. 265). The father is finally able to call the widow " 'Puttana!' " and leave with his son for home and the spring.

Fante's first published novel suggests much of the author's later work; as Fante states in the preface: " . . . all of the people in my writing life, all of my characters are to be found in this early work." Fante sets the stage for Arturo's later incessant, and often tiresome, bitterness toward the American way of life, and the "handicap" of his Italian heritage. It is interesting that in the remaining "saga of Arturo Bandini" his father is dead, and the boy is either alone with his mother and sister (brothers disappear in some novels, reappear in others), or is in Los Angeles trying to sell his stories.

The short stories which Fante published in the 1930s, and which were later collected in *Dago Red* (1940), are short, often bittersweet, sketches of his Catholic boyhood. We have pictures of the young boy (here named Jimmy) worshipping old photographs of his mother: "I would stare at that strange picture, kissing it and crying over it, happy because once it had been true" (p. 12). The story "First Communion," centers upon the boy's reception of two Blessed Sacraments, and his reaction after his first confession is typical: "I came out of the confessional . . . very happy. I knelt at the altar and said my penance. . . . I never felt so clean. I was a bar of soap. I was fresh water. I was bright tinfoil"

(p. 35). In "Altar Boy," we see clearly how the young boy receives and interprets decisions from his elders, in this case a priest, and blames them on his family's poverty. His friend, Allie, whose father owns a drugstore, gets to serve Mass from the right side, the most important, while Jimmy, whose father does not bother to attend Mass on Sundays, is relegated to the secondary position. Fante's collection of stories is filled with such well-written vignettes, but it also contains a story whose theme he elaborates further in the novels and novellas of Arturo Bandini—hatred of heritage.

"The Odyssey of a Wop" embodies the theme. The young narrator resents all who label him with the names "wop" or 'dago," from the corner grocer to the parish priest—inevitably loathing his own people. "I avoid Italian boys and girls who try to be friendly. I thank God for my light skin and hair . . . choose my friends by the Anglo-Saxon ring to their names" (p. 137). The boy's attitude is exacerbated by the fact that "Italians use Wop and Dago much more than Americans."

In *Ask the Dust* (1939), Fante's second published novel, a bitter Arturo is living in Los Angeles trying to make a living from his short stories. The plot of the novel centers on his relationship with a Mexican-American girl, Camilla. Arturo, filled with his own brand of self-loathing, inflicts it upon the girl for the most foolish reasons: " 'Do you have to emphasize the fact that you always were and always will be a filthy little greaser?'" (p. 44). In the last scene of the novel, the young author inscribes his first novel to Camilla, but he throws it out into an empty desert, where the half-crazed girl has run off insane with grief for another man who savagely rejected her.

The Road to Los Angeles (1985), Fante's first written novel, which is much more satisfying, clearly and comically shows us the roots of Arturo's bitterness. In this novel he still lives at home with his silent, suffering mother and a sister, Mona, who wishes to be a nun. His father is dead. Arturo's Uncle Frank shows up every few chapters to complain about Arturo's lack of ambition. Arturo is hip deep in Nietzsche and Schopenhauer, reveling in his blasphemous, anti-Catholic rhetoric which horrifies his mother and sister. One of the book's major qualities is its comedy, Arturo spewing pedantic words and phrases at a family who half the time does not understand him, and half the time thinks he is mad. His Uncle Frank finally gets him a job at a canning factory on the coast, and here again we see Bandini's hatred of heritage come through as he projects it upon the many Filipinos who work there. Yet, even with all of this to bar him from success—the difficult books he attempts to read, the family—he is able to write an inspired novel in a frenzied matter of several days. It is of course horrible, and his family tells him so. He punches his sister in the mouth, and his mother tells him to get out. This incident becomes his provocation to go to Los Angeles.

1933 Was a Bad Year (1985), a posthumously published novella, is perhaps Fante's best book. It contains all the finest aspects of his writing—short, terse prose, clipping dialog, a young narrator's self-confidence, and his father. Dom

Molise, the young narrator, wants to be starting pitcher for the Chicago Cubs and plans to leave home (Colorado) for their spring training camp. He needs fifty dollars, which in the winter of 1933 (his father, a bricklayer, caught again in the "white prison" of winter, is out of work) is very hard to come by. The seventeen-year-old boy, however, gets an idea: he will "borrow" his father's concrete mixer, sell it, and with the money pay the bus fare to the Cubs' camp. Of course, after the boy is signed to a twenty-thousand-dollar a year contract, he will repay his father tenfold. However, in mid-theft, after prolonged consideration and guilt feelings, he returns the mixer; his father is waiting for him. After an absurd fistfight, provoked by his father's words, " 'If you can steal from me, you can fight me,' " his son convinces the depression-torn father that his pitching hopes are the family's hopes. His father, unknown to the son, days later sells the mixer for twenty-five dollars—all he can get for it. In the last scene of the novella, as Dom tries desperately to buy the mixer back from a callous mechanic, he puts his arms round it, kisses it, and cries "for my father and all fathers, and sons too, for being alive in that time, for myself, because I had to go to California now. I had no choice. I had to make good" (p. 127).

Much later, in *The Brotherhood of the Grape*, Fante changes gears somewhat. The bulk of the novel centers on the building of a smokehouse. Though it is built by the narrator, Henry Molise, and his aging father, Nick Molise, it is quite easily destroyed by a vicious rainstorm. Nick Molise, from the sweet wine he has drunk over his long life, from his association with others in a brotherhood of the grape, soon dies of diabetes. *The Brotherhood of the Grape* is Fante's most popular novel, and perhaps justly so, for, in Molise's own words, it concentrates upon the great character of his father, from whom Molise sees "death glowing through the face of an old man clinging fiercely to life" (p. 83). Though the family life of the Molises is, to say the least, less than ideal, it is infused (except in the curious case of Henry's brother, Mario) with a profound love. Fante expresses well the admiration and love he holds for his father.

West of Rome (1986) continues Henry's story into his later years, now a failing screen and television writer, and focuses on his children and the summer they all leave their parents for good. *Dreams from Bunker Hill* (1982), Fante's last effort (dictated to his wife), is a rather disappointing return to Arturo Bandini's adventures in the section of Los Angeles called Bunker Hill.

With the panorama of John Fante's writing, from the trials of Arturo Bandini, starting from his childhood days in Rocklin, Colorado, through to an aging and regretful Henry Molise, the reader can find much to applaud. In painting a picture of a young Italian-American coping with prejudices (from within as well as without), with the unyielding influences of Catholicism, a suffering mother, an ironic expression of the stifling air about an artistic soul, Fante relates, in many ways, the trials of all sons of Italian immigrants. In all of his writing, beneath the bitterness of the past, the hopelessness of the future, lies a present bursting and full of life.

SELECTED BIBLIOGRAPHY

Works by Fante: *Wait until Spring, Bandini*. Santa Barbara, Calif.: The Black Sparrow Press, 1938, 1983; *Ask the Dust*. Santa Barbara, Calif.: The Black Sparrow Press, 1939, 1980; *Dago Red*. New York: Viking Press, 1940; *The Brotherhood of the Grape*. New York: Bantam Books, 1977; *Dreams from Bunker Hill*. Santa Barbara, Calif.: The Black Sparrow Press, 1982; *The Wine of Youth*. Santa Barbara, Calif.: The Black Sparrow Press, 1982; *The Road to Los Angeles*. Santa Barbara, Calif.: The Black Sparrow Press, 1985; *1933 Was a Bad Year*. Santa Barbara, Calif.: The Black Sparrow Press, 1985; *West of Rome*. Santa Barbara, Calif.: The Black Sparrow Press, 1986; *Full of Life*. 2d ed. Santa Barbara, Calif.: Black Sparrow Press, 1988.

Works about Fante: Brown, Carole. "John Fante's *Brotherhood of the Grape* and Robert Canzoneri's *A Highly Ramified Tree*: A Review Essay." *Italian Americana* 3 (1976), pp. 256–64; Mullen, Michael. "John Fante: A Working Checklist." *Bulletin of Bibliography* 41 (1984), pp. 38–41. CA 69–72. TCA.

Victor Greto

JAMES T. FARRELL (1904–1979). After Theodore Dreiser, James T. Farrell was the leading exponent and practitioner of American literary naturalism. In a career which lasted almost fifty years, he produced seventy books (novels, short stories, poems, criticism, and casual prose).

Born on February 27, 1904, in Chicago, the second oldest of six children who lived to maturity, he was raised as a Catholic by his maternal grandparents and was educated in parochial schools. After graduating from St. Cyril High School (now Mt. Carmel), he studied at DePaul University and, later, the University of Chicago, where he decided to become a writer and broke with the Church. By 1935, after publishing *Gas-House McGinty* (1933) and *Studs Lonigan: A Trilogy* (1935), he had become a major force in American left-wing, proletarian fiction; and during the 1930s and 1940s he played an important role in leftist literary controversy, boldly and bravely defending the integrity of literature and the responsibilities of writers to tell the truth as they understood it, independent of rigid ideological lines. His reputation and role in American letters declined after 1950, but he continued his remarkable record of publication, averaging better than a book each year until his death, on August 22, 1979, in New York. He married three times (Dorothy Patricia Butler 1931–1940 and 1955–1958, and Hortense Alden 1941–1955) and was the father of two sons.

Like Dreiser, his mentor, Farrell made his major theme the American Dream—the individual aspiring to excellence in a land whose opportunities are, or seem to be, unlimited—stressing the tragic gap between promise and possibility, expectation and fulfillment. Unlike Dreiser (who though baptized and raised as a Catholic never used the Church as important subject matter), Farrell emphasized the Church's role in a society which spoils the dream and stifles the dreamer, thwarting the individual's search for self-discovery, growth, satisfaction.

No American writer of his or any other time has produced a more severe indictment of American Catholicism. The institution, as Farrell portrays it, is sectarian and xenophobic, its dogmas frozen, its pageants irrelevant to the needs of its members, its clergy not only insensitive to problems but occasionally even parasitical and exploitative. The laity—bigoted, sentimental, superstitious, guilt-ridden, and ethically coarse—inhabit moral slums, cannot cope with poverty and social change, and fail to live generatively and joyously. The quester heroes who grow and develop, whose dreams do not perish, discover that rejecting the Church is a necessary rite of initiation into maturity.

To contend that this depiction is partial—that there are dimensions to the Church that Farrell ignored—and to maintain that even the local world he experienced was richer and more complex than what he represented are necessary but rather obvious qualifications: an institution that was no more than what he portrayed could never have survived the pressures of the times. But the Catholicism of this fiction is not the product of Farrell's imagination; he was not an inventive writer. His Mariolaters and novena addicts randy for indulgences are drawn from careful observation of the kinds of abuses the reforms of Vatican II centered on. A reasoned appraisal, while recognizing the bias, should concentrate on what he presented rather than on what he ignored. To dismiss the critique as mere caricature is as wrongheaded as to accept it as authoritative.

Farrell's literary virtues and limitations are inherent in the working aesthetic he held to throughout his career: the naturalistic belief that facts, experiential data, justify themselves and ought to be directly recorded as the subject and determine the shape of fiction. Concentrating on environment rather than biology, Farrell recorded commonplace, routine, urban Irish-American life with such abundant detail and precision that even a critical reader is persuaded of its authenticity. Though many of his characters are functional types existing mainly to etch and fill in the social world, others—a whole gallery of them—are rendered so thoroughly and vividly that they remain in our memories and continue to compel our attention.

Still, even the most finely drawn characters (Studs Lonigan and Danny O'Neill, for example) are more sociological figures than fully realized fictional constructs. Environmentalism led Farrell to stress the surface, not explore the inner life; Studs and Danny are thoroughly convincing as children and adolescents, but they do not acquire depth and complexity as they grow older, do not become psychologically adult. His naturalistic concentration on fact led him to neglect form: the clumsy, shapeless narratives, the plodding and labored style were passed over or excused by critics early in his career; but in his later writings they become embarrassing even to those who admire his cumulative power.

Now it seems clear that Farrell's achievement—qualitatively—was minor. It seems equally clear that in the future his career and his chronicle will demand the engagement of literary historians.

SELECTED BIBLIOGRAPHY

Works by Farrell: NOVELS: *Gas-House McGinty*. New York: Vanguard Press, 1933; *Studs Lonigan: A Trilogy*. New York: Vanguard Press, 1935; *A World I Never Made*.

New York: Vanguard Press, 1936; *No Star Is Lost*. New York: Vanguard Press, 1938; *Father and Son*. New York: Vanguard Press, 1940; *Ellen Rogers*. New York: Vanguard Press, 1941; *My Days of Anger*. New York: Vanguard Press, 1943; *Bernard Clare*. New York: Vanguard Press, 1946; *The Road Between*. New York: Vanguard Press, 1949; *This Man and This Woman*. New York: Vanguard Press, 1951; *Yet Other Waters*. New York: Vanguard Press, 1952; *The Face of Time*. New York: Vanguard Press, 1953; *The Silence of History*. New York: Doubleday, 1963 (first of a projected multivolume chronicle); *What Time Collects*. New York: Doubleday, 1964; *Lonely for the Future*. New York: Doubleday, 1966; *A Brand New Life*. New York: Doubleday, 1968; *Invisibile Swords*. New York: Doubleday, 1971; *The Dunne Family*. New York: Doubleday, 1976; *The Death of Nora Ryan*. New York: Doubleday, 1978. SHORT STORIES: *The Short Stories of James T. Farrell*. New York: Vanguard Press, 1937; *An Omnibus of Short Stories*. New York: Vanguard Press, 1957; *Side Street and Other Stories*. New York: Paperback Library, 1961; *Sound of a City*. New York: Paperback Library, 1962; *Childhood Is Not Forever*. New York: Doubleday, 1969; *Judith and Other Stories*. New York: Doubleday, 1973. CRITICISM AND POETRY: *A Note on Literary Criticism*. New York: Vanguard Press, 1936; *The League of Frightened Philistines and Other Papers*. New York: Vanguard Press, 1945; *Literature and Morality*. New York: Vanguard Press, 1954; *Reflections at Fifty and Other Essays*. New York: Vanguard Press, 1954; *My Baseball Diary*. New York: A. S. Barnes Co., 1957; *The Collected Poems of James T. Farrell*. New York: Fleet Publishing Corporation, 1965.

Works about Farrell: Branch, Edgar M. *James T. Farrell*. New York: Twayne, 1971; Frohock, William M. *The Novel of Violence in America, 1920–1950*. Dallas: Southern Methodist University Press, 1958; O'Malley, Frank. "James T. Farrell: Two Twilight Images." *Fifty Years of the American Novel: A Christian Appeal*. Ed. Harold C. Gardiner. New York: Scribner's, 1951; Walcutt, Charles C. *American Literary Naturalism, A Divided Stream*. Minneapolis: University of Minnesota Press, 1956; Wald, Alan M. *James T. Farrell: The Revolutionary Socialist Years*. New York: New York University Press, 1978. AW. CA 5–6. CANR 9. CN. DLB 4, 9. TCA.

James L. McDonald

ERNEST FERLITA, SJ (1927–). Playwright, author, and educator, Fr. Ferlita, in his criticism of theater and film, as well as in his own plays, focuses on questions of man's origins, his nature, his future, his obligations to his fellows, his government, and his God. He sees in most literature a history of man's quest for knowledge and understanding, a pilgrimage to truth.

A Jesuit, Fr. Ferlita holds a doctor of fine arts degree from Yale, and he has been a drama professor at Loyola University in New Orleans since 1969. He has received numerous awards for his plays, and in 1980 he was a Fulbright-Hays Lecturer at the Federal University of Parana in Brazil.

The Way of the River (1977) and *Gospel Journey* (1983) provide scriptural meditations on Jesus' pilgrimages, both physical and spiritual. His *The Theatre of Pilgrimage* (1971) finds in plays from *King Lear* to *Camino Real* statements of human responsibility and a confirmation of faith despite tragedy, despair, denials of faith, and self-made prisons. *Film Odyssey* (1976) argues that modern film directors, through physical cinematographic images, suggest the psychological and the spiritual, and thereby exert a moral force, portraying man's quest for personal, social, and religious meaning achieved through suffering and experience. His *The Parables of Lina Wertmuller* (1977) applies the same perceptions to an interpretation of Ms. Wertmuller's "myth-making" films, noting her attack on systems that stifle freedom, her images of an arid, loveless world, of anarchy, and at times of hell on earth.

His plays imitate classical patterns in style, imagery, and theme, with comic messengers, choruses, and conflicts that test values; yet they grow out of the moral conflicts of his time: race relationships, conflicts of church and state, drugs, and student protest. His most striking work, *Black Medea* (1978), set in the New Orleans of 1810, raises questions of obligation amid revolution, slavery, and miscegenation. In it, an ambitious French adventurer, once saved by a black voodoo priestess from Haiti, his present mistress, decides to marry into the white power structure to improve his position. By doing so he provokes the scorn and fury of the rejected priestess, who ensures justice through a poisoned bracelet from a serpent god. The play captures the cultural, racial, and religious differences that separate the Jason/Medea pair.

In *The Mask of Hiroshima* (1977) a couple, marked with masks of scars and threatened by a cloud of death even seven years after the bombing, face old questions of guilt (why one was spared, another not; why one was left to be burned alive, while another fled) and seek renewal in a child born of love and pain. Set against images of natural beauty are the horrid realities of the dead and deformed, and a potential for apocalyptic terror to be relived. Fr. Ferlita's most striking images derive from nature: a white magnolia whose red seeds correspond to the blood that drops from a dying beauty; dark flowers of a kimono that suck in the sun and leave "their shapes upon her skin."

Amid the symbolism and madness of Mardi Gras, a philandering, defrocked priest spreads his "hip" radical gospel by lacing the coffee of the prayer group, *The Krewe of Dionysus* with LSD, an act that leads to murder. In *The Ballad of John Ogilvie* (1968) a Jacobean Jesuit must face an inquisition of Scottish Puritans for living his faith; in *The Obelisk* an El Salvadorian dictator must face a militant church and answer for his injustice and tyranny with his son's life.

At its weakest, Fr. Ferlita's work is derivative and predictable; at its best, it sheds new light on old stories and time-honored concerns.

SELECTED BIBLIOGRAPHY

Works by Ferlita: *The Theatre of Pilgrimage*. Kansas City, Mo.: Sheed & Ward, 1971; *Film Odyssey*, with May. Mahwah, N.J.: Paulist Press, 1976; *The Way of the River*. Mahwah, N.J.: Paulist Press, 1977; *The Parables of Lina Wertmuller*, with May. Mahwah, N.J.: Paulist Press, 1977; *Religion in Film*, with John P. May. Knoxville, TN: University of Tennessee Press, 1982; *Gospel Journey*. New York: Harper and Row, 1983. In addition are a number of unpublished plays: *The Ballad of John Ogilvie*, 1968; *The Krewe of Dionysus*, 1971; *The Mask of Hiroshima*, 1971 (also entitled *The City of Seven Rivers*, to be published in 1986); *The Way of the Wolf*, 1973; *Ma-fa*, 1973; *The Eye of *the Quetzal*, 1974; *Black Medea*, 1978; *Purgatorio*, 1978; *Dear Ignatius, Dear Isabel*, 1978; *The Obelisk*, 1982; *The Drum Major*, 1985.

Gina Macdonald

JEREMY FINNEGAN (1916–). Diversity of form and theme is a hallmark of this scholar-poet. Born in Chicago, Illinois, she received her bachelor's and master's degrees from the University of Chicago. After entering the Dominican Order, she earned a Ph.D. in English from Yale University in 1942, joining in the same year the faculty at Rosary College in River Forest, Illinois, where she continues to teach.

Her scholarly interests reflect not only in numerous articles on medieval literature and contemporary poetry but also poems that echo the bawdy and balladic. "The Ballad of Kynd Kittok" is a good-humored tale of a wench who died from drink and stole into heaven between two penitents and led a blameless life for seven years until the urge for drink sent her out the gate. When she wanted to return, Peter would not let her in. So out she stayed by heaven's gate to fill the pitchers and there "She will stay till Judgment Day to serve and brew and bake."

Sister Jeremy is the recipient of prizes for her poetry from the Poetry Society of Virginia and Borestone Mountain Poetry.

SELECTED BIBLIOGRAPHY

Works by Finnegan: POETRY: *Dialogue with an Angel*. New York: Devin-Adair, 1949. Also included in such magazines as *Atlantic*, *Poetry*, *Saturday Review*, *Commonweal*, *Botteghe Oscure*, *Critic*.

Mary E. Giles

JOE FLAHERTY (1936–1983). Billy Joel, from a part of Long Island farther removed than the mere miles from Brooklyn, wrote a song entitled "Only the Good Die Young." Because of his death at forty-seven, discussion of Joe Flaherty's work will inevitably engage in speculation about unrealized talent. Would he follow in the footsteps of Jimmy Breslin* and Pete Hamill*? Would he surpass them? At least one observer expected that Flaherty would have produced a work comparable to *Studs Lonigan* in stature.

The life of Joe Flaherty almost suggests a plot for a solid mid–1930s movie. Born in a tough Irish-Catholic Brooklyn neighborhood around 1936 (he never said), Flaherty enjoyed, or so his stories would have us believe, the life of a street urchin. Forays to Ebbets Field and to The City, i.e., Manhattan, are part of the landscape. His father, a union president on the docks, was murdered. Joe dropped out of high school and went to work as a longshoreman. While working as a grain handler, he started writing for *The Park Slope News* in that section of Brooklyn. In 1966 he published an article in the *Village Voice*, where he served as a staff writer from 1967 to 1977. His tour of duty as campaign manager for Norman Mailer's bid for the New York mayoralty provided the grist for his first book, *Managing Mailer* (1970). Four years later he published a collection of his journalistic pieces, entitled *Chez Joey* (1974). After his death *Tin Wife*

(1983), another novel, was published. Among the posthumous eulogies cast his way is a discussion of the home care situation for dealing with his cancer. He did not exactly rage against the dying of the light. Had his illness not been fatal, he was scheduled to become a sports writer for, of all places, the *New York Times*.

Joe Flaherty was a journalist and an author. His style clearly displayed those strengths which made him a well-respected and successful writer of magazine articles: capturing nuances of language and gesture. At the same time, he embellished his subjects well enough so that they stand as characters without straying into caricature.

Translating this skill to a novel proved difficult in *Fogarty & Co.* (1973) but was more successfully accomplished in *Tin Wife*. The loose plot which surrounds the clever musings of Shamus Fogarty does not provide adequate support for such a grandiloquent central figure. To be sure, *Fogarty & Co.* presents more sensitively the often hackneyed figure of the deserting husband and father. Fogarty's struggle with his inner conflicts rings true, often funny and invites the overt language of journalism with forced puns and overplayed paeans of alliterative allusions. The public reception of *Fogarty & Co.* did not, obviously, lead Flaherty to abandon journalism and devote himself solely to writing novels. Between *Fogarty & Co.* and *Tin Wife*, Flaherty continued to place pieces in a variety of publications, from *Esquire* to *Nation*, from *New York* to *Macleans's*.

The difficulty of dealing with a posthumous work rises with *Tin Wife*. Sissy Sullivan, the tin wife who becomes a tin widow, is such an extraordinary character that she creates a tough act for any writer to follow. Sissy sees all (or at least almost all), does all (ditto), and is in charge of her own and others' (to the extent she wishes to be) destinies. She ultimately cons the New York City Police Department into providing enough pension to pay tuition for her daughter to attend Columbia University—in other words, to break out. She gains in brief affairs with her late husband's partner and with her woman-friend writer. Sissy sees clearly how she has gotten where she is and does not engage in easy denial, even when it surrounds her. She tosses off wonderful similes: earnest young male politicians from Manhattan look like stylized toy ducks bobbing for water. And she displays the self-assuredness to admit shortcomings, such as conceding that her earlier actions and attitudes toward movement blacks were similar to those of earnest young male politicians. *Tin Wife* is at once a very good detective story (will she do it?), a strong character study with its attendant and enhancing lesser characters, and a powerful study of the dynamics of working-class aspirations and loves within a familiar Brooklyn, Irish-Catholic setting.

Again, the intrusion. Do we pay a fitting tribute? Do we ask what would have followed? Does Flaherty become, at least, a venerable in the canon of American writers by having a dissertation written about him? Or does it end here?

SELECTED BIBLIOGRAPHY

Works by Flaherty: NOVELS: *Fogarty & Co.* New York: Coward, McCann, & Geoghegan, 1973; *Tin Wife*. New York: Simon and Schuster, 1983. NON-FICTION: *Managing*

Mailer. New York: Coward-McCann, 1970; *Chez Joey*. New York: Coward, McCann, & Geoghegan, 1974. ARTICLES: "Frankie Carlin, the Bookie." *New York Times Magazine* (2 April 1967), pp. 28–29; "Right to the Jaw: That's Black Power." *Esquire* (March 1969), pp. 112–14, 116, 144; "Love Song to Willie Mays." *Saturday Review* (26 August 1972), pp. 15–16; "Radio City: a Crasher's Bore." *New York* (20 March 1978), pp. 61–63; "Working People Talk Back." *Nation* (18 October 1980), pp. 361, 376–380; "Rocky's Road." *Film Comment* 18 (1982), pp. 58–63.

Works about Flaherty: Blair, William G. "Joe Flaherty, Writer and Newspaperman Noted for His Humor." *New York Times* (17 October 1983), p. 16; Brozan, Nadine. "Supportive Home Care for Cancer Patients." *New York Times* (5 December, 1983), p. 10; Fenton, Patrick. "What Flaherty Was." *New York Times* (3 December 1983), p. 23.

John Sheridan

THOMAS JAMES BONNER FLANAGAN (1923–). Thomas Flanagan was already a respected literary critic and short-story writer when in 1979 he won popular and critical acclaim for his first novel, *The Year of the French*. Negative murmurs about the novel's occasional prolixity have been overshadowed by enthusiastic assertions that it deserves to be ranked among the finest historical novels of this century.

Born on November 5, 1923, in Greenwich, Connecticut, Thomas Flanagan received his B.A. degree from Amherst College in 1945 and his M.A. and Ph.D. degrees from Columbia University. He married Jean Parker in 1949, and the Flanagans have two daughters. Previously on the faculty of Columbia University and the University of California at Berkeley, Flanagan has been a professor of English literature at the State University of New York at Stony Brook since 1978.

The Year of the French takes place in Ireland in 1798, when Irish and French forces united in an abortive rebellion against English rule. The novel reveals Flanagan's extensive knowledge of Irish history and literature, and critics have lauded him both for his accurate portrayal of the eighteenth-century world and his timeless insights about history. The novel's most remarkable quality is its brilliant depiction of the multiplicity of history. By employing several narrators of differing backgrounds, and by combining omniscient narrative with documentary style, Flanagan presents history not as a single, coherent entity but rather as the many-faceted complexity that is human life. The author's breadth of vision enables him to be evenhanded: English and Anglo-Irish fear of the uncouth manners and unfamiliar language of the Irish Catholic peasantry is presented sympathetically, as is the brutal slaughter of that same ill-fated peasantry by Cornwallis' army. Furthermore, Flanagan's flexible prose ensures his characters' credibility: the lush imagination of an Irish poet is rendered convincingly, as is the restrained, elegant prose of an Enlightenment historian.

As a nonfiction writer, Thomas Flanagan has been praised for his insight and scholarship; in *The Year of the French* he combines scholarship with artistry to produce a historical novel that not only speaks of the eighteenth-century world but resonates in our own times.

In his massive second novel *The Tenants of Time* (1988), Flanagan returns to Irish history, this time to probe the events, emotions, and ideas driving Ireland—and England and the United States as well—between the Fenian uprising of 1867 and the fall of Charles Parnell. Eight years in the writing, *Tenants* shows Flanagan's control of story and language as he moves his narrative from points of view which include a young Irish historian, a retired schoolmaster, Fenian rebels, an American soldier, and an English earl, and from newspaper accounts, letters, and ballads. George Garret wrote in the *New York Times Book Review* that this "story of great power peopled with characters who matter, involved in events that are worth a grown-up's time and attention, will hold still for an intricate and often elaborate complexity of detail" (p. 27). It seems clear that Flanagan has emerged as one of America's most important historical novelists, one who knows that respect for history and language will help readers understand the bloody conflict between Catholics and Protestants in Ireland today.

SELECTED BIBLIOGRAPHY

Works by Flanagan: *The Irish Novelists: 1800–1850*. New York: Oxford University Press, 1959. Reprint. Westport, Conn.: Greenwood Press, 1976; *The Year of the French*. London: Oxford University Press, 1979 and New York: Holt, Rinehart, and Winston, 1979; *The Tenants of Time*. New York: A William Abrahams Book/E. P. Dutton, 1988.

Works about Flanagan: Cahalan, James M. *Great Hatred, Little Room: The Irish Historical Novel*. Irish Studies. Syracuse, N.Y.: Syracuse University Press, 1983; Donoghue, Denis. *We Irish: Essays on Irish Literature and Society*. New York: Alfred A. Knopf, 1986; Garret, George. "Young Fenians in Love and History." *New York Times Book Review* (3 January 1988), pp. 1, 24, 27; Kiely, Benedict. "Thomas Flanagan: The Lessons of History." *The Hollins Critic* 18 (1981), pp. 1–8; Morrissey, Thomas J. "Flanagan's *The Year of the French* and the Language of Multiple Truths." *Eire* 19 (1984), pp. 6–17. CA 108.

Mary Kateri Fitzgerald

G

BRENDAN GALVIN (1938–). With the publication of his first book, *The Narrow Land* (1971), poet Brendan Galvin began building a quiet, but purposeful body of work. Hardly a Catholic poet like Alan Tate*, Galvin slipped inside the land—in his case, New England—and delivered poems which spoke unromantically and vividly of nature unto itself and of its relationship to its inhabitants, both humans and wildlife. Especially in his first four collections, he has worked his intimate associations with nature and has let readers share this contact. However, in later publications he often appears to value craft over connection. Since there are moving pieces in these latter two volumes (1980 and 1983), the spark has not completely dissipated. But like Mr. Galvin's yearnings for the past, I too find greater attachment to the earlier works.

Born on October 20, 1938, in Everett, Massachusetts, Brendan Galvin has spent his entire life—except for one year teaching—in New England. He has received four degrees, all from Massachusetts' institutions: a B.S. from Boston College in 1961, an M.A. from Boston's Northeastern University in 1964, and an M.F.A. and a Ph.D. in 1967 and 1970, respectively, from the University of Massachusetts. Galvin has published eight volumes of poetry: *The Narrow Land*, *The Salt Farm* (1972), *No Time for Good Reasons* (1974), *The Minutes No One Owns* (1977); *Atlantic Flyway* (1980), *Winter Oysters* (1983), *A Birder's Dozen* (1984); *Seals in the Inner Harbor* (1985). Galvin has taught college-level English since 1963. After shuttling between Northeastern University and Pennsylvania's Slippery Rock State College, he settled in 1969 into a career as professor of English at Central Connecticut State College. Mr. Galvin has also been awarded various writing fellowships and has been affiliated with several writing conferences, including work as director of the Connecticut Writers' Conference.

Galvin has spoken of how his younger days, which were split between the "austere and muted" sea imagery of Cape Cod and the urban blight of metropolitan Boston, have greatly affected his themes and style. This dichotomy becomes apparent in several ways. First, there is the obvious division between nature poems, i.e., a solitary excursion into the New England wilds, and those pieces which depict town or city dwellers. Second, within the nature poems the poet evokes the similarities and—ultimately—the difference between humans and nature. We as people live in Nature, but we are *not* fish (or the wind or a loon) so we do not come home like the bass in "Enfield, Massachusetts (under Quabbin Reservoir)'' (*The Salt Farm*, 1972). Now having expressed that, Galvin then too wants us to know about the intermingling of human being, animal, and nature which becomes something more: spirit. Finally, when dealing with people, he not only distinguishes between city and country residents, but he also explores the expansion of the city and its effect on small-town communities.

In *The Narrow Land* (1971) Galvin develops the gap between human beings and the natural world by using various stylistic techniques. Throughout "Crows" he personifies these creatures as "raucous . . . baseball fans" and "goofy mafia" gangs; however, in the last stanza he offsets the familiar human ties by exposing the birds as distinctly alien and sinister (to us) beings. Thus, Galvin begins with comic attachment and finishes with an ominous detachment, creating both a relationship with and a respectful separation from nature. In "Blackfish Creek" we see nature surrounding the middle stanza of humans wading in the water. People are in the midst of nature but somehow remain apart from it. And in "Little Pamet River: Eclogue and Elegy," Galvin admits that despite all his intimate connections he could never read nature quite right.

Even though he remains a person with his own concerns, Galvin also recognizes the possiblity *and* the need for a merger, if only temporary, with nature. In "For Theodore Roethke" he needs the insects which help him forget his human bitterness. This nature connection creates a new situation, an awareness of something greater than just the human condition. On the other side of the coin, however, Galvin reminds us of the hardness in nature: "sea punishes this land" (from "The Hogbacks"). We can thus infer that people too are hurt because they live off the land. Regardless of whether he speaks of suffering or salvation, Galvin illustrates that connections among the elements, the land, animals, birds, and humans are necessary to tap into the spirit of life.

Galvin often works most movingly with nature when he shows people becoming threads of an environment's fabric. In "When You Go" he uses the atmosphere in and around their house to reinforce his wife's absence. At the same time, the poet subtly senses a small, but important shift that his wife's leaving has created upon the environment. Therefore, he once again gently asserts the constant interaction between people and nature, reminding us that even in loneliness we do not live in a vacuum.

Many of Galvin's recent nature poems lack a crucial element: Brendan Galvin as human interactor. He gives us fluid descriptions of young owls and river beds, but he seems strangely absent. Even though he tentatively stops through some earlier poems, he always feels connected to his images. And we learn about both his natural subjects and himself. In "February," for example, we see all the stimulating things that can begin a day; then finally we discover that for many years the poet had not allowed himself the happiness and the room inside to accept these natural occurrences. Galvin often communicates the beauty—hard and soft—of nature through *his* connection to the environment. In "The Hogbacks" from *The Narrowing Land*, he honestly paints himself as a person who cares enough about the land to recognize its heart and commune with it. In the later volume *Winter Oysters*, however, he observes from a distance that remains respectful, but unenlivened with his being.

Even though in his poems Galvin has more often walked with dogs than with people, he has turned toward overtly human relationships. As he himself has expressed, he has long been concerned with "the urban blight that infects humans who come in contact with it, especially through their work, most of which is unfulfilling and thus worthless" (*CANR 1*, p. 218). Galvin, though, rarely delves into this big city landscape; instead, he exhibits his point of view by contrasting country people with city residents. He lovingly lingers over minute details of rural living. However, he refrains from romanticizing his country friends and acquaintances. While often wishing for the sincere but evaporating good old days, Galvin also understands the dilemma of encroaching civilization. In *Winter Oyster*'s "Lost Countrymen" he laments the fading of one age, in which people *know* the details of their lives, into another, in which the modern clerk "is only a clerk" and cannot help it that he can only find the cash register. Therein, Galvin intimates, lies the quandary: we have made our choices to populate the world with machinery that destroys nature's silence, with nuclear weapons that destroy planetary life, and with modern attitudes that destroy our breath. However, we can also choose to truly notice the "hermit grass" by lying down in it. Clearly, Galvin would opt for the latter, but he also understands the folly of simply wishing away "progress"—and that humans, however much to blame, have unfortunately been caught and harmed by its spreading blight.

Brendan Galvin has tended to distance himself from his 1980's poetry. While he eloquently describes a young owl's flight, his mind/spirit seems to be wandering elsewhere. As a reader who has been moved by his poetry, I want to know about and follow his new wanderings even if they diverge from his fine nature poems. In the past Galvin has shared the quiet, but exciting discovery of his voice with his readership. Therefore, despite this apparent transitional period, Brendan Galvin's work can be highly valued for its intimate portrayals of people finding themselves in nature.

SELECTED BIBLIOGRAPHY

Works by Galvin: POETRY: *The Narrow Land*. Boston: Northeastern University, 1971; *The Salt Farm*. Fredericton, New Brunswick: Fiddlehead Books, 1972; *No Time for Good Reasons*. Pittsburgh: University of Pittsburgh Press, 1974; *The Minutes No One Owns*. Pittsburgh: University of Pittsburgh Press, 1977; *Atlantic Flyway*. Athens: University of Georgia Press, 1980; *Winter Oysters*. Athens: University of Georgia Press, 1983; *A Birder's Dozen*. Bristol, R.I.: Ampersand Press, 1984; *Seals in the Inner Harbor*. Pittsburgh: Carnegie-Mellon, 1985.

Works about Galvin: Fenza, D. W. ''Two Representative Poets: The Provincial and the Metropolitan.'' *Telescope* 4 (1985), pp. 95, 107. CA 45.

John R. Thelin

SONIA GERNES (1942–). A published poet since the late 1960s, Sonia Gernes found herself by the early 1980s—amidst a profusion of publications, including two short stories, several essays, two volumes of poetry, and a novel—a nationally acclaimed, prize-winning author. In both prose and poetry, her memorable characters and her crafted but conversational style pleased reviewers across the land, while her personal, Midwestern, and Catholic themes captivated special audiences. Whether writing about her experiences as farm girl, nun, graduate student, or woman, or about deaf mutes in a town called Sleepy Eye, or about a spinster of strict pre-Vatican Two upbringing suddenly alone in her now post-Vatican Two parish, Gernes' works explored with striking grace and luminous immediacy the transformations worked by the world without on the self within, particularly in the world of rural Midwestern America.

Born on November 15, 1942, in Winona, Minnesota, Gernes grew up on the upper Mississippi, a life of dairy farms, 4-H fairs, and a one-room schoolhouse. She earned a B.A. in English and history at the College of St. Teresa and for four years taught as a Sister of St. Francis. Refusing to be claimed by the Midwest, she traveled to Seattle for graduate study at the University of Washington. There she severed both regional and vocational bonds, only to restore them in spirit when her Midwestern Catholic upbringing inspired her first major poem (''Where Jesus Is,'' *Sewanee Review*, 1970) and when, with an M.A. in creative writing and a Ph.D. in American literature, she returned to the Midwest to join the faculty at the University of Notre Dame. She has been teaching, writing, and winning prizes there ever since.

Gernes' belief that the soul arises from the soil not only characterizes Gernes' work but distinguishes it from that of other regional writers. While the latter invariably focus their vision through lenses of historical consciousness or ethnic heritage or social philosophy or some other intervening perspective, Gernes unveils the shaping of spirit by place itself, by the soul's habitation, be that habitation a Midwestern farmstead, a Catholic parish, a private bedroom, or the limbs and senses of the body. The confinements and exposures of place, with its populations and activities, conform to the self within, thereby confronting the self-conscious spirit, whether of a fictional character or (autobiographically, one supposes) of the authorial persona, with unexpected illuminations, eerie possibilities, ominous shadows, and foreboding incidents. The effect is gothic, and not since Grant Woods' Midwestern paintings has the spirit of country gothic been more elegantly depicted than in Gernes' stories and poems. Before the generally arresting, often saddening, sometimes alarming mysteries of place, Gernes' authorial voice remains ever personal, sometimes witty, sometimes somber, but never fully assenting, always a little unsure, always succumbing a little.

Her book of poetry *Brief Lives* won the 1981 Society of Midland Authors Best Poetry Book award, and her novel *The Way to St. Ives* (1982) put her on the American Library Association's List of Notable Books, won her a First Fiction Honorable Mention from the Great Lakes Colleges Association, and was nominated for a Pulitzer. Two of her dozen or so essays have won Special Merit Awards from the Council for Advancement and Support of Education: "Faith and Art: The Vocation of Flannery O'Connor" (October 1981) and the "Dreams of Summer" (May 1983), both published in *Notre Dame Magazine*. She has thus far published two short stories and a hundred or more poems in numerous journals and collections.

SELECTED BIBLIOGRAPHY

Works by Gernes: POETRY: *Brief Lives*. South Bend, Ind.: University of Notre Dame Press, 1981; *The Mutes of Sleepy Eye*. New York: Inchbird Press, 1981. NOVEL: *The Way to St. Ives*. New York: Charles Scribner's Sons, 1982.

Works about Gernes: CA 107.

                                                                    Edward Vasta

WILLIAM GIBSON (1914–   ). Best known for his drama, William Gibson has also written poetry, fiction, criticism, and autobiography. His drama is notable for its strong female characters, historical subjects, and crisp dialogue. His work generally is naturalistic and frequently emphasizes psychological struggles, often resolved by the redeeming quality of love, a tendency which has caused some crtitics to call his plays sentimental. He is a successful popular writer, yet Gibson has lamented over the restrictions of popular theater in the chronicle, *The Seesaw Log* (1959).

Gibson was born on November 13, 1914, in New York City. He attended the College of the City of New York but dropped out after two years. He married a psychoanalyst, Margaret Brenman, in 1940 and moved to Stockbridge, Massachusetts (where he still lives), where he took a job in a psychiatric institution, an experience he used in his novel *The Cobweb* (1954), later turned into a film. A group of poems published in *Poetry* won for him the 1945 Harriet Monroe Memorial Prize, and a volume of verse, *Winter Crook*, was published in 1948.

But it is as a dramatist that Gibson has earned most fame. Early drama included *I Lay in Zion* (produced in 1943), a one-act play dealing with the life of St. Peter. Gibson's first smash was a two-character play, *Two for the Seesaw* (1958), which is about a tough Bronx, Jewish girl, Gittel, and a divorced Nebraskan lawyer, Jerry. The Broadway play starred Anne Bancroft (who later portrayed several other Gibson characters) and Henry Fonda (who complained of the lack of appeal of Jerry's character). The play's ending, where Jerry goes back to his ex-wife, has sometimes been criticized, yet it is in keepig with the rest of the play. Gibson does not give us the typical, pat, happy ending Broadway audiences often expect. But the growth of Gittel and Jerry is apparent; their lives have been enriched even though they do not choose to remain together. The play was filmed in 1972; a 1973 revival lacked the original play's power.

Gibson's most famous play, *The Miracle Worker*, was originally produced on *Playhouse 90* in 1957 and then on Broadway in 1959, and finally was made into a film in 1962. This biography-drama is best remembered as the story of the blind and deaf girl Helen Keller, but Gibson felt the more important character was the teacher, Anne Sullivan. The play, despite its poignant portrayal of the struggles between teacher and reluctant student, suffers from sentimentality. The ending, when Helen learns to "spell" words in the palm of Anne's hand, "does not grow out of the play and seems added," as Michael Moran states, "to give television viewers the warm glow they have come to expect" (Moran, p. 753). Still, the theme of the play has universal appeal and makes the play an American classic.

Gibson wrote a sequel, *Monday after the Miracle* (1982), about the triangular relationship of Helen, Anne, and Anne's husband John Macy (who helped Helen write her autobiography). Ultimately, the strong bond between the two women, though stifling at times, endures, while Anne's marriage cannot.

Gibson wrote several other plays, including *American Primitive* (1971), the story of Abigail and John Adams, which utilizes their actual words from diaries and letters plus verse written by Gibson. *A Cry of Players*, written in 1948 and produced on Broadway in 1972, is the story, with many liberties, of young Will Shakespeare, though the last name is never supplied. The quasi-Elizabethan language and story are entertaining, but the play is more a curiosity than a success. *Golda* (1977) is about the life of the Israeli premier, another in the line of strong women Gibson portrays. *Golden Boy* (1964), a musical starring Sammy Davis, Jr., was adapted from a play by Clifford Odets, Gibson's close friend and mentor.

Gibson's religious views shift considerably; for example, in *Contemporary Authors* Gibson lists no religious affiliation. However, *I Lay in Zion* (1943) and the later plays *The Body and the Wheel* (1974) and *The Butterfingers Angel* (1974) are all religious, as are *A Season in Heaven* (1974) and a largely autobiographical chronicle, *A Mass for the Dead* (1968). His interest in Catholicism seems to have been rekindled after his near death in 1971 and his subsequent study of transcendental meditation.

SELECTED BIBLIOGRAPHY

Works by Gibson: PLAYS: *I Lay in Zion*. Pr. 1943. New York: French, 1947; *A Cry of Players*. New York: Atheneum, 1969; *Dinny and the Witches: A Frolic on Grave Matters*. Pr. 1948, rev. ver. 1959. London: French, 1960; *The Ruby*. Pr. 1957. (As William Mass, libretto based on a work by Lord Dunsany, music by Norman Dello Joio). New York: Ricordi, 1955; *The Miracle Worker*. Pr. 1957 (television), Pr. 1959 (stage). New York: Knopf, 1957. London: French, 1960; *Two for the Seesaw*. Pr. 1958. Pub. as *The Seesaw Log: A Chronicle of the Stage Production with the Text of "Two for the Seesaw."* New York: Knopf, 1959; *Golden Boy*. With Clifford Odets, adaptation of the play by Clifford Odets, music by Charles Strouse, Pr. 1964. New York: Atheneum 1965; *John and Abigail*. Pr. 1969; *American Primitive* (revision of *John and Abigail*). Pr. 1971. New York: Atheneum, 1972; *The Body and the Wheel: A Play Made from the Gospels*. Pr. 1974. New York: Dramatists Play Service, 1975; *The Butterfingers Angel, Mary and*

Joseph, Herod the Nut, and the Slaughter of Twelve Hit Carols in a Pear Tree. Pr. 1974. New York: Dramatists Play Service, 1975; *Golda*. Pr. 1977. New York: Atheneum, 1978; *Goodly Creatures*. Pr. 1980; *Monday after the Miracle*. Pr. 1982. New York: Atheneum, 1984. OTHER WORKS: *Winter Crook*. New York: Oxford University Press, 1948. POETRY: *The Cobweb*. New York: Knopf, 1954. NOVEL: *A Mass for the Dead*. New York: Atheneum, 1968; *Mona Lisa Overdrive*. New York: Bantam, 1988. CHRONICLES: *Grove of Doom*. New York: Grosset and Dunlap, 1969; *A Season in Heaven: Being a Log of an Expedition after that Legendary Beast, Cosmic Consciousness*. New York: Atheneum, 1974. *Shakespeare's Game*. New York: Atheneum, 1978.

Works about Gibson: Kintgen, Eugene. "Studying the Perception of Poetry." In *Researching Response to Literature and the Teaching of Literature: Points of Departure*. Ed. Charles R. Cooper. Norwood, N.J.: Abex, 1985, pp. 128–50; Moran, Michael. "William Gibson." *Magill Critical Survey of Drama*, Vol. 2 Englewood Cliffs, N.J.: Salem Press, 1985. 747–755 CA 9–10. CANR 9. CD 292. DLB 7.

Louis J. Parascandola

FRANK GILROY (1925–). Dramatist, television and motion picture writer and director, novelist, and children's writer, Frank Gilroy was born in New York City on October 13, 1925, and was drafted into the army shortly after graduating from high school. His army experiences in Europe were recorded in his autobiographical novel, *Private* (1970), as well as in the plays *Who'll Save the Plowboy?* (1962) and *The Subject Was Roses* (1964). After finishing his army tour in 1946 Gilroy attended Dartmouth as a writing student and graduated magna cum laude in 1950. After spending a year at Yale Drama School, he began to write for television, providing scripts for the Western shows "The Rifleman" and "Have Gun, Will Travel" as well as for the "Kraft Theater," "U.S. Steel Hour," and "Playhouse 90."

Gilroy is best known for his two early plays *Who'll Save the Plowboy?* and *The Subject Was Roses*. The former won the 1962 Obie Award for the best American play produced Off-Broadway. It is about the life of Albert Cobb, a soldier who once hoped to own a farm. It is a grim, stark, but nonetheless powerful play, dealing with unsatisfactory solutions to complex problems.

After many production problems outlined in Gilroy's log "About Those Roses" (1965), *The Subject Was Roses* was produced in 1964. It played 832 Broadway performances and won many awards, including the Pulitzer Prize for Drama in 1965. The play has several autobiographical elements. Gilroy's father, like John Cleary, is a coffee broker. Timmy Cleary, like the playwright, is a young Irish Catholic who grew up in the Bronx and returns home after being in the army. Timmy thinks of attending an expensive college and becoming a writer, both of which Gilroy went on to do.

The subject matter and style of the play are typical of Gilroy's writing. *Roses*, dealing with the conflicts amog the three family members, offers no comfortable solutions, but each character gains insight. Its strength is Gilroy's sense of the tough grittiness of urban American life. The play also demonstrates Gilroy's characteristic taut, clipped dialogue.

Gilroy's other plays are less successful. *That Summer, That Fall* (1967) is a remake of the Phaedra story in which a woman falls in love with her stepson and eventually kills herself. The work, centering as usual on family struggles, is powerful until the death of Angelina. The final two scenes, without her dynamic presence, lack the necessary intensity and appear anticlimactic. *Far Rockaway* (1967) is a one-act play which takes Gilroy beyond realistic, psychological drama into the absurdist tradition. *The Only Game in Town* (1968) is a comedy dealing with two gamblers who meet and fall in love in Las Vegas. Joe's proposal to Fran indicates Gilroy's attitude toward marriage: "Granted that marriage is a most faulty, pitiful, and wheezing institution, right now it's the only game in town and we're going to play it." *Present Tense* (1973) comprises four one-act plays that were presented Off-Broadway in 1972. *Last Licks*, produced in 1979, is another partly autobiographical play reminiscent of, but not equal to, *The Subject Was Roses*.

Despite limitations in subject matter and style, Gilroy has made substantial contributions to the American popular theater.

SELECTED BIBLIOGRAPHY

Works by Gilroy: *The Middle World.* Play, pr. 1949; *The Fastest Gun Alive.* Screenplay by Gilroy and Russell Rouse, MGM, 1956; *The Gallant Hours.* Screenplay by Gilroy and Beirne Lay, United Artists, 1960; *Who'll Save the Plowboy?* Play, pr. 1962, pub. New York: Random House, 1962; *The Subject Was Roses.* Play, pr. 1964, pub. New York: French, 1965. Reprint with "About Those Roses: Or, How Not to Do a Play and Succeed," New York: Random House, 1965, screenplay, MGM, 1968; *That Summer, That Fall.* Play, pr. 1967, pub. with the teleplay *Far Rockaway.* New York: Random House, 1967; *The Only Game in Town.* Play, pr. 1968, pub. New York: French, 1967, screenplay, Twentieth-Century Fox, 1969; *Private.* Novel. New York: Harcourt, 1970; *Little Ego.* Juvenile, with Ruth Gilroy. New York: Simon and Shuster, 1970; *A Matter of Pride.* Teleplay adapted from John Langdon's "The Blue Serge Suit," pub. New York: French, 1970; *Desperate Characters.* Screenplay adapted from Paula Fox's novel, Lew Grade-Paramount, 1971; *From Noon Till Three.* Novel. Garden City, N.Y.: Doubleday, 1973. Reprint as *For Want of a Horse.* London: Coronet, 1973, screenplay, United Artists, 1976; *Present Tense: Four Plays by Frank Gilroy* (*So Please Be Kind, 'Twas Brillig, Come Next Tuesday, Present Tense*). New York: French 1973; *Last Licks.* Play, pr. 1979, also as *The Housekeeper*, pr. 1982; *The Next Contestant.* Pub. in *Best Short Plays 1979.* Ed. Stanley Richards. Radnor, Pa.: Chilton, 1979; *Dreams of Glory.* Pub. in *Best Short Plays of 1980.* Ed. Stanley Richards. Radnor: Chilton, 1980.

Works about Gilroy: Ellis, Ted. "Frank D. Gilroy." *Critical Survey of Drama.* Vol. 2. Ed. Frank Magill. Englewood Cliff, N.J.: Salem, 1985, pp. 769–82; Weales, Gerald. *The Jumping Off-Place: America Drama in the 1960's.* London: Macmillan, 1969. CA 81–84. CD. DLB 7.

Louis J. Parascandola

DANA GIOIA (1950–). The December 1984 issue of *Esquire* quoted Howard Moss, poet and editor, on the work of Dana Gioia: "He is a exceptional poet, critic and translator, perhaps the closest to a young Wallace Stevens we have in this country today." The comparison to Stevens was inevitable. Among what was already an impressive list of publications, Gioia had articles on Stevens, and a seminal essay, "Business and Poetry," had appeared in *The Hudson Review*'s thirty-fifth anniversary issue in 1983. Readers of that and other discerning quarterlies were familiar with Gioia's poetry and prose, as well as the usual terse identification of him as "a businessman living in New York." But the connection to Stevens is also possible because Gioia is a poet of extraordinary voice. In poems that quite indirectly reflect his Catholic background, he proves yet again how powerful and lucid a medium traditional verse can be. Whether Gioia will achieve the stature of Wallace Stevens remains to be see, but it is clear that he has produced a durable body of work in both poetry and prose.

Gioia was born on Christmas Eve, 1950, at the Good Samaritan Hospital in Los Angeles, California. He attended Catholic parochial schools taught by the Sisters of Providence and a Catholic high school (Junipero Serra) run by Marianists. A graduate of Stanford University, Gioia entered a Ph.D. program in comparative literature at Harvard; however, he was quickly disillusioned with the academic life, and he left Harvard for the Stanford Business School, taking his M.B.A. in 1977. His fine memoirs of Elizabeth Bishop and John Cheever come out of the Harvard and Stanford periods, but Gioia kept both of them unpublished until 1986, when he was sure he had sufficiently revised his prose. Since leaving Stanford, he has worked as a business executive at General Foods in White Plains, New York. A career that would leave most men exhausted has not prevented Gioia from turning out a steady stream of work characterized by its graceful clarity and commitment to high literary standards. He refrained from publishing his first full-length collection of poems, *Daily Horoscope* (1986), until he was thirty-five, but before then produced editions of Italian poetry (with William Jay Smith) and the short stories of Weldon Kees. Gioia lives in Hastings-on-Hudson with his wife, Mary, who is also a business executive.

The poet, Frederick Turner, has allied Gioia with an identifiable movement in contemporary poetry. Called the Expansive Movement, it is, according to Turner, composed of "natural classicists," poets who reassert literary values once debunked by the modernists: values of narrative, representation, and the classical lyric forms. Of course, to say that Modernism rejected all of these values is simplistic, and to suggest that they have not existed until recent years does a disservice to poets of an older generation. Turner suggests that a number of vigorous poets are reclaiming values that were once rejected. Whether or not Gioia would accept membership in this Expansive Movement, it is certainly true that his poetry suggests pre-Romantic possibilities, a time when the poet was not isolated from society at large, when verse could be coherent and memorable without being considered a betrayal of the modern, a time when, in fact, the poet was more a member of the demos, less a superior being cut off from the hoi polloi.

In "The Next Poem," which he chose not to collect in *Daily Horoscope*, Gioia expresses a desire for poetry that is like classicized Wordsworth. It may be that Gioia chose not to include this poem because he did not want it to be taken for an *ars poetica*, a declaration of principles, or an alliance with a "school." Some of the reviewers of *Daily Horoscope* have, while praising Gioia's art, criticized his reserve, the apparent gentleness of his effect. One critic has said that Gioia is on occasion sentimental. But what these critics misunderstand is that Gioia is a poet with real vision. He is not sentimental, but he has written acutely about sentiment ("Cruising with the Beach Boys," "His Three Women," "The Room Upstairs"). He is not overly gentle because one finds in his verse the subtle forms of punishment, violence, and madness that lie beneath surfaces we sometimes perceive as beautiful ("In Chandler Country," "The Journey, The Arrival and the Dream," "The Man Nun"). No matter how lyrical Gioia's verse may be, how apparently simple and finely wrought, it could not have been written without complete belief in man's fallen nature. There is no easy redemption from evil here, no proclamation that the body is a poem or that ugliness is really beauty. Neither is there any comment that suggests the excessively moral or religious. There is instead a fine tension between fervor and restraint, an aura of commitment to standards, and a knowledge of how often life falls short of them.

Gioia has shown himself to be adept at both free and formal verse, though most of the poems in *Daily Horoscope* are in metered lines, and some display an unstrained use of rhyme. Nowhere does his art call attention to itself in order to mask a paucity of subject. One poem, "Lives of the Great Composers," was designed as a verbal fugue (Howard Moss published an imitation of this poem in the May 1983 issue of *Vanity Fair*), but Gioia has also written with ingenuity of jazz musicians, sculptors, and the history of tobacco. He has written of suburban life, murder, the exile felt by Westerners living in the East, nightmares, airports, and the act of drinking coffee after work. He is a poet, memoirist, and critic who has learned his trades, and he speaks to us without affectation, in the natural language of verse.

SELECTED BIBLIOGRAPHY

Works by Gioia: POETRY: "The Next Poem." *Poetry* (August 1985), pp. 262–63; *Daily Horoscope*. St. Paul, Minn.: Graywolf Press, 1986. Essays: "The Achievement of Weldon Kees." *Sequoia* (Spring 1979), pp. 25–46; "Poetry and the Fine Presses." *The Hudson Review* (Autumn 1982), pp. 483–98; "Explaining Ted Kooser." In *On Common Ground*. Ed. Mark Sanders and J. V. Brummels. Ord, Nebr.: Sandhills Press, 1983; "Business and Poetry." *The Hudson Review* (Spring 1983), pp. 147–71; "The Barrier of a Common Language: British Poetry in the Eighties." *The Hudson Review* (Spring 1984), pp. 5–20; "The Sense of The Sleight-of-Hand Man." *The Hudson Review* (Summer 1984), pp. 343–52. MEMOIRS: *Letter to the Bahamas*. Omaha, Nebr.: Abattoir Editions, 1983; "Studying with Miss Bishop." *The New Yorker* (15 September 1986), pp. 90–101; "Meeting Mr. Cheever." *The Hudson Review* (Autumn 1986), pp. 419–34. REVIEWS: "Poetry Chronicle." *The Hudson Review* (Winter 1980—81), pp. 611–27. INTERVIEWS: "An Interview with John Cheever." *Sequoia* (Summer/Autumn 1976), pp. 29–35. EDITIONS: *The Ceremony and Other Stories* by Weldon Kees. Port Townsend, Wash.: Graywolf Press, 1984; *Poems from Italy*, with William Jay Smith. St. Paul, Minn.: New Rivers Press, 1985.

Works about Gioia: "The Best of the New Generation." *Esquire* (December 1984), p. 134; Brewer, Daryln. "Poets in the Corporation." *Coda: Poets and Writers Newsletter* (November/December 1985), pp. 1–18; Knoll, Robert E. Review of *Daily Horoscope*. *Prairie Schooner* (Fall 1985), pp. 122–25; McClatchy, J. D. "Mortal Listeners," *Poetry* (October 1986), pp. 31–47; Newman, Wade. "An Interview With Frederick Turner." *Southwest Review* (Summer 1986), pp. 337–56.

David Mason

CAROLINE GORDON (1895–1981). Caroline Gordon deserves a much higher critical reputation than she has received. Her fiction is filled with examples of human beings interacting in and with nature; her novels and stories present with a sense of compelling urgency some of the most profound questions that modern man must attempt to answer. If he cannot solve the problems from resources within him, he must seek the answer from without. She is, too, one of the few writers of the twentieth century who possesses the artistic discipline to control the range of vision she brings to her fiction. Though disarmingly clear, her style is filled with wit, humor, pathos, and pity.

If one may judge from her fiction, however, the acute feeling of need for some force to bring order out of the chaos of modern living was not as urgent or as protracted as it was in the life of her husband, Allen Tate.* Like her husband, she was born (October 6, 1895) and brought up in the rural areas of the upper South. As a young girl on the plantation, Mary Mount, which was her home until she left for college, the intellectual milieu to which she was exposed was a combination of Southern stoicism and Deism. Her father, who later appeared as the title character in her best-known novel, *Alex Maury, Sportsman* (1934), insisted that one could find in nature the wondrous results of God's power.

After marrying Tate, on November 2, 1924, she went with him to New York, where she lived until 1928. Life in the city and in the villages surrounding New York proved unsatisfactory. She was disturbed because the process of living and fulfilling social obligations was too time-consuming. There were too many geniuses who knew everything and insisted that one follow their solutions for bringing order out of the chaotic and disturbing world. She was brought up to believe in the imperfection of man; therefore, she could not bring herself to accept the Marxian doctrine that if the workers would unite they could create a perfect society.

Although Gordon was growing more disenchanted living in a modern urban society, she was just as unhappy at Benfolly, the Tennessee farm she and Tate acquired and occupied during the early 1930s. Entertaining the many artists who visited them, she became convinced that modern life at all levels lacked unity, purpose, and focus.

In the fiction she was producing in these years there runs an obvious vein of pessimism. From *Penhally* (1931) through the *Garden of Adonis* (1937), a series of protagonists struggle to find meaning in their lives, some permanent values to stand against death and oblivion. Without exception they all fail. Even the strongest of her heroes, Alex Maury, who comes nearest to living beyond the demands of unrestrained materialism, finally finds that devotion to the rituals and the hunt do not sustain him.

Only the acceptance of religious faith (she joined the Catholic Church in 1947) gave her life direction and purpose, order and structure. "In life," she wrote near the end of hers, "as well as in the writing of novels, faith is the key to the puzzle, the puzzle doesn't make any sense until you have the key." It seems only now "when I am nearly fifty years old" that I have found "the plot of the novel that I have been writing all my life." Life lacked purpose until "I discovered that art is the handmaiden of the church" ("The Art and Meaning of Faith," 1950).

SELECTED BIBLIOGRAPHY

Works by Gordon: FICTION: *Penhally.* New York: Scribner's, 1931; *Alex Maury, Sportsman.* New York: Scribner's, 1934; *None Shall Look Back*, New York: Scribner's, 1937; *The Garden of Adonis.* New York: Scribner's, 1937; *Green Centuries.* New York: Scribner's, 1941; *The Women on the Porch.* New York: Scribner's, 1944; *The Forest of the South.* New York: Scribner's, 1945; *The Strange Children.* New York: Scribner's, 1951; *The Malefactors.* New York: Harcourt, Brace, 1956; *Old Red and Other Stories.* New York: Scribner's, 1963; *The Glory of Hera.* New York: Doubleday, 1972. *Collected Stories.* New York: Farrar, Straus, Giroux, 1972. In 1972 Cooper Square Publishers of New York reprinted *Old Red and Other Stories* plus seven earlier novels. CRITICISM: *How to Read a Novel.* New York: Viking, 1957; *A Good Soldier: A Key to the Novels of Ford Madox Ford.* Davis: University of California Press, 1963. TEXTBOOK: *The House of Fiction, edited with Allen Tate.* New York: Scribner's, 1951.

Works about Gordon: Brinkmeyer, Robert H., Jr. *Three Catholic Writers of the Modern South.* Jackson: University Press of Mississippi, 1985; Landess, Thomas, ed. *The Short Fiction of Caroline Gordon.* Irving, Tex.: University of Dallas Press, 1972; Wood, Sally, ed. *The Southern Mandarins: Letters of Caroline Gordon to Sally Wood.* Baton Rouge: Louisiana State University Press, 1984. AW. AWW. CA 11–12. (1952). CN. DLB 4, 9. TCA.

Thomas Daniel Young

MARY GORDON (1949–). With the publication of her second novel in 1981, Mary Gordon achieved the reputation as the foremost novelist of the Catholic experience in the United States. Praised for her understanding of the profound impact of Catholicism on the world view of her characters and for her rendering of emotion into powerful, precise image, she has nonetheless been criticized for her failure to create realistic sexual male characters. Even in her most recent novel, *Men and Angels* (1985), Gordon retreats from the challenge of entering the minds and emotions of men to represent them with compassion and understanding as believable living characters. As skilled and successful as she is, it remains to be seen whether Mary Gordon will transcend the limitations of her own beautifully rendered imaginative world.

Born on the Feast of the Immaculate Conception, December 8, 1949, in Far Rockaway, New York, Mary Gordon was raised in Valley Stream, Long Island,

and was educated in Catholic schools until she earned a scholarship to Barnard College. After graduating from Barnard in 1971, Gordon went to Syracuse University to earn a Ph.D., but her professional writing of fiction interfered with work on her dissertation. Once married to James Brain, she now lives in New Paltz, New York, with her second husband, Arthur Cash, and their two children. In addition to her three novels, *Final Payments* (1978), *The Company of Women* (1980), and *Men and Angels*, Gordon has published many short stories in, among other publications, *The Virginia Quarterly*, *Ms.*, and *Mademoiselle*, and she writes critical essays, especially book reviews.

Gordon herself has spoke of the central theme of her work as the fate of women disempowered by surrendering themselves to the will of men, a fate dramatized most potently in the short story called "Murder," but apparent as well in such as "A Serious Person," "Kindness," and "The Other Woman." Sometimes the disempowering men are fathers, as in *Final Payments* where Isabel Moore sacrifices her youthful energies to the caretaking of her invalid father; sometimes the men are priests, as in *The Company of Women* where, with the other significant women in her life, Felicitas surrenders her will into the powerful hands of the traditionalist Roman Catholic priest, Father Cyprian. In these two examples, the men share important characteristics: both are old enough to be the biological father of the main female character, both are essentially asexual, both are authoritarian, and both embody the values of traditional Roman Catholicism.

Attempting to escape the rigid, aged sterility of their Catholic heritage, Isabel and Felicitas fall into tortuous love affairs with men who lack not only common human sensitivity but also the redemptive quality and heavenly authority of a religious vocation. Isabel, for example, lets John Hughes, married and sporting an apparently raised consciousness, define the boundaries of her emotional, physical, and spiritual reality. In *The Company of Women*, Felicitas falls innocently and easily into the exploitative clutches of her English professor at Columbia University, Robert Cavendish, who stands out as a typical Gordon male, insensitive to anything but the need to satisfy his own ego by controlling the lives of others, particularly young women. Charismatic and good-looking, Cavendish flaunts his professorial expertise and his sexual energy like the chain necklace he wears dangling on his exposed chest. Like most of Gordon's male characters—Catholic or non-Catholic—Cavendish shows little understanding of women except as notches to be worn on the handle of his sexual prowess.

These novels demonstrate the dilemma Gordon confronts in trying to balance goals which at times seem incompatible. On the one hand, she would like to remain committed to the values of a feminist ethic in which her female characters find self-expression outside of relationships with men, but on the other hand, she is drawn simultaneously to the substantive, durable values of ritual and the learned tradition of the Church. The two sets of values often conflict, as Gordon herself has noted, remarking, for instance, on her uneasiness with the Church's stand on women in the priesthood. In Gordon's writings, the strength of the

Church apparently rests squarely and historically on the shoulders of its male believers, particularly its priests, while women remain relegated to subordinate and even passive roles.

Gordon's problematical commitment to both a male-dominated religious institution and to modern feminist principles accounts in part for the ambivalence and ambiguity which occur at the end of her first two novels. It is never clear, for example, why Isabel Moore in *Final Payments* must contribute her fortune to the care of the abhorrent Margaret unless we understand that Isabel remains tied to the values of the Catholic Church which demand the final payment of self-sacrifice and suffering for someone else. Rescuing herself from the self-righteous cruelty of the pious Margaret means that Isabel must pay a (literally) high price—$20,000. But the emotional price may be even higher; Isabel's departure from Margaret's apartment in the company of her supportive female friends seems only a preparation for a return to the arms of her lover Hugh, who formerly usurped Isabel's right to her own emotional identity. At the end of *The Company of Women*, it remains questionable that Felicitas' daughter should be raised among all these women, loving though they be, or that Felicitas herself should see fit to sacrifice her own autonomy—and that of her daughter—to the values of the rigid and aging Father Cyprian.

Unlike her predecessors in *Final Payments* and *The Company of Women*, the heroine of *Men and Angels*, Anne Foster, is not a religious person. But like the men in the earlier novels, Anne's husband is a shadowy insubstantial figure, leaving Gordon once again to face the problem of creating believable male characters.

In *Men and Angels*, Gordon returns to another dilemma displayed in Isabel's relationship with the monstrously selfish Margaret and left unresolved at the end of *Final Payments*: is it possible to love the apparently unlovable? As Gordon says in an interview about *Men and Angels* in *The New York Times* on March 31, 1985, "I wanted to show the limits of love and the failure of love, particularly for a good person." For Anne Foster, the commitment to loving her children involves the rejection of the pathetic and unlovable Laura Post, the counterpart to Margaret in *Final Payments*. Thus, at times, the good of loving the most lovable (children, for example) means betraying the unlovable. And for at least some of Gordon's characters, loving the unlovable involves a greater emotional sacrifice but earns a superior redemptive reward. Is a spiritual satisfaction worth the cost of emotional torture? In spite of loathing the task, Anne must show her children that "life is terrible and they are never safe." Love and its motivations, like loyalty to the self in the face of loyalty to the Church, involves irresoluble ambiguities.

In the end, however, Gordon's ambiguous attitude toward secular, family, and Church values may constitute her finest contribution to Catholic writing. Gordon at once depends on the powerfully symbolic language of the Church for her characteristically imagistic prose even as her stories and novels criticize certain fossilized forces of oppression within the predominantly male structures of Church authority. Although this ambivalent attitude never resolves the essential conflict between a woman's need for self-power and the masculine dominance of the Catholic Church, it nonetheless represents realistically a dilemma familiar to many contemporary Catholics, both men and women. Is it possible to reconcile the humanity of Church members like Isabel and Felicitas with the divine expectations of Jesus Christ and his male spokesmen, the Pope, bishops, and priests? Is it possible to love others—even children—without inflicting pain? Is the only painless love in today's world one which does not involve human contact, namely, the love of God? In spite of certain shortcomings in the creation of character, Mary Gordon demands respect for the courage she shows to confront the difficult and even unsolvable moral problems of modern life.

SELECTED BIBLIOGRAPHY

Works by Gordon: NOVELS: *Final Payments*. New York: Random House, 1978; *The Company of Women*. New York: Random House, 1980; *Men and Angels*. New York: Random House, 1985. SHORT STORIES: *Temporary Shelter*. New York: Random House, 1987.

Works about Gordon: Cooper-Clark, Diana. "An Interview with Mary Gordon." *Commonweal* (May 1980), pp. 270–73; Levine, Paul, ed. *Recent Women's Fiction and the Theme of Personality*. Budapest: Akademiai Kiado, 1984; Rigney, Barbara. *Lilith's Daughter: Women and Religion in Contemporary Fiction*. Madison: University of Wisconsin Press, 1982; Review of *The Company of Women*. *New York Times Book Review* (15 February 1981), p. 1; Review of *Final Payments*. *New York Times Book Review* (16 April 1978), p. 1; Review of *Men and Angels*. *New York Times Book Review* (31 March 1985), p. 1; Review of *Temporary Shelter*. *New York Times Book Review* (19 April 1987), p. 8. CA 102. DLB 6.

Daniel J. Tynan

FRANCINE DU PLESSIX GRAY (1930–). Francine du Plessix Gray's three novels, *Lovers and Tyrants* (1976), *World without End* (1981), and *October Blood* (1985), depict an intervowen, multicolored tapestry of the female experience from the 1930s to the 1980s—lives which for many women are defined by a succession of lovers and tryants, often in the same person.

In her largely autobiographical first novel, *Lovers and Tyrants*, the story of Stephanie, Gray writes of a Parisian childhood molded by her Russian emigré mother, her aristocratic French father (killed in the Resistance) who wanted a male Stephen not a female Stephanie, a world of artsy and articulate aunts, an extended family proficient in high drama, rivalry, and infighting, and a suffocating and hypochrondriacal governess who wrapped her in "gauze veiling" and woolen mufflers, "checked her temperature twice a day," and "scrubbed, spruced, buffed, combed, [and] polished [her], year round, like a first communicant" (p. 13). The experience of the protected pedestal—enervating, cloistered, and lonely—is shared by many women.

Stephanie's early childhood was "muted, opaque, and drab, the color of gruel and of woolen gaiters, its noises muted and monotonous as a sleeper's pulse" (p. 13). Stephanie moves to New York where she is again odd woman out, the token poor student at an exclusive girl's school (Francine du Plessix Gray attended

Spence under similar circumstances), returns to France where she spends her time in bed with a patronizing French prince who thinks he is "style incarnate," and emerges from this to marry (at thirty) an architect and bear two sons. These experiences of growth encased in images of confinement and imprisonment parallel the vita of Francine du Plessix Gray—the daughter of Bertrand du Plessix, a diplomat, and Tatiana Iacovleff and the wife of Cleve Gray, a painter. She has two sons.

Gray's novels are about "the tyranny of love" (*Contemporary Authors*, p. 234), and her non-fiction review of Catholicism in the 1960s, *Divine Disobedience: Profiles in Catholic Radicalism* (1970), similarly records the experience of radical priests who loved and were tyrannized by the Catholic Church. In *Lovers and Tyrants* Gray says that "Every woman's life is a series of exorcisms, from the spells of different oppressors: Nurses, lovers, husbands, gurus, parents, children, myths of the good life. The most tyrannical despots can be the ones who love us the most." Stephanie "lights out for the territory" (Leaving her husband at home), an icy, intellectual female wanderer, seeking her own truths and acting as a slightly confused exemplar for other women who she says " . . . are killing each other in our doll's houses." She wants "to be free, to be a boy, to be God." This journey, in the final section of the book, from the restrictions of things past, is written in the third person and introduces a radical Jesuit as a love object and a whining, unappealing young homosexual as traveling partner.

The problems with *Lovers and Tyrants*, as many critics have noted, are twofold: Stephanie's feminism conflicts with her identification with men, and in the end the book becomes obsessed with its own cleverness and intelligence. *World without End* also records a search for truth, continuity, and meaning, this time by three middle-aged friends on a tour of Russia. Here, familiarity breeds contentment although the three characters—Sophie, a superstar journalist; Edmund, a painter and art critic, and Claire, a political activist—are in love with themselves and each other.

Du Plessix Gray has an advanced degree from the City University of New York; she has taught at Yale, Columbia, and City College; she was educated at Bryn Mawr, Barnard, and Black Mountain College; and she is a distinguished scholar of philosophy, religion, painting, and literature. As she has said,

[S]uch wide-ranging passions can have their drawback. . . . I'm always eager to talk about Titian's iconography of the Resurrection or Pascal's theory of grace. That's the language I was brought up on, and you can't help being what you are. I might never have a very wide audience with such specialized novels, but I don't write for an audience—I think that's an odious idea. (*Contemporary Authors* interview)

It is precisely that overwhelming intelligence that undermines the novel.

October Blood explores the glitzy world of four generations of the Fitzsimmons women—the Edwardian Georgia; her daughter, Nada, editor of the world's most powerful fashion magazine, *Best*; Nada's daughter, Paula, an actress; and Paula's daughter, another Georgia. There are actually two families—the second consists of individuals at *Best*—providing the reader with interwoven worlds of elusive reality, illusion, and appearance, materiality, style, and substance. In this novel love emerges victorious over tyranny, and the women prevail in a world of narcissistic, odious French men.

In a radio interview on WQXR in New York, Gray spoke of her novelistic attempts to transcend sex and time and of the importance of androgyny and sexual ambivalence in her fiction. In each novel, she says, there is one central character who represents "the search for androgyny which marks [her] work." Gray spoke too of her childhood which left her with the fear of being alone, the fear of solitude which, she acknowledged ironically, is the daily experience of each writer's life. She spoke of her childhood reading of the tales of "virile heroism," of how she wanted then (and sometimes now) "to be a boy," of the evil and sentimentality of the Nazis whose regime so affected her youth. She says that she "always seem[s] to have a character in search of God in [her] novels" which reflects her search for her own father and the "search for the Father, search for God, part of the same problem" (*Contemporary Authors* 240).

She writes, finally, of our disparate drives and desires, of the female lust for both freedom and identity, and the difficulty of reconciling expectation and experience.

SELECTED BIBLIOGRAPHY

Works by du Plessix Gray: NOVELS: *Lovers and Tryants*. New York: Simon & Schuster, 1976; *World Without End*. New York: Simon & Schuster, 1981; *October Blood*. New York: Simon & Schuster, 1985. NON-FICTION: *Divine Disobedience: Profiles in Catholic Radicalism*. New York: Knopf, 1970; *Hawaii: The Sugar-Coated Fortress*. New York: Random House, 1972; "The French: Portrait of a Country through a Family." *The New York Times Sunday Magazine* (October 13, 1985), p. 26–29; 116–126.

Works about du Plessix Gray: Bell, Pearl K. "Self-Seekers." *Commentary* (August 1981), pp. 56–60; Braendlin, Bonnie Hoover. *Alther, Atwood, Ballantyne, and Gray: Secular Salvation in the Contemporary Feminist Bildungsroman*. Boulder, Colo.: Frontiers: A Journal of Women Studies 4 (1979), pp. 18–22; Stelzmann, Rainulf A. *Katholizismus und Frauenemanzipation: Die Romane Francine du Plessix Grays und Mary Gordons*. Munich, Germany: Stimmen der Zeit, 1981. CA 61–64. CANR 11.

Mickey Pearlman

ANDREW GREELEY (1928–). Roman Catholic priest, sociologist, university professor, researcher, theologian, prolific writer, columnist, television personality, and sexuality counsellor, Andrew Greeley has been called "the Howard Cosell of the Catholic Church." A witty, charming workaholic much like Father Blackie Ryan and "Ace" McNamara of his fiction, he is a curious mixture of conservative and liberal, opposing abortions and supporting celibacy and slow change, but also favoring birth control, divorce, and the ordination of women. He firmly opposes the radical and the charismatic movements, personally attacking Daniel Berrigan* and all who emulate him and associating the charismatics with madness and sexual hysteria. However, he also denounces conservative church leadership as anti-intellectual, power-hungry, and "religiously bankrupt"; its stand on human sexuality he declares inhumane and insensitive and its procedure for selecting popes and cardinals, anti-democratic intrigue ultimately dangerous to the Church. His *Virgin and Martyr* (1985) vividly depicts the confusion and frustration produced by Vatican II; his *The Cardinal Sins* (1981) and *The Making of the Popes 1978: The Politics of Intrigue in the Vatican* (1979) concern the Machiavellian machinations of papal elections. He enthusiastically endorses human sexuality and inventive marital sex, compares erotic and divine love, and refers to the Divine "She" as the ultimate creative and regenerative force. He praises Hans Kung's stand on honesty in the church. He is nothing if not controversial.

Educated at St. Mary of the Lake Seminary (A.B., 1950; S.T.B., 1952; S.T.L., 1954) and the University of Chicago (A.M., 1961; Ph.D., 1962), he is a Chicagoan at heart. From 1961 to 1968, he was senior study director for the National Opinion Research Center there, and Lecturer in sociology of religion and education there; his fiction which, in the main, is set there, vividly depicts the horrors of the Daley era: the corruption, repression, hatred, and intolerance of the political machine, the Mafia, and the Church. His novel *Death in April* (1980), for example, delineates abuses of the grand jury process in Daley's Chicago. Greeley has received a number of awards for his radio broadcasts and his books for young people, and his fiction has repeatedly made the best-sellers list. He has been professor of sociology at the University of Arizona (Tucson) since 1978, and hence he speaks knowledgeably of the tenure process in *Lord of the Dance* (1984).

His writing, whether clearly theological or indirectly so in his novels, aims to challenge and to shock in order to force readers to reconsider "the religious possibilities in their own lives." For him American Catholicism is pluralistic, diversified, and decentralized, with a high potential for new vision and new insights into what remains fossilized in European (particularly Italian) Catholicism. His New World priests may be lustful and vain, repressed, and insecure, but his Old World ones are decadent, narrow, Machiavellian, and perverse. Drawing on his experiences as a priest, as assistant pastor of the Church of Christ the King (Chicago, 1954–1964), and as lecturer on "The Catholic Hour," Greeley personally attests to the trials and temptations of the ministry, the conflicts of duty and honor, desire and hypocrisy. He depicts priests as human, limited by flesh, ridden with doubts, forced to deal with envy, stupidity, homosexuality, and corruption within the Church, burdened by the effects of social change as the Church battles within itself to reconsider and review an ancient faith in the light of modern social progress. His characters include a lecherous cardinal blackmailed into supporting a Mafia-controlled, would-be pope (*The Cardinal Sins*); a nun whose sexual hysteria involves her in nefarious illegal activities in Latin America and a greedy Communist priest turned Judas to gain a fortune (*Virgin and Martyr*); parish priests who must deal with repressive, senile, psychotic superiors (*Ascent into Hell*, 1983, *The Cardinal Sins*); and a religious talk show host undermined by the jealousies of his fellow priests (*Lord of the Dance*). *Thy Brother's Wife* (1982) traces a priest's journey from conservative to crusader. In other words, Greeley deals with the controversies embroiling the modern Church, and he portrays priests as dealing with the essential human questions both for themselves and for their parishioners.

Critics accuse Greeley of being just another "Harold Robbins" in clerical garb, but Greeley considers his novels parables, inculcating moral lessons as they entertain and carefully reflecting the concerns of his theological canon. They are carefully structured and dramatically conceived. *Lord of the Dance*, a gripping murder mystery about dark family secrets, and *Happy Are the Meek* (1983), a locked room puzzle with Father Blackie Ryan as detective, unlocking secrets of the human soul, are typical. Greeley lets his characters speak for themselves and his readers judge for themselves. He solves the problem of providing multiple perspectives by mixing an epistolary style with first-person narration or third-person records of first-person responses, so that the point of view changes from chapter to chapter. In that way he can give the illusion of objectivity while allowing characters to damn or redeem themselves. He depicts human frailty, but also strength, love, and meekness of spirit that, despite or because of physical and mental anguish, is nourished and, in his central characters, wins out. Suspenseful and compassionate, his stories usually focus on a family group—Chicago Irish, wealthy, influential, part of the power structure, and hence to some degree tainted—and trace their lives over twenty to thirty years as they grow, mature, and flee God and love, self-knowledge, and self-acceptance, only to ultimately face the reality of their lives and the limits or potentials of their faith. His characters struggle with environment, family, and inner self until they learn the lesson of the Irish Christian king of Greeley's mythological tale, *The Magic Cup* (1979): what one seeks in distant places is always there in one's heart if one only learns to truly see. By learning to accept themselves and to truly love another, his characters find God's love.

Most of Greeley's novels include women who are degraded, dehumanized, raped, and brutalized, their sense of self underminded, their creative and intellectual capacities ignored. But usually they learn to reject the passive, submissive roles forced upon them by society, family, and lovers and to act and think for themselves. They continue their education, set their own terms for a relationship, enter the business world, and create meaningful relationships through maturity, self-discipline, and love. In *Happy Are the Clean of Heart* (1986), for example, as the brutalized heroine hovers near death, Father Blackie Ryan provokes self-righteous, self-justifying denunciations of that talented woman who dared to worship through her cinematic art, and in so doing uncovers envy so strong that it demanded horrifying violence, but love and a sense of dedication so strong that all could be overcome. For Greeley, sexual love is at its best a powerful nurturing force that reflects the creative and regenerative powers of a loving Deity—a female who revels in sexuality that involves giving and yielding, and thereby deep pleasure and communion with the best in the spirit of man. His anthropomorphized God touches the celibate priest, the broken teenager, the despairing housewife with the intimacy and fulfillment of a physical encounter. His latest book, *God Game* (1986), breaks new ground in a provocative way: a computer game, struck by lightning, produces a "real" world of human beings, fighting, living, and loving on the player's screen, invading his dreams with their pain and passion, calling on him to play God out of his growing love and compassion for them.

Despite the "moral" nature of Greeley's novels, they are moving sagas, so realistic and so accurately drawn as to be taken for romans à clef. Greeley has a good sense of the female psyche, prides himself on his ability to accurately delve the teenage mind, and praises sharp-tongued wit, self-honesty, and resiliance. He demonstrates man's ability to transcend limitations, God's pursuit of man, and the splendor of that grand "whore," the Church, despite its lethargy, corruption, and at times irrelevance.

SELECTED BIBLIOGRAPHY

Works by Greeley: Greeley has written well over sixty non-fictive works; the following are typical of his canon. *The Jesus Myth*. Garden City, N.Y.: Doubleday, 1971; *That Most Distressful Nation: The Taming of the American Irish*. Quadrangle, 1972; *The Devil, You Say!: Man and His Personal Devils and Angels*. Garden City, N.Y.: Doubleday, 1974; *Ecstasy: A Way of Knowing*. Englewood Cliffs, N.J.: Prentice-Hall, 1974; *The Mary Myth: On the Femininity of God*. New York: Seabury, 1977; *Everything You Wanted to Know about the Catholic Church but Were Too Pious to Ask*. Chicago, Ill.: Thomas More Press, 1978; *The Making of The Popes 1978: The Politics of Intrigue in the Vatican*. Kansas City, Mo.: Sheed Andrews, 1979. FICTION: *The Magic Cup: An Irish Legend*. New York: McGraw, 1979; *Death in April*. New York: McGraw, 1980; *The Cardinal Sins*. New York: Warner Books, 1981; THE PASSOVER TRILOGY: *Thy Brother's Wife*. New York: Warner Books, 1982; *Ascent into Hell*. New York: Warner Books, 1983; *Lord of the Dance*. New York: Warner Books, 1984; *Happy Are the Meek*. New York: Warner Books, 1983; TIME BETWEEN THE STARS: *Virgin and Martyr*. New York: Warner Books, 1985; *Angels of September*. New York: Warner Books, 1986; *God Game*. New York: Warner Books, 1986; *Happy Are the Clean of Heart*. New York: Warner Books, 1986.

Works about Greeley: Anderson, David D., ed. *Essays on the Works of Andrew Greeley*. East Lansing, Mich.: Midwestern Miscellany, 1987; Review of *Ascent into Hell*. *America* (22 October 1983), p. 236; Review of *The Cardinal Sins*. *Time* (10 August 1981), p. 69; Review of *Thy Brother's Wife*. *Time* (12 July 1982), p. 70; Review of *Why Can't They Be Like Us*. *New England Quarterly* 46 (1973), p. 643. CA 7–8. CANR 7.

Gina Macdonald

ROSE BASILE GREEN (1914–). Rose Basile Green is a distinguished poet and an accomplished critic, essayist, translator, and lecturer, whose documentary *The Italian-American Novel* (1974) is a definitive analysis of the fictional writings of Americans of Italian ancestry. Her finest work, however, is found in her nine books of verse, chiefly in sonnet form, in which she spins out fluid narratives of her adopted Philadelphia and Pennsylvania; her poetic themes feature Woman as a coparticipant in the creative process of the universe, heralding the equality of the sexes under God.

A descendant of Roman Italians, Green was born in New Rochelle, New York, and earned her B.A. (cum laude) from the College of New Rochelle, her M.A. in Italian studies from Columbia University, and her Ph.D. in American civilization from the University of Pennsylvania. Subsequent to a variety of prestigious educational positions, she is former department chairman and professor of English at cabrini College. She has received numerous honorary doctorates for her scholarly achievements. She is married to Raymond S. Green, board chairman of the Franklin Broadcasting Company, and is the mother of a son and a daughter. Dr. Green's many current activities include leadership roles in the National Italian American Foundation, the Free Library of Philadelphia, the Balch Institute of Ethnic Studies, the World Affairs Council, and the American Association of University Women.

To Reason Why (1971) comprises fifty-two sonnets, one for each Sunday of the traditional Roman Catholic Church year—from the first Sunday of Advent to the twenty-fourth Sunday after Pentecost. In these poems, Green explicates some of the questions which the faithful have been asking for generations. The perfection of the classic artistry of these poems is an enticing invitation to her later works.

In *Primo Vino* (1974), Green sings the varied songs of the Italian-American in the New World—from the *bocce* courts to Fiorello La Guardia and Filippo Mazzei, from Little Italy to Mother Cabrini and Constantine Brumidi.

Songs of Ourselves (1982) reveals the poet in her most intensely personal mood, as she remembers her *nonno*, the death of her brother, and her son's commencement day. As an Italo-American woman, she is "new Ruth, she is a rose in alien corn." And while these sonnets celebrate her own ethnic saga, they tell equally the story of all American women.

In *Woman, the Second Coming* (1977), the prevading quality of the verse shines through the fusion in them of images of modernity and classical allusions. The author is equally at home with Juno and Aurora as she is with protons and quarks, thereby illuminating an odd scene of universal reconcilement of all time and all matter.

In *The Pennsylvania People* (1984), the poems articulate that the population of ethnic areas has come from various nations from which the newcomers have retained characteristics of their origin to share with others the shaping of the total American. Timing the lines with the progress of individuals within these groups, Green enhances the theme of pursuing this dream with the elevating sound of iambic pentameter verse in the poetic forms of an earlier school.

The poet does not probe into the seamier aspects of our present world. And yet in this demurrer may well lie the warmest praise of Green's poetry as a historian-bard who sings of the good things of today's world in the disciplined forms that poets used in the past.

SELECTED BIBLIOGRAPHY

Works by Green: POETRY: *The Violet and the Flame*. Radnor, Pa.: Cabrini College, 1968; *Lauding the American Dream*. Radnor, Pa.: Cabrini College, 1971; *To Reason Why*. Cranbury, N.J.: A. S. Barnes & Co., 1971; *Primo Vino*. New York: A. S. Barnes & Co., 1974; *76 for Philadelphia*. New York: A. S. Barnes & Co., 1975; *Woman, The Second Coming*. New York: A. S. Barnes & Co., 1977; *Century-Four*. Philadelphia: Women for Greater Philadelphia, 1982; *Songs of Ourselves*. New York: Cornwall Press, 1982; *The Pennsylvania People*. New York: Cornwall Press, 1984. CRITICISM: *The Italian-American Novel*. Rutherford, N.J.: Fairleigh Dickinson University Press, 1974. Translation: *The Life of St. Frances Cabrini*. New York: Cornwall Press, 1984.

Works about Green: Review of *The Italian-American Novel*. *Choice* 11 (1974), p. 592. CA 41–44. CANR 15.

Robert M. Sebastian

JOHN GUARE (1938–). Among both the most prolific and most honored American playwrights, John Guare challenges the conventions of modern realistic drama by combining absurdist farce with domestic tragedy. His style has kept him from much mainstream success, though the much-praised revival of his masterpiece *The House of Blue Leaves* (1970) and his award-winning screenplay for Louis Malle's *Atlantic City* (1981) may signal that he is finally being recognized.

Guare was born in New York City on February 5, 1938, to John and Helen Clare (Grady) Guare. He was educated in Catholic schools, St. Joan of Arc Grammar School in Queens, St. John's Prep in Brooklyn, and Georgetown University (B.A. in 1960). He studied under John Gassner at the Yale Drama School and received an M.F.A. in 1963. He went to Hollywood briefly and then into the Air Force Reserve. He later returned to Yale to study screenwriting and began to write his first successful plays.

Muzeeka (1968), his first hit in New York, earned him his first Obie Award. Guare takes aim at some of his favorite targets, aspects of modern culture which distance people from genuine emotions and actions. His treatment of the Vietnam War as played out by soldiers under contract to rival television networks is especially telling satire. *Cop-Out* (1969) and *Home Fires* (1969) both depict the homogenization of American society. The characters give up their individuality, their family ties, and their emotional lives to become part of the club. Guare has no patience with such foolishness.

The House of Blue Leaves remains Guare's best work. It is also his most personal play, autobiographical in that "everything in the play happened in one way or another . . . and some of it happened in dreams and some of it could have happened and some of it, luckily, never happened." Guare sees the seed of the play in the fantasies of the nuns who taught him in grammar school during the "wild years before Daniel Berrigan" (See also Daniel Berrigan, SJ). They, like the characters in the play, were obsessed with seeing the Pope. More directly, the play was influenced by Guare's watching Laurence Olivier bring the same level of intensity to August Strindberg's drama and Feydeau's farce. Guare imagines *The House of Blue Leaves* as the child of a magical marriage of those two dramatists and their contrasting styles.

In the play, Guare exposes pretension and delusion with comic abandon, while he also depicts real pain. Guare's hero, Artie Shaughnessy, faces a serious situation: a meaningless job, a disastrous marriage to the unbalanced Bananas, and pressure from his success-driven girlfriend, Bunny. In the end his dreams of success have evaporated, his girl has left him, and all he has left is Bananas' dependence on him. Strangling Bananas is the final act of the most desperate man. Guare understands the frustrations of ordinary Americans who have been promised too much and cannot take continual disappointment: "why do my dreams, my wants, constantly humiliate me?"

If Guare feels deeply the frustrations of our time, he also knows whom to blame. In *The House of Blue Leaves* he attacks the purveyors of illusion with such savage satire as this:

Come see the Pope. Pray. Miracles happen. He'll bless you. *Reader's Digest* has an article this month on how prayer answers things. Pray? Kneel down in the street? The Pope can cure you. The *Reader's Digest* don't (sic) afford to crap around.

Bunny and Artie are sucker victims of what the culture feeds them. Hollywood tells them how to love; the Catholic Church tells them how to get lucky; Walter Winchell tells them how to handle grief—with a $5 gift to the Damon Runyon Cancer fund. They have been conditioned by a vast behavioral experiment gone awry. Apparently Artie and Bananas once had real emotions. But now Artie and Bunny feed Bananas pills to keep her quiet, and Artie is reduced to repeating helplessly, "Bananas, sometimes I miss you so much."

Bosoms and Neglect (1979) finds Guare at his most playful. The play is a Freudian shaggy dog story. Scooper has spent six years in analysis trying to understand a recurring dream. His eighty-two-year-old, blind mother, Henny, holds the key to his nightmare: it actually happened when Scooper was a child. But when Henny explains this to Scooper, he is not there; he has left to find his vacationing psychiatrist in Haiti.

If Scooper's dedication to psychiatry is foolish, his mother's superstition-laden Catholicism is also ridiculous. Henny's first love made her feel like "my father in heaven was paying attention to me and had sent Don to me as a heavenly present." When she is afflicted with breast cancer, she chooses to pray to a plastic statue of St. Jude, patron of lost causes, rather than seek medical help. Guare also considers St. Jude his patron: this play and others are copyrighted under St. Jude Productions.

Guare's screenplay for *Atlantic City* (released in 1981) is among his best work. Guare and director Louis Malle create a group of down-and-outers surrounded by the glossy decadence of the new gambling capital. Lou, an old man who once worked for the mob, has sunk to running fifty-cent numbers and caring for Grace, the widow of his boss, and her poodle. It takes Guare's unconventional imgination to redeem all of Lou's past mistakes through outrageous coincidences in a seedy and violent cocaine scheme. Grace's character echoes Henny (and was played by the same actress, Kate Reid). In many ways, Lou is an older Artie Shaughnessy who gets another chance and somehow makes it work. The screenplay is Guare's ringing salute to the losers who still dream of good times.

SELECTED BIBLIOGRAPHY

Works by Guare: PLAYS (year of first New York production in parentheses): *The Loveliest Afternoon of the Year* and *Something I'll Tell You Tuesday* (1966). New York: Dramatists Play Service, 1968; *Muzeeka* (1968), *Cop-Out* (1969), and *Home Fires* (1969) in *Three Plays by John Guare*. New York: Grove Press, 1970; *Kissing Sweet* and *A Day for Surprises*. New York: Dramatists Play Service, 1970; *The House of Blue Leaves* (1970), *Landscape of the Body* (1977), *Bosoms and Neglect* (1979) in *Three Exposures*. New York: Harcourt Brace Jovanovich, 1982; *Two Gentlemen of Verona* (1971), musical adapted from Shakespeare by John Guare and Mel Shapiro, lyrics by John Guare, music by Galt MacDermott. New York: Holt, Rinehart and Winston, 1973; *Marco Polo Sings a Solo* (1977). New York: Dramatists Play Service, 1977. SCREENPLAYS: *Taking Off*, coauthor with Milos Forman. New York: New American Library, 1971; *Atlantic City* (1981), directed by Louis Malle.

Works about Guare: Bernstein, Samuel J. *The Strands Entwined: A New Direction in American Drama*. Boston: Northeastern University Press, 1980; Cohn, Ruby. ''Camp, Cruelty, Colloquialism.'' Festschrift article in *AN* 70, 1, 131, 201, 303. CA 73–76. CD. DLB 7.

Willem O'Reilly

H

RICHARD HAGUE (1947–). Though a promising writer of short fiction, Richard Hague has made his mark primarily as a poet of woods and streams, of particular people and places, and of voices within and without. He writes concretely with his eye on the object, but, as Jim Wayne Miller notes, his poems "shade off into depths . . . express an invisible part" of life.

Hague was born on August 7, 1947, in Steubenville, Ohio, on the Appalachian Plateau. He graduated from Steubenville's Central Catholic High School (1965) and earned his B.S. (1969) and his M.A. in English (1971) from Xavier University in Cincinnati. Since 1969 he has taught at Purcell-Marian High School in Cincinnati and has been adjunct lecturer at Edgecliff College and Xavier University. The recipient of many poetry awards, he has been actively involved in creative writing workshops, and he served as writer-in-residence at the Kentucky Institute for the Arts in Education, University of Louisville, in 1984.

Hague's poetry is not notably innovative; in many ways it is refreshingly traditional: sound grammar, conventional punctuation, and coherent expression. But he has found his own voice in a crisp-phrased free verse that pulses with a mind earning its truths. His poetry is filled with a sense of place, often reflected in his titles: "Fire in Steubenville," "Women on Porches outside Hannibal, Ohio." He searches out the universal in the particular, the oneness in the diversity.

The slender *Crossings* (1978) is more than a promising first book; it contains some of his finer poems such as "Snag" and "Lesson," which acknowledge his debt to nature. *A Week of Nights Down River* (1982) is a quest volume: a canoe trip down the Ohio generates a series of epiphanies as the river "scours down to truth the muddy meaning of our native hills." The three sections of *Ripening* (1984), with epigraphs from Eliade and Exodus, present three stages in the poet's search for meaning in a sacramental universe. Although Hague's impulses are basically religious, his faith is tempered by a Keatsian negative capability. If the world is the mask of God—and Hague is sure of that—it masks a mystery.

SELECTED BIBLIOGRAPHY

Works by Hague: POETRY: *Crossings*. Cincinnati: Cincinnati Area Poetry Press, 1978; *A Week of Nights Down River*. Cincinnati: Privately printed, 1982; *Ripening*. Columbus: Ohio State University Press, 1984. POEMS, STORIES, AND ESSAYS: In numerous journals such as *Appalachian Heritage*, *Appalachian Journal*, *Hiram Poetry Review*, and the *Ohio Journal*.

Works about Hague: Collins, Robert J. "Crossings." *Ohio Journal* 5 (1979), pp. 48– 49; Finkelstein, Norman. "Country Matters." *Athenaeum* 68 (1984), pp. 25–28; Miller, Jim Wayne. "Ripening." *Mountain Life and Work* 60 (1984), p. 29; Steel, Frank. *Appalachian Journal* 12 (1985), pp. 348–354.

Joseph H. Wessling

PETE HAMILL (1935–). Hamill a journalist turned novelist, who brings to his fiction the compact precision, the quick character sketch, the evocative descriptive detail, the clear sense of place and time and action of newspaper coverage at its best. His territory is The City, New York; his characters, its extraordinary ordinary men and women.

Born on June 24, 1935, in Brooklyn, New York, of Belfast Catholic immigrants and educated first in Jesuit schools, then at Pratt Institute (1955–1958) and Mexico City College (1956–1957), Pete Hamill has travelled widely, living at times in Barcelona, Dublin, Rome, and Puerto Rico, and visiting in Australia, Malaysia, Vietnam, North Africa, and most of Europe, but he has always considered himself a New Yorker, and in particular a Brooklynite at heart. In fact, his opening essay in *Irrational Ravings* (1971) eulogizes and criticizes that city. Hamill says he grew up poor and Irish and angry, nurtured on stories of injustices in Northern Ireland, outraged by class and racial differences, distressed by fat priests who maintained privileged positions through "mumbo jumbo," as he calls it. It is this strong sense of outrage at corruption and sham and injustice, whether in city or federal government, that has dominated his news stories, his novels, and his life. His first employment was as a sheet-metal worker, then an advertising designer, and finally a reporter. He worked for the *Saturday Evening Post* for a year, but most of his newspaper career was as a political columnist and war corespondent for the *New York Post*. His highly personalized accounts of the waste and horror of the Vietnam War and later of the Watergate conspiracy are among his most powerful, springing from a deep-seated sense of outrage; whether descriptive narrative or polemic they can still wring the emotions. He received the Newspaper Reporters Association Special Award in 1962 for his series on police, and, from the Columbia University Graduate School of Journalism, the 1962 Meyer Berger Award for distinguished journalism, particularly for his series on slums. Since then he has continued to contribute to periodicals from the *Village Voice* to *Reader's Digest*, from *Playboy* to *New York Times Magazine*. In addition he has written screenplays, authored television scripts, and produced a series of novels.

Pete Hamill's stories and novels grow out of the city. They are products of his experiences observing people intimately, their exhaustion and fear and loneliness, their joys and heartaches. Sometimes his glimpse is sentimental, but more often there is a hard-edged realism, as he describes saloons and dance halls, gyms, and tiny flats from Brooklyn to Greenwich Village to Queens and the Lion's Head. His sketches in *The Invisible City* (1980) focus on the smaller dramas of life: a hoodlum boxer murdered for turning stool pigeon, an abandoned soldier returning for his old girlfriend's funeral, a doomed affair with a Puerto Rican mailman who tells Polish jokes. Typically they turn on chance encounters, random episodes, and surprising twists, with strong feelings and rounded characters packed into a small space. *The Gift* (1973) focuses on a seventeen-year-old Hamill, who comes home to Brooklyn from the navy for Christmas, loses his girl, but finds a sense of manhood and family pride when he, for the first time, makes human contact with his father, as they drunkenly sing sentimental Irish songs, and together beat up three strangers who laugh. In *Flesh and Blood* (1977) Bobby Fallon, a streetwise Irish bar brawler from Brooklyn whose oversized punch and hot temper land him in the pen, fights his way toward the top of his class in the ring but has to fight against the street kid's need to make it too fast, to take the easy way out and end up a sucker. But this story is more than a realistic *Rocky*; it is also the story of a son's obsessive and incestuous love for a mother who has been the only beauty, the only stability he has ever known, a modern Oedipal myth with the son meeting the father he has hated and loved all his life and realizing he can never take his father's place in his mother's love. The simplicity of these works, the clarity, the rightness of place and diction, terse but intense, is Hamill at his best. What might be grotesque in other's hands is human here.

Hamill's disillusionment with the modern church is the basis for his first novel, *A Killing for Christ* (1968). Therein he traces a plot to assassinate the Pope, spawned by an aging cardinal and an Italian count, implemented by an American Nazi Jew, and foiled by a fallen priest in love with a prostitute. It is the priest's ability to love, to see his own inadequacy and to quit the church, and yet to stand up to evil, that for Hamill is true redemption.

Three of Hamill's novels are a mystery series with Sam Briscoe, former crack columnist for a New York City daily newspaper, now turned free-lance and finding himself caught up in murder and mayhem. The hard-boiled and savvy Briscoe is very much like Hamill pictures himself: divorced, a disillusioned socialist, a skeptic, a loner. In *Dirty Laundry* (1978) a terrified call for help from an old flame ends in a suspicious car wreck and a trail of embezzlement, dirty tricks, assassination attempts, and murder that leads to Mexico, the CIA, and a cold, ruthless, greedy killer. *The Deadly Piece* (1979) begins with a murder at a salsa concert and the disappearance of Sam's cousin and millions in missing diamonds; it ends in Puerto Rico with an Israeli connection and greed and betrayal. In *The Guns of Heaven* (1984) Briscoe's Irish sympathies involve him in terrorism; to win an interview with a rebel strategist, he agrees to carry back a package that proves deadly, and the sinister obsessions of Belfast plunge Briscoe into a race with time to prevent an explosion in Manhattan. These novels suffer from the general faults of the genre, but they are valuable for loyalties questioned, old values rethought, fanaticism and greed condemned, innocents protected, and quick wits and a suspicious nature praised.

SELECTED BIBLIOGRAPHY

Works by Hamill: *A Killing for Christ*. New York: World Publishing, 1968; *Irrational Ravings*. New York: Random House, 1971; *The Gift*. New York: Random House, 1973; *Flesh and Blood*. New York: Random House, 1977; *Dirty Laundry*. New York: Random House, 1978; *The Deadly Piece*. New York: Random House, 1979; *The Invisible City*. New York: Random House, 1980; *The Guns of Heaven*. New York: Random House, 1984.

Works about Hamill: Casey, Daniel J. "Heresy in the Diocese of Brooklyn: An Unholy Trinity." *Irish-American Fiction: Essays in Criticism*. Ed. Daniel J. Casey and Robert E. Rhodes. New York: AMS, 1979, pp. 153–72. CA 25–28. CANR 18.

Gina Macdonald

LUCILE HASLEY (1909–). Her jaunty personal essays, which blended humor with family life and Catholicism, brought Lucile Hasley into national prominence in the late 1940s and made her a worthy forerunner of Jean Kerr and Erma Bombeck. He first collection, *Reproachfully Yours* (1949) was immensely successful and brought her fan mail and speaking engagements from Boston to Spokane, from Minneapolis to Mobile and Dallas. She has published four books, all issued in both America and Great Britain by Sheed & Ward. Besides personal essays, there are sketches and a few short stories, one of which, "The Little Girls," won a national contest.

Lucile Charlotte Hardman was born on August 6, 1909, in South Bend, Indiana. She attended Milwaukee-Downer College and the University of Wisconsin, after which she became a convert from Presbyterianism to Catholicism. In 1935, she married Louis Hasley, a professor in the Notre Dame English Department, and they are the parents of three.

Bedridden for a stretch in 1944, she began writing as an escape from boredom and her principal literary standard demands that she never bore the reader. Her tens of thousands of enthusiastic readers testify that she lives up to that principle. Her style is vivid, casual, effervescent, and veined in the vernacular, with sudden shifts and unsuspected humorous turns that feed on human foibles or express the joys of Christianity with engaging irreverence.

SELECTED BIBLIOGRAPHY

Works by Hasley: *Reproachfully Yours*. New York and London: Sheed & Ward, 1949; *The Mouse Hunter*. New York and London: Sheed & Ward, 1953; *Saints and Snapdragons* (British title: *Play It Cool, Sister*). New York and London: Sheed & Ward, 1957; *Mind If I Differ*. New York and London: Sheed & Ward, 1964. The last entry is a sprightly dialog with Unitarian coauthor Betty Mills.

Works about Hasley: Romig, Walter. *The Book of Catholic Authors.* 5th ser. Grosse Pointe, Mich.: Walter Romig Publisher, n.d., pp. 132–38; CA 33–36. Cat A (1952) 235–37.

Louis Hasley

SAMUEL HAZO (1928–). Poet, essayist, professor Sam Hazo and his brother Robert grew up in their birth city of Pittsburgh, Pennsylvania, where Sam attended grade school at St. Paul's and high school at Central Catholic. After graduating magna cum laude as an English major from Notre Dame University (1948), he earned a Master's degree in English at Duquesne University (1955), and a Ph.D. at the University of Pittsburgh (1957).

Samuel Hazo began his teaching career at Shady Side Academy (1953–1955). By 1961, when he became dean of Arts and Sciences at Duquesne, he had completed his studies, served as a captain in the Marine Corps (1950–1958), and married. He has one child. Hazo became a professor of English at his alma mater in 1965, director of the International Poetry Forum there in 1966, and editor of the Forum's *Byblos* Editions in 1976.

Hazo's academic distinctions include honorary degrees, study grants, and awards, notably Pittsburgh's "Man of the Year in the Arts" (1984); and in 1986, the Governor's Hazlett Award for Excellence in Literature and the World Council's David Glick Award.

During his years of teaching and publishing poetry, Hazo managed to write articles for more than forty leading periodicals and to lecture at over fifty universities in America and abroad.

Under the aegis of the State Department, Hazo lectured (1965) in Lebanon and Jordan, in Cairo, and in Athens and Salonika. For the U.S. Information Service, he edited (1977) the poetry section of the Russian and Polish versions of *American* and the Arabic issue of *Mundus Artium.* Among his own translations is *The Growl of Deeper Waters,* from the French by Denis de Rougemont.

Hazo's books of poetry include *Discovery and Other Poems* (1958), followed by *Quiet Wars* (1962), *My Sons in God* (1965), *Blood Rights* (1968), *To Paris* (1981). For a special volume titled *Once for the Last Bandit* (1972), Hazo chose poems from his five earlier volumes. He published *A Selection of Contemporary Religious Poetry* (1963), introduced by his essay on poetic art. Hazo's lyrics cover a wide range of themes: God, faith, morals, time, students, mythology, and voodoo. Realism, incisive vigor, and tight language characterize Hazo's style.

Of Hazo's prose works, the most prominent is *Hart Crane: An Introduction and Interpretation.* Other prose writings include reviews, critiques, and a book of lyrical essays *A Feast of Icarus* (1964).

Hazo's essays offer insights into the art and role of a poet: "the poet is a child of his time", "the poet sees through and with the eye". For the poet, "the world is as multiple as man's imaginings." One of Hazo's own statements is a veritable summary of his works: "Poems are a poet's way of christening the world with words, for his own sake and for the sake of anyone."

SELECTED BIBLIOGRAPHY

Works by Hazo: *Discovery and Other Poems*. Kansas City, Mo.: Sheed, 1958; *Quiet Wars*. Kansas City, Mo.: Sheed, 1962; *Listen with the Eye*. Kansas City, Mo.: Sheed, 1963; *The Christian Intellectual* (ed.). 1963; *My Sons in God*. Kansas City, Mo.: Sheed, 1965; *Blood Rights*. Kansas City, Mo.: Sheed, 1968; *Once for the Last Bandit*. Pittsburgh: University of Pittsburgh, 1972. *Nightwords*. New York: Sheep Meadow Press, 1987. Articles: "The Death of John Berryman." *Commonweal* (25 February 1972), pp. 489–90; "One Sibling with Gleb Derujinsky," an interview. *Commonweal* (9 February 1973), pp. 424–26; "Belief and the Critic." *Renascence* 25 (Summer 1973), pp. 235–47; "Maritain and the Poet." *Renascence* 34 (Summer 1983), pp. 229–44; "The World with the Word." *Studies in Formative Spirituality* 4 (1983), pp. 47–60.

Works about Hazo: Review of *Once for the Last Bandit. Choice* 9 (1972), p. 150; Review of *Quartered. Choice* 12 (1974), p. 130. CA 7–8. CANR 8.

Sister Ann Edward Bennis

MIKE HENSON (1947–). Mike Henson writes chiefly of Appalachians in the urban North, usually Cincinnati, with occasional shifts to their mountain homelands. His fiction reflects a moral earnestness, a deep feeling for his characters, and a controlled rage against institutions that subjugate the poor.

Born in Sidney, Ohio, Henson graduated from Sidney's Holy Angels High School (1965), received has A.B. (1969) from Xavier in Cincinnati, and taught one year in a small Appalachian community before earning his M.A. in English (1971) from the University of Chicago.

Henson was deeply affected by the life of Jesus Christ and the societal teachings of the Catholic Church. Choosing to live in the way of the poor, he took up residence in 1971 in Over-the-Rhine, perhaps the poorest and least safe neighborhood in Cincinnati. His three daughters by his first wife still live there and attend school. Henson now lives in the inner city with his second wife, Lissa Pogue, and he works as a counselor for chemical-dependent adolescents.

In the novel *Ransack* (1980), drug-dependent Seth, leaving behind a jail term, venereal disease, and a battered woman, travels to Cincinnati's Over-the-Rhine where he undertakes the tortuous, stumbling struggle for self-mastery and for a meaningful, redemptive life in the face of a living ghost from his antiheroic past. *Ransack* shares with "*A Small Room with Trouble on My Mind*" *and Other Stories* (1983) the strange combination of intense realism and a Utopian belief in the human spirit. In the title novella, Randall and Rosetta Martin try to maintain control of their own lives as they struggle to survive. Disabled and too proud to live as a dependent, Randall ultimately prefers death. Rosetta, proud but survival oriented, is planning her sons' future even as she plans the funeral of her disturbed, impulsive husband. The other stories, written earlier, generally need more development.

Praised for his "class feeling," Henson still draws criticism for a lack of balance in his work. Institutions—welfare, law enforcement, health care—are viewed negatively, perhaps unfairly. His is not an overview of society but a view from down under, where institutions become antagonistic forces.

Though Henson is the voice of the poor, he is not a populist writer. Narrative movement is sacrificed to density of often poetic detail. Interior monologues abound, and frequent unannounced shifts of speaker and setting challenge even the sophisticated reader. But the reader's effort brings entrance into the little known, seldom expressed world of the urban Appalachian, viewed sentimentally on occasion, but always with immediacy, respect, love, and a ring of authenticity.

SELECTED BIBLIOGRAPHY

Works by Henson: NOVEL: *Ransack*. Minneapolis: West End Press, 1980. SHORT STORIES: *"A Small Room with Trouble on My Mind" and Other Stories*. Minneapolis: West End Press, 1983. Poems and other stories in various journals.

Works about Henson: Finkelstein, Norman. " 'A Small Room with Trouble on My Mind' and Other Stories." *The Minnesota Review* NS23 (1983), 196–97.

Joseph H. Wessling

GEORGE VINCENT HIGGINS (1939–). A lawyer who has served both prosecution and defense in state and federal courts and an assistant attorney general turned author, George Higgins draws on his personal knowledge of the criminal justice and political systems to write about real people making their way in a real world.

Born in Brockton, Massachusetts, on November 13, 1939, and educated at Boston College (B.A., 1961; J.D., 1967) and Stanford University (M.A., 1965), Higgins first worked as a reporter, then as a bureau correspondent, before joining a Boston law firm as a researcher. Admitted to the Massachusetts Bar in 1967, he progressed up the scale from legal assistant in charge of organizing the crime section to deputy assistant attorney general, then to assistant attorney general from 1969–1974, and finally to head, then partner in his own law firm (Higgins, 1973–1978; then Griffin & Higgins, 1978–1982). During this time he acted as an instructor in law enforcement programs for Northeastern University, in trial practice for Boston College Law School, and as a consultant for the National Institute of Law Enforcement and Criminal Justice. Now he is a full-time writer.

Most of Higgins' novels, and especially his early ones, are closet dramas in novel form. There is almost no description, only a few "stage directions" to guide our attention. Speech alone carries the plot and develops the character and setting, as the protagonists talk, talk, talk. No one is—or could be—taciturn in a Higgins novel; every character, even the most minor, has a pressing need to explain himself, to soliloquize on his life. The model of communication is less that of a tennis match's volleys back and forth than that of a military engagement: a salvo of big guns that goes on for paragraphs, to be answered at like length by the opposition.

Higgins' blocks of speech raise interesting questions about the nature of plays, of novels, and, ultimately, of speech itself. As closet drama, Higgins' novels give up the overwhelming advantage that comes with most novels, the narrative apparatus that can depict the novelist's mind in intimate detail, relying instead on our understanding of the rules of conversation. In doing so they raise questions about what these rules are, what factors of power and decorum make us decide to speak or remain silent, how we signal "turns" or opportunities to respond, what general dynamics govern the flow of speech. Higgins answers these questions with models that are certainly synthetic and "false"—his stories are art, not documentary recordings—but in a way that is persuasive of their reality as acts of speech. The illusion of natural speech is created through simple techniques of grammar (ironically, often those of incompetent, beginner's prose) which suggest the confusion of people actually talking: unclear pronoun references (often forcing the reader to stop and reread), simple repetition, the constant use of comma splices, and incredibly lengthy run-on sentences. Yet these conversations would remain affectations without Higgins' ear for street rhythms and style. When the formula works, it creates an unforgettable portrait.

Higgins' characters talk about all the subjects stereotypical gangsters and hoodlums talk about: making a big score, jail, the police, rival gangsters, and the like. Yet they also are humanized as they complain about their wives and families and their problems in paying the light bill. They gossip constantly about their friends and competitors, and they are as nervous about their status and financial security as any junior executive of a Fortune 500 firm. Higgins' cops and lawyers are sometimes hard to distinguish from the criminals they chase; the choice of sides is less important than a love of the rough and tumble of street life. Both groups share the same idiom and thus, though from opposing viewpoints, the worldview their speech entails.

The Friends of Eddie Coyle (1972), *The Digger's Game* (1973), and *Cogan's Trade* (1974) all focus on petty hoodlums. The first looks at a small-time criminal who is caught in an attempt to catch a bigger criminal; Coyle's "friends" turn out to be no friends at all. The second presents the day-to-day world of a professional minor-league criminal: obsessively self-interested while trapped and limited in a narrow male subculture existing parallel to the working-class mainstream. In debt to a loan shark after gambling away eighteen thousand dollars in Las Vegas, "the Digger" must frantically try to find an out. Higgins involves us to the point of identification with his violent, amoral hero, despite his foulmouthed and sleazy ways. *Cogan's Trade* also has us identify with an amoral character in the person of Cogan, a hit man establishing his business and his personal business style. Cogan has a firm sense of criminal decorum which must not be violated, yet his rules are also chillingly self-serving; as in *Eddie Coyle*, the reader is given a society devoid of affect in which human life and human relationships are evaluated in terms of utility. What makes these stories so coldblooded and original is the foucs on the small-time, rather than the master, criminal. The offenses of these little fish, while not trivial, should nevertheless not be mortal, but in a world quite literally ruthless, the death penalty is casually administered.

A City on a Hill (1975) is a less successful attempt to apply the same techniques for dealing with Boston lowlife to dealing with the more complex milieu of Washington politics; it tries to give a sense of political machinations and respectable crime, but it lacks the previous novel's feel of authenticity. Beyond its clever title, *The Friends of Richard Nixon* offers little that is original about Watergate. Higgins seems less comfortable in Washington, far from the rhythms of Boston Irish speech; also, the familiar Watergate story lends itself poorly to Higgins' strengths as a writer.

Back to Boston and surer territory, Higgins' *The Judgment of Deke Hunter* (1976) plays off a policeman, with a nagging wife, a smug boss, and a problem mistress, against a bank robber caught up in the machinations of the representatives of justice. It is notable for its heated argument between detective and prosecutor about whether to cover up the key defense witness' plan to perjure himself and for its explanation of why a testifying officer should not practice one-upmanship on a pushy lawyer.

Kennedy for the Defense (1980) and *Penance for Jerry Kennedy* (1985) share the protagonist, Jerry Kennedy, and examine a criminal trial lawyer's hustling life defending the guilty. Higgins delineates the professional life of a middle-class man fascinated with his work involving the underworld, and hence caught between two worlds. In the second novel Kennedy is older, more disillusioned; as the book proceeds, he finds himself out of the favor of an influential judge, investigated by a television reporter, and drinking too much. For Higgins, Kennedy is a dying breed.

The Rat on Fire (1981) is a tragicomic romp through the complexities of torching buildings. The fiery rat of the title is an unwitting arsonist, aided by many of his rodent fellows, who are also torched by a couple of inept insurance-scam criminals. We see a slice of the lives of arsonists, arson investigators, a lawyer, and a tenant, and develop a sympathy for all, in spite of their unsavory natures. The novel ends abruptly and is not entirely satisfying; the depth and richness of its character portraits promise complications and convolutions that are not delivered.

The characters in *Dreamland* (1977) are a radical departure from Higgins' previous pattern. Instead of the usual lowlifes of the underworld, *Dreamland*'s two main characters are an establishment Boston lawyer and a top-ranked Washington journalist. The lawyer, Daniel Compton Wills, is a fourth-generation member of a conservative financial district law firm, a stuffy and inhibited traditionalist who seemingly lives a life of stultifying order and predictability. He is possibly a half brother to Andrew Collier, the journalist, who lives in the fast lane. Language in Higgins' earlier novels is always a double-edged instrument, concealing and revealing by turns as his almost obsessively loquacious characters insist on telling their stories at length, but in doing so, often show their weaknesses and vulnerabilities. Here, the language is the measured periods of Daniel Wills' first-person narration, polished, oblique, as controlled and polite as the life he apparently lives. Daniel shares the stage uneasily with Andrew, whose speech is also professionally polished but also slangy, profane, and as unpredictable in its leaps and bounds as is its creator's "Bedouin" lifestyle. The measure of Higgins' skill and ambition in this novel is that we begin to distrust our initial and natural sympathy for Daniel as his prevarications and contradictions mount, and we gradually realize that his version of things is not to be trusted. What begins as linguistics ends as philosophy: truth lies neither in the speech of Daniel nor of Andrew, but rather to the extent that the "truth" of a long-past event can be known at all, in an uneasily shifting range of possibilities whose indeterminacy satisfies no one. This is a journalist's lesson, or a trial lawyer's, and it leaves the reader with the satisfaction of a puzzle naggingly left open in spite of all pieces being accounted for, the feel, almost, of real life and of biography.

Dreamland thus represents a movement toward the "respectable" novel for Higgins himself, away from the less honored crime-novel format which has included some of the most readable and exciting American fiction but which has never been taken as seriously as the well-formed novel about upper middle-class characters. It is perhaps Higgins' most impressive book, for it shows skills far transcending facility at straightforward narrative and a fine ear for dialogue.

Imposters (1986) returns like *Dreamland* to secret sin and crime among Boston's fashionable. As in the earlier novel, sexual relationships become a means of maneuvering for advantage and protection, as private obsessions corrupt every relationship.

SELECTED BIBLIOGRAPHY

Works by Higgins: SHORT STORIES: "All Day Was All There Was." *Arizona Quarterly* (Spring 1963); "Something of a Memoir." *Massachusetts Review* (Summer 1969); "Mass in Time of War." *Cimarron Review* (September 1969); "Something Dirty You Could Keep." *Massachusetts Review* (Autumn 1969); "Dillon Explained That He Was Frightened." *North American Review* (Autumn 1970); "The Habits of Animals, The Progress of the Seasons." *North American Review* (Winter 1972); "Two Cautionary Tales: Donnelly's Uncle and The Original Watercourse." *North America Review* (Winter 1974); "The Judge Who Tried Harder." *Atlantic Monthly* (April 1974). NOVELS: *The Friends of Eddie Coyle*. New York: Knopf, 1972; *The Digger's Game*. New York: Knopf, 1973; *Cogan's Trade*. New York: Knopf, 1974; *A City on a Hill*. New York: Knopf, 1975; *The Friends of Richard Nixon*. Boston: Little, Brown, 1975; *The Judgment of Deke Hunter*. Boston: Little, Brown, 1976; *Dreamland*. Boston: Little, Brown, 1977; *A Year or So With Edgar*. New York: Harper, 1979; *Kennedy for the Defense*. New York: Knopf, 1980; *The Rat on Fire*. New York: Knopf, 1981; *The Patriot Game*. New York: Knopf, 1982; *A Choice of Enemies*. New York: Knopf, 1984; *Penance for Jerry Kennedy*. New York: Knopf, 1985; *Imposters*. New York: Holt, 1986; *Outlaws*. New York: Holt and Co., 1987.

Works about Higgins: Levenson, E. A. "Literary Dialect in George V. Higgins' *The Judgment of Deke Hunter*." *English Studies* 62 (1981), pp. 358–70; Review of *The Digger's Game*. *New York Times Book Reivew* (25 March 1973), p. 2; Review of *Dreamland*. *Time* (21 February 1972), p. 74; Review of *The Friends of Richard Nixon*. *New*

York Times Book Review (26 October 1975), p. 28; Review of *The Judgment of Deke Hunter*. *Virginia Quarterly Review* 53 (1977), p. 65. CA 77–80. CAN 17. CN. DLB 2.

Andrew F. Macdonald

DAVID HOPES (1953–). Tough, angry, and hopeful are notes in the often unsettling song of this man who was confirmed a Catholic in his twenty-sixth year. A native of Akron, Ohio, he completed his work for the bachelor's degree at Hiram College in Hiram, Ohio, and continued study at Syracuse University, where he earned a master's degree and in 1980 a doctorate. He currently teaches at the University of North Carolina at Asheville.

Whether the subject is the nativity or the passion of Jesus, the Virgin or Lucifer, there is a "dark night" quality to the poetry in tone, imagery, and the harsh thrust of lines. "We are not in our right minds," he says in the poem of Julian of Norwich, "Heart flaps in dawn wind crying *betrayed*." No hint of pious affectation mars the rigor of this faithful poetry. Already an accomplished poet with many publications, he will continue to be heard from.

SELECTED BIBLIOGRAPHY

Works by Hopes: POETRY: *The Glacier's Daughters*. Amherst, University of Massachusetts Press, 1981. Winner of Juniper Prize (1981) and Saxifrage Prize (1982). CRITICISM: *A Sense of the Morning: Nature through New Eyes*. New York: Dodd, 1988. Also in such magazines as *The New Yorker, Audubon, Poetry Northwest, Kansas Quarterly, Hiram Poetry Review, Salmagundi, Bennington Review, Southern Poetry Review, Greensboro Review, Studia Mystica, Stone Country*, and *Laurel Review*.

Works about Hopes: Review of *The Glacier's Daughters*. *Hudson Review* 35 (1982), p. 328. CA 109.

Mary E. Giles

STEVEN HOPKINS (1953–). Steven Hopkins believes that poetry allows for deep revelations about the self and worth—almost like epiphanous moments. Born in Van Nuys, California, his first love was music; he has played most of his life and continues improvisational composing for poetry-theatre events. He began writing about ten years ago, fiction and poetry as well as articles and reviews. He has been a California Poet-in-the-Schools and spent several years studying comparative religion. Currently he is doing doctoral studies in the history of religions and South Asia studies, with emphasis on Sanskrit literature. Greek Christianity and Camaldolese_ Benedictine monasticism inform his Catholicism.

Pain centers the poetry of Steven Hopkins, the pain of war and violence, of families parted by time and death, as in the sequence for his grandmother entitled "First Light: A Canadian Letter." "I will mark the dead ones," he sings, "where they worked."

Pain is epiphany and the road to epiphany. The face of a peasant is Jesus; through him the poet is moved, beyond visions, into the center of pain, and beyond.

Steven Hopkins is a young poet, mature in poetic vision and voice.

SELECTED BIBLIOGRAPHY:

Works by Hopkins: STORIES: *The Leaving*. Mudborn Press, 1978. POEMS AND STORIES: In such magazines as *Orpheus*, *Northeast*, *Kultur* (Berlin), *Rockbottom*, *One Fare*, *i.e.*, *Eye Magazine*, *Santa Barbara Magazine*, *Epiphany*, *Contemplative Review*, *Studia Mystica*. Articles and reviews in *Cross Currents* and *Anthropos* (Barcelona).

Works about Hopkins: Review of *The Leaving*. *Booklist* (15 October 1979), p. 335.

Mary E. Giles

PAUL HORGAN (1903–). Truly a man of letters, Paul Horgan has had one of the longest, most versatile, and most panoramic literary careers of this century. Best known for his fifteen novels and his historical and biographical works, Horgan has also written over a hundred short stories and novellas, poetry, drama, and essays. Horgan's history of the Rio Grande, *Great River* (1954) and his biography, *Lamy of Santa Fe* (1975) both won the Pulitzer Prize. He has won numerous other literary awards, beginning when his first novel, *Men of Arms* (1931), won the Harper Prize Novel Contest. Horgan did no major work in poetry or drama, but was adept at writing fiction in both the novel and shorter forms. Sometimes called a regionalist because of his intense interest in the land, its people, and its history, Horgan identified too strongly with both East and West and was too engrossed in universal human concerns to be a regionalist in the narrow sense.

Paul George Vincent O'Shaughnessy Horgan was born in Buffalo, New York, on August 1, 1903. His parents, Edward Daniel and Rose Marie Rohr Horgan, moved the family from Buffalo to Albuquerque, New Mexico, in 1915 in hopes of improving his father's health. Horgan attended Albuquerque public schools and the New Mexico Military Institute before going to the Eastman School of Music in 1923, two years after his father's death. He became the librarian of NMMI in 1926 on the condition that he spend mornings on his own writing. The productive artistic habitus thus established was interrupted and regained with effort following service in the army during World War II. Upon discharge, Horgan lectured at the University of Iowa Writers Workshop, assisted the president of NMMI, and held two Guggenheim Fellowships. He was Fellow at the Wesleyan Center for Advanced Studies for two years before being appointed its director in 1962. In 1967, he resigned this position to teach English at Wesleyan University and has been, since 1969, Professor of English and Permanent Author in Residence there. Horgan never married; he lives on the university campus.

Horgan's fictional output is quite evenly divided by a hiatus of several years surrounding the war. Prolific as a novelist for over fifty years, his fiction has always been accompanied by historical and biographical treatments of much of the same material. His work has strong autobiographical components, from his first two novels, *The Fault of Angels* (1933) and *No Quarter Given* (1935), both closely tied to his experience at Eastman, through his Richard trilogy, published in the 1960s and 1970s. Though certain themes and situations recur in his work,

Horgan continually deepens and expands his range rather than merely repeats himself, and his historical and biographical concerns prevent in-growness in his treatment of personal experience and convictions.

Beginning with *Main Line West* (1936), Horgan focused primarily on the Western and Southwestern regions of the country, using settings contemporary to himself as well as from the area's earliest history. His stories usually entail a confrontation of cultures, whether that of the three ethnic groups which converge in the Southwest—the Anglo-American, Native American, and Hispanic— or of the character transplanted from the cultured East to the barely civilized West. Whether historical or more recent, Horgan is typically concerned with humane values and their development in the young, and with the dignity of the human person as fostered by the Catholic Church.

In the two military novels published just after World War II, Horgan does not deal with the conflict in which he had just participated, but with the Civil War and subsequent Apache uprisings. Horgan has been criticized for his presupposition that the conquest of Native Americans was inevitable and desirable, and that the Apaches' proper role was to accept this situation and assimilate gracefully into the culture of the invaders. Though there is some validity to this, Horgan did not condone the inhumane practices of the soldiers in subduing the Apaches, and he presented Native American characters as real persons, of equal worth and dignity to their conquerors.

Though somewhat mannered in style, Horgan's writing shows such a hopeful and redemptive view of man's worth and possibilities as to offset this, and his meticulous craftsmanship overrides any tendency toward sentimentality in what might be regarded as old-fashioned ideals. All of Horgan's novels or stories make good reading on their own, but his contribution is best assessed in its expansive entirety. Critics who read Horgan's work feel that he deserves more of a readership and more critical attention than he has had, and it would be useful if Horgan's numerous shorter pieces that remain uncollected and difficult to obtain were to be gathered.

SELECTED BIBLIOGRAPHY

Works by Horgan (Post-war fiction): NOVELS: *Give Me Possession*. New York: Farrar, Straus and Cudahy, 1957; *A Distant Trumpet*. New York: Farrar, Straus and Cudahy, 1960; *Things As They Are*. New York: Farrar, Straus, 1964; *Memories of the Future*. New York: Farrar, Straus and Giroux, 1966; *Everything to Live For*. New York: Farrar, Straus and Giroux, 1968; *Whitewater*. New York: Farrar, Straus and Giroux, 1970; *The Thin Mountain Air*. New York: Farrar, Straus and Giroux, 1977; *Mexico Bay*. New York: Farrar, Straus and Giroux, 1982. SHORTER WORKS: *Humble Powers*. New York: Image Books, 1955; *The Saintmaker's Christmas Eve*. New York: Farrar, Straus and Cudahy, 1955; *The Peach Stone*. New York: Farrar, Straus and Giroux, 1967.

Works about Horgan: Gish, Robert. *Paul Horgan*. Boston: Twayne Publishers, 1983; Gish, Robert. "Paul Horgan and the Biography of Place." *Prairie Schooner* 55 (1981– 1982), pp. 226–32; Hansen, Terry L. "The Experience of Paul Hogan's *The Peach*

Stone." South Dakota Review 22 (1984), pp. 71–85. CA 13–14. CANR 9. Cat A(1947). CN. TCA.

Linda Schlafer

MAUREEN HOWARD (1930–). Maureen Howard is a witty and perceptive chronicler of Irish-Catholic family life in mid-twentieth-century America. Her subject matter, shaped by personal experience, portrays the tension experienced by those who have passed through the rites of assimilation into mainstream middle-class America while retaining the memories of an ethnic sensibility. This is familiar territory in American literature, but Howard is an extraordinarily gifted storyteller capable of creating characters who command attention. In an interview with Sybil Steinberg for *Publishers Weekly*, Howard described herself as a "Depression kid" who cultivated economies. This self-description provides a key to understanding the craftsmanship which graces her prose and infuses even the trivial with meaning.

Howard was born on June 28, 1930, in Bridgeport, Connecticut, to William L. and Loretta Burns Kean both of whom are central figures in her autobiographical memoir *Facts of Life* (1978). After attending Saint Patrick's Grammar School (Bridgeport) and Laurelton Hall-Academy of Our Lady of Mercy (Milford, Connecticut), she matriculated at Smith College where she recieved a A.B. degree in 1952. Her first two marriages to academicians Daniel F. Howard and David J. Gordon ended in divorce. She presently resides with her third husband in New York City. She has one daughter by her first marriage.

In addition to her writing career, Howard has worked in publishing and advertising, but in recent years she has complemented her own creative life by book reviewing, editing anthologies, and serving as visiting lecturer at a number of colleges and universities. A partial list includes the University of California (Santa Barbara), the New School of Social Research, Columbia University, Amherst, Brooklyn College, and Fairfield University. Besides the critical acclaim garnered over the years, she has been the recipient of numerous awards and recognition for her literary achievements including: the O'Henry Prize for Short Stories (1962), a Guggenheim Fellowship (1967–1968), a Fellowship to Radcliffe Institute (1967–1968), the National Books Critics Circles for General Non-Fiction (1978), and a nomination for the PEN/Faulkner Award for Fiction (1983).

When Maureen Howard recounted the critical details of her life in the autobiography *Facts of Life*, she provided her readers an insight into the emotional backdrop of her creative life. Raised in Bridgeport, a northeastern industrial city, by a refined, college-educated, but religiously scrupulous mother and an irreverent, flamboyant, ex-seminarian father, young, bright Maureen received a classic Irish-Catholic education with the paradoxical agenda of aspiring to gentility while mocking all who make claim to it. She writes of her father that he "was a terrible man . . . it is no mystery that he is the model for the charming, self-dramatizing men I'm drawn to . . . a barroom Paddy delivering himself of wise and witty observations. . . . I learned more from his cruelty than from my mother's care" (*Facts of Life*). The funny but taunting insults of her reactionary father toward her intellectual development provide ample clues to the source of Howard's own disarming wit. Examining her religious ethnic heritage, Howard sees both its grandeur and absurdity. "Religion was a serious business, but the Irish were fair game. In laughing at them [fellow Irish-Catholic parishioners] we laughed at ourselves, didn't we, Catholics in good standing pure potato-famine Irish, gone fine with our cut glass and linens from McCutcheon's."

Her first novel *Not a Word about Nightingales* (1962) is a curious and unrepresentative Howard work. A fifty-ish professor Albert Sedgely is captivated by the charms of Perugia, Italy, while taking a semester sabbatical; after a few days' stay, he decided to extend his visit, much to his wife's bewilderment. The seduction of a Yankee by the easy charm of Italy is familiar Jamesian territory. His seventeen-year-old daughter Rosemary is sent abroad to bring her father to his senses (echoes of Lambert Strether in *The Ambassadors*) only to find herself undergoing a similar transformation. After several melodramatic episodes, the novel reverts to form, as the professor, having spent all of his savings, finds it necessary to return home and resume teaching eighteenth-century English literature to indifferent students. Writing about this apprentice novel in *Facts of Life*, Howard noted her own reservations:

If there is any strength there (I will never look back to see) it can only be what I wanted that book to reflect: a sense of order as I knew it in the late fifties and early sixties . . . that was the enormous joke about life—that our passion must be contained if we were not to be fools.

Not a Word about Nightingales is a minor work containing flashes of wit and ample evidence of a disciplined stylist, yet it contains no hint of the explosive energy of her second novel *Bridgeport Bus* (1965), in which Howard gives a stunning portrait of a thirty-five-year-old virginal secretary, Mary Agnes Keeley, who is attempting to escape from the spiritual and intellectual suffocation imposed by family, job, friends, and community. "When I [Mary Agnes] go home my mother and I play a cannibal game; we eat each other over the years, tender morsel by morsel until there is nothing but bone and wig. She is winning." Mary Agnes is no match for her pious, neurasthenic, novena-going mother who blocks her daughter's every attempt to escape, even the single evening class of French literature which is her only reprieve from the tedium of everyday life. Mrs. Keeley invokes all potential allies in admonishing her daughter: "God knows . . . you were brought up a good Catholic girl, that you should choose a lot of dirty French books over your religion. And thank the good Lord (with a tremolo) your father is not here to see you as an ingrate to your mother."

Mary Agnes eventually lives her flight fantasy by taking a bus from Bridgeport to New York City. Although Mary Agnes has none of the self-conscious grandeur of James Joyce's Stephen Dedalus, she repeats the familiar journey of provincial to cosmopolite in a similar fashion as she acquires both intellectual and carnal knowledge. With her assimilation into New York City, Mary Agnes transforms herself into a new, freer, bawdier, life-giving force. By novel's end she shocks the youthful attending physician with her disarming candor as an expectant mother who is giving birth to a fatherless child. The strength of this novel is in characterization. Mary Agnes finds in the city the freedom to release herself from all her jailers—mother, brother, friends, community, and church—but, like James Patrick Donleavy's* Sebastian Dangerfield in *The Ginger Man*, the reader is left awed and a bit bewildered with the ultimate fate of the new Dionysian Mary Agnes.

Her third novel *Before My Time* (1974) is more a series of vignettes than a conventional novel. A tale within the novel, entitled "Cogan Wins," however, demonstrates Howard at her best. She describes a patriarchal Jewish tycoon, Hoshie Feinmark, and his developing friendship with Cogan, a luckless salesman. Both are clear-eyed commentators on life's absurdities from the differing perspectives of the materially successful but aging Feinmark and the failed, middle-aged salesman Cogan. When Hoshie dies, his children assume that Cogan's friendship had been based upon an expectation of money from their father's estate, and they decide to reward him for his time spent with the deceased. To the bewilderment of Feinmark's children, Cogan refuses this money. His friendship for their father had been a true one, and he chooses not to taint it after Hoshie's death. In this episode in the novel, Howard touches upon that peculiar Irish tendency to reject the things of the world—in this case for the memory of a friendship.

Her most recent novel *Grace Abounding* (1982) set in the suburbs of Fairfield County and New York City contains both the expected strengths and weaknesses of Howard's longer fiction. Brief brilliant passages are linked by a fragile plot structure. Maude Dowd Lasser is a middle-aged child psychologist who has survived widowhood, a shabby affair, and the angry sacrifice of raising her only daughter Elizabeth to be an opera singer, only to see her marry a corporate lawyer and settle into suburban complacency in Scarsdale. Maude's second marriage to Bert Lasser is a welcome mid-life relief. Her past had been a series of quiet adjustments to disappointments. There are, however, consolations for both Maude and Bert. As Bert quotes Santayana's "The acme of life is to understand life," Maude achieves a quiet peace by novel's conclusion accepting her inability to change the course of events. Her own peaceful resolution is mirrored in her husband Bert and daughter Elizabeth who share the bountiful grace of that peace.

Maureen Howard is a writer who surprises; she does not repeat herself except in the skillful command of language and her discerning good humor. The theme of accommodation is central to her most recent fiction. In her introductory comments to *The Penguin Book of Contemporary America Essays* (1984), she observed: "Perhaps we have had too much to keep track of in this country lately. . . . Perhaps we have finally lost our American innocence . . . and we'll not be caught wearing youthful illusions like a party hat on graying hair." Maureen Howard could well be describing her own development from a novelist writing imitative academic fiction to a clearheaded commentator on her own everchanging world.

SELECTED BIBLIOGRAPHY

Works by Howard: NOVELS: *Not a Word about Nightingales*. New York: Atheneum, 1962; *Bridgeport Bus*. New York: Harcourt, Brace, and World, 1965; *Before My Time*. Boston: Little, Brown & Co., 1974; *Grace Abounding*. Boston: Little, Brown & Co., 1982. AUTOBIOGRAPHY: "Charting Life with a Daughter." *New York Times*, (1 June 1977), Sec. C, pp. 1, 14; *Facts of Life*. Boston: Little, Brown & Co., 1978; "The Making of a Writer: Before I Go I Have Something to Say." *New York Times Book Review* (25 April 1982), pp. 7, 16.

Works about Howard: Ahearn, Kenneth. "Pursuing the Self: Maureen Howard's *Facts of Life*." *New Republic* (9 September 1978), pp. 37–38; Pollitt, Katha. "Midlight Writing." *Saturday Review* (28 October 1978), pp. 43–44; Sale, Roger. "The Realms of Gold." *Hudson Review* 28 (1975–1976), pp. 616–28; Sale, Roger. "Staying News." *Sewanee Review* 83 (1975), pp. 212–24; Taliaferro, Frances. "Facts of Life." *New Republic* (9 September 1978), pp. 37–78. AWW. CA 53–56; *DLB*, 1983.

Leo F. O'Connor

I

ALBERT INNAURATO (1947–). The plays of Albert Innaurato that have been produced on Broadway, *Gemini* (1977) and *Passione* (1981), are set in Italian neighborhoods of South Philadelphia. In these plays critics have found a collection of distinct and original characters who evoke both laughter and pity as they take pride in, survive, or try to escape from their ethnic and local peculiarities. They offer a welcome departure from the standard fare of characters and conflicts presented on the current stage. Some critics believe, however, that Innaurato compromised his talents in these plays, that he sacrificed art for popularity and entertainment. These critics see more imagination and satirical power in his Off-Broadway productions, where social misfits pass through scenes of grotesque violence and nightmarish absurdity.

Albert Innaurato was born in Philadelphia on June 2, 1947. He attended St. Monica's School in South Philadelphia from 1953 to 1961 and spent one year at Bishop Neumann High School (now St. John Neumann) before he transferred to Central High School and graduated in 1965. After five years at Temple University and one year at California Institute of the Arts, he entered Yale School of Drama in 1971, where he collaborated with Christopher Durang on such plays as *The Idiots Karamazov* (1981), and received a Master of Fine Arts in 1974. He now resides in New York City.

In discussions about his plays and in the plays themselves, Innaurato accuses contemporary society of exaggerating materialistic values and social conformity. It is useless for an artist to arrange conflicting values into beautiful harmonies when society does not recognize any values that conflict with its systems. Rather, agreeing with Flannery O'Connor,* Innaurato believes that the artist must create grotesque images of materialism and conformity to show society how distorted it is, and oppose these with equally grotesque images of spirituality and personal uniqueness, since this society will perceive unconventional values only in their distorted forms.

In *Urlicht* (1974) and *Wisdom Amok* (1980), struggling male artists have to defend themselves against the threatening domination of Catholic nuns, who represent the abuse of both physical and spiritual values. The nuns renounce marriage and children, but compensate with a ghoulish craving to devour male flesh. In the background of many Innaurato plays a young man is carried in procession by nuns to a presumed sacrificial death and banquet. This may mean that the theater can redeem a sick culture by ritual purification and nourishment, but the ceremony is gruesome, and the artist often considers himself the victim. In *The Transfiguration of Benno Blimpie* (1977), Benno Blimpie admires and copies the geometric designs in Leonardo's ''Last Supper,'' but this abstract art does not satisfy him or appeal to a society interested only in consumerism and sex, so he unconsciously parodies the fresco's theme by ritually eating himself to death—in despair and protest, but perhaps also in redemptive transfiguration. Artists like Benno are victimized in Innaurato's plays because they are fat and ugly, but especially because their sexuality is ambiguous. They are males, but they share the creative power of women—that is why they antagonize the nuns— and sometimes, to stress their countercultural status, they assume postures of androgyny. The opera buff in *Earth Worms* is a drag queen, and the writer, Bernard, feels most comfortable in female attire of the 1890s.

Francis Geminiani is not an artist in *Gemini*, but he is chubby and he enjoys opera. When he comes home for the summer to South Philadelphia from Harvard and prepares to celebrate his twenty-first birthday, he suffers a ''homosexual panic.'' He seems unsure whether he loves Judith, a trim Wasp classmate, or her gymnast brother Randy. His deeper struggle, however, is between Harvard and Philadelphia. At this turning point in his life, Francis is terrified by Philadelphia, which for him represents the usual burdens of adulthood: hard work, marital friction, raucous neighbors, overeating, and minor physical ailments. The homosexual option would make him a pariah and free him from all this. Unfortunately, he sees no way that he can be both a normal Philadelphian and a cultured Harvard man. He cannot mix the physical with the spiritual. *Passione* explores the same conflict through the image of being a wop in a Wasp culture. It sets the food, family, and accumulated junk of a Philadelphia Italian against the diet, feminism, and sterile cleanliness of his estranged wife from North Carolina.

Innaurato wants the theater to be the center of life, to be serious, but popular and commercial too. His later plays, however, seem to argue the impossibility of this. In *Ulysses in Traction* (1978), a college drama department tries to rehearse for a play during a race riot, and in *Coming of Age in Soho* (1985), a writer has to isolate himself from family and politics to pursue his art. These plays have the same rigid dichotomies and sexual ambiguities, but they also have the sacrificial deaths and meals that promise society some form of redemption.

SELECTED BIBLIOGRAPHY

Works by Innaurato: PLAYS: *The Transfiguration of Benno Blimpie*. New York: Dramatists Play Service, 1977; *Gemini: A Play in Two Acts*. New York: Dramatists Play

Service, 1977; *Ulysses in Traction*. New York: Dramatists Play Service, 1978; *Bizarre Behavior: Six Plays*, with introduction by author. New York: Avon, 1980; *The Idiots Karamazov*, with Christopher Durang. New York: Dramatists Play Service, 1981; *Passione*. New York: Dramatists Play Service, 1981; *Coming of Age in Soho*. New York: Dramatists Play Service, 1985. *The Best Plays of Albert Innaurato*. New York: The Gay Press of NY, 1987.

Works about Innaurato: Katz, Marc. "Interview with Albert Innaurato." *New York Arts Journal* (July-August 1978), pp. 7–9; Ventimiglia, Peter James. "Recent Trends in American Drama: Michael Cristofer, David Mamet, and Albert Innaurato." *Journal of American Culture* 1 (1978), pp. 195–204. CA 115. CD.

Anthony J. Berret, SJ

K

JAMES J. KAVANAUGH (Father Joseph Nash) (1934–). From the traditions of Roman Catholicism to the gratifications of California's human potential movement, James Kavanaugh has wandered, a self-described "searcher" after life's "ultimate secret" and for "everything good and beautiful." Along the way, Kavanaugh has written nearly twenty volumes, including ten books of poetry and two novels.

Born on September 17, 1934, in Kalamazoo, Michigan, Kavanaugh earned his B.A. from Xavier University in Cincinnati in 1954. He was ordained in 1956, taught at the Catholic University of America nursing school from 1961 to 1963, and became an instructor in theology there in 1964. From 1964 to 1966, he taught theology at Trinity College in Washington, D.C. Kavanaugh has earned an M.A. (1963) and a Ph.D. (1966) from Catholic University of America, and another Ph.D. (1973) from U.S. International University in San Diego. From 1966 to 1972, he was a marriage counselor at the Human Resources Institute in La Jolla, California, while he also served as a professor of graduate psychology at International University. In 1967 he resigned his priesthood. An actor, Kavanaugh has appeared on stage and television and has written (with Darrell Fetty) a musical review called *Street Music*, which was first performed in 1974 at Theatre 40 in Los Angeles. Kavanaugh is a clinical psychologist and the founder of the James Kavanaugh Institute (1984).

Kavanaugh's controversial first book, *A Modern Priest Looks at His Outdated Church* (1967), contains the core of the ideas that he explores later in his two novels. Essentially, Kavanaugh objects to the legalistic structures of the Catholic Church which have tended to smother "personhood" and the potential for a free response to God in faith. Rigid, institutionalized codes governing every aspect of Christian life—but especially sexual feelings—overrun human feelings and replace them with pain and despair. In response, Kavanaugh calls for a return to the simple message of Christ: "Love one another as I have loved you."

In his first novel, *A Coward for Them All* (1979), Kavanaugh concentrates on questions of (among others) Church authority, homosexuality, celibacy, and birth control. Raised in an Irish-American family with strong roots in the traditions of the Roman Catholic Church, Thom Maguire gives up a promising football career and a powerful sexual drive to enter the priesthood. Thom's vocation faces temptations from women and from the drive to power within the Church hierarchy. Petty jealousies, however, stymie Thom's political ambitions, and sexual cravings threaten his vow of celibacy. Ultimately, Thom leaves the priesthood, submerges himself in his sexual passions, marries, builds a successful business, divorces, marries again, divorces again, and on his own for the first time finds strength in his separateness. In spite of leaving the priesthood, however, Thom wants to remain a part of the Church: " . . . there was a Catholicism, and even a priesthood, beyond modern anxieties and ancient hostilities" (p. 513), "a Catholicism that cared about the sick, that fought for the workingman, that protected children, sanctified marriage, built universities, and protected artists. And battled to make of man more than a greedy, destructive savage on earth" (p. 514). This Catholicism, Thom believes he can accept.

The rage resulting from the conflict between the abstract legalisms of canon law and simple human love keeps the novel moving, but ultimately, *A Coward for Them All* is too long. When it succeeds, it contracts and dives, looking deeply into the pain in individual hearts; when it falters, however, the novel sweeps across years and decades and family members and historical events in an effort to recreate the power of the Catholic tradition and history that envelopes the main characters. Too often, this grand scale obscures the cry for a simple love which rests at the heart of the novel.

As its title suggests, Kavanaugh's second novel *The Celibates* (1985) deals primarily with the place of human sexual love within the priesthood. Its two main characters, Father Ted Santek and Father Gerry Beauvais, are good priests forced from the priesthood by the Church which cannot abide their relationships with the women whose compassion and love, ironically, strengthen the priests' ministry. Even the crucial question of celibacy, however, hides a more profound problem: how can the traditional Church bound in its stifling legalisms accommodate a modern Church breathing the fresh air of Pope John XXIII's gift of love? The response, in this novel anyway, is that the modern Church will fall back on the rigidity of canon law; it is the way of the Church, apparently, to make all-or-nothing decisions; there is no room for compromise, for consideration. The Church hierarchy drives Gerry Beauvais from his parish because he is living with a woman, even though Beauvais and Peggy sanctify their relationship with their own vow of celibacy. The consequences of the Church's intransigence are heartbreak, physical pain, loneliness, lost vocations, and, in the case of Father Gerry, suicide. What little flexibility the American Church hierarchy reveals at odd moments in this novel ultimately gets stifled by the constitutively more rigid rule of Rome.

Like *A Coward for Them All*, *The Celibates* shows well Kavanaugh's great compassion for human pain, his intolerance of the Church's destructive obsession with humanity's sexual nature, and his belief that love must be "the free choice of the spirit of man and God" (p. 421). But the novel also suffers from the sensationalism of event and language made popular by Andrew Greeley's* pot-boiler novels of priests' illicit sexual liaisons. Kavanaugh's rage at the Church as an institution too often overpowers his obviously tender feelings for certain characters.

Not unlike his fiction, Kavanaugh's poetry ranges from the effective to the banal, from the compassionate to the self-centered. At its best, it finds appropriate metaphor for the pain of loneliness and spiritual vacuity which Kavanaugh discerns at the core of contemporary human experience. "The Football Game" from *There Are Men Too Gentle to Live among Wolves* (1971) explores in a Sunday football game "A proper ritual" for weak, lonely men tired of "hymns and sacraments too subtle" for life's viciousness. In "Lonely Numbered Cards," the poet discovers that sexual union can make even strangers connect for a moment "[d]espite the fantasy of place and fated deal" and can ease the pain and fear usually suffered in loneliness. "My Easy God Is Gone" contemplates with anger the loss of a childhood belief but finds solace in "the call of creation" and "the mystery of loneliness and love" which the adult embraces.

Kavanaugh's poetry slips into the simplistic when it attempts cleverness. Even a poem like "Of Women and Men," which flirts humorously with formal constraints, reduces the complexity of human relationships to "What it takes to sustain an erection."

Overall, Kavanaugh's poetry tends to reduce all human experience and even all material reality to the poetic self. An irritating narcissism governs his poetic vision. "Doom Prophets Say" slaughters empathy for others to record a litany of woes for the planet which affect, apparently, only the poet's self which occupies the center of the universe: "My . . . Streams I've fished in" all face extinction; the final line of the poem collapses the fate of the earth into the fate of the poet: "I don't die easily."

With similar egotism, "Ode To a Relationship" explores the causes of the poet's spiritual discontentment after experimentation with every faddish form of the California human potential movement. The poem succeeds at capturing the specific details of a moment in time but finally ascribes the poet's unhappiness only to his relationship with an unnamed other. The poet yells "I'm splitting" because "You piss me off!"

After a while, such poetic self-absorption grates and perplexes more than it enriches, even though many readers might find inspiration in some of Kavanaugh's words.

Kavanaugh seems to have found expression for the great energies of his expansive self. In 1984, he founded the James Kavanaugh Institute for "*searchers* . . . a haven where men and women in . . . painful transitions . . . can meet with kindred spirits." While Kavanaugh seems to have left far behind the legalistic repressiveness of the Catholic Church, he has redefined for himself a new kind of priesthood which combines a vocation as writer with training in contemporary psychological theory to "provide the healthy, joyful, loving environment that people need for total healing."

SELECTED BIBLIOGRAPHY

Works by Kavanaugh: *There's Two of You*. New York: Newman, 1964; *A Modern Priest Looks at His Outdated Church*. New York: Trident Press, 1967; *The Struggle of the Unbeliever*. New York: Trident Press, 1968; *The Birth of God*. New York: Trident Press, 1969; *There Are Men Too Gentle to Live among Wolves*. New York: Dutton, 1971; *The Poetry of James Kavanaugh*. Mesa, Arizona: Nash Press, 1974; *Sunshine Days and Foggy Nights*. New York: Dutton, 1975; *Winter Has Lasted Too Long*. New York: Dutton, 1977; *A Coward for Them All*. New York: Bantam, 1979; *Maybe If You Loved More*. New York: Dutton, 1982; *The Celibates*. New York: Harper, 1985; *Search: A Guide for Those Who Dare to Ask of Life Everything Good and Beautiful*. New York: Harper, 1985.

Works about Kavanaugh: Review of *A Modern Priest Looks at His Outdated Church*. *New York Times Book Review* (10 July 1967), p. 10; Review of *Sunshine Days and Foggy Nights*. *Booklist* (15 September 1975), p. 111. CA 13–14. CANR 17.

Daniel J. Tynan

WILLIAM KENNEDY (1928–). Beginning in 1983, good things happened in a great rush for novelist William Kennedy. The MacArthur Foundation gave him one of its "genius awards," the National Book Critics Circle named *Ironweed* (1983) the year's best book of fiction, and *Ironweed* won the 1984 Pulitzer Prize. Kennedy became an important literary figure overnight. Kennedy's four novels and book of non-fiction are all set in Albany, New York, where his ancestors settled five generations ago. Kennedy writes about what he knows best: his subject matter, his point of view, and his imagery come out of growing up in a working-class family in an Irish-Catholic neighborhood in his native city.

Born on January 16, 1928, Kennedy earned his B.A. at Siena College in 1949. He immediately began a career in journalism and continued newspaper writing in the army. After reporting for the Albany *Times-Union* from 1952 to 1956, Kennedy left Albany for Puerto Rico where he worked as a journalist and began to write fiction. Kennedy's biography reflects his extraordinary devotion to writing: he has always been a novelist waiting for the professional and economic opportunity to make it his sole occupation. Saul Bellow spotted Kennedy's talent more than twenty-five years ago when he had him as a student in Puerto Rico. More recently, Bellow fought to get *Ironweed* published and to have Kennedy recognized as an important American writer. Kennedy published his first novel *The Ink Truck* in 1969; his three best books—now known as his Albany cycle—came out in 1975, 1978, and 1983. In 1984, he coauthored the screenplay for Francis Ford Coppola's *The Cotton Club*, and his novels have been optioned for future Hollywood productions.

In *The Ink Truck* Kennedy's hero is Bailey, a reporter involved in a prolonged newspaper strike. The novel is a vigorous period piece of surrealistic black humor (which invites comparison with the work of Kurt Vonnegut, Jr.). Bailey, like all Kennedy's heroes, is an outsider. He keeps trying to make connections, but he finds no solace in the orgies, drugs, or violence which motivate others. He makes defiant gestures against the system which serve only to affirm life's essential absurdity. For Bailey, born of the Jansenist strain in Irish Catholicism, sin, guilt, suffering, and punishment are certainties, salvation merely a possibility. Yet, no matter how corrupt or violent his environment, Bailey, a true comic hero, lands on his feet. *The Ink Truck* is a joyful book.

A detailed exploration of evil, *Legs* (1975) chronicles the rise and fall of Albany's greatest celebrity of the 1920s and 1930s, the stylish gangster Jack "Legs" Diamond. The narrator of *Legs*, Marcus Gorman, an Albany lawyer, a Democrat and a Catholic, is just as much a sucker for Jack's glamor as are the readers of the yellow press. To Marcus, Legs is bigger than life, to which Kennedy playfully refers by having both men read from Rabelais' *Gargantua*.

The main characters of *Legs*, Jack, his wife Alice, and Marcus are all products of ethnic Catholicism. Jack considers his rosary beads good luck, and Alice hopes they will magically convert him to conventional piety. Alice is Jack's madonna, the showgirl Kiki his magdalene. In one of the most effective scenes in the book, Jack dances with them both in a moment of supreme happiness shortly before his death. In the climactic courtroom drama, Marcus, whose rhetorical techniques are derived from speeches at Knights of Columbus communion breakfasts, invents a character reference for Jack, ostensibly from an old nun, the kind who looks Jack in the eye and is as "certain as I am of God's love that . . . he is not an evil man." Kennedy also returns to his themes of sin, guilt, and punishment, expressed in Marcus' assessment of Jack's character: "He was also a venal man of integrity, for he never ceased to renew his vulnerability to punishment, death, and damnation."

Billy Phelan's Greatest Game (1978) might easily be subtitled "Fathers and Sons." Kennedy uses the Biblical story of Abraham and Isaac to help unify the plot, which concerns the kidnapping of the son of one of the city's political bosses. The narrator, Martin Daugherty, "age fifty," is trying to come to terms with his dying father and his soon-to-be-a-priest son and also takes a very fatherly interest in Billy Phelan himself. One of the kidnappers is the no-good son of a politician opposed to the bosses. In this book it is extremely difficult for fathers to love sons and for sons to love fathers. Fathers cannot mold sons like themselves, and sons lose whether they follow their fathers' wishes or rebel against them.

Billy Phelan is a mature work; it has none of the wildly improvisational scenes of *The Ink Truck* or the sometimes awkward juxtapositions of fact and fancy in *Legs*. It points forward to Kennedy's masterwork *Ironweed*, in which he develops the story of Billy's father, Francis Phelan.

Ironweed is, like its two predecessors, set in Albany in the 1930s. This time Kennedy looks at the lower depths of the city through the eyes of a skid row bum. Several elements contribute toward making *Ironweed* an exceptional work.

In this novel Kennedy is the absolute master of his narrative voice. There is no clumsy machinery: the story unfolds as Francis' inner monologue, punctuated with startling visions of the past and present that make the living and dead seem part of the same reality. Kennedy has created the psyche of his protagonist so convincingly that the everyday, the mysterious, and the miraculous believably coexist, as when Francis contemplates a picture of himself in his prime, when he was a ballplayer:

The flight of the ball had always made this photo mysterious to Francis, for the camera had caught . . . two instants in one: time separated and unified, the ball in two places at once . . . a Trinitarian talisman (a hand, a ball, a glove) for achieving the impossible.

Francis, who seems at first a victim or merely a survivor, is much more: he is a hero who defends the powerless with his natural strength of body and will. In the climax of the book, Francis fights off a mob of vigilantes who invade a hobo camp. He then carries a stricken comrade to a hospital where his friend dies. Francis is at the point of running away again but instead goes home to his family—to his wife Annie, his children, and his grandchildren. Francis' personal odyssey ends; he is able to go home again because he finally conquers his guilt and believes he has atoned for his crimes.

Kennedy's non-fiction book *O Albany! Improbable City of Political Wizards, Fearless Ethnics, Spectacular Aristocrats, Splendid Nobodies, and Underrated Scoundrels* (1983) was published after his novels, but it reflects his intense, intimate relationship with the city and its people which has inspired his fiction. The book's opening sentence is a fitting summary: "I write this book . . . as a person whose imagination has become fused with a single place, and in that place finds all the elements that a man ever needs for the life of the soul." Kennedy's imagination has already produced some distinguished American fiction and promises more fine work to come.

SELECTED BIBLIOGRAPHY

Works by William Kennedy: NOVELS: *The Ink Truck*. Garden City, N.Y.: Dial Press, 1969, reprinted New York: Viking Press, 1984; *Legs*. New York: Coward, McCann & Geogheghan, 1975; *Billy Phelan's Greatest Game*. New York: Viking Press, 1978; *Ironweed*. New York: Viking Press, 1983; *Quinn's Book*. New York: Viking Press, 1988. NON-FICTION: *O Albany! Improbable City of Political Wizards, Fearless Ethnics, Spectacular Aristocrats, Splendid Nobodies, and Underrated Scoundrels*. New York: Viking Penguin, 1983. SCREENPLAYS: *The Cotton Club*, with Francis Ford Coppola, 1984; *Legs*, 1984.

Works about Kennedy: Bonetti, Kay. "An Interview with William Kennedy." *The Missouri Review* 8 (1985), pp. 71–86; Reilly, Edward C. "The Pigeons and Circular Flight in Kennedy's *Ironweed*." *Notes on Contemporary Literature* 16 (1986), p. 8; Whittaker, Stephen. "The Lawyer As Narrator in William Kennedy's *Legs*." *Legal Studies Forum* 9 (1985), pp. 71–86. CA 85–88. CANR 14.

Willem O'Reilly

X. J. KENNEDY (1929–). A poet who excels in many different verse types as well as an editor, critic, and anthologist, X. J. Kennedy has enthralled, baffled, and often angered critics because of the breadth and, of late, the perceived aimlessness of his career. His first poetry collection was the Academy of American Poets' Lamont Poetry Selection in 1961; however, nothing he has written since has been quite so successful, and consequently Kennedy is viewed more harshly and perhaps more unfairly than he would be had he made a long, slow climb toward literary greatness.

Born on August 21, 1929, in Dover, New Jersey, he was originally named Joseph Charles Kennedy and allegedly took the pseudonym to distinguish himself from the patriarch of the celebrated Massachusetts clan. Kennedy received a bachelor's degree from Seton Hall University in 1950 and a master's from Columbia in 1951, and he attended the Sorbonne and the University of Michigan. Kennedy is married and has five children; he has taught at colleges and universities in the United States and England and is currently a professor of English at Tufts University. His poetry collection *Nude Descending a Staircase* (1961) was the Lamont Poetry Selection in 1961, and his children's book *One Winter Night in August* (1975) was named an Outstanding Book of the Year in 1975 by the *New York Times Book Review*; other awards and honors include a Bread Loaf Fellowship (1961), the Bess Hokin Prize from *Poetry* magazine (1961), the Shelley Memorial Award (1970), and a Guggenheim Fellowship (1973–1974). He has contributed reviews and criticism to *The Atlantic*, *The Nation*, and other journals.

There is a marked concern with worldly affairs in Kennedy's poetry, a quality that his readers have used both to praise and damn him. Such critics as M. L. Rosenthal have noted that Kennedy is satirical, wry, and astringent in the manner of the classical ironists; others have lamented what they see as a descent into comic poetry and so-called society verse. While Kennedy does write light verse and topical poetry, he handles his material skillfully and perceptively, in the manner of W. H. Auden and John Updike, rather than in that of the more accessible Ogden Nash ("I am never after laughs for their own sake," said Kennedy in the anthology *A Controversy of Poets*). Kennedy reveals his priorities in his latest collection, *Cross Ties* (1985), which alternates sections of poems on serious subjects with songs, light verse, epigrams, and children's poetry. To regain his stature in the eyes of critics with a narrow range of vision, Kennedy will probably have to publish an extended collection limited to serious poems in the manner of his earliest work or that of the remarkable if unheralded *Celebration after the Death of John Brennan* (1974), an elegy to a talented student who committed suicide.

SELECTED BIBLIOGRAPHY

Works by Kennedy: *Nude Descending a Staircase*. Garden City, N.Y.: Doubleday, 1961; *Celebrations after the Death of John Brennan*. Lincoln, Mass.: Penmaen, 1974; *Cross Ties*. Athens, Ga.: University of Georgia Press, 1985.

Works about Kennedy: Holmes, Theodore. "Wit, Nature and the Human Concern." *Poetry* 100, 5 (August 1962), pp. 319–24; Rosenthal, M. L. "Poetic Power—Free the Swan!" *Shenandoah* 24, 1 (Fall 1972), pp. 85–91. DLB 5.

David Kirby

JACK KEROUAC (1922–1969). There is as yet little critical agreement about the work of Jack Kerouac. He has been praised as a major stylistic innovator for his experiments with jazz rhythms; others have dismissed his style as merely "typewriting." Similarly he has been celebrated and condemned for his subject matter—the beat generation of young Americans who found themselves looking for alternatives to middle-class norms and patterns in the late 1940s and 1950s. For some, Kerouac's explorations of life on the road and of characters poised between escapism and questing has seemed to reach back to such nineteenth-century works as *Huck Finn* while prophetically foreshadowing the counterculture of the 1960s. Some have even claimed Kerouac's best known novels, *On the Road* (1957) and *The Dharma Bums* (1958), were in part the cause of that era's experimentations. Others have more simply denounced Kerouac's portrayals as vicious and nihilistic, a "know-nothing bohemianism." In all, most of the praise and damnation has centered on Kerouac's own public persona and his material. The novels and poems he has published have as yet generated little sustained critical discussion. By contrast, Kerouac has been the subject of five lengthy biographies.

Born on March 12, 1922, in Lowell, Massachusetts, Kerouac was raised in the French Canadian neighborhoods of that city. Kerouac spoke mostly French until he shifted from the parochial school system to the public junior high school. Kerouac graduated from high school at the age of sixteen and played football for a year at Horace Mann prep school before enrolling on a football scholarship at Columbia. The outbreak of World War II, disagreements with the coach, and Kerouac's own sense of dislocation as he tried to adjust to the big city led him to drop out of college, and by the end of the war he had held various odd jobs, worked as a merchant seaman, and done a brief stint in the navy before being discharged for psychological reasons. From 1946 until his death, Kerouac wrote twenty published novels and collections of poetry. He completed most of this writing between 1951 and 1957 when he worked in virtual anonymity. During his most productive period, Kerouac alternated periods of wandering and various short-term jobs with periods of writing while living with his mother in the New York area. He was married briefly three times, but his most lasting relationships were with his fellow beat writers: William Burroughs, Allen Ginsberg, and John Clellon Holmes and with Neal Cassady, the model for the character Dean Moriarity in *On the Road*. Kerouac died on October 21, 1969, in St. Petersburg, Florida from esophageal hemorrhaging brought on at least in part by alcoholism.

On the Road will probably continue to be Kerouac's best known work, but that novel's concern with narrating events is at odds with much of the rest of Kerouac's practice where the emphasis is, instead, on writing as a kind of meditation. In a letter written a few months after he completed *On the Road*, Kerouac claims that the book is somehow false to the imaginative depth of the experiences even though "it's the one that happened." After *On the Road* Kerouac concentrated on what he first termed "sketching" and later codified as "Spontaneous Prose." In books like *Visions of Cody* (1972), *Doctor Sax* (1959), and *The Subterraneans* (1958), Kerouac chose to understate the "horizontal," or narrative dimension of his work and concentrated instead on recording the "vertical, metaphysical" qualities of his material. In a sense, Kerouac sought to collapse the distance between perception and expression by merging them in a single act. In "Essentials of Spontaneous Prose," he explained that writing "spontaneously" meant starting from "a definite image-object" (either actual or from memory) and then tracing out the associations the writer has for that "image-object," "swimming in sea of language to peripheral release and exhaustion." Kerouac stressed that this process proceeded "not from preconceived idea of what to say about image but from jewel center of interest in subject at *moment* of writing." Kerouac's "spontaneous" aesthetic is in some ways a parallel to bop improvisation and action painting, two other developments of the same period, and Kerouac's emphasis after *On the Road* on writing as a variety of performance, as a real-time response to an image or memory, became a way of attempting to possess the world imaginatively by using language to create a space and then fill it with motion.

In spite of the emphasis on writing as meditation in "Spontaneous Prose," most discussions approach Kerouac's work as autobiographical narrative. Kerouac's own charisma, his actual experiences, and the beat generation controversy all helped focus attention on Kerouac himself. And certainly Kerouac did draw heavily on the material of his own life, but rather than use that material to create an autobiographical story, Kerouac used it to provide occasions for the narrator to meditate on a series of thematically and tonally related images that become, as they repeat, vary, and evolve, the structure and action of the books. If one misses this, one misses as well Kerouac's extended exploration of whether imaginative literature's task is to bear witness to reality, or whether imaginative literature creates its own reality. In spiritual terms, Kerouac related this to the conflicting allegiances he felt to Catholicism and Buddhism.

To Kerouac, the Catholicism of his youth stressed the reality of life and suffering and offered redemption only if one could meet the terms of the world with patience and charity. Buddhism for Kerouac implied the unreality of incarnated existence and promised relief from suffering only if one could accept the world as illusion. For several years prior to *On the Road*'s publication, Kerouac seriously explored Buddhism, but the work of his last few years increasingly returned to explore the Catholicism of his youth, especially in the novel *Visions of Gerard* (1963), the story of Kerouac's brother who died at the age of nine when Kerouac was four. In the novel, Kerouac presents Gerard as a suffering child saint to whom he is still loyal. From novels like *Visions of Gerard* and *Big Sur* (1962), it is clear that Kerouac's Catholicism is less a matter of theology and doctrine than of textures and images he associated with the French Canadian neighborhoods of his early years. (And indeed there is now some interest in Kerouac as a minority writer on the part of some French Canadian critics who wish to place Kerouac in the Quebecois tradition.) For Kerouac, Catholicism was St. Francis and not Aquinas, and that perhaps points to the strengths and weaknesses of his work as a whole. Like Charlie Parker and Jackson Pollock, Kerouac responded to the world intuitively, and that, matched with his incredible ear and sense of language, led to intense and brilliant recordings of his own conflicts and the conflicts of the world around him. It also meant that he was often unable to resolve or mediate those conflicts either in his life or in his art.

SELECTED BIBLIOGRAPHY

Works by Kerouac: *The Town and the City*. New York: Harcourt, Brace, 1950; *On the Road*. New York: Viking Press, 1957; *The Dharma Bums*. New York: Viking Press, 1958; *The Subterraneans*. New York: Grove Press, 1958; *Doctor Sax*. New York: Grove Press, 1959; *Maggie Cassidy*. New York: Avon Books, 1959; *Mexico City Blues*. New York: Grove Press, 1959; *Lonesome Traveler*. New York: McGraw-Hill Book Company, 1960; *The Scripture of the Golden Eternity*. New York: Totem/Corinth Books, 1960; *Tristessa*. New York: Avon Books, 1960; *Book of Dreams*. San Francisco: City Lights Books, 1961; *Pull My Daisy*. New York: Grove Press, 1961; *Big Sur*. New York: Farrar, Straus and Cudahy, 1962; *Visions of Gerard*. New York: Farrar, Straus and Company, 1963; *Desolation Angels*. New York: Coward-McCann, 1965; *Satori in Paris*. New York: Grove Press, 1966; *Vanity of Duluoz*. New York: Coward-McCann, 1968; *Pic*. New York: Grove Press, 1971; *Scattered Poems*. San Francisco: City Lights Books, 1971; *Visions of Cody*. New York: McGraw-Hill Book Company, 1972.

Works about Kerouac: Charters, Ann. *Kerouac: A Biography*. San Francisco: Straight Arrow Books, 1973; Hunt, Tim. *Kerouac's Crooked Road: Development of a Fiction*. Hamden, Conn.: Archon Books, 1981; Kerouac, Jack. *On the Road*. Ed. Scott Donaldson. New York: Viking Critical Library, 1979; Nicosia, Gerald. *Memory Babe: A Critical Biography of Jack Kerouac*. New York: Grove Press, 1983; Tytell, John. *Naked Angels: The Lives and Literature of the Beat Generation*. New York: McGraw-Hill Book Company, 1976. CA 5–6. DLB 2.

Tim Hunt

GALWAY KINNELL (1927–). Since the publication of his first volume of poems *What a Kingdom It Was* (1960), Galway Kinnell has been acclaimed as one of America's most distinguished poets of the twentieth century. The centerpiece poem of that collection, "The Avenue Bearing the Initial of Christ into the New World," was celebrated by poets and critics alike as a rare achievement in American poetry in which the Whitmanesque vision of Kinnell inspired both awe and promise. Kinnell has since written five major volumes of poetry and compiled *Selected Poems* (1982) for which he received both the American Book Award and the Pulitzer Prize. Although there have been some dissenting opinions on Kinnell's oeuvre, he continues to attract a significant and supportive audience to the steady dramatic evolution of his poetic vision.

Kinnell was born on February 1, 1927, in Providence, Rhode Island, to James Scott and Elizabeth Mills Kinnell. After serving in the U.S. Navy (1945–1946), he received an A.B. degree from Princeton University in 1948 and an M.A. from the University of Rochester in 1949. Married to Ines Delgado de Torres, he has two children; all of them appear in his autobiographical poems. Kinnell spent three years (1951–1954) supervising the liberal arts program at the University of Chicago (Downtown) before accepting a Fulbright Fellowship which brought him to teaching assignments at the University of Grenoble (1956–1957) and the University of Iran (1959–1960). As with so many other twentieth-century

poets, Kinnell has functioned as both an educator and a poet. He has taught at
an extraordinary number of colleges and universities, including Reed College,
the University of Washington, the University of Hawaii, Columbia University,
Brandeis University, and the City University of New York. He is currently a
professor at New York University.

Kinnell has been the recipient of numerous awards and grants; the following
is a select chronological list: Ford Grant (1955), Fulbright Fellowship (1955–
1956), two Guggenheim Fellowships (1961–1962 and 1974–1975), National
Institute of Arts and Letters Grant (1962), two Rockefeller Foundation Grants
(1962–1963 and 1968), Amy Lowell Travelling Fellowship (1969–1970), Brandeis University Creative Arts Award (1973), Shelley Prize from the Poetry
Society of America (1974), Medal of Merit from the National Institute of Arts
and Letters (1975), the American Book Award for Poetry-Co-Recipient (1983),
and the Pulitzer Prize for Poetry (1983).

Kinnell has been and continues to be fundamentally a religious poet who uses
a variety of images in his search for transcendence and immortality. As Richard
Howard noted in *Alone with America: Essays on the Art of Poetry in the U.S.
Since 1950* (New York: Atheneum, 1963):

The poetry of Galway Kinnell . . . is an Ordeal of Fire. . . . It is fire—in its constant
transformations, its endless resurrection—which *is* reality, for Kinnell. . . . The agony of
that knowledge—the knowledge or at least the conviction that all must be consumed in
order to be reborn, must be reduced to ash in order to be redeemed—gives Galway
Kinnell's poetry its extraordinary resonance (p. 259)

Thus the speaker in "The Avenue Bearing the Initial of Christ into the New
World" encountering the urban chaos of New York's Lower East Side is reminded of that larger twentieth-century chaos, the Holocaust, but unlike other
contemporary voices, Kinnell is not paralyzed by either horrors seen or imagined.
Rather, it is a prelude to a resurrection of the spirit which begins with the creative
act of the poet. The resonance, identified by Richard Howard, is derived from
the fundamental cycle of the Christian tradition in which the gift of faith tempers
and finally conquers suffering.

Alan Williamson noted in *American Poetry Since 1960* (1974) that Galway
Kinnell suffers a recurring ordeal in poem after poem "accepting death in order
to be able to accept life, and concomitantly—like his Thoreau in 'The Last
River'—accepting cruel appetites in order to accept his full animal being" (p.
63).

In his second volume, *Flower Herding on Mount Monadnock* (1964), the
urban landscape of *What a Kingdom It Was* is replaced by his encounter with
nature, and although Kinnell is frequently identified with the romantic tradition,
his natural order is not curative in the conventional sense. Chance encounters
in nature provide an occasion to renew with sharpened awareness the fragility
of life. "I know half my life belongs to the wild darkness." Such knowledge
creates in Kinnell's poetry the nightmare vision which has led him to describe

himself as being a "Damned nightmarer," who illuminates the wakened world with poetic messages from the nether regions of the urban and natural orders. He sees without being devastated; he confronts the horrors—personal, social, historical—and he moves on.

With *Body Rags* (1968), his third volume which received special meritorious mention from the National Book Awards, Kinnell assumed an imaginatively submissive persona in the animal poems. A dramatic rendering of Emerson's "transparent eyeball" is the device of quest poems such as "The Porcupine" and "The Bear," where meaning is sought through sublimation into the consciousness of dying animals. The religious overtones of this quest are made explicit in the "Saint Sebastian of the Sacred Heart" mask adopted by the Speaker in "Porcupine" and the bear hunter deriving sacramental union with the bear by ingesting his blood-soaked excrement to achieve salvation as bear-man. These poems are harrowing and celebratory as the various speakers discover secrets in the dumb creatures which occasion wonder and transcendence. Kinnell extends our humanity by sensitizing the reader to suffering outside of the self, extending it to all living creatures.

The Book of Nightmares (1971), his fourth and pivotal work, is a single 1400-line poem in ten sections. It falls broadly into the genre of confessional poetry. Beginning with the birth of his daughter Maud in Part One, the speaker explores the wild darkness of life via a variety of nightmarish topics from the imminence of death through the trials of human affection and the vulnerability of fatherhood to the angst of meaninglessness. The poem concludes with his son's birth in Part Ten and a tentative resolution "Living brings you to death, there is no other road." This poem is his most personal, and its consuming power seems to explain Kinnell's reluctance to leave it behind, and perhaps explains the relative silence of the next nine years; the poet who reappears in the fifth volume *Mortal Acts, Mortal Words* (1980) is quite different. The "damned nightmarer" had been deposed by a more relaxed and lighthearted Kinnell. The metamorphosis bewildered some; others were relieved to see the nightmarer banished. For all the change in tone, there is thematic continuity woven throughout the most apparently disparate poems. Kinnell believes that the death of the self in poetry gives over to new life more open to nature and still more generous. With all the tonal variations, the existential paradox is indeed central to an understanding of Kinnell's poetic vision.

The Past (1985) finds Kinnell employing Frost's New England landscape as the imaginative instrument for linking past and present. Like Frost, his language is concrete, precise, and economical. When Kinnell describes lighting a box stove in "Break of Day," the reader encounters immediate experience in an economy of images. The musical gift always present in Kinnell's poetry is now in service to a less haunted voice. The tender wisdom of his elegies to fellow poets James Wright in "Last Holy Fragrance" and Richard Hugo in "On the Oregon Coast" answers eloquently a speculation raised by *The Book of Night-*

mares: could Kinnell join his nightmare vision with a brighter, lighter more hopeful view of life?

Kinnell has emerged from the nightmare vision with gift in tact. There is a bond between the nightmarer and his middle-aged usurper; the harmonies of concern and compassion make them companions not adversaries, but the new voice is wiser, wittier, and more temperate. One suspects that Kinnell has not finished with surprising and delighting his loyal readership.

SELECTED BIBLIOGRAPHY

Works by Kinnell: POETRY: *What a Kingdom It Was*. Boston: Houghton Mifflin, 1960; *Flower Herding on Mount Monadnock*. Boston: Houghton Mifflin, 1964; *Body Rags*. Boston: Houghton Mifflin, 1968; *Poems of Night*. London: Rapp and Carroll, 1968; *First Poems, 1946–1954*. Mount Horeb, Wis.: Perishable Press, 1970; *The Book of Nightmares*. Boston: Houghton Mifflin, 1971; *The Avenue Bearing the Initial of Christ into the New World*. Boston: Houghton Mifflin, 1974; *Mortal Acts, Mortal Words*. Boston: Houghton Mifflin, 1980; *The Past*. Boston: Houghton Mifflin, 1985; *Walking Down the Stairs*. Ed. Donald Hall. Ann Arbor: University of Michigan Press, 1988. TRANSLATIONS: Rene Hardy's *Bitter Victory*. Garden City, N.Y.: Doubleday, 1956; Henry Lehmann's *Pre-Columbian Ceramics*. New York: Viking, 1962; *The Poems of Francois Villon*. New York: New American Library, 1965, rev. ed., Boston: Houghton Mifflin, 1977; Yves Bonnefoy's *On the Motion and Immobility of Douve*. Athens: Ohio University Press, 1968; Yvan Goll's *Lascawanna Elegy*. Fremont, Mich.: Sumac Press, 1970. NOVEL: *Black Light*. Boston: Houghton Mifflin, 1966.

Works about Kinnell: Evert, William B., and Barbara White, comps. "Galway Kinnell: A Bibliographical Checklist." *American Book Collector* (July-August, 1984), pp. 22–32; Hilgers, Thomas, and Michael Molloy. "An Interview with Galway Kinnell." *Modern Poetry Studies* 11 (1982), pp. 107–12; Molesworth, Charles. "The Rank Flavor of Blood: Galway Kinnell and American Poetry in the 1960's." *Western Humanities Review* 27 (Summer 1973), pp. 225–39; Perloff, Marjorie G. "Poetry Chronicle: 1970–71." *Contemporary Literature* 14 (Winter 1973), pp. 97–131; Stitt, Peter. "Dimensions of Reality." *The Georgia Review* 34 (Winter 1980), pp. 887–94; Taylor, Jane. "The Poetry of Galway Kinnell." *Perspective* 15 (Spring 1968), pp. 189–200. CA 11–12. CANR 10. DLB 5.

Leo F. O'Connor

W. S. (JACK) KUNICZAK (1930–).

Gilbert Highet compared *The Thousand Hour Day* (1966), W. S. Kuniczak's first novel, "with the broad sweep of *Doctor Zhivago* and the tragic heroism of *For Whom the Bell Tolls*," insisting that "These claims may seem extravagant, but they are justified in every chapter." Indeed, Highet's comparisons not only define the achievement of *The Thousand Hour Day*, they accurately identify a major influence which has shaped Kuniczak as a writer and suggest the dilemma of this writer trapped between two worlds— a dilemma which raises important questions about the very nature of American literature.

Wieslaw Stanislaw Kuniczak was born on February 4, 1930 in the ancient Polish city of Lwow; his father was a career soldier, his mother a talented pianist. The Kuniczak family was committed to a fiercely patriotic tradition of service, and its life revolved around the father's military career. Constantly uprooted by his father's various assignments, young Kuniczak was educated largely by tutors, and he turned to books for stability, reading anything from Balzac to the encyclopedia but becoming "absorbed" in the *Trilogy* of Henryk Sienkiewicz, a vast sprawling historical work set in the final years of Poland's preeminence in the seventeenth century. This work became the yardstick by which Kuniczak would later measure his own writings.

Kuniczak's childhood ended in 1939 when the Nazi and Soviet invasions of Poland destroyed his home. By separate and frequently dangerous routes, the father and family escaped to Britain where they were reunited late in 1940. Once again, Kuniczak turned to books, exploring Charles Dickens and other English Victorians but deriving a sense of classical form and style from the nineteenth-century Russian writers who were favorites of his English tutor. Then Kuniczak discovered Ernest Hemingway. Within six months he had read everything Hemingway had written to date and then took up F. Scott Fitzgerald, John Dos Passos, Thomas Wolfe, and John Steinbeck. These writers fired Kuniczak's imagination, and he determined to become an "American" novelist.

Kuniczak finished his secondary education in Scotland and earned a B.S. in political science from the London School of Economics. In 1950, pursuing his goal, Kuniczak arrived in the United States. He worked at a variety of jobs and attended Alliance College in northwestern Pennsylvania, but he soon found himself in Korea as a machine gunner and then a platoon sergeant in the 31st U.S. Infantry. Back in the United States, Kuniczak earned an M.S. in journalism at Columbia University and worked as a newspaper reporter in New York, Ohio, and Pennsylvania. In 1958 Kuniczak became a United States citizen. In the 1950s and early 1960s, while working as a journalist and advertising agent, Kuniczak practiced fiction extensively but made no attempt to publish. At that time his style was derivative. Because he was determined to be an American novelist, Kuniczak picked contemporary American themes with which he lacked both direct experience and emotional involvement. As a result, his work, although reasonably well written, lacked insight and substance.

Under the guidance of novelist Don Robertson, Kuniczak came to realize that he must write about the things for which he cared; and he made contact with Dial Press, to which he sold the as-yet-unfinished *The Thousand Hour Day*, a novel treating the 1939 invasion of Poland.

Driven now by a need to write, twice married and divorced, Kuniczak moved to Mexico in order to work in seclusion. There, he completed *The Thousand Hour Day*, began *The Sempinski Affair* (1969) and *The March* (1979), and experimented with the idea of translating the Sienkiewicz *Trilogy* into modern English.

In 1966 Dial Press published *The Thousand Hour Day* which immediately met with amazing success. The novel was chosen for the May 1966 selection of the Book of the Month Club; the Modern American Library bought the reprint rights; and ten major European publishers contracted for translations. Its popular success and critical acclaim around the United States and Europe notwithstanding, *The Thousand Hour Day* was generally ignored by the New York literary establishment which found little of interest in the novel's subject matter.

Despite the success of *The Thousand Hour Day* and the publication of *The Sempinski Affair* in 1969, Kuniczak's life and career soon ran aground. Disappointed by the New York response to his novels, Kuniczak stopped writing for almost two years and left for Europe where at the end of 1969 he was arrested in Greece and sentenced to ten years in prison when drugs were found in the car in which he was riding. In 1972 Kuniczak was pardoned, partially through the efforts of novelist Jerzy Kosinski, then president of the American P.E.N. Center.

From 1972 to 1974 Kuniczak lived in Cypress, where he worked on *The March* but took out time to serve as an ambulance driver in the Israeli Yom Kippur War. After returning to the United States, Kuniczak completed *The March*, an 860-page sequel to *The Thousand Hour Day*, which deals with the fate of Poles in the Soviet Union during World War II. The novel was published by Doubleday, chosen as an alternate selection for the Literary Guild, and published abroad in 1982.

During the next four years, Kuniczak, now apparently convinced that an American writer need not deal exclusively with American experiences, began work on an autobiographical novel entitled *Journeys*, researched a possible biography of Pope John Paul II, and completed *Valedictory* (1983), the last volume of his Polish trilogy, which was picked up by five publishing houses in Europe where the novel became a comparative best-seller.

Today Kuniczak is Writer-in-Residence at Mercyhurst College in Erie, Pennsylvania, where he has put aside *Journeys* and, returning to his literary beginnings, has begun work on a "transformation" of the eight-volume, 5,000-page *Trilogy* of Henryk Sienkiewicz into a "twentieth-century American novel" which he hopes to complete by his sixtieth birthday.

To date, Kuniczak's reputation rests on the strength of his war trilogy. In the three novels which constitute the trilogy—novels which have invited comparison not only with Boris Pasternak and Hemingway but Leo Tolstoy and Aleksandr Solzhenitsyn—Kuniczak displays considerable literary skill; but three qualities especially stand out.

Like the writers to whom he has been compared, Kuniczak provides realistic and vivid portrayals of places, experiences, and people unknown to most Americans. In the trilogy Kuniczak creates a living, complex world which is convincing not because it resembles things as we know them but because it possesses an inner truth and vitality all its own. Furthermore, Kuniczak peoples his world with a wide range of three-dimensional, complex, and dynamic human beings. His best characters are Poles and Jews, but his works include a remarkable cross-section of individuals—Russians, Mongols, Nazis, Americans—who display differing backgrounds, temperaments, and points of view.

This points to a second feature of Kuniczak's trilogy: its polyphonic nature. There is no main hero in the individual novels or in the trilogy as a whole; instead, the works are structures with many competing centers of attention and are marked by shifts from one viewpoint to another, many of which challenge the author himself. This polyphonic method, utilizing, among other things, personalism and pluralism, affects every aspect of the novel's art,—and is largely responsible for the great sweep and universality of Kuniczak's work. Here one might note that, although Kuniczak has ambivalent feelings about Catholicism, it seems clear that his Roman Catholic heritage and the cultural and political pluralism of pre-war Poland have shaped this very significant and distinguishing feature of his writings.

One final consideration is worth noting. Reviewers have repeatedly used the word "epic" to describe Kuniczak's novels. Perhaps picking up on this tendency, a recent study, "The War Trilogy of W. S. Kuniczak," has argued that Kuniczak's trilogy is epic not just in a descriptive or adjectival manner but in a generic sense. Considering first nominal and formal criteria, the study links the trilogy to the traditional epic, pointing out that, although the trilogy is a modern prose narrative excelling in the literary qualities peculiar to the novel, it is directed by the goals of the classical epic and relies heavily on the strategies and conventions of that genre. Beyond this, the study insists that the epic is "a perennial mode of the human spirit" (p. 85) and uses a famous essay by E.M.W. Tillyard to define Kuniczak's work as an example of that mode.

Although caught between two worlds, Jack Kuniczak has become a successful novelist. His works have been published in seventeen languages and in twenty-two countries; they have met with almost universal praise. The only question that remains to be answered is whether the United States will embrace him as an American novelist or deny him because of his subject matter.

SELECTED BIBLIOGRAPHY

Works by Kuniczak: *The Thousand Hour Day*. New York: Dial Press, 1966; *The Sempinski Affair*. New York: Doubleday & Company, 1969; *The March*. New York: Doubleday & Company, 1979; *Valedictory*. New York: Doubleday & Company, 1983.

Works about Kuniczak: Krzyzanowski, Jerzy R. "W. S. Kuniczak's *The March*: A Polyphonic Novel." *Polish American Studies* 37, 1 (Spring 1980), pp. 52–64; Mocha, Frank. "History As Literature." *The Polish Review* 12, 3 (Autumn 1967), pp. 78–83; Napierkowski, Thomas J. "The War Trilogy of W. S. Kuniczak." *The Polish Review* 32, 1 (Spring 1987), pp. 85–92. CA 85–88.

Thomas J. Napierkowski

L

MARY LAVIN (1912–). Nearly fifty years have passed since a young, slim, dark-haired American-born teacher of French at the Loreto convent school in Dublin was notified that two of her earliest stories had been accepted for publication, one by the *Atlantic Monthly*, the other by the *Dublin Magazine*. Moreover, both editors were eager to see more examples of her work. Abandoning her partially completed dissertation for a Ph.D. in English literature, she turned full time to the writing of fiction. Lord Dunsany was her chief mentor. Frank O'Connor soon became one of her strongest supporters. Today, with an international reputation based on two full-length novels, four short novels, two children's books, eighteen volumes of short stories, and uncollected stories, poems, and essays, Mary Lavin is still writing full time. Translated into a dozen languages and published in as many and more countries, scripted for two films and an opera, widely anthologized, her work has won literary prizes and awards in the United States, England, and Ireland. In recent years she has been spoken of seriously by critics and journalists as a possible candidate for a Nobel Prize in literature.

Born on June 11, 1912, in East Walpole, Massachusetts, Mary Lavin spent her American childhood among friends and neighbors who were for the most part either Irish by birth, like her parents, or first-generation Americans, like herself. In this comfortable if not affluent environment far removed from the poorer Irish immigrant neighborhoods of large Eastern cities, her father, who had left his native County Roscommon to strike out on his own while still an adolescent, was happy. Her mother, however, the daughter of well-to-do Athenry, County Galway, shopkeepers who missed her large family and was uncomfortable with what she regarded as a lack of decorum in the community to which she had been brought as a new bride, never felt at home in her adopted country. In 1921 she took Mary, her only child, back to Athenry, for what was proposed as a long visit but from which she refused to return. The following year Thomas Lavin joined his wife and daughter in Ireland, and together they moved first to Dublin, where Mary was enrolled in the Loreto school, and then to nearby County Meath, an area of prosperous farms and fine estates, among them that of Lord Dunsany. After graduating from the Loreto school, Mary Lavin took an undergraduate degree at University College Dublin, where she earned first honors in English; her master's thesis on Jane Austen also was awarded honors; at the time when she abandoned her studies toward the doctorate to pursue her writing career, she was at work on a dissertation on Virginia Woolf. Although she did not return to the United States until she was a young woman and then lived in her native country only intermittently, on long visits or, later, as a visiting writer-in-residence at American universities, until his death her father repeatedly reminded her that she was an American by birth. Thus Mary Lavin grew up with the dual ethnic identity of Catholic Irish-American and Irish Catholic.

In 1942, the year in which *Tales from Bective Bridge*, Mary Lavin's first volume of short stories, was published, she married William Walsh, an Irish barrister. In 1943, the year in which she was awarded the James Tait Black Memorial prize for *Tales from Bective Bridge*, her first daughter was born. Soon there was a second daughter, four more volumes of short stories, and two novels. Then, in 1954, one year after the birth of her third daughter, Mary Lavin was widowed. Her father was dead; her fragile mother often seemed like still another child to be cared for. Writing became even more of an essential source of additional income and an essential diversion from the kind of daily life, depicted in her fiction, that society often imposes on widows in their thirties with three growing children and an elderly mother. Her stories appeared with increasing regularity not only in the *Atlantic Monthly* but in such other noted magazines and journals as the *New Yorker*, *Harper's Bazaar*, the *Kenyon Review*, and the *Southern Review*. Awarded two Guggenheim Fellowships, she traveled through France with her daughters and settled for a time in Italy where, remote from both cultures that had provided the matrix of her writing, she hoped to achieve an objective perspective on the creative process in general and her own creative methods in particular.

Between 1956 and 1971, seven more collections of Mary Lavin's short fiction were published, one of her novellas was republished as a separate volume, and her first children's story appeared, first in the United States and then in Ireland. In 1961 she was awarded the Katherine Mansfield Prize. Invitations to sit on quasi-governmental boards and committees concerned with arts administration in Ireland also provided evidence of the respect and recognition accorded her work. They served, in addition, to strengthen her ties to the country of her principal residence which had been increased by changes in her personal life: her mother had died; her two eldest daughters had married, giving her Irish sons-in-law; Irish grandchildren had been born. From his native Australia, Michael MacDonald Scott, a college friend, had returned to Ireland where he was appointed dean of the School for Irish Studies. In 1969 they were married.

Since 1971 Mary Lavin has continued to write and to receive recognition and awards on both sides of the Atlantic. She has been the recipient of the Eire Society of Boston Gold Medal (1974), the Gregory Medal (1975), and the American Irish Foundation Literature Prize (1979). She was among the first writers appointed to Ireland's newly constituted Aos Dana, a national academy of writers and artists similar in purpose, organization, and membership qualifications to the French Academy and the American Academy of Arts and Letters.

Readers will find in this brief sketch of Mary Lavin's life and work the correlative themes of her fiction. Human feelings and relationships fascinate her most, in the sense of why things happen rather than what happens. That she regards the latter as "only history" answers critics who have labeled her work autobiographical. What she has seen, heard, or experienced often provides the seeds of a story, but their cultivation in the imagination depends upon her perceptions of universal truths. For the same reason, those who identify naturalism as antecedent to her method of characterization are but partially correct. Although influenced by heredity and environment, the fate of a Mary Lavin character is determined by the accidentals of existence that have forced choices on the individual human heart. Psychological realism is perhaps a more appropriate term for her fiction, but it also uses poetic symbolism to glimpse the deeper aspects of life. What some critics have described as her double vision thus identifies as purposeful a quality of her artistic method: the versatility with which she combines the comic and the lyric, the satiric and the tragic. Mary Lavin herself acknowledges the accuracy of observations that an underlying tone of sadness characterizes much of what she writes. Awareness that ultimately all life ends in death never has been far from the surface of her own mind, she says, since childhood. Inevitably it is revealed in her fiction. Closely related is an understanding of the human capacity for venial sin although it does not, as in the fiction of James Joyce, inevitably lead to moral paralysis, chiefly because along with selfishness, pettiness, dishonesty, disloyalty, greed, envy, and cowardice, Mary Lavin's characters may have, in individual measure, a capacity for happiness and for love.

Many of Mary Lavin's stories focus on women. Mothers, daughters, wives, sisters, aunts, friends, widows, women not yet married and women who never will marry, homemakers, lodgers, educated women, uneducated women, professional women, and women who work at a variety of occupations: for readers concerned with the question of how and to what extent the stages of women's lives have been depicted in twentieth-century literature, the spectrum is broad. But there are also many stories that focus on men: fathers, sons, husbands, brothers, uncles, lovers, some educated and professional, some truckers, shopkeepers, artisans, gardeners, farmers, or fishermen, fully and skillfully developed. Questions of religious vocation and other aspects of religious life center on nuns, monks, priests, and bishops. Religious issues that affect individual and family life are debated by women and men, by priests and lay Catholics, and by Catholics and Protestants. Stories of children, boys as well as girls, alone or within a context that includes adults, are presented with a particular sensitivity. In short, Mary Lavin's fictional world is neither segregated nor segmented.

Economy is the hallmark of Mary Lavin's writing style. Her method, when she begins to write a story, is first to see it as a whole, with perceivable opening, development, and conclusion, then to see it clearly, by expanding preliminary drafts to explore cause and consequence of every recorded thought and deed. Not until all are related by inevitability as well as logic does she move on to the next stage of artistic development: the cutting, shaping, and compressing of what often has grown into a novel-size manuscript. Citing the favorable reception of her early full-length novels, reviewers sometimes suggest that longer works would indicate greater maturity of her talent. Mary Lavin disagrees: it would be easier but less satisfying to author and reader alike, she says, if she were to give free rein to the analytic mind through which she examines the relations of variables as a story develops. But only the disciplined imagination can create the synthesis of idea and expression that distinguishes art.

SELECTED BIBLIOGRAPHY

Works by Lavin: NOVELS: *The House in Clewe Street*. London: Michael Joseph, 1945, and Boston: Little, Brown, 1945, Reprint, New York: Penguin, 1988; *Mary O'Grady*. London: Michael Joseph, 1950, and Boston: Little, Brown, 1950, Reprint, New York: Penguin, 1986. COLLECTIONS, NOVELLAS, AND SHORT FICTION: *Tales from Bective Bridge*. Boston: Little, Brown, 1942, and London: Michael Joseph, 1943, rev. ed., Dublin: Poolbeg, 1978; *The Long Ago and Other Stories*. London: Michael Joseph, 1944; *The Becker Wives and Other Stories*. London: Michael Joseph, 1946, and *The Becker Wives*. New York: New American Library, 1971; *At Sallygap and Other Stories*. Boston: Little, Brown, 1947; *A Single Lady and Other Stories*. London: Michael Joseph, 1951; *The Patriot Son and Other Stories*. London: Michael Joseph, 1956; *Selected Stories*. New York: Macmillan, 1959; *A Great Wave and Other Stories*. London and New York: Macmillan, 1961; *The Stories of Mary Lavin*. Vol. 1. London: Constable, 1964; *In the Middle of the Fields and Other Stories*. London: Constable, 1967, and New York: Macmillan, 1969; *Happiness and Other Stories*. London: Constable, 1969, and Boston: Houghton Mifflin, 1970; *Collected Stories*. Boston: Houghton Mifflin, 1971; *A Memory and Other Stories*. London: Constable, 1972, and Boston: Houghton Mifflin, 1973; *The Stories of Mary Lavin*. Vol. 2. London: Constable, 1974; *The Shrine and Other Stories*. London: Constable, 1977; *Mary Lavin: Selected Stories*. Harmondsworth, UK: Penguin, 1981.

Works about Lavin: Bowen, Zack. *Mary Lavin*. Lewisburg, Pa.: Bucknell University Press, 1975; Dunleavy, Janet Egleson. "The Fiction of Mary Lavin: Universal Sensibility in a Particular Milieu." *Irish University Review* 7 (Autumn 1977), pp. 222–36; Harmon, Maurice, ed. Mary Lavin Special Issue. *Irish University Review* 9 (Autumn 1979) (includes bibliography by Heinz Kosok and essays by Janet Egleson Dunleavy, Marianne Koenig, and Bonnie Kime Scott); Kelly, Angeline A. *Mary Lavin: Quiet Rebel*. Dublin: Wolfhound, 1980; Peterson, Richard F. *Mary Lavin*. Boston: Twayne, 1978. CA 9–10. Cat A (1947). CN. DLB 15. TCA.

Janet Egleson Dunleavy

KATHLEEN ROCKWELL LAWRENCE (1945–). Kathleen Rockwell Lawrence's first novel, *Maud Gone* (1986), is a late entry in a genre best described as "Catholic girl grows up, talks dirty and about the kind of sex that would propel any nun or priest who taught her into the confessional, writes book, and provides the Catholic and non-Catholic reader with lots of laughs" about the "subculture . . . in the laundry room," about popping Stressaways during baby's naptime, and about the number of insomniacs on Staten Island.

Maud Malone Devlin, nine-months "gone" with her first child, is married to Jack, who, predictably, has a one-night stand with the ludicrous and luscious Xenia Olssen (of the deep purple leotard and lavender tights), their Swedish "painless birth instructor," who hands out "Chuckle Bags" to her pregnant clientele. Maud is soon "gone" from their New York apartment, after kicking Jack where it is not painless. She is wobbling up 14th Street at 3 A.M. in search of a cab when she meets Serge (the 1980s answer to the good-hearted prostitute?), driver of "a Pimpmobile, a Ho Hauler, a Drug Abuse Center, a Perpetrator's Palace," but actually the Pepto-Bismol pink Lincoln of this urban knight. Serge gallantly delivers Maud to the Greenwich Village apartment of Joanna Di-Robertis, her former roommate at the "women's college for the brainiest Catholic women in the country" who has apparently slept with every man in New York who is not incarcerated, incapacitated, or impotent; Joanna quickly falls for Serge. Maud is so far "gone" emotionally that, shortly after her baby's birth, she returns not to Jack, but to the Hoboken office of her Cuban emigré psychiatrist, Daisy Santiago, and later to the upstate home of her physician father and a brother who lives in a trailer parked on the front lawn. She is retrieved by Jack who wants her back about as badly as William Butler Yeats wanted the original Maud Gonne.

Lawrence contributes to the "Hers" column in the *New York Times*, and she has written for *Redbook* and other journals. She was the National Arts Club Scholar in fiction at Breadloaf in 1984.

SELECTED BIBLIOGRAPHY

Works by Lawrence: NOVEL: *Maud Gone*. New York: Atheneum, 1986. SHORT STORY: "With this ring . . . " *Redbook* 165 (August 1982), p. 58.

Works about Lawrence: Leber, Michelle. *Library Journal* 111 (16 July 1986), p. 110; Steinberg, Sybil. *Publishers Weekly* 229 (23 May 1986), p. 91.

Mickey Pearlman

SR. M. THERESE LENTFOEHR (1902–1981). In the 1940s and 1950s, American Catholic poetry was likely to be thought of in terms of a small group of Midwestern nuns, particularly Sr. Madeleva and Sr. M. Therese Lentfoehr. Ironically, by the time Sr. Therese's best work appeared, she was much overshadowed by John Frederick Nims,* John Logan,* and Robert Lowell,* among others.

Sister Therese was born on July 18, 1902, in Oconto Falls, Wisconsin. At the age of twenty-one she entered the Sisters of the Divine Savior (Salvatorians) and professed vows in 1925. She received a B.A. at Marquette in 1933, an M.A. in 1938. She later continued graduate work. From 1946 to 1970, she taught at several institutions, among them Marquette, Loretto Heights College, Georgetown, and Mount Saint Paul. From 1970 to 1974 she was poet-in-residence at Dominican College in Racine, Wisconsin.

Apart from her three volumes of poetry and an anthology, she published an excellent short volume on Marianne Moore's poetry, but her most notable literary interest was in Thomas Merton,* who became a close friend. They corresponded about their poetry, and at his death she had a significant collection of manuscripts, drafts of poems, articles, and autobiographical material. Subsequently, she published *Words and Silence: The Poetry of Thomas Merton* (1979) and *Contemplation and Social Concerns in the Writings of Thomas Merton* (1980), the chief occupations of her later years. She died following a stroke on October 31, 1981.

As a poet, Sr. Therese was comfortable writing in some form, even the most flexible—free verse but for some syllabic pattern or cadence. The poems of her first volume *Now There Is Beauty* (1940) are almost all religious in subject and conventional in form—mostly sonnets, some praising friends, several evoking women saints and Mary. One, "Son of the Nun," declares for continuation of her first vocation; "Magnificat" imagines its first singing.

Her second volume *Give Joan a Sword* (1944) begins with a war-time call upon the "God of peace" to send Joan down; the war preoccupies her, turns her to public affairs. But a Mary group, which includes a rich description of Fra Angelico's *Annunciation* and a poem that collects songs of Rome, makes it clear that recording encounters with holiness is Sr. Therese's most frequent theme.

"Moment in Ostia," the title poem of her third volume, heralds a tighter if longer, more original, tougher verse with polysyllables abounding. In presenting Monica at prayer, Augustine listening, she lets the poem find its own form. She goes farther afield, pondering the thoughts of gazing dogs, considering that her "father's work is done," likening a long-dormant lotus flower to the parousia. "To No One Other" and "Quo Vadis" are representative of her increased power.

Sentimentality slides along the pages of Sr. Therese's first two volumes, but reviewers of her final volume praised her intellectual reach, enlarged vision, wider lyrical range, the richness of her allusions, and her command of the craft.

SELECTED BIBLIOGRAPHY

Works by Lentfoehr: *Now There Is Beauty*. New York: Macmillan, 1940; *Give Joan a Sword*. New York: Macmillan, 1944; *Moment in Ostia*. Garden City, N.Y.: Hanover House, 1959.

Works about Lentfoehr: Review of *Words and Silence*. *America* (22 September 1979), p. 131. CA 97–100.

William H. Slavick

ELMORE "DUTCH" LEONARD (1925–   ). According to *Newsweek*, Leonard is "the best American writer of crime fiction alive, possibly the best we've ever had" (22 April 1985). Readers justly skeptical of critical hyperbole nevertheless will recognize that Leonard's achievement as a writer of Westerns, crime novels, and screenplays, is substantial.

Born on October 11, 1925, in New Orleans, Louisiana, Leonard was raised as a Catholic. In 1934 his family moved to Detroit, where he attended Catholic elementary and secondary schools. After serving thirty months with the Seabees in World War II, he attended the University of Detroit and received his Ph.D. in English and philosophy in June 1950. For more than ten years he earned his living as an advertising copywriter while writing Westerns in his spare time. His first novel appeared in 1953; *Hombre* (1961) was voted one of the twenty-five best Westerns of all time by the Western Writers of America. In 1961 he left advertising, produced scripts for educational and industrial films, and began writing scripts for Hollywood—such films as *Hombre, Joe Kidd,* and *Mr. Majestyk.* When the market for Westerns dried up, he turned to writing the crime novels that recently have earned him the reputation as a master of the genre: *LaBrava* received the 1984 Edgar Award, an American mystery writer's equivalent of an Oscar; *Glitz* (1985) moved David Lehman to rank him with G. K. Chesterton, Arthur Conan Doyle, and Dashiell Hammett among the top ten mystery writers of all time. In the 1970s he joined Alcoholics Anonymous. Divorced in 1977, he married Joan Shepard in 1979.

Leonard's crime novels offer the staples readers expect from the genre. The locales (primarily Detroit and Miami) are represented realistically, with cultural fact—local color, manners, and mores, the vernaculars of the streets, informing scene and setting. Plots are intricate and suspenseful, centering on detection of crime and the working out of retribution. The criminal elements, urban predators, embody moral corruption: hoodlums, sociopaths, racketeers, and psychopaths, who destroy society's illusions of comfort and security. Rogue protagonists— street smart, suspicious, resilient—attempt to understand themselves, cope with corruption, and strive for justice in terms of a personal code, often outside the law. Perhaps most Catholic in his assumption of human corruptibility, Leonard sees little hope for redemption in institutionalized Catholicism.

Sex and violence are among the staples, but Leonard does not exploit sex and violence for cheap ends. His model and conscience is Ernest Hemingway (a 3-1/2-by–4-foot photo hangs in Leonard's office), who saw the writer's task as a moral one: to write accurately, with restraint, etching a world in clean, clear lines; to be, in short, a careful, conscientious craftsman. Leonard depicts sexuality and graphically renders violence because not to do so would falsify his subject matter, for the world is sexual, painful, cruel, even brutish; but he does so in order to probe his characters and dramatize his themes.

Leonard's strengths are his style and his humor, and they point to his artistic stance. The style is blunt, bare, gritty, laced with the vulgarities of a profane world. And this world is comic. Leonard's villains, however depraved and menacing, are bumblers, incompetents: they blunder their ways to disaster through stupidity, or they outsmart themselves. His heroes are only steps removed from their antagonists: hard-boiled but sentimental, perceptive but limited by simple reason and decency, they stumble toward workable solutions through trial and error, and the errors frequently undercut the solutions, a droll, wry irony twisting the hero's role and underscoring its limitations.

Leonard skillfully manipulates the conventions of the crime novel. Unlike Graham Greene, he does not attempt to transform the genre into serious literature. To search his works for complexities and profound insights invites disappointment and leads to distortion. In *LaBrava* Leonard anticipates and dismisses overreading through his protagonist, who reports two reactions to an exhibit of his photographs:

I heard one guy at the gallery—it was his wife or somebody who said I was dispossessed, unassimilated, and the guy said, "I think he takes pictures to make a buck, and anything else is fringe." I would've kissed the guy, but it might've ruined his perspective.

This modest appraisal, devoid of cant or humbug, is typical of Leonard, an honest entertainer who neither makes nor accepts any higher claims. Within the limits he has set for himself, his position is secure.

SELECTED BIBLIOGRAPHY

Works by Leonard: NOVELS: *The Bounty Hunters*. New York: Houghton Mifflin, 1954; *The Law at Randado*. New York: Houghton Mifflin, 1955; *Escape from Five Shadows*. New York: Houghton Mifflin, 1956; *The Lawless River*. London: Robert Hale, 1959; *Hombre*. London: Robert Hale, 1961; *The Moonshine War*. London: Robert Hale, 1969; *The Big Bounce*. London: Robert Hale, 1969; *Fifty-Two Pickup*. New York: Delacorte, 1974; *Swag*. New York: Delacorte, 1976; *Unknown Man #89*. New York: Delacorte, 1977; *The Switch*. London: Secker and Warburg, 1978; *City Primeval*. New York: Arbor House, 1980; *Split Images*. New York: Arbor House, 1981; *Cat Chaser*. New York: Arbor House, 1982; *Stick*. New York: Arbor House, 1983; *LaBrava*. New York: Arbor House, 1984; *Glitz*. New York: Arbor House, 1985; *Freaky Deaky*. New York: Morrow, 1988.

Works about Leonard: Dunn, Bill. "Dutch Treat." *Writer's Digest* (August 1982), pp. 26–29; Lehman, David. "Thrillers." *Newsweek* (22 April 1985), pp. 58–61; Prescott, Peter S. "Making a Killing." *Newsweek* (22 April 1985), pp. 62–67. CA 81–84. CANR 12.

James L. McDonald

JOHN LOGAN (1923–). John Logan's poetry has often been highly praised by critics. James Dickey compares his work with that of Thomas Merton* and Robert Lowell.* Robert Bly exclaims that "John Logan is one of the five or six finest poets to emerge in the United States in the last decades" (p. 77).

John Logan was born in Red Oak, Iowa, on January 23, 1923. Raised a Protestant, Logan converted to Catholicism at the age of twenty-three; he has nine children with Mary Minor, from whom he is divorced.

Despite much acclaim, Logan is sometimes criticized as merely a religious writer because his first volume contains many poems with religious themes (and was given the title, chosen by the publishers, *Cycle for Mother Cabrini*, 1955). However, the later volumes have taken a less overtly religious tone; in addition, even the poems with religious subjects are accessible to nonbelievers. As Dickey writes of Logan's work: "The churchly bookishness is not dry and dead; it is oddly alive and *felt*, for in addition to being a Catholic, Logan is a man for whom intellectual excitement lives." Logan himself sees no room for pious soppiness in poetry, but believes that religious ideas need forceful and aesthetically satisfying treatment.

Cast inaccurately as a "confessional poet," Logan does express intense, personal feeling, but he believes that "what is 'confessed' is what is in the reader, in a sense—as much as what is in the author."

James Dickey has written of Logan:

His technical abilities are relatively slight, and really begin and end with an uncommon capacity for coming up with a strangely necessary and urgent observation and setting it among others by means of ordinary, unemphatic but rather breathless language which makes his lines read something like a nervous, onrushing prose. (p. 166)

John Carpenter notes,

The poems have few pinnacles or startling cliffs one can admire; they proceed by very small increments and build into large, deliberate structures with a high point at the end which we realize is high only after the rather flat voice has stopped, the poem ends, and we are falling from it. (p. 172)

While it is true that Logan uses commonplace language, he is not without technical skill. Rather, to use the words of his great master, which he paraphrased in "Homage to Rainer Maria Rilke," "I love the poor, weak words." The splitting of words is characteristic of Logan's poetry. He often experiments with slant rhyme and metrics (e.g., the ten-syllable lines in "Shore Scene" and the thirteen-syllable lines in "Monologues of the Son of Saul") and internal rhyme based on musical relationships.

Logan is something of an academic poet. With a master's degree in English from the University of Iowa and a strong background in philosophy, theology, psychology, and science, he has taught at several universities (State University of New York at Buffalo since 1966). Logan sees himself as part of a poetic continuum, which is clearly evidenced from the number of poems addressed to other poets, including, among others, Dylan Thomas, Christina Rossetti, John Keats, Arthur Rimbaud, Lord Byron, and Hart Crane.

But Logan's poetry is not pedantic and is not about academics. It is of a more personal nature. He often writes of death with quiet power. His major theme, however, is not death but love which he helps us to understand and accept. There is a lushness and a delight in life, and Logan's poems are humanistic to the core.

SELECTED BIBLIOGRAPHY

Works by Logan: POETRY: *Cycle for Mother Cabrini*. New York: Grove Press, 1955; *Ghosts of the Heart: New Poems*. Chicago: University of Chicago Press, 1960; *Spring of the Thief: Poems 1960–1962*. New York: Knopf, 1963; *The Zig-Zag Walk: Poems 1963–1968*. New York: Dutton, 1969; *The Anonymous Lover: New Poems*. New York: Liveright, 1973; *Poem in Progress*. San Francisco: Dryad Press, 1975; *Aaron Siskind: Photographs/John Logan: Poems*. Rochester, N.Y.: Visual Studies Workshop, 1976; *The*

Bridge of Change. Brockport, N.Y.: BOA Editions, 1979; *Selected Poems: Only the Dreamer Can Change the Dream*. New York: Echo Press, 1981; *The Transformation: Poems January to March 1981*. San Francisco: Pancake Press, 1983. OTHER WORKS: *Of Poems, Youth, and Spring*. New York: French, 1962, play; *Tom Savage: A Boy of Early Virginia*. Chicago: Encyclopaedia Britannica, 1962, juvenile; *The House That Jack Built: or, a Portrait of the Artist As a Sad Sensualist*. Omaha: Abattoir, 1974, novel; *A Ballet for the Ear: Interviews, Essays, and Reviews*. Ed. A. Poulin, Jr., Ann Arbor: University of Michigan Press, 1983.

Works about Logan: Bly, Robert. "The Work of John Logan." *Sixties* 5 (1961), pp. 77–87; Carpenter, John. "The Anonymous Lover." *Poetry* 125 (December 1974), pp. 171–72; Dickey, James. *Babel to Byzantium: Poets and Poetry Now*. New York: Farrar, Straus & Giroux, 1968; Mazzaro, James. "The Poetry of John Logan." *Salmagundi* 2 (1968), pp. 78–95; Murray, Dan. "John Logan." *Dictionary of Literary Biography 5: American Poets since World War II. Part 2*. Detroit: Gale, 1980, pp. 18–23. CA 77–80. DLB 5.

Louis J. Parascandola

BARRY HOLSTUN LOPEZ (1945–). In the seven books he has published over a period of twelve years, Barry Lopez, who has recently dropped his mother's maiden name, has consistently returned to a central theme: the widely sensed and deeply felt relationship between people, animals, and physical nature. From the slim volume of *Desert Notes* (1976) to the compendium of *Artic Dreams* (1986), Lopez combined first-person description and reflection on the natural world with accounts of imagined and historical individuals and events. *Crossing Open Ground* (1988) is a collection of essays in the same vein. Some of Lopez's books are closer to fact, others to fiction, but such a distinction would be irrelevant to him, for one of his main concerns is the inadequacy of analysis. Lopez approaches the universe through myth and mystery, not quantification. He believes that Western man would be wiser to try to hold a conversation with the land and all that belongs to it, as the Native American, the Eskimo, and the animals have, rather than to try to master it to meet his self-determined material needs.

Lopez was born on January 6, 1945, in Port Chester, New York, to a Spanish father and a mother of early American stock. According to Peter Wild, in *Barry Lopez*, he "gives thanks for the intellectual rigors of sweating through the strict curriculum of a Jesuit high school" (p. 7). The classical elements from this schooling and his education at Notre Dame (A.B., 1966, M.A.T., 1968) have been matched throughout his life by a compelling interest in American Indians and the American West. He has lived in Oregon since his twenties. In addition to six books, he has published numerous articles and short stories.

Desert Notes: Reflections in the Eye of a Raven and *River Notes: The Dance of Herons* (1979) illustrate the coming together of the humanist and the naturalist in a devotional spirit. These notes record characters and events, but they are essentially meditations intended to enable the reader to become an intimate friend of organic nature. The strongest thread in each volume is the voice of the protagonist who lies on the desert under an Indian blanket and looks around at the mountains; who tries to grasp the meaning of the bend of the river; and who recalls the character of the raven, the heron, and the salmon. *Desert Notes* is starker and more abrupt than *River Notes*; the desert's emptiness lacks the natural unity of the river.

In the three years between these two sets of notes, Lopez published two books quite different from either of them and from each other. *Giving Birth to Thunder, Sleeping with His Daughter: Coyote Builds North America* (1977) is a collection of the folktales of the hero-trickster Old Man Coyote, whose antics provided the Indians of many tribes with an interpretation of the natural world. In adapting the folktales he had combed from scholarly sources into sixty-eight stories with the sex, scatology, and creation myths of the hero intact, Lopez was aiming at "the needs of a modern, literate audience."

The second book of this period, *Of Wolves and Men* (1978), is a handsomely illustrated study of mankind's self-revelation in its treatment of the *canis lupus*. Framed as the author's personal account, it begins innocently enough as a biological description of the wolf. The remainder of the book demonstrates Lopez's hypothesis that men "create" their own animals. The Indians and the Eskimos can bring one closer to the nature of the wolf than the wildlife biologists can: they have observed them, thought about them, and faced the same problems in hunting for survival. But civilized man has justified his slaughter of the wolf for sport or protection of pasture by arguments that the animal is "the Devil in disguise" and "has to be rooted out." Lopez looks to myth and history for "the stories we made up when we had no reason to kill." If man could find a new myth for the wolf, "it would mean that he had finally quit his preoccupation with himself and begun to contemplate a universe in which he was not central."

Lopez's two most recent books are divided in method between the approach to the desert and the river and the study of the wolf. In *Winter Count* (1981) he enlarged the scale of his notes to varied settings, civilized and primitive, of the North American world, adding a number of characters, dead and living, whose experiences bring *Winter Count* to the border between fiction and non-fiction. Lopez calls his collection a "winter count" after the images that the Plains Indians use to record significant events "pictographically on a buffalo robe or spoken aloud."

The narrator of much of *Winter Count*, who is a mildly protean figure, a white man, an academic with a background broadly resembling Barry Lopez's, finds greater truth in primitive myth than in civilized fact. He learns of a French aristocrat on the frontier who believed that in North America animals were "the owners of the landscape, or even, in theological terms, equal with men." The mind of an elderly historian delivering a paper on winter counts at an academic meeting is filled with the realities of the Northern plains as the academic language of his colleagues flies past his ears. A nineteenth-century naturalist rejects the logic of the white man when it fails to explain the Pawnee myth of a disappearing river; more than a hundred years later, the narrator affirms the truth of this story.

If *Winter Count* evolves from the notes, *Arctic Dreams: Imagination and Desire in a Northern Landscape* (1986) is a direct successor to *Of Wolves and Men*. It is motivated by the danger to a forbidding region just as the earlier book is occasioned by the threat to a despised animal. Lopez shows that civilized man has been captivated by a frozen North in which he is a stranger. The musk-ox, the polar bear, and the narwhal who belong there surround the mystery of the arctic which the author perceives from an open boat, the sea ice, a campsite, or an airplane. Lopez finds the heart of the mystery in the northern lights, in the fantastic shapes of the icebergs, in the "country of the mind" that the Eskimo builds to mirror the outer reality of a world that cannot be completely portrayed in maps. The mystery of this metaphysical realm is now endangered by the white man's search for natural resources. Lopez hopes to avoid a "profound collision of human will with immutable aspects of the natural order" and to preserve the "wisdom . . . that lies in the richness and sanctity of a wild landscape" that can soothe the "troubled human spirit."

Lopez is not only a naturalist; in his concern for human values, the epicycles of his interests and beliefs cross the orbit of Thomas Merton* as well as those of Edward Abbey and Peter Matthiessen. Lopez is a Romantic visionary. He recreates the icy caves, stormy seas, and dream-like lands of Samuel Coleridge as he stands, like Wordsworth, in contemplation of the least adorned, and therefore the best, of nature and human nature. He is more transcendental than William Wordsworth; his *pensées* have grown toward narrative but have remained essentially non-linear and meditative. But there is a stress line, the beginnings of a flaw, in the compendious studies of the wolf and the Arctic; here Lopez is in danger of contradicting his aim with his method. All the personal vistas and imaginative invocations of *Arctic Dreams* cannot absorb the volume of information that the author has amassed. One gets the feeling, as myth and history accumulate, that scientific fact and the bookish past may overwhelm the subjective apprehension which is the key to his advocacy of the undervalued and overthreatened components of the natural world. Perhaps it is Lopez's weakness as well as his strength that he has applied a humanistic Catholic education and a passion for the primitive to a vision which brings together scientific observation and spiritual epiphany.

SELECTED BIBLIOGRAPHY

Works by Lopez: *Desert Notes*. Kansas City, Mo.: Sheed, Andrews and McMeel, 1976; *Giving Birth to Thunder, Sleeping with His Daughter*. Kansas City: Andrews and McMeel, 1977; *Of Wolves and Men*. New York: Scribner's, 1978; *River Notes*. Kansas City: Andrews and McMeel, 1979; *Winter Count*. New York: Scribner's, 1981; *Arctic Dreams*. New York: Scribner's, 1986; *Crossing Open Ground*. New York: Scribner's, 1988.

Works about Lopez: Wild, Peter. *Barry Lopez*. Boise, Idaho: Boise State University (Western Writers Series, no. 64), 1984. CA 65–68. CANR 7.

Neale R. Reinitz

ROBERT LOWELL (1917–1977). As a major poet who combined criticism of culture with elements from his own troubled life Lowell built poetry which can be described as paradigmatic of a changing American poetic landscape. His work, often complex, challenging, and innovative, reflects much about him and culture. While his early spirited endorsement of Catholicism was replaced by muted spiritual concerns, always at the core of his work remained a preoccupation with questions about the nature of society, spirituality, and ultimately the waning of religious belief.

Stylistically his art changed radically over the years but autobiographical preoccupation remained at its center. For such reasons, questions of belief, or its absence, are important throughout. Lowell was born in Boston on March 1, 1917. As a young man, Lowell knew he wanted to be a poet. He entered Harvard to cultivate this desire, but the poetry completed by then brought little satisfaction, and when he showed a poem to Robert Frost, no encouragement. Disappointments at Harvard in 1935 and 1936, in conjunction with private anguish about his family, led to his departure from college, but luckily also to the suggestion that he seek out Allen Tate* for poetic advice, which he did by travelling to Tennessee in April 1937. Tate's encouragement was, apparently, what Lowell needed, and he found a poetic father. Also Lowell decided not to return to Boston, but to enroll in Kenyon College where he would study with John Crowe Ransom. While a student at Kenyon, Lowell married Jean Stafford, an aspiring novelist. He also converted to her religion, Roman Catholicism. Upon graduation he taught at Kenyon, did graduate study at Louisiana State University, and was employed by Sheed and Ward, a Catholic publishing house, during a period when he wrote little and published nothing.

Late in 1942 he returned to visit Allen Tate. During that stay at Monteagle, Tennessee, he wrote (or rewrote) the poems of *Land of Unlikeness* (1944), a volume that was privately printed. Tate's presence seemed to inspire Lowell. As Steven Axelrod has argued, Tate provided examples of style and theme as well as a conviction that Lowell might also achieve a life completely devoted to art. The best of the poems written during this period were revised and included in *Lord Weary's Castle* (1946), the volume which established Lowell as a significant poet.

Lord Weary's Castle utilizes Christian images, sometimes derived from the Puritanism which Lowell considered to be debased, especially as fused in his poetic imagination as part of a modern landscape which seemed so completely separated from hope. War, materialism, and senseless death haunt this poetry. Lowell imagines the Church within this apocalyptic Christian myth as a sign of hope in a world largely bent on self-destruction.

Often Lowell's life was troubled. His first marriage ended in divorce, and in 1950 he married Elizabeth Hardwick. His bouts with mental illness and hospitalization, his affair with Caroline Blackwood, and his subsequent divorce of Elizabeth Hardwick in 1972—to whom he returned when he returned to the United States before his death by heart failure in 1977—suggest those difficulties and stand as harbingers of the poetry he would produce which would be less and less like his earliest production.

As early as 1947, Tate seems to have begun to recede from Lowell's consciousness as a poet model. Lowell sensed he needed another style, and in that year he reviewed William Carlos Williams's *Paterson*. Lowell himself was moving toward a different variety of writing, one which would utilize more of his own anguish while it would be more open, less formal, and more concerned with narrative.

Subsequent volumes were less overtly devoted to inquiry into subjects relating to Christianity, while many questions about culture and value inform all the remaining work. *The Mills of the Kavanaughs* (1951) contains seven poems. Two are successes. The first, "Falling Asleep over the Aeneid," is an attempt to achieve a mystical vision which is not possible; the second, "Mother Marie Therese," is a tribute to a nun who was able to live her life as the " 'emigree in this world and the next.' " It achieves its intention and reveals, Jerome Mazzaro states, Lowell's "new humanity." Though one of the best poems Lowell had written, ironically it is one of the last to deal in a sustained way with a Christian subject.

Life Studies (1959) exhibits striking changes in style. Lowell became more interested in plot and character. His earlier hopes for a society with a Catholic framework can be seen in "Beyond the Alps." Its title echoes the first half-line of "Falling Asleep," but in this poem man is no longer able to cope with the miraculous: science and technology have taken precedence. "For George Santayana" deals with a similar theme: Santayana is portrayed as close to the Church while paradoxically an unbeliever and a martyr. The last poems in *Life Studies* put an end to the "mythic" vision which informs Lowell's earlier poetry. In still later volumes overt concern with religious belief is gone.

As the poetry develops into the final decade of Lowell's production, its speakers are often reduced to fragile individuals unable to make sense of their worlds. *Notebook 1967–68* (1969) is essentially a disorder which goes in many directions. (Lowell recognized its failure. In 1973 he reorganized and rewrote the poem for the third time.) In *History* (1973), cut from a larger body of material, Lowell utilizes the past by bringing to life historical figures, including St. Thomas More, "my patron saint as convert." In *The Dolphin* (1973) the poet recounts his allusive search for joy and confesses loss in a world where there is "No Messiah." Nevertheless Lowell continues to raise questions about fundamental spiritual matters.

The late poetry reflects the mind of a troubled Christian. While for him Christianity dimmed, Lowell's poetry exists as the record of a poet frequently lost in a post-Christian age. As a major writer, honest in his poetic cries, Lowell's oeuvre is more valuable than much writing that never raises such questions, nor mirrors the loss and despair so basic to his career.

SELECTED BIBLIOGRAPHY

Works by Lowell: *Land of Unlikeness*. Cummington Press: Cummington, Mass., 1944; *Lord Weary's Castle*. New York: Harcourt Brace, 1946; *The Mills of the Kavanaughs*. New York: Harcourt Brace, 1951; *Life Studies*. New York: Farrar, Straus & Cudahy, 1959; *Imitations*. New York: Farrar, Straus & Giroux, 1961; *For the Union Dead*. New York: Farrar, Straus & Giroux, 1964; *The Old Glory*. New York: Farrar, Straus & Giroux,

1964, rev. ed., New York: Farrar, Straus & Giroux, 1968; *Near the Ocean*. New York: Farrar, Straus & Giroux, 1969; *Notebook 1967–68*. New York: Farrar, Straus & Giroux, 1969; *Notebook*. New York: Farrar, Straus & Giroux, 1970; *History*. New York: Farrar, Straus & Giroux, 1973; *For Lizzie and Harriet*. New York: Farrar, Straus & Giroux, 1973; *The Dolphin*. New York: Farrar, Straus & Giroux, 1973; *Day by Day*. New York: Farrar, Straus & Giroux, 1977.

Works about Lowell: Axelrod, Steven Gould. *Robert Lowell, His Life and Art*. Princeton, N.J.: Princeton University Press, 1978; Mazarro, Jerome. *The Poetic Themes of Robert Lowell*. Ann Arbor: University of Michigan Press, 1965; Perloff, Majorie G., *The Poetic Art of Robert Lowell*. Ithaca, N.Y.: Cornell University Press, 1973; Procopiow, Norma. *Robert Lowell: The Poet and the Critics*. Chicago: American Library Association, 1984; Siedel, Frederick. "Interview with Robert Lowell." *Paris Review* (Winter-Spring 1961) pp. 56–95, reprinted in *Robert Lowell: A Portrait of the Artist in His Time*. Ed. Michael London and Robert Bizes. New York: David Lewis, 1970. CA 9–10. DLB 5. TCA.

Victor A. Kramer

CLARE BOOTHE LUCE (1903–1987). Clare Boothe Luce was a woman for all seasons: outspoken and controversial for her time, an editor, news correspondent, fashion plate and socialite, playwright and novelist, congresswoman, ambassador, and mother. As a writer, she is best known for her brilliantly satiric spoofs of upper-crust society, their pretensions, their hypocrisy, their snobbery, their sugarcoated viciousness, and their boorishness, but her impassioned attacks on Hitler and Stalin and her pleas for American involvement in World War II and for the defense of democracies worldwide are memorable too.

Born on April 10, 1903, in New York City, the daughter of a violinist and an actress, she married first George Tuttle Brokaw and later Henry Robinson Luce, the head of the Time/Life empire. Clare Boothe Luce proved herself glamorous, witty, and formidable; she evoked gossip and envy, respect and admiration. She first made her name in American letters as an associate, then managing, editor of *Vanity Fair* magazine. She was a war correspondent for *Life*, a magazine she originally planned and designed (1940), and for *Time*, *Life*, and *Fortune* (1941–1942); a member of the House of Representatives (R–Conn., 1943–1947); the American ambassador to Italy (1953–1957); and a columnist for *McCalls* (1960–1967). She served on innumerable committees—for refugees and immigrants, for wildlife and oceanography, for the press, arts, and religion, and she received numerous awards, including the Cardinal Newman Award, the American Statesman Medal, the Knight of the Grand Cross of the Order of Merit of the Italian Republic, and the Order of Lafayette Freedom Award. She moved in circles of power and wealth as a personal friend of Winston Churchill, Douglas MacArthur, the Kennedy family, and Madame Chiang Kai-shek; she was an outspoken critic of Franklin D. Roosevelt and a fervent opponent of both communism and nazism. Throughout her career, she gave substance in her writing to her strongly held Catholic and political ideals.

Her two most enduring works, *Stuffed Shirts* (1933) and *The Women* (1937), are plucky, flippant attacks on Society, à la Oscar Wilde, full of regal put-downs, sneers, and innuendo, the type of intelligent chat that made *Vanity Fair* so popular. *Stuffed shirts*, a title based on a phrase Luce claimed to have coined, is a series of satiric short stories, interlocked by shared characters and a semi-chronological arrangement; it focuses on the gamesmanship and tactics of survival amid the wealthy and established, the Towerlys and Toppings, as Wall Street topples around them. It is a record of social gaffes and social triumphs, of drawing-room hostilities, of daughters sold and artists bought, of the nouveau riche competing for a place with the established arbitrators of taste, of the scandals and hypocrisies, and the ironic twists of love and fate that made up 1920's life among the New York and Newport aristocracy. Its attack is most direct in its portrait of a writer who is applauded for his fantasies about the rich but scorned for his realistic portraits of them as he comes to know them better.

The Women, an international success, is good theater, with its scintillating one-liners and its on-stage bath scene (so scandalous for the time). It mocks the catty rich, whose envy and disillusionment lead them to try to steal or destroy what they cannot have, a happy marriage. It focuses on a basically good woman who at first does not know how to cope with infidelity, but who learns to be "the other woman" and to fight back. What makes both these works so successful, however, is not simply the vividness and accuracy of the portraits, the wit and rightness of the dialogue, but the ability to both scorn and pity, to point out the absurdity but to provide a sense of weak humanity beneath the grand poses.

World War II spawned two of her more impassioned works, an anti-Nazi play, *Margin for Error* (1940), written two months after Hitler invaded Poland, and *Europe in the Spring* (1940), a chatty, personal recollection of conversations among Europeans in the spring of 1940 aimed at warning Americans about the dangers of complacency. The central confrontation of *Margin* is between a Nazi consul and a Jewish cop, who, despite his wisecracks, speaks for civilization and humanistic values, but the plot really turns on the staging of a murder amid the distractions of a Nazi Bund rally. *Europe* is full of funny, and sometimes devastating, sketches, but it has a deadly serious argument: that 1940s America had no real foreign policy and that what happened to the French might well happen to the English, and then to America, because of the Allies' failure to take the Germans seriously enough, to read the warning signs, and to prepare to defend, not just their piece of land, but democracy itself. As in *The Women*, Luce warns about what is lost when one gives up too easily, a theme echoed throughout her career, and argues that one must fight evil, not negotiate with it. She begins with cynical dinner table talk among politicians and businessmen and ordinary citizens from a number of countries, openly records her own mistaken assumptions and the steps that led her to reevaluate them, weaves in conversations in which men try to regroup their theories or seek scapegoats as the Germans draw nearer, and ends with a series of rhetorical questions based on analogies with France and England.

Less memorable and less effective are *Abide with Me* (produced November 22, 1935), the story of a young woman married to a rich old alcoholic; *Kiss the Boys Goodbye* (1939), a satirical spoof lampooning overblown Hollywood movie promotions which Luce tried unsuccessfully to pass off as a political allegory about American fascism; and a screenplay called *Come to the Stables* (1949), a sentimental, rather simplistic story of the efforts of two nuns to found a hospital for crippled children in Bethlehem. These exemplify her writing at its weakest: poor plotting, dependence on coincidence, and a tendency to lecture and over-simplify. Nonetheless, they also demonstrate what has made her best works endure: her attempts to come to terms with her own experiences through her art, her commitment to religious and political convictions, and her willingness to laugh at herself (in this case, in her portrait of a vulgar newspaperman and his wife with delusions of being Southern plantation owners).

What Luce proclaimed in her introduction to *Saints for Now* (1952) sums up the beliefs upon which her writing career was founded: "ideas have conse-quences," and actions must be judged "in the context of history."

SELECTED BIBLIOGRAPHY

Works by Luce: *Stuffed Shirts*. New York: Liveright, 1933; *The Women*. New York: Random House, 1937; *Kiss the Boys Goodbye*. New York: Random House, 1939; *Margin for Error*. New York: Random House, 1940; *Europe in the Spring*. New York: Knopf, 1940; *Saints for Now*. New York: Sheed and Ward, 1952.

Works about Luce: Baldridge, Letitia. *Of Diamonds and Diplomats*. New York: Lanewood Press, 1969; Shadegg, Stephen. *Clare Boothe Luce*. New York: Simon and Schuster, 1970; Sheed, Wilfrid. *Clare Boothe Luce*. New York: E. P. Dutton, 1982. AWW. CA 45–48. Cat A(1947). TCA.

                                                                    Gina Macdonald

M

PETER MAKUCK (1940–). Peter Makuck's career demonstrates a diversity of interests and talents. In 1981 and 1982, two major works appeared—*Breaking and Entering*, a collection of short stories, and *Where We Live*, a volume of poetry. In addition, Makuck collaborated on a poetry textbook, *Poetry: Sight and Insight*. He continues to serve as editor of *Tar River Poetry* and to teach classes in American literature and creative writing at East Carolina University.

Makuck was born in New London, Connecticut, in 1940 and was educated at St. Mary's Elementary School and New London High School. He received a B.A. from St. Francis College, an M.A. from Niagara University, and a Ph.D. from Kent State University. In 1974–1975 he was a Fulbright Lecturer on modern American poetry at Université de Savoie, France, and since 1976 he has taught at East Carolina University in Greenville, North Carolina.

Makuck's critical interests range from post-modern American fiction and poetry to film and French literary criticism. His fiction and poetry are also diverse, emphasizing the sense of place, the influence of the past, and the threat of evil. Makuck admits that the Catholic Church is largely responsible for his being a writer because it sensitized him to language through Latin and created a conscience and other impulses that lead to "inking up paper." Catholicism is also important in his two major works, *Where We Live* and *Breaking and Entering*, in which Makuck draws on his own experiences in Catholic school and Catholic neighborhoods to provide details and images for his characters, who often must confront their consciences and anxieties. In a number of his short stories, nuns and priests embody childhood fears and admonitions which his adult characters must come to terms with. Makuck laughingly admits to playing devil's advocate at times and says that Catholic images and phrases will continue to be part of his work.

SELECTED BIBLIOGRAPHY

Works by Makuck: ESSAYS AND REVIEWS: In *Tar River Poetry* on the poetry of Louis Simpson, Laurence Lieberman, Samuel Hazo,* Stephen Dunn, Brendan Galvin,* and others. POEMS AND SHORT STORIES: In *The Sewanee Review*, *The Hudson Review*, *The Nation*, *The Yale Review*, *The Virginia Quarterly*, *Ploughshares*, *The Southern Review*, *North American Review*, *Yankee*, *Ohio Review*, and *Chicago Review*. BOOKS: *Breaking and Entering*. Champagne-Urbana: University of Illinois Press, 1981; *Where We Live*. Brockport, New York: BOA Editions, 1982; *Poetry: Sight and Insight*. New York: Random House, 1982; *Pilgrims*. Ampersand Press (forthcoming).

Works about Makuck: Review of *Breaking and Entering*. *American Notes and Queries* 20 (1981), p. 56; Review of *Where We Live*. *Hudson Review* 36 (1983), p. 402.

James Craig Holte

ROBERT MARASCO (1936–). Robert Marasco was the first Catholic playwright of his generation to make it on Broadway. *Child's Play* (1970), a gothic tale of unchecked envy set in a Catholic boys' school, earned Marasco the New York Drama Critics' Citation as the year's most promising playwright. Marasco has continued to write in the gothic vein in two novels which demonstrate his skill at narrative and suspense, *Burnt Offerings* (1973) and *Parlor Games* (1979).

Marasco, born in the Bronx, New York, on September 22, 1936, attended the Jesuit Regis High School in Manhattan, graduated from Fordham University, and returned to his high school to teach English, Latin, and Greek for nine years. This experience gave him the background for *Child's Play* and also the material for the screenplay which became his first novel, *Burnt Offerings*. In the latter the central figures are a teacher and his family who desperately seek a quiet summer.

In *Child's Play* Joe Dobbs, a senior member of the faculty, despises his colleague Jerome Malley. Dobbs' malice creates a climate of fear and violence among the students. But no one suspects he is its cause: Dobbs is apparently loved by the boys while Malley is feared and hated. When the violence gets out of hand, the traditional priests who run the school cannot control it. Dobbs has sold his soul for the power to destroy his rival, and the good fathers either fail to recognize the evil or flail helplessly before it. By the end of the play Dobbs has destroyed Malley, but he confesses his crimes to the boys and faces his inevitable punishment at their hands.

The novel *Burnt Offerings* links evil and human obsession. In this case, a woman's seemingly ordinary desire for material comfort makes her an easy victim for an unusual haunted house. The Rolfes—Marian, Ben, and son David—rent a once glamorous Long Island estate for the summer. But the spirit of the owner's dead mother completely takes over Marian's mind and body. Marasco's plot is much too predictable, but the atmosphere and details of Marian's fate are generally well done.

If *Burnt Offerings* sometimes seems clumsy, *Parlor Games* is skillfully constructed. This story of incestuous love between brother and sister is a complex psychological study, a good murder mystery, and an involving love story. Marasco deftly shifts the narrative voice in the novel to capture the emotions of his highly charged characters, Peter Drexler, his jealous sister Gail, his lover Maggie, and Joanne Ellis, the mother of his dead girlfriend. The evil in *Parlor Games* is far less mystical than in the other two works. In this book the characters have the mistaken impression that they are still in control. But here again Marasco depicts evil as overwhelming, and he creates characters too blind or flawed to fight it.

SELECTED BIBLIOGRAPHY

Works by Robert Marasco: PLAY: *Child's Play*. New York: Samuel French, 1970. NOVELS: *Burnt Offerings*. New York: Delacorte Press, 1973; *Parlor Games*. New York: Delacorte Press, 1979.

Willem O'Reilly

PAUL MARIANI (1940–). Books on Gerard Manley Hopkins and William Carlos Williams and a collection of essays place Paul Mariani high in American poetry criticism. His three volumes of poems since 1979 give him a high rank as well among contemporary Catholic poets.

Born in New York City on February 29, 1940, Mariani holds a B.A. from Manhattan College, an M.A. from Colgate, and a Ph.D. from the City University of New York. He began teaching at the age of twenty-three and is now a professor at the University of Massachusetts at Amherst. He is frequently at Bread Loaf in the summer and is much in demand as a lecturer.

Unsurprisingly, Mariani's poetry reflects his interests in the tradition—what he calls the "poetics of unselfconsciousness" of Hopkins—akin to the dramatic quality of William Shakespeare; to Williams' stories with "little moral judgments"; to Robert Penn Warren, Robert Creeley, and John Montague; to John Berryman's* "genius for the unexpected," the coarse, vulgar, tragic, and profound; to Thomas Merton's* *Literary Essays* which took him on a spiritual journey; and to Robert Pack, a "strong son of Frost."

From the first poem in *Timing Devices: Poems* (1979), Mariani's course is set—his kin, their experience, his love—rich in concreteness and significance. An asthma attack: "We were all drowning in my brother's heaves." His grandmother: "my earliest guardian," an aunt who "kept tenacious watch over this clan." A portrait of Allen Mandelbaum, "The Dancing Master." Imagining the Last Judgment coming to the figures in the Torcello mosaics. Here memory and imagination meet, the concrete becomes universal, the passion of life and death in an intimate world where God is as familiar as "crazy Angelo," though more important. A poet in love with living.

Crossing Cocytus: Poems (1982) includes a "song with love in it" for his exhausted mother. "Replaying the Old Morality Play" is another rescue of his mother from suicide. He meditates on the fire of First Communion only smoldering and again on his friend Cathy's death by cancer: "our drinks turned to gold before us"; his son's first football injury: "*What, what do I do now, Dad?*" One of the best is "The Old Men Are Dying"—his father's brothers, one by one, drifting away through "familiar channels for the last trip north." And the title poem, in which father and son forgive one another.

Mariani's power grows in *Prime Mover: Poems* (1985): "Matadero, Riley and Company" is an audacious leap from a childhood fight to Good Friday; "Some Sort of Answers" dramatizes meeting Williams at the refrigerator; the self finds "the woman in yourself" in "The Easter Point Meditations"; and the final prayer asks for courage "to still sing to thee, *how great thou art.*"

SELECTED BIBLIOGRAPHY

Works by Mariani: *Timing Devices: Poems.* Boston: Davis R. Godine, 1979 (Pennyroyal Press Limited, signed edition, 1978); *Crossing Cocytus: Poems.* New York: Grove Press, 1982; *Prime Mover: Poems.* New York: Grove Press, 1985.

Works about Mariani: Review of *William Carlos Williams: A New World Naked. Antioch Review* 41 (1983), p. 232; Review of *William Carlos Williams: The Poet and His Critics. American Literature* 48 (1976), p. 402. CA 29–32. CANR 12.

William H. Slavick

MARY McCARTHY (1912–). An essayist and novelist whose first professional work was published in 1933 and whose novels are of exceptional quality, Mary McCarthy became a best-selling author when *The Group* was published in 1963. Because it deals with eight Vassar graduates of the class of 1933, it focuses on the attitudes and life-styles of upper middle-class college graduates rather than on the problems of being Catholic in the United States. Nevertheless, works like *The Company She Keeps* (1942), *The Groves of Academe* (1952), *Memories of a Catholic Girlhood* (1957), and *Cannibals and Missionaries* (1979) show that McCarthy is concerned with the Catholic and, more generally, the Judeo-Christian experience and their impact on modern life. McCarthy's writings and her life reflect both her independence and her interest in contrasts.

McCarthy was born on June 21, 1912, in Seattle, Washington, the eldest of four children. Her father was an Irish Catholic, and her mother, the daughter of a Protestant father and a Jewish mother, was a convert to Catholicism. When their parents died of influenza in 1918, McCarthy and her three brothers were placed in the care of their great-aunt and her husband; in *Memories of a Catholic Girlhood*, McCarthy recounts the censorious form of Catholicism in which the children were reared. In 1923, McCarthy returned to Seattle to live with her maternal grandparents, who sent her to a Catholic school for two years; McCarthy relates that there she encountered a positive version of Catholicism among the nuns—tolerant, uplifting, and inspiring. Nevertheless, she lost her faith and was sent first to public school and then to the Episcopalian Annie Wright Seminary in Tacoma, Washington. After graduation in 1929, she attended Vassar, where she received her A.B. in 1933. She has been married four times; her second husband, Edmund Wilson, the father of her only child, encouraged her to write fiction. In addition to being a professional writer, McCarthy worked for *The Partisan Review*, has taught at Bard College and Sarah Lawrence College, and has received several Guggenheim Fellowships.

McCarthy writes both her essays and her novels from personal observation and research. She travelled in North Vietnam prior to writing *Vietnam* (1967) and *Hanoi* (1968); while living in Europe, she set *Cannibals and Missionaries* in Holland, depicting Americans of the type whom she observed in Europe. A recurring critical commonplace is that McCarthy's novels are fictionalized essays. She deals with the thoughts and actions of her characters rather than with their feelings, describing them through monologues, letters, and journal entries that discuss ideas. Her characters are lively, although her comic characters are more vivid than her serious ones, and her female characters tend to be more fully developed than her male. Her physical descriptions of characters and settings are excellent. She uses action to help characterize the people she depicts, so that the actions become symbolic of the people, and she is especially good at writing dialogue that is lively and appropriate.

In essays and novels, McCarthy demonstrates a special interest in political themes, emphasizing the importance of balance and contrast. Like her novels, her essays reflect her Catholic upbringing despite her adult unbelief. Her two books on Vietnam express serious criticism of the war, emphasizing that Americans should use free will and act in an independent and moral manner to end the war. At the same time, they are not naive and simplistic depictions of left-wing values, for McCarthy criticizes the cynicism of the left that permits the military to act as it does. In *The Mask of State: Watergate Portraits* (1974), written before President Nixon's resignation and pardon, McCarthy discusses the fascistic mentality behind Watergate and theorizes that Nixon must have been behind the break-in. Many of her fictional characters are drawn from life, as are the women in *The Group*—based on McCarthy's Vassar classmates—and Margaret in *The Company She Keeps*, a socialistic lapsed Catholic whose childhood was unhappy and who, like many McCarthy heroines, resembles McCarthy herself.

Although McCarthy is not a practicing Catholic, her works reflect Catholic training. Her concerns are moral, affirming her belief in free will rather than the modern idea of corporate guilt. In *The Oasis* (1949) she depicts intellectuals who found a colony called Utopia but who fail because they cannot abandon self-interest to work for the common good. The heroine of *A Charmed Life* (1955) is Martha Sinnot, whose name recalls the Biblical Martha and Christ's command, "Sin not." When Martha is seriously tempted, she uses Christ's words, "Father, let this cup pass from me," and she freely chooses the moral way. *The Company She Keeps* includes the episode "Ghostly Father, I Confess," which deals with Margaret's visits to a psychoanalyst. Margaret's substitution of a secular confessor for a priest is not successful, because the psychoanalyst tries to persuade her to eliminate her "festering conscience" by denying that evil exists. Margaret refuses the false hopes held out by secular society, and she prays to the God whom she officially no longer worships: "If the flesh be blind, let the spirit see." One of McCarthy's few practicing Catholic characters, and one of her best male figures, is Senator James Carey in *Cannibals and Mis-*

sionaries. Because he occasionally makes retreats and feels that God is ''the only person'' to whom he can talk, the media labels him a ''spoiled priest.'' Because this alienates ''not only Jews and Protestants but Catholics,'' he cannot realize his ambition to be president. Such themes and characters examine moral preconceptions, both good and bad.

SELECTED BIBLIOGRAPHY

Works by McCarthy: NOVELS: *The Company She Keeps*. New York: Simon and Schuster, 1942; *The Oasis*. New York: Random House, 1949; *The Groves of Academe*. New York: Harcourt, Brace & Co., 1952; *A Charmed Life*. New York: Harcourt, Brace & Co., 1955; *The Group*. New York: Harcourt, Brace, and World, 1963; *Birds of America*. New York: Harcourt Brace Jovanovich, 1971; *Cannibals and Missionaries*. New York: Harcourt Brace Jovanovich, 1979. STORIES: *The Hounds of Summer and Other Stories*. New York: Avon Books, 1981. AUTOBIOGRAPHY: *Memories of a Catholic Girlhood*. New York: Harcourt, Brace & Co., 1957. *How I Grew*. New York: Harcourt Brace Jovanovich, 1987. ESSAYS: *Sights and Spectacles 1937–1956*. New York: Farrar, Straus, and Cudahy, 1956; *On the Contrary*. New York: Farrar, Straus, and Cudahy, 1961; *Vietnam*. New York: Harcourt, Brace, and World, 1967; *Hanoi*. New York: Harcourt, Brace, and World, 1968; *Medina*. New York: Harcourt Brace Jovanovich, 1972; *The Mask of State: Watergate Portraits*. New York: Harcourt Brace Jovanovich, 1974; *Ideas and the Novel*. New York: Harcourt Brace Jovanovich, 1980; *Occasional Prose*. New York: Harcourt Brace Jovanovich, 1985.

Works about McCarthy: Hardy, Willene Schaefer. *Mary McCarthy*. New York: Frederick Ungar Publishing Co., 1981; McKenzie, Barbara. *Mary McCarthy*. New York: Twayne, 1966; Stock, Irvin. *Mary McCarthy*. Minneapolis: University of Minnesota, 1968. AW. AWW. CA 7–8. CANR 16. CN. DLB 2. TCA.

Alexandra Hennessey Olsen

JOE McGINNISS (1942–   ). Although he has written one novel, Joe McGinniss is best known for his non-fiction. In all his writings, from his early journalistic pieces to his latest best-seller, he combines an eye for detail and an ear for dialogue with an unsparing honesty that has angered some but won him the respect of many.

Born on December 9, 1942, in New York City, Joe McGinniss was raised in Rye, New York. He attended Catholic schools, graduating in 1964 from the College of the Holy Cross. He began a highly successful career as a journalist. In June 1968, however, he resigned from his position as a columnist with the *Philadelphia Inquirer* to work on a book about the role of advertising agencies in that year's presidential election. The result was *The Selling of the President 1968* (1969), which brought McGinniss instant fame. He has since written four more books; *Fatal Vision* (1983) returned him to the best-seller lists. Meanwhile, in 1976, McGinniss married for the second time. He lives in Williamstown, Massachusetts, and he teaches at Bennington College.

McGinniss bases his writing on first-hand experience and personal knowledge although it has little direct interest in Catholic concerns. *Going to Extremes* (1980) came out of eighteen months' travel in Alaska; for *Fatal Vision*, Mc-

Ginniss lived with his subject, Jeffrey MacDonald, for seven weeks during MacDonald's murder trial. His one novel, *The Dream Team* (1972), similarly rooted in personal experience, features as its protagonist a young best-selling author on tour promoting his book. In it as in all his works, McGinniss demonstrates a remarkable gift for creating scenes vividly and succinctly.

His novel also reflects his honesty. Whether writing of Richard Nixon, or of MacDonald or, in *The Dream Team*, of himself, McGinniss records what he sees with unremitting truthfulness. The portraits that emerge are not always endearing. In fact, in his novel and in *Heroes* (1976), McGinniss at times depicts himself in a less than flattering light. Given his honesty, however, one is always left with the conviction that he is a writer not only of ability but of integrity as well.

SELECTED BIBLIOGRAPHY

Works by McGinniss: NOVELS: *The Dream Team*. New York: Random House, 1972. NON-FICTION: *The Selling of the President, 1968*. New York: Trident, 1969; *Heroes*. New York: Viking Press, 1976; *Going to Extremes*. New York: Knopf, 1980; *Fatal Vision*. New York: Putnam, 1983; *Blind Faith*. New York: Putnam, 1989.

Works about McGinniss: Kornbluth, Jesse. "Talking with Joe McGinniss." *New York Times Book Review* (September 1980), pp. 35–36. CA 25–28.

Charles Trainor

WILLIAM PETER McGIVERN (1927–1985). William McGivern was a prolific writer, the author of twenty-three novels, several children's books, numerous short stories, and scripts for both movies and television. Though best known for his tight characterizations of police and criminals, his novels vary in type and focus: war, espionage, homicide detection, psychic suspense, political corruption, crooked cops, mad capers, and psychopathic horror.

Born in Chicago, Illinois, on December 6, 1927 and educated at the University of Birmingham (1945–1946), McGivern joined the U.S. Army in 1943, received the Soldier's Medal in 1944, and was discharged at the rank of master sergeant in 1946. His military experience formed the basis for one of his most popular books, *Soldiers of '44* (1979), as well as for such later treatments of the military mind as *A Matter of Honor* (1984) and *Night of the Juggler* (1975). He married writer Maureen Daly in 1948; they have two children and have produced several books jointly (*Mention My Name*; *Unscheduled Adventures* 1958, *The Seeing* 1980). He was a reporter and reviewer for the Philadelphia *Evening Bulletin* between 1949 and 1951, after which he worked as a self-employed writer, living in a dozen countries, until his death from cancer on November 18, 1985, at his Palm Desert, California, home. He received the Mystery Writers of America's Edgar award in 1952 for *The Big Heat* (1953).

McGivern's early works are straightforward analyses of the human psychology of crime and corruption, focusing on men molded by their upbringing and environment and their physical and psychological compulsions; his later works, however, became increasingly complex, with intricate, multithreaded plots, in-depth characterization, and more psychoanalysis of motives and behavior. At his best he deals with men, thrown together by circumstance, trying to survive the prejudices and violence of their comrades amid the dangers of war or crime, or with men trained for combat and survival trying unsuccessfully to cope with ordinary life. Often these men find that their special skills for hunting, tracking, and killing the enemy are needed to protect the lives of innocents, threatened by the animals who roam the urban or corporate or international jungles. His Catholic sensibility confronts human motives and human guilt; his central characters search their souls, trying to cope with their past acts, to establish contact with people they love, to control their obsessions. They question their own perceptions and motives, but ultimately they learn to trust their instincts. McGivern shows good men trapped in frightful, morally ambiguous circumstances, making decisions about right and wrong amid the confusing morass of contradictory evidence. Often his central figures feel alone, cut off from humanity, though McGivern reveals how closely intertwined their lives are despite their antagonism and their adversarial relationships. Occasionally there is a Catholic priest who admits his inadequacies but whose trust in the good proves a firm foundation that the central figure at first denies but eventually confirms.

McGivern frequently explores the question of revenge. In *Reprisal* (1974) three grieving fathers whose children have died from drug overdoses on a sunny California beach seek to assuage their personal guilt by tracking down and killing the drug dealers responsible, but they find too late that toying with death is addictive and that revenge exacts revenge. In *The Big Heat* a hard-nosed, uncompromising detective, compelled by his sense of right, reinforced by reading philosophy (especially St. John's *Ascent of Mount Carmel*), refuses to bow to political pressure, and stalks city streets seeking the reason for the suicide of a fellow officer, only to have his wife killed by a bomb meant for him; though he abandons his faith to pursue revenge, his friends, the little guys of the city, show him that ordinary men, sticking together, can overcome the mob, destroy corrupt politicians, and exact revenge legally and morally. In *A Matter of Honor* a bitter philosophical conflict over the Vietnam War is resolved posthumously as the general avenges his policeman son's death, taking on the son's mission himself, exposing corruption within the military itself.

McGivern's characters struggle with questions of obligation and right and wrong. In *Rogue Cop* (1955) a corrupt cop tries to save his honest brother and thereby saves himself. In *Soldiers of '44* a war-weary lieutenant must decide whether to help cover up the initial cowardice of a general's son and let his heroic death stand on record or to pass on that son's letter explaining his fears and cowardice in hopes that the general will better understand what really makes a man a hero. McGivern's most famous book, *Night of the Juggler*, explores the power of a father's love as he tries to outwit both professional law officers and a twisted psychopath to save his kidnapped daughter; ironically it is the combination of his harsh wartime training that allows him to approach horror coldly and methodically and of his daughter's instinct for pity and sympathy that produces success. A touching father-daughter relationship also dominates *Summitt* (1982); therein the hero's brother is killed and his daughter is raped to hide a frightening military experiment in mind and memory control. Tight, penetrating characterization; hurtling, suspenseful action; and a deep moral sense make McGivern's novels well worth reading.

SELECTED BIBLIOGRAPHY

Works by McGivern: *But Death Runs Faster*. New York: Dodd, Mead, 1948; *Heaven Ran Last*. New York: Dodd, Mead, 1949; *Very Cold for May*. New York: Dodd, Mead, 1950; *Shield for Murder*. New York: Dodd, Mead, 1951; *Blondes Die Young*, as Bill Peters. New York: Dodd, Mead, 1952; *The Crooked Frame*. New York: Dodd, Mead, 1952; *The Big Heat*. New York: Dodd, Mead, 1953; *Margin of Terror*. New York: Dodd, Mead, 1953; *Rogue Cop*. New York: Dodd, Mead, 1955; *The Darkest Hour*. New York: Dodd, Mead, 1955; *The Seven File*. New York: Dodd, Mead, 1957; *Night Extra*. New York: Dodd, Mead, 1957; *Odds against Tomorrow*. New York: Dodd, Mead, 1957; *Savage Streets*. New York: Dodd, Mead, 1959; *Seven Lies South*. New York: Dodd, Mead, 1960; *The Road to the Snail*. New York: Dodd, Mead, 1961; *A Pride of Pride*. New York: Dodd, Mead, 1962; *Police Special*. New York: Dodd, Mead, 1962; *A Choice of Assassins*. New York: Dodd, Mead, 1963; *The Caper of the Golden Bulls*. New York: Dodd, Mead, 1967; *Lie Down, I Want to Talk to You*. New York: Dodd, Mead, 1968; *Caprifoil*. New York: Dodd, Mead, 1973; *Reprisal*. New York: Dodd, Mead, 1974; *Night of the Juggler*. New York: Dodd, Mead, 1975; *Soldiers of '44*. New York: Dodd, Mead, 1979; *The Seeing*, with Maureen McGivern. New York: Dodd, Mead, 1980; *Summitt*. New York: Dodd, Mead, 1982; *A Matter of Honor*. New York: Dodd, Mead, 1984; *Shield for Murder*. New York: Berkley Pub., 1988.

Works about McGivern: Review of *The Caper of the Golden Bulls*. *New York Times Book Review* (6 March 1966), p. 36; Review of *Caprifoil*. *The New Yorker* (14 October 1972), p. 170; Review of *Night Extra*. *New York Times* (7 April 1957), p. 22; Review of *Odds against Tomorrow*. *New York Times* (3 November 1957), p. 54. CA 49–52. CANR 7.

Gina Macdonald

TOM McHALE (1941–1982). A writer most notable for his imagination and his vision, Tom McHale published six novels before his early death. With an imagination that critics called fecund, "prodigal," and "spendthrift," McHale presents a grotesque, tragicomic, and blackly humorous vision of the world. His characters (in his early novels, Irish and Italian Catholics) live amid the lies and corruptions of family, marriage, Church, business, and society. Death and funerals abound—often mixed with comedy—and his protagonists, always men and usually Irish and unhappily married, seek stability and hope, if such can be found. His plots are picaresque, his style serviceable at best. Though most reviewers saw a decline after his first two novels, McHale's work continuingly shows an exuberance, an overwearing energy, and under his wild comedy lies a deep compassion for the human as victim.

Born in Avoca, Pennsylvania, on May 29, 1941, Thomas Arthur McHale attended the Jesuits' Scranton Preparatory School (1955–1959) and Temple University in Philadelphia (B.A., biology, 1963). After a semester he withdrew from Hahnemann Medical College, took creative writing courses at the University of Pennsylvania, and worked as a caseworker for the Department of Public Assistance. He visited Israel in 1964 for a friend's wedding and spent three years in Israel, Paris, and Spain, doing some study at the Sorbonne. He then attended the Writer's Workshop at the University of Iowa (M.F.A., 1969), where he continued work on his developing first novel.

The critics celebrated the "rococo extravagance" and black hilarity of *Principato* (1970) and *Farragan's Retreat* (1971). In 1974 he published *Alinsky's Diamond* and held a Guggenheim Fellowship; *School Spirit* followed in 1976, winning the Thomas More Medal. No longer considering himself a Catholic, McHale published his two New England (and more secular) novels, *The Lady from Boston* (1978) and *Dear Friends* (1982). All these novels were reviewed in such magazines as *Time*, *The New Yorker*, the *New York Times Book Review*, and London's *Times Literary Supplement*. During these years he was married (in Bombay) and divorced, did some teaching, enjoyed outdoor activities, and lived in New Jersey, Vermont, Maine, and Massachusetts. He moved to Florida, where he worked in various jobs (teaching, writing, public relations with a Miami firm, assistant manager of a movie theatre) and died, a suicide, on March 30, 1982, in Pembroke Pines near Miami. He was scheduled to begin teaching creative writing at the University of Pennsylvania the following autumn.

At the heart of every McHale novel is a comic victim, always male, who seeks integrity and truth amid the corruption of institutions and persons. The McHale hero—a likeable loner—is usually Irish in descent (although Italian in *Principato* and WASP in the last two novels), drinks too much, and has had an unhappy marriage. Internally howling at life's pain and suffering (and sometimes at the God who permits it), he manages at best to survive and to cope, though occasionally he actively fights for justice. His foes are multiple: family or in-laws, cold wives, dull children, venal priests, the Philadelphia or Boston establishments, old lies and cover-ups, abuses of power by church or state, America's loss of its former values, personal loneliness, and ultimately death. The hero's few consolations come from the human warmth of friend, mistress, or family (especially an Italian family); his own pain and loneliness give him a deep and immense compassion for fellow sufferers. At times the hero's life is put in a larger political context, and McHale's creative years—1964–1982—chronicle a time of great social change in America. McHale's novels, in any case, focus on his solitary hero, and his themes are always explicitly stated (at least in passing) somewhere in the novel. A summary of his vision is perhaps clearest in *The Lady from Boston* when the nearly mythic Dwight David Aldrich, from the Midwest heartland of Abilene, Kansas, reflects that "All of existence [is] something like a melting snow bridge over a bottomless chasm."

McHale communicates this vision through plot, character, situation, and, especially, a distinctive black comedy. His plots are episodic, picaresque, and often frantic as the hero keeps off some destructive force or figure. In *Alinsky's*

Diamond and *The Lady from Boston*, particularly, the plots and characters wander all over the place, making the two novels lively but unfocused. His characters, like his plots, are a curious mix of the realistic and the grotesque: the Pope (in *Alinsky's Diamond*), mafia figures (in *Principato* and *School Spirit*), an effeminate, bisexual hairdresser who refers to himself in the third person (in *Dear Friends*), or (in *The Lady from Boston*) a Mohawk Indian who graduated from Harvard Law, reads the Sunday *Times*, works in construction, and lives with his cousin, named "Sybaritic Hawk," in a dump in Saugus, Massachusetts.

His situations and big scenes, similarly, are frantic in mood and grotesque in conception: wild parties at a wake, a nun leaving her convent and immediately phoning her lover, suicides that aren't, or a fake crusade-pilgrimage from France to Jerusalem. His humor, spawned by an imagination that makes unusually strange linkings, is situational rather than verbal, and McHale enjoys creating medical doctors who want to kill, a man having an erection in the Pope's presence, a couple making love in a car wash, or the death scene of an Italian padrone complete with caterer, band, and multiple priests. Through this humor, he jests at institutions and hypocrisies, but underlying his humor is a wounded innocence, an unsatisfied quest for hope, and the sense of a world falling apart. Many people die in McHale's novels, many others drink, and his endings, though they may conclude a book, do not clean up the deeper human mess.

McHale's greatest weaknesses are his ill-crafted prose, sprawling plots, and overabundant characters. He seems impatient with novelistic convention, and it is not easy for him to rein in his intense, quirky, irreverent, inventive imagination. Nor, truly, can he fully control his vision; he is not sure whether to laugh or cry, and his mixed tone—as well as his distinctive voice—grows out of his ambivalence. As a novelist he is rarely neat, but his lively, inventive imagination and his bizarre mix of incongruities provide his unique signature: Tom McHale, grotesque-comic novelist, victim, and frantic chronicler of the American middle-class in religious and cultural transition.

SELECTED BIBLIOGRAPHY

Works by McHale: NOVELS: *Principato*. New York: Viking, 1970; *Farragan's Retreat*. New York: Viking, 1971; *Alinsky's Diamond*. Philadelphia: Lippincott, 1974; *School Spirit*. Garden City, N.Y.: Doubleday, 1976; *The Lady from Boston*. Garden City, N.Y.: Doubleday, 1978; *Dear Friends*. Garden City, N.Y.: Doubleday, 1982. SHORT STORIES: "Why We Gave Up Kidnapping." *McCall's* (December 1970), pp. 40, 120; "Farragan's Retreat." *Cosmopolitan* (August 1971), pp. 176 ff.; "A Society of Friends." *Playboy* (July 1973), pp. 76 ff., apparently the original last chapter, later discarded, of *Farragan's Retreat*.

Works about McHale: Brennan, Todd. "The Prime of Tom McHale" (with interview). *The Critic* (Summer 1977), pp. 62–66; Browne, Joseph. "Rejoicing in a Man's Life and His Art: An Appreciation." *Philadelphia Inquirer* (30 April 1982), sec. D., p. 1; McCormick, Bernard. "The Crack-up of Tom McHale." *Philadelphia Inquirer Magazine* (9 October 1983), pp. 32 ff; Polak, Maralyn Lois. "Tom McHale: 'The World's Worst Irishman.' " *Authors in the News*. Ed. Barbara Nykoruk, vol. 1. Detroit: Gale,

1976, pp. 332–33; Taylor, Mark. "McHale's Retreat." *Commonweal* (14 March 1975), pp. 459–63; Reply, *Commonweal* (25 April 1975), pp. 93–94. CA 77–80. CN.

Joseph J. Feeney, SJ

RALPH McINERNY (1929–). Scholar, educator, philosopher, critic, editor, journalist, and novelist, Ralph McInerny is among the most versatile and accomplished of contemporary American Catholic writers. As philosopher and scholar, McInerny has achieved over the past three decades an international reputation as one of the world's foremost living Thomists, author of more than ninety scholarly articles and books, including a two-volume *History of Western Philosophy* (1970) and the TWAS (Twayne World Authors Series) volume on *St. Thomas Aquinas* (1982); since 1976 he has been editor of *The New Scholasticism*, and he has served on the editorial boards of learned journals as diverse as *Center Journal* and *The American Journal of Jurisprudence*. Almost in counterpoint to these and other imposing credentials, McInerny is also a prolific writer of popular fiction. In more than twenty-five novels written since 1967, McInerny has displayed a rich fecundity of imagination, the flow of his thematic interests having branched into three principal tributaries that often crisscross: the droll academic novel, the serious psychological study of post-conciliar crisis in the Church, and, most abundantly, the detective thriller. The third tributary itself has branched into two very popular series of mysteries, each series named for the clerical sleuth who is the principal character: Father Dowling and Sister Mary Teresa. (For his novels in the Sister Mary Teresa mystery series, McInerny goes by the pen name Monica Quill.) In his novels, however light or profound the subject matter, McInerny exhibits a quiet authority that commands attention, inviting his readers to share in his own wry bemusement over the human condition—a condition at once lovely and grotesque, coherent and preposterous, deadly serious and wildly farcical. His language—although flawed now and then by careless lapses into the formulaic or by a sometimes excessive wordplay— is usually precise and evocative. His ample wit is served well by a seemingly effortless sense of plotting and timing—and, above all, by a shrewd and very attentive sense of character.

An Irish-Catholic Midwesterner, Ralph Matthew McInerny was born in Minneapolis on February 24, 1929. He grew up in the Twin Cities, served a year (1946–1947) with the U.S. Marine Corps, and entered the diocesan seminary in St. Paul, Minnesota. By 1951, when he received his bachelor's degree at St. Paul Seminary, McInerny had decided on an academic career in lieu of the priesthood. He earned a master's degree in philosophy and classics at the University of Minnesota (1952), and went on to take his Ph.D. (summa cum laude) at Laval University in 1954. On January 3, 1953, he married Constance Terrill Kunert (the Connie to whom many of his books are dedicated), who has borne him six children. After a one-year teaching stint at Creighton University, McInerny and his wife settled in South Bend in 1955, where he took on an instructorship in philosophy at the University of Notre Dame. He advanced steadily through the academic ranks until he became professor of philosophy in 1969. Since 1978, he has been the Michael P. Grace Professor of Medieval Studies at Notre Dame, director of the Jacques Maritain Center, and (until 1985) director of the Medieval Institute. The recipient of two honorary doctor of letters degrees, McInerny has been guest lecturer at more than thirty colleges and universities nationwide, and he holds active membership in more than a dozen professional associations.

Early in his academic career, while he was still at Creighton, McInerny wrote an essay on "Plot, Fate and Providence" (1955) for the Jesuit magazine *America*. The essay indicates something of the affinity between McInerny's then budding aspirations—which were always literary as well as philosophical.

It is just because the meaning of life is not at all clear to us in actual, concrete existence that we have need of the palliative of art. . . . Art's difference from life is the very reason for its relation to life: it enables us to view human acts as meaningful.

Like philosophers, artists try to make sense of human existence, so in 1963, after having put aside his literary aspirations to concentrate on his academic career, McInerny began to try his hand at fiction, using some of his free time to dash out stories for popular magazines, usually under the pen names Harry Austin and Ernan Mackey.

But his energy required a broader canvas, so he turned to the novel, and in 1967 Doubleday published his *Jolly Rogerson*, a blend of high farce (the very real academic politics and personal wrangling of the mythical Fort Elbow State College) and bittersweet psychological probing (the mid-life crisis of Matthew Rogerson, failed professor of humanities, whose deliberate efforts to fail are themselves a failure as the efforts start to gain him unwanted popularity and respect). A barbed sequel to *Jolly Rogerson* appeared nine years later in *Rogerson at Bay* (1976), wherein Professor Rogerson is ambushed by the erotic cravings of middle age as his wife Marge becomes entangled in feminist enthusiasms.

Meanwhile, between the publication dates of his two Rogerson works, McInerny produced his three most important novels. *A Narrow Time* (1969) stands out as perhaps his best novel and certainly his least classifiable; it belongs in a category of its own. One of the very few in which he writes in the first person, *A Narrow Time* displays McInerny's strongest suits as a novelist: deft plotting, penetrating psychological insight, and remarkably unsentimental compassion. The first-person narrator is an uncertain Mortimer Ballinger, a Midwestern dairy products salesman whose indolence is of a sort peculiar to his "Catholic distrust of the world." Mortimer takes the reader on an odyssey of suicidal despair (uplifted by farce, a regular ingredient of McInerny's fiction) as Mortimer finds that the vague pieties of his Catholic upbringing do not seem to jibe well with life's irrationality—i.e., with the death of his two-year-old daughter Marie. "When the world loses the power to make one feel at home," Mortimer reflects, "when things are what they are and nothing more, a fear begins which is both solemn and silly."

Somewhat less artful but vastly more successful commercially was *The Priest* (1973), the novel for which McInerny is best known—with two book-club entries and over a million copies sold in paperback. *The Priest* is a sensitive portrait of young Father Frank Ascue (the pun on the last name is intentional), who, on his first parish assignment, is caught between conflicting forces in the Church: tight triumphalists on one side and trendy radicals on the other. Richly nuanced and often playful, *The Priest* is partly a roman à clef (e.g., a haughty itinerant lecturer named Manspricht Deutsch is an obvious allusion to Hans Küng), but the principal theme of this sprawling, slow-paced novel is serious—and recurrent in McInerny's fiction: that the ordinary and largely ignored orthodox Roman Catholic is the one who suffers the most dislocation in a post-conciliar Church of battling "liberals" and "conservatives."

The same theme is echoed with sharper effect in *Gate of Heaven* (1975), a novel about the obscure Catholic Order of St. Brendan, which is dying out because of encroaching secularism and receding vocations. There is a bitter division in the order regarding the proposed destruction of an old seminary building to make room for a new college dormitory. Nearly lost among the warring factions is the thoughtful minor character Father Garrity, who is troubled by the pitting of "a false nostalgia for the past against a thoughtless hurtling into the future."

Romanesque (1977), a thriller about terrorism and stolen Vatican documents, marks a turn toward the popular mystery novel. In the same year, McInerny published *Her Death of Cold*, the first in his ongoing Father Dowling mystery series—an enterprise which has invited comparisons with G. K. Chesterton and the Father Brown stories. Roger Dowling, erstwhile canon lawyer, is a Midwestern parish priest of precise mind and sympathetic temperament. With his friend Phil Keegan of the local police department, Father Dowling unravels convoluted mysteries, always involving great suspense and some degree of mayhem. Another mystery series, begun in 1981 with *Not a Blessed Thing!*, turns on the adventures of Sister Mary Teresa Dempsey. She is an elderly member of the almost defunct Order of Martha and Mary ("the M&M's" inevitably—the McInerny wink again), and with the help of her young aides Sister Kim and Sister Joyce, the scholarly "Emtee" Dempsey untangles the violent mysteries into which she and her aides more or less improbably drift. Amid all this elegant potboiling, McInerny often takes time to dwell seriously on character and to explore the predicament of a collapsing orthodoxy in the modern Church.

In 1982, under the auspices of the Jacques Maritain Center at Notre Dame, McInerny cofounded with Michael Novak *Catholicism in Crisis* (now called *Crisis*), a journal of lay Catholic opinion, to which McInerny frequently contributes. Created out of dissatisfaction with contemporary Catholic intellectual discourse, this new Catholic magazine aims to revitalize liberal Catholic thinking. Avoiding both reactionary response and unchained radicalism is dramatized in McInerny's recent *Connolly's Life* (1983) and *The Noonday Devil* (1985), two wry theological thrillers which, like all of Ralph McInerny's prodigious literary and scholarly work, continue to exhibit that most distinctive quality of Catholic Christian orthodoxy: a tough mind leavened by a tender heart.

SELECTED BIBLIOGRAPHY

Works by McInerny: NOVELS: *Jolly Rogerson*. New York: Doubleday, 1967; *A Narrow Time*. New York: Doubleday, 1969; *The Priest*. New York: Harper & Row, 1973; *Gate of Heaven*. New York: Harper & Row, 1975; *Rogerson at Bay*. New York: Harper & Row, 1976; *Romanesque*. New York: Harper & Row, 1977; *Her Death of Cold*. New York: Vanguard, 1977; *Spinnaker*, Chicago: Gateway-Regnery, 1977; *The Seventh Station*. New York: Vanguard, 1977; *Quick As a Dodo*. New York: Vanguard, 1978; *Bishop As Pawn*. New York: Vanguard, 1978; *Lying Three*. New York: Vanguard, 1979; *Abecedary*. Notre Dame, Ind.: Juniper, 1979; *Second Vespers*. New York: Vanguard, 1980; *Thicker Than Water*. New York: Vanguard, 1981; *Not a Blessed Thing!*, as Monica Quill. New York: Vanguard, 1981; *The Frozen Maiden of Calpurnia*. Notre Dame, Ind.: Juniper, 1982; *Loss of Patients*. New York: Vanguard, 1982; *Let Us Prey*, as Monica Quill. New York: Vanguard, 1982; *Connolly's Life*. New York: Atheneum, 1983; *The Grass Widow*. New York: Vanguard, 1983; *And Then There Was Nun*, as Monica Quill. New York: Vanguard, 1984; *Getting a Way with Murder*. New York: Vanguard, 1984; *The Noonday Devil*. New York: Atheneum, 1985; *Nun of the Above*, as Monica Quill. New York: Vanguard, 1985; *Rest in Pieces*. New York: Vanguard, 1985; *The Basket Case*. New York: St. Martin's, 1987. LITERARY ARTICLES: "Plot, Fate and Providence." *America* 93 (1955), pp. 392–49; "The Greene-ing of America." *Commonweal* 95 (1971), pp. 59–61; "The House of Burgess." *Commonweal* 95 (1972), pp. 290–91; "A Clerical Collage." *Commonweal* 95 (1972), pp. 494–99; "The Wearing o' the Greene." *The American Spectator* 14, 2 (February 1981), pp. 16–18; "Waugh at Peace." *The American Spectator* 14, 5 (May 1981), pp. 16–18; "Maritain and Poetic Knowledge." *Renascence* 34 (1982), pp. 203–14; "Flannery O'Connor, Hillbilly Thomist." *The American Spectator* 16, 7 (July 1983), pp. 22–23.

Works about McInerny: Carroll, James. "Between Life and Death." *Catholic World* 210 (1970), pp. 239–40; Dunlap, John R. Review of *Connolly's Life*. *The American Spectator* 16,11 (November 1983), pp. 44–45; Greeley, Andrew. "The Moles of the Vatican." *New York Times Book Review* (31 March 1985), p. 19. O'Connell, David. Review of *Gate of Heaven* and *Rogerson at Bay*. *Commonweal* 104 (1977), pp. 184–86; Schroth, Raymond A. "Up against the Wall, Father." *Commonweal* 98 (1973), pp. 432–35. CA 21–22. CANR 12.

John R. Dunlap

CLAUDE McKAY (1889–1948). Though Jamaican by birth, Claude McKay is most strongly associated with the Harlem Renaissance writers of the 1920s, even though personality conflicts, ideological differences, and McKay's own foreign travel actually put him at the fringes of the movement rather than at its heart. Often characterized as "unpolished" and "uneven," McKay's works depict, often quite angrily, an oppressive white society that prevents blacks, primarily in the United States but also in other parts of the world, from realizing their potential, from living unencumbered by racial barriers, and from achieving a healthy racial identity.

Born on September 15, 1889, in Jamaica, British West Indies, Festus Claudius McKay lived first on the family farm in Clarendon Parish, then with his older

brother, Uriah Theophilus McKay, a schoolteacher, near Montego Bay. Following his grammar school education and a short apprenticeship with a wheelwright
and cabinetmaker, he moved to Kingston, where he joined the Jamaican con-
stabulary. In 1912, McKay published two volumes of dialect poetry, *Songs of
Jamaica* and *Constab Ballads*, and went to the United States to study at Tuskegee
Institute, where he quickly felt hostility and racial tension, and then at Kansas
State College. Receiving a cash gift from an "English admirer" of the Jamaican
poetry, McKay moved to New York, where, after a short attempt as a businessman and a husband, he held numerous odd jobs and began to write poetry
again, later contributing regularly to Max Eastman's *The Liberator* (formerly
The Masses). Here he gained national recognition with "If We Must Die," still
his best-known poem, in 1919, and quickly became a leading voice of black
protest. After travelling to London and beginning his long, but tentative interest
in Marxism, McKay became an associate editor of *The Liberator* in 1921 and
a coeditor in 1922, publishing his first volumes of poetry since moving to the
United States: *Spring in New Hampshire and Other Poems* (1920) and *Harlem
Shadows* (1922). For twelve years, McKay lived as an expatriate in Russia,
Europe, and North Africa, where he produced a large body of fiction: three
novels—*Home to Harlem* (1928), *Banjo: A Story without a Plot* (1929), and
Banana Bottom (1933)—and a collection of short stories, *Gingertown* (1932).
Following his return to the United States, McKay produced two works of non-
fiction—*A Long Way from Home* (1937), an unusual autobiography that largely
focuses on his world travels and his literary associations, and *Harlem: Negro
Metropolis* (1940), a disappointing, bitter collection of essays on New York's
black community and its leaders. In 1944, he converted to Catholicism. After
a long illness, McKay died in a Chicago hospital on May 22, 1948. He was
buried in New York.

Even in his earliest works, the dialect poetry, McKay's enduring concerns are
already apparent. While he vividly presents the beauty and richness of the exotic,
primitive life in harmony with the earth, the poet also indicts the strangling
effect of the city and of the oppressive structures, generally white, often con-
tagious, that deny the Jamaican peasants—and blacks elsewhere—self-realization
and make a healthy racial identity impossible.

Despite the conventionality of his verses—sonnets and other traditional
forms—McKay gives voice to direct, anguished statements of outrage, as in
such protest poems as "The Lynching," "The White House," and "The White
City." Although "If We Must Die"—his most famous, most frequently reprinted
work—crosses all barriers—national, racial—in voicing resistance to forces of
oppression, it is this poem that placed McKay at the forefront of black protest
and gave him national recognition.

Home to Harlem and *Banjo*, tellingly subtitled "a story without a plot,"
reflect a greater interest in character and self-image than in a strong plot line.
In several ways, these novels reflect McKay's own life story and his own quest
for resolution of conflicting forces of instinct and intellect. *Home to Harlem*

became an immediate hit, the first black best-seller. At the same time, however, many resented the stereotypical images of black life that pervade the novel. Although no real influence existed between it and Carl Van Vechten's earlier *Nigger Haven*, the obvious similarities drew similar criticisms. W.E.B. DuBois, who had earlier scorned *Nigger Heaven*, was now repulsed by *Home to Harlem*'s drunkenness, fighting, and sexuality.

As *Home to Harlem* presents the free and easy life of unencumbered blacks in America, *Banjo* focuses on the lives of those in Europe, including *Home to Harlem*'s Ray, who, in many respects, speaks for McKay himself and demonstrates the conflict between intellect and instinct that will be more articulately stated and more artistically resolved in *Banana Bottom*. Less concerned with a strong plot than with the black man's place in the world and the development of several black characters, *Banjo* presents a microcosm of the black world through his collection of black Americans, West Indians, and Africans. The theme of racial identity dominates. Like *Home to Harlem*, *Banjo* shows that white prejudice and bigotry promote self-hatred in blacks themselves.

In *Banana Bottom*, generally recognized as his highest achievement in fiction, McKay accomplishes a unification of the conflicting intellectual and instinctual aspects of life. Like McKay himself, Bita Plant, appropriately named in a story about natural growth, is born in Jamaica, receives a foreign education, and benefits from a white person, Squire Gensir (Walter Jekyll in McKay's life). On the one hand, McKay presents a world of the intellect. At its most complete, this world—the Craigs, respectability, education, Christianity, light-skinned natives in civil service jobs—is still inadequate for the whole person. But so is the world of instinct of primitivism—the primitive god Obeah, freedom in sexuality, the spontaneity and sensuality of the natives' "tea meetings." The struggle between the contradictory forces is eventually resolved in Bita's marriage to Jubban, her father's drayman, an uneducated peasant who, despite his low social position, is the picture of strength, self-respect, confidence, and competence. Most importantly, this triumphant union allows for Bita's personal growth but prevents her manipulation by forces outside herself.

In 1944, McKay joined the Catholic Church, a decision that originated with his association with Ellen Tarry, a Catholic author of children's books, but his conversion should be seen not as a rejection of his earlier interests, despite his attempts to dismiss much of the earlier work, but as the "final hurdle," as McKay phrased it, in a long progress toward unifying the conflicting forces in his life. The Church, he wrote in the pages of *Ebony*, "is the greatest stabilizing force in the world today—standing as a bulwark against all the wild and purely materialistic isms that are sweeping the world." Prior to his death, McKay served as a consultant on racial problems and radical politics to Bishop Bernard Sheil, worked with Chicago's Catholic Youth Organization, wrote poems and essays on his move to Catholicism, and worked on various projects in progress. At his death, he left behind several unpublished manuscripts.

SELECTED BIBLIOGRAPHY

Works by McKay: POETRY: *Songs of Jamaica*. 1912. Miami: Mnemosyne, 1969; *Constab Ballads*. London: Watts, 1912; *Spring in New Hampshire and Other Poems*. London: Richards, 1920; *Harlem Shadows*. New York: Harcourt, 1922; *Selected Poems of Claude McKay*. 1953. New York: Harcourt, 1969; *The Dialect Poetry of Claude McKay: Two Volumes in One*. Freeport, N.Y.: Books for Libraries, 1972, reprints *Songs of Jamaica* and *Constab Ballads*. NOVELS: *Home to Harlem*. 1928. Chatham, N.J.: Chatham Bookseller, 1973; *Banjo: A Story without a Plot*. 1929. New York: Harcourt, 1957; *Banana Bottom*. 1933. Chatham, N.J.: Chatham Bookseller, 1970. SHORT STORIES: *Gingertown*. 1932. Freeport, N.Y.: Books for Libraries, 1972. AUTOBIOGRAPHY: *A Long Way from Home*. 1937. New York: Harcourt, 1970. OTHER BOOKS: *Harlem: Negro Metropolis*. 1940. New York: Harcourt, 1972. *The Passion of Claude McKay: Selected Poetry and Prose, 1912–1948*. New York: Schocken Books, 1973. UNCOLLECTED PIECES: "Harlem Runs Wild." *The Nation* (3 April 1935), pp. 382–83; "Lest We Forget." *Jewish Frontier* (7 January 1940), pp. 9–11; "On Becoming a Roman Catholic." *The Epistle* (Spring 1945), pp. 43–45; "Why I Became a Catholic." *Ebony* (March 1946), p. 32; "The Middle Ages." *Catholic Worker* (May 1946), p. 5; "Boyhood in Jamaica." *Phylon* (Summer 1953), pp. 134–35.

Works about McKay: Conroy, Sister Mary. "The Vagabond Motif in the Writings of Claude McKay. *Negro American Literature Forum* 5 (Spring 1971), pp. 15–23; Cooper, Wayne. *Claude McKay: Rebel Sojourner in the Harlem Renaissance*. Baton Rouge: Louisiana State University Press, 1987; Giles, James R. *Claude McKay*. Boston: Twayne, 1976; Greenberg, Robert M. "Idealism and Realism in the Fiction of Claude McKay." *CLA Journal* 24 (1981), pp. 237–61; Kent, George E. "The Soulful Way of Claude McKay." *Black World* 20 (1970), pp. 37–51. CA 104. Cat A (1947). DLB 4, 45. TCA.

Robert A. Russ

CARMELITA McKEEVER (1914–). Poetry alone does not define the career of this woman who has spent most of her life as a Sister of St. Joseph of Carondelet, but since 1981 when she turned to writing what she calls "contemporary poetry," it has sharpened awareness of herself as part of the flux of things. Born on August 10, 1914, in Englewood, New Jersey, she earned a B.S. from the College of Saint Rose and an M.S. from the State University of New York at Albany. She taught both elementary and high school classes before becoming assistant registrar at the College of Saint Rose in 1967. She held various positions before retiring in 1984 and is at present a part-time administrative assistant in the Experienced Adult Program.

Sister Carmelita had several poems published in religious magazines between 1945 and 1953, but it has been since 1981 that she stretched her poetic vision, finding a larger audience for her poems in journals as diverse as *Parnassus*, *Studia Mystica*, and *Up against the Wall Mother*.

Nature, especially the Adirondacks, informs her poetry, as does, now, the sense of aging. "On Growing Old," with its haunting opening "My rock is closer now as I begin" was awarded Honorable Mention in *The Lyric* 1984 annual contest. A quiet, firm awareness of God's presence attracts the reader, as does the clean imagery and the simple line.

SELECTED BIBLIOGRAPHY
   Works by McKeever: POETRY (in anthologies): *Ashes to Ashes, American Poetry Anthology*. Boulder: Westview Press, 1975; the 1984 *Anthology of Magazine Verse and Yearbook of American Poetry*. Beverly Hills, Calif.: Monitor Book Company. Also over thirty magazines, including *The Christian Century, The Lyric, New Voices, Poetry Today, Review for Religious, Spirit*, and *Studia Mystica*.
                                                                    Mary E. Giles

THOMAS MERTON (1915–1968). *The Seven Storey Mountain* (1948) made its author, a cloistered monk in Kentucky, a nationally recognized writer, and the success of this autobiographical book, which articulated concerns of the post–World War II generation, has continued to affect the writer's reputation even to the present. Merton insisted that he had grown immensely beyond the simple pieties of this early enthusiastic account of conversion and vocation; thus it is ironic he was, and continues to be, so recognized for this book. In fact, he wrote much biographical prose and poetry in the years preceding and following *Seven Storey Mountain*. He claimed to be surprised by its immense sales. As his reputation strengthened in the decades following, however, and earlier unpublished books appeared (*The Secular Journal of Thomas Merton*, 1959, and *My Argument with the Gestapo: A Macaronic Journal*, 1969), it became clear that Father Louis (Merton's name as a Cistercian) had always aspired to be a man of letters. His decision to enter the Abbey of Gethsemani combined to provide materials beneficial to literary development and to achievements as one of the major Christian writers of this century.

   In the twenty years since his first wide recognition and before his accidental death in 1968 while travelling in Asia, Merton demonstrated enormous energy which was channeled into poems, essays, translations, reviews, journals, and a huge correspondence. Such a diversity of interests, along with his ability to reflect upon aspects of the Church in process of change provided him with a wide audience which included many non-Christians. His odyssey stands as a symbol of what many have experienced in an era when Christianity moved from modern to post-modern.

   Merton's vast writings reflect his quest as pilgrim within a church which in the 1940s might stress its connections with medievalism but later learned to become less preoccupied with the past. Merton's many writings about the East, such as *Mystics and Zen Masters* (1967), are one indication of this change. He was born on January 31, 1915 of artist parents in France and saw much of Europe during periods of residence and education. Later, after his parents had died, he came to live in New York City with his father's parents. He attended Columbia University as an undergraduate and a graduate student; he converted to Catholicism; and he found himself mysteriously drawn to the priesthood. Twenty-seven years of wandering brought him to the relative stability of a monastery. He documents much of those years himself, and his principal biographer, Michael Mott, provides considerable detail about the complexity of the life. *The Secular*

Journal of Thomas Merton (1959) is the earliest sustained record of Merton's spiritual pilgrimage. It covers the period from 1939 to his entrance in December 1941. The grace to go to Gethsemani changed Merton's life, and as a novice he felt so content within that routine that he was apparently willing to give up any ambition to be a writer. Nevertheless, poems written in the 1930s had been saved. They were shown to his old mentor from Columbia, Mark Van Doren, who sent them to James Laughlin, an editor at New Directions, who was destined to become Merton's poetry editor and friend.

Many books appeared in the 1940s. The first, *Thirty Poems* (1944) consisting of pre- and early monastery poems, reflects a calmness and serenity. *A Man in the Divided Sea* (1948) followed; the title suggests Merton felt he had been delivered from the chaos of the world. Even more intense was *Figures for an Apocalypse* (1948) which might be described as a castigation of the secular world. By 1949, when a small volume of poems, *The Tears of Blind Lions*, appeared, Merton implied that it might not be possible to be both a poet and a contemplative.

This was, of course, possible but many questions had to be resolved before Merton learned how best to resolve his questions about monastic and public responsibilities. From 1941 through 1949 he had prepared to be a priest, and he was ordained on May 26, 1949. Gradually he assumed duties as a teacher, master of students, and novice master. In 1955 he began a ten-year term as novice master. Those duties were demanding, but during those years his literary output was enormous. Apparently his teaching, daily contact with novices, and reading stimulated writing. Books about the psalms, the Eucharist, the monastic life, and solitude and books of poetry appeared in the mid-fifties. *The Strange Islands* (1957) shows a willingness to experiment as a poet.

During this same period Merton wrote extensively about issues beyond just the spiritual life. He began making more connections about race, war, bureaucracy, violence, and renewal. He wrote more about matters beyond Western monasticism. Stylistically his range expanded; thus, while a book like his autobiography is quite conventional, as he developed in the 1950s, he sought ways to make connections beyond the conventional.

A way to observe some changes in Merton's writing would be to compare *Seeds of Contemplation* (1949) with the greatly expanded text, *New Seeds of Contemplation* (1961). In the second book, Merton adds material which reflects his appreciation of meditative traditions beyond the Christian. Clearly he was moving beyond the predictable patterns of a cloistered Catholic. Many books in the 1960s (*Disputed Questions*, 1960, *The Behavior of Titans*, 1961, *The New Man*, 1961, and *Conjectures of a Guilty Bystander*, 1966) reflect an openness to the world. Full of insights about a world to be loved, these books document Merton's growing compassion.

During the 1960s Father Louis was involved in much writing about peace and war. Increasingly he was convinced that questions about spirituality must not be separated from those about the world. During this time, while his poetic production was not as prolific as in the 1940s, Merton's willingness to experiment also made it possible for him to produce a new variety of engaged poetry. *Emblems of a Season of Fury* (1963) and *Cables to the Ace* (1968) reflect this concern for the world.

Cables is the overflow of a busy contemplative, who by then was living as a hermit near Gethsemani Abbey, who could not abandon the world. These poems, experimental and often ironic, reflect the poet's acknowledgement that the modern world is cluttered and noisy to the point of distraction. But Merton's point is to remind readers that the wholeness of God's universe remains. The posthumously published *The Geography of Lograire* (1969), a book-length poem (a "purely tentative first draft" insisted Merton), provides an elaborate record of reading, dreaming, and writing. Merton crafted a poem in the manner of Ezra Pound, modified by the attention to words of someone like William Carlos Williams or Louis Zukofsky, which both indicated Western civilization and celebrated God's love for all mankind.

Merton's life ended abruptly. He died in Asia when he accidentally touched a fan wire while in attendance at a conference of religious superiors in Bangkok. His *The Asian Journal of Thomas Merton* (1973) compiled from several notebooks—travel, personal, reading—is a detailed account of his final months.

Many other books have been published posthumously including the enormous *The Collected Poems of Thomas Merton* (1977) and *The Literary Essays of Thomas Merton* (1981). These volumes, plus the first volume of selected correspondence, *The Ground of Love* (1985) reveal the immense range of his interests and the tremendous energy of this unusual monk.

Merton's entire production demonstrates that his was a continuing quest for God. The writing, which often began as a personal record, is proving to have great value for a wide variety of readers. Many scholarly works about him and a stream of manuscripts are being published, ensuring continued interest.

SELECTED BIBLIOGRAPHY

Works by Merton: AUTOBIOGRAPHY: *The Seven Storey Mountain.* New York: Harcourt, Brace, 1948; *The Sign of Jonas.* New York: Harcourt, Brace, 1953; *The Secular Journal of Thomas Merton.* New York: Farrar, Straus & Cudahy, 1959; *Conjectures of a Guilty Bystander.* Garden City, N.Y.: Doubleday, 1966; *The Asian Journal of Thomas Merton.* Ed. from notebooks by Naomi Burton, Brother Patrick Hart, and James Laughlin. New York: New Directions, 1973; *Day of a Stranger.* Intro. by Robert E. Daggy. Salt Lake City: Gibbs M. Smith, 1981. DEVOTIONAL: *Exile Ends in Glory.* Milwaukee: Bruce, 1948; *What Is Contemplation?* Notre Dame, Ind.: Holy Cross, 1948; *Seeds of Contemplation.* New York: New Directions, 1949; *What Are These Wounds?* Milwaukee: Bruce, 1950; *No Man Is an Island.* New York: Harcourt, Brace, 1955; *Praying the Psalms.* Collegeville, Minn.: Liturgical Press, 1956; *Thoughts in Solitude.* New York: Farrar, Straus & Cudahy, 1958; *New Seeds of Contemplation.* New York: New Directions, 1961; *Contemplative Prayer.* New York: Herder & Herder, 1969. Also published as *The Climate of Monastic Prayer.* Kalamazoo, Mich.: Cistercian Publications, Cistercian Studies Series, no. 1; *Opening the Bible.* Collegeville, Minn.: Liturgical Press, 1970; *He Is Risen.* Niles, Ill.: Argus Communications, 1975. ESSAYS: *Bread in the Wilderness.* New York: New Directions, 1953; *Disputed Questions.* New York: Farrar, Straus & Cudahy, 1960; *The Behavior of Titans.* New York:

New Directions, 1961; *The New Man*. New York: Farrar, Straus & Cudahy, 1961; *Life and Holiness*. New York: Herder & Herder, 1963; *Seeds of Destruction*. New York: Farrar, Straus & Giroux, 1964; *Seasons of Celebration*. New York: Farrar, Straus & Giroux, 1965; *Raids on the Unspeakable*. New York: New Directions, 1966; *Mystics and Zen Masters*. New York: Farrar, Straus & Giroux, 1967; *Zen and the Birds of Appetite*. New York: New Directions, 1968; *Faith and Violence*. Notre Dame, Ind.: University of Notre Dame Press, 1968; *Contemplation in a World of Action*. Garden City, N.Y.: Doubleday, 1971; *Ishi Means Man*. Greensboro, N.C.: Unicorn Press, 1976; *The Monastic Journey*. Ed. Brother Patrick Hart. Kansas City, Mo.: Sheed, Andrews & McMeel, 1977; *Love and Living*. New York: Farrar, Straus & Giroux, 1979; *Thomas Merton on St. Bernard*. Kalamazoo, Mich.: Cistercian Publications, 1980; *The Literary Essays of Thomas Merton*. New York: New Directions, 1981. FICTION: *My Argument with the Gestapo: A Macaronic Journal*. Garden City, N.Y.: Doubleday, 1969. POETRY: *Thirty Poems*. New York: New Directions, 1944; *A Man in the Divided Sea*. New York: New Directions, 1948; *Figures for an Apocalypse*. New York: New Directions, 1948; *The Tears of Blind Lions*. New York: New Directions, 1949; *Selected Poems*. London: Hollis & Carter, 1950. First English edition; *The Strange Islands*. New York: New Directions, 1957; *The Tower of Babel*. Hamburg, West Germany: Laughlin, 1957; *Selected Poems of Thomas Merton*. New York: New Directions, 1959; *Original Child Bomb*. New York: New Directions, 1962; *Emblems of a Season of Fury*. New York: New Directions, 1963; *Cables to the Ace*. New York: New Directions, 1968; *The Geography of Lograire*. New York: New Directions, 1969; *The Collected Poems of Thomas Merton*. New York: New Directions, 1977. OTHER WORKS: *The Waters of Siloe*. New York: Harcourt, Brace, 1949; *The Ascent to Truth*. New York: Harcourt, Brace, 1951; *The Last of the Fathers*. New York: Harcourt, Brace, 1954; *The Living Bread*. New York: Farrar, Straus & Cudahy, 1956; *The Silent Life*. New York: Farrar, Straus & Cudahy, 1957; *Spiritual Direction and Meditation*. Collegeville, Minn.: Liturgical Press, 1960; *A Thomas Merton Reader*. Ed. Thomas P. McDonnell. New York: Harcourt, Brace, 1962; *Thomas Merton on Peace*. Ed. Gordon C. Zahn. New York: McCall, 1971, republished as *The Non-Violent Alternative*. New York: Farrar, Straus & Giroux, 1980; *A Catch of Anti-Letters*. Kansas City: Sheed, Andrews & McMeel, 1978 (letters by Merton and Robert Lax); *Geography of Holiness: The Photography of Thomas Merton*. Ed. Debra Prasad Patnaik. New York: Pilgrim Press, 1980. COLLECTIONS EDITED BY MERTON: *Breakthrough to Peace*. New York: New Directions, 1963; *Ghandi on Non-Violence*. New York: New Directions, 1965. TRANSLATIONS: Lao Tzu, *The Wisdom of the Desert*. New York: New Directions, 1960; Titus Flavius Clemens, *Clement of Alexandria*. Verona, Italy: Stamperia, Valdonega, 1962; Chuang Tzu, *The Way of Chuang Tzu*. New York: New Directions, 1965.

Works about Merton: Hart, Patrick, ed. *The Message of Thomas Merton*. Kalamazoo, Mich.: Cistercian Publishers, 1981; Kramer, Victor A. *Thomas Merton*. Boston: G. K. Hall, 1984; Labrie, Ross. *The Art of Thomas Merton*. Fort Worth: Texas Christian University Press, 1979; Lentfoehr, Therese. *Words and Silence: On the Poetry of Thomas Merton*. New York: New Directions, 1979; Mott, Michael. *The Seven Mountains of Thomas Merton*. Houghton Mifflin, 1984. CA 5–6. Cat A (1947). DLB 48. TCA.

Victor A. Kramer

WALTER M. MILLER, JR. (1923–). Walter M. Miller, Jr., is one of the most important science fiction authors in America. A classic of post–World War II science fiction, *A Canticle for Leibowitz* (1959) shows how the Catholic Church provided continuity to a world ravaged by atomic holocaust.

Miller was born in New Smyrna Beach, Florida, on January 23, 1923, and he graduated from the University of Tennessee in 1942. During World War II he served in the U.S. Army Air Corps, participating in the bombing raid on February 15, 1944, against the Abbey of Monte Cassino in Italy. In 1947, he converted to Catholicism, and in 1950, he began to write science fiction. In 1959, he revised three stories about the monks of the Albertian Order of Leibowitz into *Canticle*.

Miller's science fiction reflects his reading in Catholic literature; *Canticle*, which deals with theological and liturgical matters, also demonstrates Miller's familiarity with the lives of the Desert Fathers. In addition, it reflects his scientific studies and his experiences during the war, which showed that science and technology threaten civilization and the human race when used exclusively in the service of war. His work is of especial interest because he deals with the importance of Catholic values in an age when science and technology promote the view that the Church is irrelevant. The central theme of *Canticle* is the conflict in human life between original sin and the Redemption, and the central question is whether men can use their free will to break out of what seems to be an eternal cycle that repeats the Fall.

The first book of *Canticle*, ''Fiat Homo,'' depicts the Church as the one institution that can save both humanity and human knowledge; Rome has been destroyed, but the papacy has moved to ''New Rome'' on the American continent. At the end of the third book, when a small group leaves earth, it takes along apostolic succession, the power of the Papacy which can never be destroyed. The second book, ''Fiat Lux,'' depicts a world wherein the light of knowledge, separated from the Church, becomes diabolical. The third book, ''Fiat Voluntas Tua,'' depicts the second atomic war: ''Lucifer is fallen'' is the code for the bombing that begins it. The war causes the death of the earth, but by introducing a character with two heads, one representing man's fallen nature and the other, which awakens just as the bombs fall, representing a being of Edenic innocence which gives hope for the resurrection, Miller shows that fallen humanity can achieve redemption.

Miller's short stories include the same themes found in *Canticle*. In the most intriguing story, ''Dark Benediction'' (1951) (Collected in *Conditionally Human*, 1962), Miller treats his subject and characters with the same wit that makes *Canticle* memorable, and he includes a love story that shows that hope for the world lies in love as well as in cooperation between science and the Catholic Church. The hero of the story is Paul who, like St. Paul on the road to Damascus, undergoes a spiritual conversion. An extraterrestrial plague has spread among mankind, transmitted by ''the gray and slippery hands'' of an infected person in a gesture that recalls the biblical ''laying on of hands.'' Paul learns that the plague causes its host to have deepened sensory responses and heightened mental efficiency, and the question he must face is whether the human race is still human when people have evolved past the stage that we consider human. Although the story provides a dark vision of the breakdown of civilization, it holds out hope that the potential "benediction" of what appears to be a plague can be realized if, under the guidance of the Church and of scientists with consciences, people learn to control their evil impulses and work for the spiritual advancement of the human race. Such stories provide allegorical statements about our modern world and the place of science, religion, and love.

SELECTED BIBLIOGRAPHY

Works by Miller: *A Canticle for Leibowitz*. New York: Lippincott, 1959; *Conditionally Human*. New York: Ballantine Books, 1962; *The View from the Stars*. New York: Ballantine Books, 1965; *The Science Fiction Stories of Walter M. Miller, Jr*. Boston: Gregg Press, 1978. *The Best of Walter M. Miller, Jr*. New York: Pocket Books, 1980.

Works about Miller: Griffin, Russell M. "Medievalism in *A Canticle for Leibowitz*." *English Journal* 59 (1970), pp. 484–89; Samuelson, David N. "The Lost Canticle of Walter M. Miller, Jr." *Science Fiction Studies* 3 (1976), pp. 3–26. CA 85–88. DLB 8.

Alenandra Hennessey Olsen

JOHN MOFFITT (1908–1987). John Moffitt created a poetry of faith, hope, and love, rooted in close observation of the sensible universe and in the dual visions of Hinduism and Christianity.

Moffitt was born on June 27, 1908, in Harrisburg, Pennsylvania, and he received his A.B. in 1928 from Princeton University. He graduated from the Curtis Institute of Music in 1932 and spent twenty-five of the next thirty years as a member of the Ramakrishna order, advancing from probationer to novice in 1949 and to monk in 1959. In 1963, Moffitt became a Roman Catholic and in the same year joined the staff of *America*, where he served as poetry editor. In addition to his poetry, he wrote extensively on monasticism and was a leader in bringing East and West together in a common spiritual quest.

Though Moffitt can convey carnal passion ("Marauder") or move us with a simple elegy ("When Yama Came"), his poetry is chiefly transcendental. He creates from religions and mystical contexts, and for the mystical poet the chaotic modern world is not basically different from the world a mystical poet would have experienced in earlier times. Although his style, though modern, is not particularly innovative, it eschews fashion, and his vision is ageless and universal. Though in some poems ("The Cantata," for example) the transcendent vision seems too easily won, his better poems—whether Hindu or Christian in context—celebrate with conviction his "sense of union with the timeless creative spirit, as incarnated in time." He is at his best when, as in "Palinode," he stands humbly but with keenly observant eye before the prolific miracles of nature, striving to understand "What fathoms fathered them."

John Moffitt died of cancer on July 10, 1987, in Hershey, Pennsylvania.

SELECTED BIBLIOGRAPHY

Works by Moffitt: POETRY: *This Narrow World*. New York: Dodd, 1958; *The Living Seed*. Harcourt, Brace & World, 1962; *Adam's Choice*. Francestown, N.H.: Golden Quill, 1967; *Escape of the Leopard*. New York: Harcourt Brace Jovanovich, 1974; *Signal Message*. Francestown, N.H.: Golden Quill, 1982. NON-FICTION: *A New Charter for Monasticism* (editor and contributor). South Bend, Ind.: University of Notre Dame, 1970;

Journey to Gorakhpur. New York: Holt, 1972; *The Road to Now*. New York: Crossroad, 1982.
   Works about Moffitt: Hendon, Venable. *"Adam's Choice." America* (22 April 1968), pp. 116–598. CA 25–28. CANR 10.

                                                              Joseph H. Wessling

ALBERT J. MONTESI (1921–). With the publication of his second book, *Windows and Mirrors*, in 1977, Al Montesi found a balance between the vicious and the worshipful, between autobiography and nostalgia, between—in his words—fin de siècle and fin du race. Bound by the blood and bone of his Southern and Italian heritage, Montesi is, in the words of a student, "a cross between Truman Capote and Sylvester Stallone." His critical essays, performances, reviews (*Globe Democrat* and *Universitas*), plays for the Catholic Radio Hour, children's books, and cultural evenings at local pubs resonate with the world of the urban pioneer. Long, florid narratives echo the Southern Fugitives, his spiritual fathers, and the subject of his book-length work, *Radical Conservatism: The Southern Review (1935–1942)*. Four volumes of poems trace the texture of the man: that son of a peasant kingdom, the decadent aristocrat, the skilled textual exegete, the slum-dwelling sybarite, the religious cicerone-in-training who is cheerfully doomed to take on the "mouth chopping intellectuals" in his latest volume, *Robots and Gardens* (1985). From the rocky fields of Ancona to the Ruhr Valley, from the whores of Essen to the old boarding houses of Lafayette Square, St. Louis, Montesi storms the poetic world with his poems, punching out a slangy, streetwise portrait of the artist as an old rat—a gentled old rat.
   For nearly thirty-five years, he has been a legend at St. Louis University. Generations of students have courted Al Montesi and have immortalized him in their memoirs, letters, tributes, even novels (see John Coyne's* *The Legacy*). Recently a permanent fund of $10,000 was established at St. Louis University, the A. J. Montesi Achievement Award, given each spring to the university's most promising creative student.
   Born in Memphis, Tennessee on January 10, 1921, of Italian immigrant parents, Al Montesi attended CBC High School there, and from 1941 to 1943 served as control tower operator in the Army Air Corps. His B.A. from Northwestern and M.A. from the University of Michigan were followed by a Ph.D. from Pennsylvania State University. Montesi has taught at The Citadel, Penn State, State University of New York at Buffalo, Wesleyan, The University of Ruhr (Bochum, Germany) and St. Louis University where, since 1952, he has been on the English Department faculty. Editor (*Talisman, Twentieth Century Literature*), lecturer (Trinity University in Dublin, and Frankfurt, Germany), critic, and poet, Montesi is also one of the founders of the M-Circle, the Mississippi riverfront literary movement in St. Louis.
   In his most important volume, *Windows and Mirrors*, the poet is a St. Francis manqué, dispensing "order and tenderness" in his search for the giant-pawed father, Aleco, for "Nonno" with her "spaghetti gothic" of clothes and houses,

and for Zia Sofia who sang "Tre, sientra-tre" on radio's Italian Hour. As he moves from Memphis to the boarding houses of the Midwest, this tarnished visionary makes a restless pact with peace, hope, and love. Like the old men of Essen in another poem, he performs a charade, "not of attraction, but of neglect." Al Montesi's futuristic vision of "cement and steel capitals" is Yeatsian, but with the violent bite of a Flannery O'Connor* tinged with a bit of early T. S. Eliot.

With the spirit of Philip Larkin, he culls power—and "by degrees, some presence"—from old churches, "Pfingsten" in "Der Dom zu Munster," a focal poem in *Windows and Mirrors*. In his vision, "fitful buttresses," rounded arches and mulberry windows rise again. Gazing at the old masonry, the poet finds himself "moved to stone center," unnamed. Hope and promise are renewed by the glimpse of a plaque which contains a remnant stone from the ruins of Coventry—another cathedral destroyed by another armada in another war: "Let us forgive each other as Christ forgave us," the poet urges.

Tributes to students (Bettina, Hans, Manfred), futuristic visions ("Whiteness"), sadomasochistic battles between motorcyclists and dogs ("The Death of Literature") surround this stately monumental poem like the aggregate stones around the old cathedral. *Windows and Mirrors* blends rage and restoration, warning and graciousness. Surely Al Montesi is a master builder whose poetic hands return all readers, even the unbelieving, to the solid, broad strokes of humanity.

SELECTED BIBLIOGRAPHY

Works by Montesi: POETRY: *Micrograms*. St. Louis: Maryhurst Press, 1971; *Windows and Mirrors*. St. Louis: Cornerstone Press, 1977; *Five Dinners to Quick Lunch*, with Richard Hill. Liverpool, England: Toulouse Press, 1980; *Robots and Gardens*. St. Louis: Cornerstone Press, 1985; *Peter Bentley: The Detective Cat*. St. Louis, Nevertheless Press, 1986; *Poems Sweet and Sour*, with Richard Hill. St. Louis: Cornerstone Press, 1986. Criticism: *Radical Conservatism: The Southern Review (1935–1942)*. PLAYS: Montesi has written four plays, one of which, *Sidestep*, was produced in St. Louis.

Works about Montesi: "Authentic Reflections." *St. Louis Post-Dispatch* (25 September 1977); Jablonsky, B. "Montesi, I Heard You Been out on the Streets." *The University News* (19 November 1979); "Poems by Al Montesi: A Portrait of the Poet As Old Rat," *Saint Louis Literary Supplement* I, (November/December 1977). CA 37–40.

Mary Lynn Broe

BRIAN MOORE (1921–). Brian Moore's childhood and adolescence in the Roman Catholic community of Belfast, Northern Ireland, and his subsequent relocations to Europe, Canada, and the United States provide the themes and settings for his fiction. The harsh nature of the church of his youth in particular had a profound impact on his imagination. Moore's stirring characterizations depict individuals, often ordinary people from the Old World or the New, who are facing a moment of crisis in their lives, as the overwhelming importance of their past thrusts itself into the present. His well-paced and compelling stories are written in sparse, lucid prose, although the resolution of his character's confrontation is not always clear, and his consistent adherence to the traditional conventions of narrative realism frequently produces "flat" characters involved in melodramatic plots.

Moore, one of the nine children of James Brian and Eileen McFadden Moore, was born on August 25, 1921. In 1940 he left St. Malachy's College for military service and other employment in several European cities; in 1948, he emigrated to Canada. During these years, he worked as a proofreader, a reporter, and a writer of pulp fiction. *Judith Hearne*, his first novel and, according to some critics, his best, was published in 1955. Awarded a Guggenheim Fellowship in 1959, he moved to New York, and although he retains his Canadian citizenship, he resides in Malibu, California, with his wife, Jean Denny, whom he married in 1966. Other awards are the Author's Club first novel award, 1956; the Quebec Literary Prize, 1958; the Governor General's Award for Fiction, 1960; the National Institute of Arts and Letters fiction grant, 1961; the Canada Council fellowship for travel in Europe, 1962; the W. H. Smith Literary Award, 1972; and the James Tait Black Memorial Award, 1975.

For several of his own works he has written screenplays as well as the screenplay for Alfred Hitchcock's *Torn Curtain* (1966). In addition to film work, short stories, and numerous contributions to periodicals, he teaches a weekly writing course at the University of California at Los Angeles. His non-fiction books include *Canada* (with the editors of Life), Time-Life, 1963 and *The Revolution Script*, Holt, 1971.

Moore's belief in the primary importance of the past, especially the familial past, relates to the contemporary anguish over individual identity and the meaning of human existence. Moore states, in an interview for the *National Catholic Reporter*, that many of his books "deal with the point in people's lives when what they believed in is taken away." When this event occurs, no matter what the gender, setting, or time, Moore's protagonists totter on the brink of failure. Parental relationships and the religion of parents lie at the base of these conflicts; as the writer-hero of *Fergus* (1970) remarks, "parents form the grammar of our emotions." When confronted with their illusions, Moore's first two protagonists, Judith Hearne and Diarmuid Devine, fail utterly to face the implications of their discoveries. By contrast, in *The Emperor of Ice-Cream* (1965), a coming-of-age novel whose title and structure rely on the poetry of Wallace Stevens, the young Gavin Burke distinguishes the real from the unreal and arranges his life accordingly.

The conclusions of several of Moore's novels, however, remain ambiguous. At the end of *Catholics* (1972), for instance, a novel about a future Catholic Church more concerned about world unity and social service than about the existence of a transcendental deity, readers may wonder whether the loving abbot of Muck is merely facing a dark night of the soul or whether he is heroically accepting what he fears to be the truth about the emptiness of the tabernacle. In addition to the problematic endings, the strategies of conventional realism do not always work in Moore's stories. The unconscious drives of some of his characters are often hazy because of too many trivial details about trips and reservations. Thus, in *The Doctor's Wife* (1976), the persistent descriptions of the superficial activities of Shelia Redden obscure the true motives for her sudden erotic behavior.

Central to all Moore's fiction, either directly or indirectly, is the activity of the artist. Several of his protagonists are writers or artists themselves. These characters experience certain artistic pitfalls, events such as the punitive restrictions that religion and family can place on the creative imagination as well as the temptation of the artist to compromise his integrity in order to ensure commercial success. In Moore's own life the restrictions imposed by his Roman Catholic background were graduallly rejected in favor of the supremacy of his own imagination. In this substitution of art for religion, he was heavily influenced by James Joyce.

A self-labelled agnostic, Moore nevertheless continues, as he says, "to wonder about" the existence of God. In *Cold Heaven* (1983) he considers the shabbiness that surrounds miraculous visions and an individual's freedom to reject such events. In *Black Robe* (1985) he depicts the crisis of faith in a seventeenth-century French missionary to the Indians of Canada. No longer certain of his religious beliefs, the priest nonetheless is finally able to utter "a true prayer," because he has learned to love the "Savages." Paradoxically, he, and perhaps his creator as well, has attained spiritual growth through negation.

SELECTED BIBLIOGRAPHY

Works by Moore: NOVELS: *Judith Hearne*. New Orleans, La.: Collins, 1955, published as *The Lonely Passion of Judith Hearne*. Boston: Little, Brown & Co., 1956, rep. 1978; *The Feast of Lupercal*. Boston: Little, Brown & Co., 1957; *The Luck of Ginger Coffey*. Boston: Little, Brown & Co., 1960; *An Answer from Limbo*. Boston: Little, Brown & Co., 1962; *The Emperor of Ice-Cream*. New York: Viking Press, 1965; *I Am Mary Dunne*. New York: Viking Press, 1968; *Fergus*. New York: Holt, 1970; *Catholics*. J. Cape, 1972, New York: Harcourt, 1973; *The Great Victorian Collection*. New York: Farrar, Straus & Giroux, 1975; *The Doctor's Wife*. New York: Farrar, Straus & Giroux, 1976; *The Mangan Inheritance*. New York: Farrar, Straus & Giroux, 1979; *The Temptation of Eileen Hughes*. New York: Farrar, Straus & Giroux, 1981; *Cold Heaven*. New York: Holt, 1983; *Black Robe*. New York: Dutton, 1985; *The Color of Blood*. New York: Dutton, 1987.

Works about Moore: Flood, Jeanne A. *Brian Moore*. The Irish Writer Series. Lewisburg: Bucknell University Press, 1974; Flood, Jeanne A. "*The Doctor's Wife*: Brian Moore and the Failure of Realism." *Eire-Ireland*. 18, 2 (1983), pp. 80–102; McSweeney, Kerry. *Four Contemporary Novelists: Angus Wilson, Brian Moore, John Fowles, V. S. Naipaul*. Montreal: McGill-Queens University Press, 1983, pp. 56–99. CA 2. CANR 1. CN.

Anne Keeler McBride

JULIAN LANE MOYNAHAN (1925–). Julian Lane Moynahan, a master of style, writes in the tradition of Saul Bellow and Anthony Burgess, and can be compared to the earlier Evelyn Waugh or Anthony Powell. He is a distinguished literary scholar who has published important studies on stylistics and on the works of Charles Dickens, D. H. Lawrence, Vladimir Nabokov, and Thomas Hardy; he has written essays and reviews for *The Observer*, *New York Times Book Review*, *The New Statesman*, *The Washington Post*, *Modern Fiction*, *English Literary History*, and other periodicals. He also wrote poetry until 1960 when he was so taken aback at being asked to record some of his work for the Harvard Vocarium Archives of Contemporary Poets that he gave up poetry altogether. He has five novels, all diverse, but all characterized by an underlying contempt for hypocrisy and an appreciation for truth no matter how shocking or how unconventional. He is interested in human psychology and human interaction, the way people use and abuse each other, the way they support and lend credence to each other. His novels incorporate the tragic and the comic, the witty and the heartrending, and, overriding all, an awareness of the absurd. While looking at turning points in the lives of individuals, Moynahan captures the social, political, and human climate and is most perceptive in his depiction of parent-child and sibling relationships. His works reflect the values he enunciates in his introduction to *The Deed of Life* (1963): they illuminate "the muddle of the human condition," are animated by "deep insight into human behavior and into the workings of society," and face the really difficult problems of life and death "in the terms of common life" and in "the strange texture of human experience" (pp. xiii, xxi).

Born in Cambridge, Massachusetts, on May 21, 1925, the son of salesman Joseph Leo and Mary Moynahan, Julian Moynahan is a professional scholar, writer, and university professor. Like the protagonist of *Pairing Off* (1969), he worked as Russian cataloguer in a library, was an intermittent student, and, as the Morrow book jacket notes, was an occasional layabout. After marrying Elizabeth Reilly, a noted architect, on August 6, 1945, he settled down to serious efforts at Harvard University, from which institution he received an A.B. in 1947, an A.M. in 1951, and a Ph.D. in 1957. He began his teaching career as an instructor in English at Amherst College (1953–1955) and then as asssitant professor and later bicentennial preceptor at Princeton (1955–1963). After a Fulbright to University College, Dublin, Moynahan joined the faculty of Rutgers University, where he is currently a full professor, though he occasionally takes leave to act as a visiting professor or visiting scholar to other universities. He has received numerous awards for scholarship, including the American Council of Learned Societies grant-in-aid, the Fulbright-Hays award, the American Philosophical Society grant, the National Endowment for the Arts sabbatical leave award, a Rutgers Research Council faculty fellowship, the Ingram-Merrill Foundation award, and the National Endowment for the Humanities award. Moynahan has three daughters and currently resides with his family in Princeton, New Jersey.

His first novel, *Sisters and Brothers* (1960), is a depression era story in which the disintegration of a family necessitates boarding the two sons, aged six and eight, at a Catholic institute for boys, mainly orphans. It is a scathing denunciation of the cruelty and viciousness of nuns who take advantage of their position to inflict their own warped sensibilities on those too innocent, too young, and too naive to fight back effectively. Its third-person narrative follows the experiences, perceptions, and psychological transformation of the two boys as they learn firsthand about hypocrisy, puritanism, and hatred. Moynahan explores simple truths and asks probing questions through the fresh and guileless eyes of children whose traumatic experiences make them wise beyond their years. The nuns of Moynahan's story opt for profit over providing healthy exercise, fresh produce, and a potential livelihood for their charges, and they thrive on rich food while the children under them languish on thin gruel and moldy bread. Their public appearances and propaganda brochures create the illusion of beatific devotion, while their reality is a sadistic obsession with discipline and punishment—projecting on the children the nuns' own adult motivations and weaknesses, beating them with rubber truncheons, playing on their fears and guilt, and dressing them like girls to alienate them from their peers. Stackpole, a perceptive rebel for whom the institute is a prison worth any amount of suffering to escape, denounces all nuns as proud, arrogant, and self-convinced of their superiority, and concludes that heaven and hell are lies and that the nuns like everyone else will end up "in a dark hole . . . —soul and body—with icy water coming down" (p. 118). Moynahan's final attack is made through the shocked and angry mother, who finds her youngest son nearly dead from a severe head wound which an embittered nun perversely ignored and who thereafter learns that her eldest son has been severely beaten and the younger one labelled "pathological" and "psychotic" for sharing his fantasy dreams with others. She takes her sons away, but the reader is left with disturbing concerns: How many other mothers, hearing of the cruelty of the order, would still blind themselves to its reality, as did this mother, for the sake of financial expediency? What about the orphans like Stackpole who had no mother to speak up for them?

Moynahan's second novel, *Pairing Off*, received much critical acclaim for its verbal brilliance and sardonic wit; "farcical and verbally brilliant" (Thomas Dowling); "devastatingly witty," "highly intelligent," and "very accurate" (Alison Buriel); "the perfect Moynahan cocktail, Bourbon and Irish, with a dash of hysterica passio, scattered with ashes of Roses and the Past, and a drop of eternal Celtic sorrow, brewed in heaven and matured in hell, and drunk to soft, sad music out of the western isles" (Sean O'Faolain). It is a funny, erudite, virtuoso performance. Its hero, Myles McCormick, is a randy librarian who spends his days cataloguing books in odd alphabets, fantasizing about various relationships pursued in and out of the stacks, and trying to come to terms with such stark realities as death and suffering and personal identity. Like Thomas Pynchon's *The Crying of Lot 49*, it is a compelling mixture of black humor, philosophical musing, and absurdist images. McCormick's normal devil-may-care life-style is broken when he discovers that his latest flame is dying of cancer and that their relationship is only a "stumbling in the dark . . . , each exploiting the other's warmth as a meagre substitute for a bed and a fire." As he helps her through her final hours, he searches for clues to his own ancestry, takes on the responsibility of her half brother, and begins a relationship that leads ultimately to self-acceptance and a deeper love relationship, the "pairing off" of the title.

Garden State (1973) makes a bid for preserving trees and race relationships in the urban wasteland of New Jersey. Its protagonist, Howard Butler, is a man adrift in the materialism and boredom of suburban life. Alienated from wife and daughter and self, on the verge of perpetual drunkenness, he tries to bury himself in his tree farm, but, when a major pharmaceutical corporation determines his property is vital to the new research complex they are trying to railroad through the local city government, he is forced to decide about his life and his relationship to the land, to his community, and to his fellows. The corporation's scheme to take over 200 acres designated for a community park, using bribes, donations, and kickbacks to assure support, is cynically conceived and ecologically destructive. Butler, lured by large sums, at first acquiesces, but when his failed employee and drinking companion commits suicide, his would-be black mistress appeals to him for help amid the racial turmoil of her Newark community, and his estranged daughter confides in him for the first time, he takes a long look at his life, decides corporations "lack brains, hearts, and other organs and faculties possessed by moral beings" (p. 261), and he exposes the corporation's underhanded illegalities at a public meeting to rezone the park land. He returns to his wife and family a new man—one whose values and sense of self have been confirmed by error.

Critics praise Moynahan's fourth novel, *Where the Land and Water Meet* (1979), for its beautiful writing, innovative narrative, rich portrayal of the American persona in charge and comic balance between innocence and wickedness. It is told by the younger boy from *Sisters and Brothers*, Irish-American Felix "Lefty" Murray, at the point of his coming of age the summer of his sixteenth year, as he gets his first real jobs, tries his first drink, lives independently for the first time, attempts his first sexual encounter, and tries to come to intellectual and emotional terms with both the world at large and the lesser world of family and friends (alcoholic father; alienated brother; precocious sister; plucky, resourceful, and unforgiving mother; and best friend, his companion in his voyage of discovery). Set in the suburbs and coastal towns of Greater Boston amid the poverty and despair of pre-war years, it is a novel of maturation as Felix gradually gives up his idealism and illusions and learns to look more realistically and with greater understanding at the world around him. Moynahan is a master at convincingly capturing the thoughts, conflicts, interests, fantasies, and circumlocutions of the teenage male mind. His narrative voice follows the diary, letters, and notes of sixteen-year-old Felix, but is interspersed with memories from childhood and with the more mature recollections of the older, adult Felix testing out his teenage interpretations of people and events. The hopes and dreams of youth, the petty conflicts and childish pranks, the growing awareness of the hypocrisy and viciousness of man as well as his kindness and goodwill are humorously and sympathetically rendered. Felix asks what it all means and concludes that there is "no message out there to be gleaned, either from beneath or above the stars," that the "bald, unvarnished truth" is always "a big disappointment," and that being "conned" and "suckered" is just a natural part of life (p. 243). "Desire is endless, satisfaction is in short supply," quips Felix's best friend Ace as the two boys embark on their homeward journey, their journey into adulthood (p. 287).

Moynahan is a master of humorous and convincing description and dialogue, much of which is satiric or barbed. A militarist—who thinks FDR a traitor, Truman soft on communism, and McCarthy misguided but an old-fashioned patriot—responds to the ejaculation " 'Jesus Christ' " with " 'Sir!' Although he personally preached a form of creeping socialism, wiser heads prevailed in later times and made his religion suitable to the ideals of old-fashioned Hamiltonian republicanism" (p. 132). Another character, musing on the sort of heaven Yankee tycoons go to, adds "plastered saints" and "Jesuits with poison rings" to his girlfriend's description of Irish Catholic heaven as "tinselled Infant Saviours from Prague and a lot of Bishops and Popes riding around in litters with their girlfriends fanning them. And the whole place stinking of incense" (p. 98). Librarian McCormick, enumerating *ad infinitum* the tedious steps involved in preparing a new collection for public display, including "descending to such niceties as 'signatures,' 'foxing,' 'colophons,' 'water marks,' and 'chain lines' where unavoidable" and entering "into correspondence with several dozen university pedants on bibliographical fine points," concludes that, to assure its popularity with the public, "he, or rather the unfortunate person who would take the job over in a few months, if all went well, had to compose the printed bibliography, climb up on the roof, and leap five floors down, head first, into the courtyard fountain" (pp. 54–55). With Moynahan always beneath the humor is a moral outrage at blind allegiance, smug hypocrisy, and unrelenting materialism. His values are humanistic. For him the true heroes of modern life are those weak and muddled humans who learn to face themselves and their world honestly, no matter how bleak the reality, who take their fate in their own hands and act with resourcefulness and tenacity to battle indifference and inhumanity, and who ultimately learn to care about others.

SELECTED BIBLIOGRAPHY

Works by Moynahan: NOVELS: *Sisters and Brothers*. New York: Random House, 1960; *Pairing Off*. New York: Morrow, 1969; *Garden State*. Boston: Little, Brown & Co., 1973; *Where the Land and Water Meet*. New York: Morrow, 1979. NON-FICTION: *The Deed of Life: The Novels and Shorter Fiction of D. H. Lawrence*. Princeton, N.J.: Princeton University Press, 1963; *Vladimir Nabokov*. Minneapolis, Minn.: University of Minnesota Press, 1971.

Works about Moynahan: Bloom, Edward. "Hermeneutic Hesitation: A Dialogue between Geoffrey Hartman and Julian Moynahan." *Novel: A Forum of Fiction* 12 (1979), pp. 102–12; Spilka, Mark; Price, Martin; Moynahan, Julian. "Character As a Lost Cause." *Novel: A Forum on Fiction* 11 (1978), pp. 197–219. CA 2. CANR 1.

Gina Macdonald

N

JOHN FREDERICK NIMS (1913–). In the foreword to his *Selected Poems* (1982), John Frederick Nims wrote, "Form is what I thought poems came into the world with, as plants and animals do." He is not one to use the word "form" loosely; its properties include symmetry, isotropy, harmony, or, in the case of poetry, meter, and rhyme. Nims has been characterized as a formal poet who has survived years in which such formality was more than a little unpopular. But his engagement with form cuts through the surface characteristics of his poetry. It is the engagement of a man who has developed his spiritual nature without losing sight of the gritty exteriors of modern life. In addition, Nims is among our most learned critics and translators. His urban vision attaches itself to tradition, a fact which caused him to call one early collection of poems *The Iron Pastoral* (1947). As an editor of *Poetry*, an educator, and an author of one of the best recent poetry textbooks, *Western Wind* (2nd Edition, 1983), Nims has had a quiet but pervasive influence on contemporary poetry. Yet it is as a poet, translator, and essayist that Nims chiefly demands to be known.

Born in Muskegon, Michigan, on November 20, 1913, Nims attended the University of Notre Dame, where he received his A.B. in 1937 and his M.A. in 1939. After earning his Ph.D. from the University of Chicago in 1945, Nims Married Bonnie Larkin and fathered five children, one of whom died at an early age. Nims has taught at numerous universities, and has spent a good portion of the 1950s teaching in Milan, Florence, and Madrid. From 1965 until his retirement, he taught at the University of Illinois at Chicago Circle.

Though not a devotional poet, Nims has always been associated with literature of Catholic experience. He was one of the earliest and most perceptive critics of Thomas Merton* and Robert Lowell*, placing them succinctly in the tradition of religious poetry:

Because of the immanence and transcendence of religious experience and because it must be expressed, if at all, in a language implemented for quite different functions, genuine religious poetry is rare and difficult. ("Two Catholic Poets," 255)

While praising the "tension" and "conflict" in Lowell's work, Nims quickly and shrewdly perceived Lowell's weaknesses: "There is an emphasis on detail at the expense of total effect: too often the verse seems imbricated rather than cellular. The very brilliance of technique is a distraction." From these passages it is possible to pinpoint not only Nims' acuity as a critic—which he has brought to bear on a wide variety of subjects—but his poetic concerns as well. The spiritual, even the specifically religious has a place in his poetry, yet he uses "a language implemented for quite different functions," cognizant of strip joints, train wrecks, and girlie magazines, of both Latinate elegance and urban slang. And there is, in his best work anyway, an effort to write whole poems, not merely brilliant phrases or lines.

If his poetic voice has changed at all in forty years, it is difficult to say precisely why or how. Some early works (even a few omitted from his *Selected Poems*) speak with as much skilled irony as his more recent collection of epigrams, *Of Flesh and Bone* (1967). From *Five Young American Poets* (1944), his "Scherzo: Writers' Conference" shows a talent for satire that has never left him (in this he somewhat resembles J. V. Cunningham*). In addition, Nims has always displayed a preoccupation with the great themes, love and death, in their most ironic correspondences. Nims' faith is apparently stronger than Cunningham's because, in his poetry at least, death is both a hard fact and an assurance. "Evergreen," his most beautiful elegy for the son who died in infancy, hints that the destination of the dead is not oblivion, but pleasure. "The Masque of Blackness," his sonnet sequence on the same subject, suggests a darker prospect: "No millenium/Here."

Nims has done a famous translation of St. John of the Cross, and his own work can sometimes seem a toning down of that poet's anguished sensuality; he observes the prospects of various living hells, but, outside his moving elegies, he seems not to feel them. He is tremendously good at catching the *haecceity* of ironic love. Love is his subject, and the fact of death forces him to be an ironist.

Nims is a deft practitioner whose poems are worked out with mathematical precision. He brings the same precision and formal dedication to the art of translation. He may not be our most exuberant translator, but he is certainly among our most assiduous. In an important essay, "Poetry: Lost in Translation?" (*Sappho to Valery*, 1971) he calls on translators to be poets, to make new English poems rather than productions that are accurate but lifeless. He makes this demand without sacrificing his dedication to the originals; he has worked from at least six languages, and on occasion he has been successful at matching the original sounds with English cadences.

While not, perhaps, a major poet, Nims is a writer of broad accomplishment who offers poems of survival and humor, as well as of modern observation. He has educated us in the formal rigors of the art and in the vocation of translation. The handful of his best poems deserve a place in the anthologies of our time.

SELECTED BIBLIOGRAPHY

Works by Nims: BOOKS: *Five Young American Poets*, by Nims and others. Norfolk, Conn.: New Directions, 1944; *The Iron Pastoral*. New York: Sloane, 1947; *A Fountain in Kentucky and Other Poems*. New York: Sloane, 1950; *Knowledge of the Evening: Poems 1950–1960*. New Brunswick, N.J.: Rutgers University Press, 1960; *Of Flesh and Bone*. New Brunswick, N.J.: Rutgers University Press, 1967; *The Kiss: A Jambalaya*. Chicago: University of Chicago Press, 1982; *Selected Poems*. Chicago: University of Chicago Press, 1982; *A Local Habitation: Essays on Poetry*. Ann Arbor: University of Michigan Press, 1985. TRANSLATIONS: *The Poems of St. John of The Cross*. New York: Grove Press, 1959; *Andromache*. In *The Complete Greek Tragedies, Euripides III*. Ed. David Grene and Richmond Lattimore. Chicago: University of Chicago Press, 1959; *Sappho to Valéry: Poems in Translation*. New Brunswick, N.J.: Rutgers University Press, 1971, rev. ed. Princeton, N.J.: Princeton University Press, 1979.

ADDITIONAL ESSAYS: "Two Catholic Poets." *Poetry*. (February 1945), pp. 264–68; "Dedalus in Crete." In *Dedalus on Crete: Essays on the Implications of Joyce's Portrait*. Los Angeles: Saint Thomas More Guild, 1956; "Yeats and the Careless Muse." In *Learners and Discerners: A Newer Criticism*. Ed. Robert Scholes. Charlottesville: University Press of Virginia, 1964; "The Poetry of Sylvia Plath: A Technical Analysis." In *The Art of Sylvia Plath: A Symposium*. Ed. Charles Newman. Bloomington: Indiana University Press, 1970.

Works about Nims: Blackmur, R. P. Review of *Five Young American Poets*. *Kenyon Review* (Spring 1945), pp. 339–52; Ciardi, John. "John Frederick Nims and the Modern Idiom." *University of Kansas City Review* (Winter 1947), pp. 105–10; Shaw, Richard O. "Sanctity and the Poetry of John F. Nims." *Renascence* (Autumn 1960), pp. 84–91; Wilbur, Richard. Review of *A Fountain in Kentucky and Other Poems*. *Poetry* (November 1950), pp. 105–7. CA 15–16. CANR 6. Cat A (1952). DLB 5. TCA.

David Mason

O

JOYCE CAROL OATES (1938–). In her recent book, *On Boxing* (1987), Joyce Carol Oates argues, with plenty of blunt, statistical, gory evidence, that boxing is not a metaphor—boxing is boxing. People love to fight, love to bet on fighting, love to watch fighting. *On Boxing* is not a fiction; it is an American truth. The "very long" essay is, perhaps, a relatively new form for Oates, although she is no stranger to non-fiction. It is, perhaps, most accurate to say that she is no stranger to any literary pursuit, having written well in every genre imaginable, including an absurdist play and film criticism. To say she is prolific does not completely account for her multiple, yearly publications and her intense critical involvement in American letters. Oates has won many awards for her work, among them a National Book Award for *them* (1969), several O. Henry Awards, and an election to the National Academy and Institute of Arts and Letters.

Once called the dark lady of American letters, Oates creates protagonists who struggle to escape their fates and their worlds, but succeed only through death or madness. Oates might also be called a realist, a naturalist, a feminist, a Catholic allegorist, or even a moralist, eager to convince her audiences that the isolated self is an impossibility; living's chiefest virtue is in recognizing that humanity is bonded together in a universe it cannot ignore or control. In an essay on Sylvia Plath, Oates says "tragedy is cultural, mysteriously enlarging the individual so that what he has experienced is both what we have experienced and what we need not experience—because of his, or her private agony" (*Southern Review* 501–2). To catalogue the violent, the grotesque, or the bizarre events in Oates' fiction is a favorite pastime of critics, but such cataloguing ignores one of her crucial purposes in composing: to encourage human reciprocity.

Joyce Carol Oates was born on June 16, 1938, in rural Lockport, New York, to an Irish-Catholic working-class family. She graduated Phi Beta Kappa in 1960 from Syracuse University with a B.A. in English and earned an M.A. in 1961 from the University of Wisconsin. Oates taught English at the University of Detroit for six years, a period encompassing the race riots that she documented in *them*. The University of Windsor in Ontario employed Oates and her husband Raymond J. Smith, from 1967 to 1977; both taught literature. They now live in Princeton, New Jersey, where Oates is writer-in-residence at Princeton University.

In a lecture given at Claremont College in October 1986, Joyce Carol Oates argued that the "happiest people are amateurs, because when you get serious, when your work becomes important, it becomes your arena of competition . . . writing has [for me] become that arena, that brightly lit ring." She also spoke of writing novels that almost killed her, of her need during her career to insist that she was not a woman writer, but a writer.

There is little doubt that Joyce Carol Oates is a consummate professional, a writer whose craft and art are a way of life for her. That that life is a demanding one is evidenced by the quality and breadth of her fiction.

Some critics have argued that Oates' best work is found in her short stories. One of her most anthologized stories, "Where Are You Going, Where Have You Been," is a typically powerful, haunting piece of short fiction. An almost allegorical "seduction of Eve" tale, this story chronicles the encounter between demon-lover Arnold Friend and Connie, an adolescent on the brink of young womanhood, who craves excitement, who flirts with promiscuity. This story's bleak ending—Connie is seduced, lost—was not retained in the PBS film version called "Smooth Talk"; instead, Connie returned to and was comforted by her family, an ending probably deemed necessary to make the story more palatable for mass audience. Indeed, many of Oates' fictions are not particularly palatable. Rather, they are disturbing, carefully wrought visions of characters who do not fit in their worlds.

Another of Oates' best-known short stories, "In the Region of Ice," reveals the turmoil resulting when a nun, Sister Irene, is confronted by a university student who demands more than Irene is comfortable giving. When his need is greatest, Irene refuses to relinquish her isolation, confirming she is a dweller in the region of emotional ice, shutting herself off from reciprocity. Oates' selection of religious protagonists in this and several other stories, is not, however, crucially significant; more important is their human nature, which everyone in our species shares, and which, in Oates' world, means a tendency to deny the interconnectedness of all things. Of course, religious characters *are* often isolated from humanity by design, making them likely subjects.

When asked by a *Writers at Work* interviewer if there was a religious basis to her work, Oates responded:

I have beliefs, of course, like everyone—but I don't always believe in them. Faith comes and goes. God diffracts into a bewildering plentitude of elements—the environment, love, friends, and family, career, profession, "fate," biochemical harmony or disharmony, whether the sky is slate-gray or a bright mesmerizing blue. These elements then coalesce again into something seemingly unified. But it's a human predilection, isn't it?—our tendency to see, and to wish to see, what we've projected outward upon the universe from our own souls? (*Writers at Work* 375)

Oates has written an entire novel, *Son of the Morning* (1978), that she herself calls a prayer, because it is a first-person narration by a man addressing himself, throughout, to God. Therefore, in this novel Oates calls her ideal reader God; everyone else, including Oates, is secondary (*Writers at Work*, 375). Nathanael Vickry, the pentecostal preacher in *Son of Morning*, who rises and falls from near deification, displays an overt concern with religion not evidenced since Oates' first novel, *With Shuddering Fall* (1964).

In *With Shuddering Fall* Oates establishes a writing style rich in detail, portraying life as a nineteenth-century novelist might. Indeed her writing was in this novel, and continues to be, extraordinarily powerful. When she is most successful, the reader is swept into the consciousness of the character, suffering with him or her, and comes to a realization of the greater life force of which we are all a part.

With Shuddering Fall is an initiation story where a virginal, religious girl, Karen, leaves her godlike father, Herz, for a violent young man, Shar. Karen discovers she has left her identity behind as well, and after enduring rape, beatings, and Shar's suicide, she returns, recognizing the value of place and family and rejecting freedom.

All of Oates' subsequent novels, including the National Book Award winner, *them*, describe her characters' attempts to escape their worlds, only to learn real freedom exists in connectedness. The violence of *them* is not just the sociological upheaval of a race riot, but a life rhythm. In such a dangerous universe, freedom creates vulnerability. The characters in *them* begin to find peace only when they begin to search for association and union.

Although much of Oates' work is thematically similar, her later fiction reveals an evolution of form and an interest in the novel as an aesthetic object. For example, the characters in *The Assassins: A Book of Hours* (1975) are revealed through a series of separate streams of consciousness, each character isolated from his fellows, just as the book is a series of isolated sections. In *Childwold* (1976) the characters' voices are manipulated and shifted to represent successive generations, a formal imitation of the book's theme: all humanity is subject to temporal change; we cannot isolate ourselves from the evolution of our world.

Bellefleur (1980), *A Bloodsmoor Romance*, (1983), *Mysteries of Winterthurn*, (1984), *Solstice* (1985), and *Marya: A Life* (1986) are representative (though not inclusive) of Oates' fiction during the last six years. Her themes are consistent, but she has become increasingly fascinated with the gothic and the fantastic; her latest books might legitimately be called twentieth-century gothic, and as such, have earned her best-seller status and a wider reading public. Her critical essays and books have variously explored tragedy, the visionary experience in literature, and feminism. Her witty, readable essays and reviews reveal a broad knowledge of literature, philosophy, and psychology. And she is a most competent, even moving, poet and playwright. It is not unreasonable to predict that Joyce Carol Oates will continue to be an influential presence in American letters for some time to come. Her moral vision of humanity—placed in a world it cannot transcend, but must reconcile through union with one's fellows—is her fictional (and non-fictional) obsession.

SELECTED BIBLIOGRAPHY

Works by Oates: NOVELS: *With Shuddering Fall*. New York: Vanguard, 1964; *A Garden of Earthly Delights*. New York: Vanguard, 1967; *Expensive People*. New York: Vanguard, 1968; *them*. New York: Vanguard, 1969; *Wonderland*. New York: Vanguard, 1971, Greenwich, Conn.: Fawcett, 1973, with rev. ending; *Do With Me What You Will*. New York: Vanguard, 1973; *The Assassins: A Book of Hours*. New York: Vanguard, 1975; *Childwold*. New York: Vanguard, 1976; *The Triumph of the Spider Monkey*. Santa Barbara, Calif.: Black Sparrow Press, 1976; *Son of the Morning*. New York: Vanguard, 1978; *Unholy Loves*. New York: Vanguard, 1979; *Bellefleur*. New York: E. P. Dutton, 1980; *A Bloodsmoor Romance*. New York: Warner Books, 1983; *Mysteries of Winterthurn*. New York: Berkley Publishing, 1985; *Solstice*. New York: E. P. Dutton, 1985; *Marya: A Life*. New York: E. P. Dutton, 1986; *You Must Remember This*. New York: E. P. Dutton, 1987; *American Appetites*. New York: E. P. Dutton, 1989. COLLECTED SHORT STORIES: *By the North Gate*. New York: Vanguard, 1963; *Upon the Sweeping Flood*. New York: Vanguard, 1966; *The Wheel of Love*. New York: Vanguard, 1970; *Marriages and Infidelities*. New York: Vanguard, 1972; *The Goddess and Other Women*. New York: Vanguard, 1974; *The Hungry Ghosts: Seven Allusive Comedies*. Los Angeles: Black Sparrow Press, 1974; *The Poisoned Kiss and Other Stories from the Portugese*. New York: Vanguard, 1975; *The Seduction and Other Stories*. Los Angeles: Black Sparrow Press, 1975; *Crossing the Border*. New York: Vanguard, 1976; *Night-Side*. New York: Vanguard, 1977; *All the Good People I've Left Behind*. Santa Barbara, Calif.: Black Sparrow Press, 1979; *A Sentimental Education*. New York: E. P. Dutton, 1982; *Last Days: Stories*. New York: E. P. Dutton, 1984; *Raven's Wing: Stories*. New York: E. P. Dutton, 1986. POETRY: *Women in Love and Other Poems*. New York: Albondacani Press, 1968; *Anonymous Sins and Other Poems*. Baton Rouge: Louisiana State University Press, 1969; *Love and Its Derangements*. Baton Rouge: Louisiana State University Press, 1970; *In Case of Accidental Death*. Cambridge, Mass.: Pomegranate Press, 1972; *Wooded Forms*. New York: Albondacani Press, 1972, single poem; *Angel Fire*. Baton Rouge: Louisiana State University Press, 1973; *Dreaming America and Other Poems*. n.p.: Aloe Editions, 1973; *A Posthumous Sketch*. Los Angeles: Black Sparrow Press, 1973; *The Fabulous Beasts*. Baton Rouge: Louisiana State University Press, 1975; *Women Whose Lives Are Food, Men Whose Lives Are Money*. Baton Rouge: Louisiana State University Press, 1978. OTHER FICTION: *Scenes from American Life: Contemporary Short Fiction*, ed. Oates. New York: Random House, 1973; "The Death Throes of Romanticism: The Poems of Sylvia Plath." *Southern Review* (Summer, 1973), pp. 501–22; *Miracle Play*. Los Angeles: Black Sparrow Press, 1974; *Three Plays*. Ontario Review, 1980. CRITICAL BOOKS AND ARTICLES: *The Edge of Impossibility: Tragic Forms in Literature*. New York: Vanguard, 1972; *The Hostile Sun: The Poetry of D. H. Lawrence*. Los Angeles: Black Sparrow Press, 1973; *New Heaven, New Earth: The Visionary Experience in Literature*. New York: Vanguard, 1974; *Contraries: Essays*. New York: Oxford University Press, 1981; *The Profane Art: Essays and Reviews*. New York: E. P. Dutton, 1983.

Works about Oates: Bibliographies: Catron, Douglas M. "A Contribution to a Bibliography of Works by and about Joyce Carol Oates." *American Literature* 49 (1977), pp. 399–414; McCormick, Lucienne P. "A Bibliography of Works by and about Joyce Carol Oates." *American Literature* 43 (1971), pp. 124–32. Critical studies: Creighton, Joanne. *Joyce Carol Oates*. Boston: G. K. Hall (Twayne), 1979; Friedman, Ellen G. *Joyce Carol Oates*. New York: Ungar Publishing Co., 1980; Grant, Mary Kathryn, R.S.M. *The Tragic Vision of Joyce Carol Oates*. Durham, N.C.: Duke University Press, 1978; Plimpton, George, ed. *Writers at Work*: The Pane Review Interviews New York: Viking Press, 1981; Wagner, Linda W., ed. *Critical Essays on Joyce Carol Oates*. Boston: G. K. Hall & Co., 1979; Waller, Gary F. *Dreaming America: Obsession and Transcendence in the Fiction of Joyce Carol Oates*. Baton Rouge: Louisiana State University Press, 1978. AWS pt. 2. AWW. CA7–8. CN. DLB 2, 5.

Linda Bannister

TIM O'BRIEN (1946–). Tim O'Brien's novel, *The Nuclear Age* (1985), is a departure of sorts from his earlier work which depicts the experience of American soldiers in and after the Vietnam War. In *If I Die in the Combat Zone* (1973), O'Brien chronicles his own observations as a combat soldier in Vietnam, and in *Going after Cacciato* (1978), his second novel, he explores the war experience through the thoughts and dreams of a soldier who embarks on an imaginative quest to make sense out of the Vietnam ordeal. O'Brien's first novel, *Northern Lights* (1975), portrays the intense rivalry of two brothers (one a wounded Vietnam veteran) as they struggle to understand the nature of courage and to forge a way to live by their discoveries.

In *The Nuclear Age* O'Brien's focus is on the nuclear peril, and with it he gives us the story of a man struggling to come to grips with our precarious existence overshadowed with the threat of nuclear annihilation. His hero's fears and frustrations, which surface in a number of bizarre ways, are embodied in one of his many laments/polemics:

What's wrong with me? Why am I alone? Why is there no panic? Why aren't governments being toppled? Why aren't we in the streets? Why do we tolerate our own extinction? Why do our politicians put warnings on cigarette packs and not on their own foreheads? Why don't we scream it? Nuclear war!

Yet despite this overriding concern about our nuclear predicament, much of *The Nuclear Age* takes place in the 1960s and 1970s when the novel's hero becomes involved in the war protests and the political underground. So in a larger sense we are back to Vietnam—except this time we are at the home front.

Born on October 1, 1946, in Austin, Minnesota, O'Brien grew up in the rural prairie country of southern Minnesota and graduated with honors from Malcalaster College. Soon afterward, at the age of twenty-two, O'Brien was drafted by the army, and after basic training was sent to Vietnam in 1969. After his tour of duty ended, O'Brien entered Harvard Graduate School to pursue a doctorate in government. O'Brien finished *If I Die in a Combat Zone* while he was in graduate school. In 1973 he took a leave from school to work as a reporter on the national desk of the *Washington Post*. While at the *Post*, he completed *Northern Lights*. After this first novel was published, O'Brien devoted himself full-time to writing, working on his second novel and contributing frequently to magazines, including *Playboy*, *Esquire*, and *Redbook*. When *Going after Cacciato* appeared in 1978, it won the National Book Award for the year; *The Nuclear Age* was published in 1985. O'Brien now lives in Cambridge, Massachusetts.

Despite the profound influence that O'Brien's war experience has had upon his thinking and writing, he does not consider himself a war writer. When asked in an interview with Larry McCaffery if he saw himself as primarily a "Vietnam writer," O'Brien said that he did not, although he added that it was true that

Vietnam was the impetus and spark for *becoming* a writer. When I returned from Vietnam, I had something to say: I had witnessed things, smelled things, imagined things which struck me as startling and terrifying and intriguing in all sorts of ways. At that point I didn't care much about technique or language or structure or any of that craft stuff. All I had was a body of acquired experience that impelled me to write.

As O'Brien has made clear, he believes that the writer needs more than experience to make his or her work meaningful; the writer needs an understanding of the ideas that experience embodies. He calls this knowledge "substance." "The writer needs a passionate and knowledgeable concern for the substance of what's witnessed," he has said, "and that includes the spiritual and theological and political implications of raw experience. All my fiction is governed by this concern for substance—ideas with philosophical meat to them." O'Brien believes that while fiction should not be philosophy, it become peripheral and finally insignificant if it lacks what he calls "the true core of fiction"—"the exploration of substantive, important human values." "Thought is the critical element in writing," O'Brien told McCaffery. "Hard, vigorous, disciplined thought."

One human value that O'Brien has consistently explored in his fiction is that of courage. In *If I Die in the Combat Zone* and *Going after Cacciato*, O'Brien focuses on the trials of the foot soldier, not only in battle but, more important, in his own mind, probing to understand the significance of and the reasons behind his actions. This dual concern for physical bravery and mental awareness is also central in *Northern Lights*, where two brothers face an ordeal in the wilderness, their responses to which—together with the knowledge derived from their responses—ultimately shape the course of their lives. In *The Nuclear Age*, the hero continually wrestles with the problem of how to live with courage and conviction in a world gone awry. Perhaps the clearest statement of O'Brien's concept of bravery comes in *If I Die in the Combat Zone*. Drawing from Plato, O'Brien says courage is a virtue deriving ultimately from wisdom. "Without wisdom men are not truly courageous," he writes. "Men must know what they do is courageous, they must know it is right, and that kind of knowledge is wisdom and nothing else." "Courage," he adds, "is more than the charge."

O'Brien's greatest strength as a writer is portraying men (but not women) in ordeals that allow for discovery and clarification of human values. As he himself has admitted, he has trouble with indoor scenes and with domestic dialogue. *The Nuclear Age* is by far O'Brien's best effort to overcome these rather severe limitations, and yet even here he is not entirely successful. As striking as O'Brien's talent is, the significance of his future work will in all likelihood be determined by how well he can overcome these limitations of his otherwise rich and full imagination.

SELECTED BIBLIOGRAPHY

Works by O'Brien: NOVELS: *Northern Lights*. New York: Delacorte Press/Seymour Lawrence, 1975; *Going after Cacciato*. New York: Delacorte Press/Seymour Lawrence, 1978; *The Nuclear Age*. New York: Knopf, 1985. SHORT STORIES: "Darkness on the Edge of Town." *Feature* (January 1979), pp. 42–49; "Ghost Soldiers." *Esquire* 95 (March 1981), pp. 90–93. NON-FICTION BOOKS: *If I Die in the Combat Zone*. New York: Delacorte Press, 1973. ESSAYS: "Violent Vet." *Esquire* 92 (December 1979), pp. 96–104.

Works about O'Brien: Busby, Mark. "Tim O'Brien's *Going after Cacciato*: Finding the End of the Vision." *CCTE Proceedings* 47 (September 1982), pp. 63–69; Couser, G. Thomas. "*Going after Cacciato*: The Romance and the Real War." *Journal of Narrative Technique* 13 (Winter 1983), pp. 1–10; McCaffery, Larry. "Interview with Tim O'Brien." *Chicago Review* 33 (Winter 1982), pp. 129–49; Varnatta, Dennis. "Theme and Structure in Tim O'Brien's *Going after Cacciato*." *Modern Fiction Studies* 28 (Summer 1982), pp. 242–46. CA 85–88.

Robert H. Brinkmeyer, Jr.

EDWIN O'CONNOR (1918–1968). In his three well-received and highly popular major novels, *The Last Hurrah* (1956), *The Edge of Sadness* (1961), and *All in the Family* (1966), Edwin O'Connor has provided one of the best fictional portraits we have of the political, religious, and familial concerns of the urban American Irish coming to terms with the mid-twentieth century. If there is one abiding theme common to these novels, as well as his other works, it is change, the changes, both public and private, wrought upon the Irish-American experience by acculturation. O'Connor sensitively records the gains and especially the losses incurred in that transformation from ethnic insularity to the American cultural mainstream. Although intentionally conventional in form and occasionally melodramatic in plot, all of O'Connor's work is characterized by an original comic vision, encompassing both the profound and the everyday absurdities of human existence.

Edwin O'Connor was born on July 29, 1918, in Providence and was raised in Woonsocket, Rhode Island. He was the eldest son of second-generation Irish Americans; his father was a doctor, his mother a school teacher. After receiving Catholic schooling, he attended Notre Dame, where he showed an interest in broadcasting and journalism, and he was graduated cum laude in 1939. Before and after World War II, during which he served in the U.S. Coast Guard, O'Connor was involved in radio broadcasting in and around Boston; he worked as an announcer, script writer, and newspaper critic before turning full-time to fiction. O'Connor's broadcasting experience provided the material for his first novel, *The Oracle* (1951), a satirical account of the vicissitudes of a fatuous radio news commentator. Although O'Connor did not marry until into his forties, he was popular among the wide variety of literary personalities who gathered on Cape Cod, and with one of whom, Edmund Wilson, he collaborated on an unfinished novel. He died of a cerebral hemorrhage on March 23, 1968, at the age of forty-nine.

O'Connor's first novel to explore in depth the theme of change in the Irish-American experience is *The Last Hurrah*, which focuses on Frank Skeffington, a long-time political boss of a large, old eastern city. With humor and gusto the author depicts the demise, both politically and physically, of Skeffington, who dies after losing a hard-fought campaign for another term as mayor. O'Connor shows the rough-and-tumble, ward-heeling, personal style of politics Skeffington represents, losing out to a bland coalition backing a modern, made-for-television candidate. The Pulitzer Prize winning *The Edge of Sadness*, a more controlled, introspective novel, continues O'Connor's examination of change—this time the evolving role of the Catholic Church in the daily lives of both priest and parishioner. The public role of the Church is dramatized in the contrast between two parishes, one old and impoverished, ministering to the needs of the indigent and ethnically diverse, the other prosperous but spiritually complacent. Similarly, the private role of the Church is revealed in the contrast between two priests, the narrator, Father Hugh, who struggles heroically with his pastoral vocation, and Father John Carmody, who is brilliant but morally and emotionally depleted. In O'Connor's last novel, *All in the Family*, the exploration of change is extended to the shifting complexities within a wealthy Irish-American family, the Kinsellas, which becomes involved in power politics. Again, changes in both the public and private spheres are scrutinized, and as public pressures inexorably destroy one branch of the family, the individual human need and capacity for love and understanding salvages another.

An inevitable corollary to the theme of change in O'Connor's fiction is the theme of generational conflict, primarily between the middle-aged main characters and the veritable gallery of irascible old men who populate these novels. This conflict dominates *I Was Dancing* (1964), originally a Broadway play, which concerns old Dan Considine's efforts to remain a guest in his son's home rather than go to a home for the elderly. In O'Connor's fiction this is grounds for comedy, just as so often elsewhere in his novels O'Connor seizes every opportunity to exploit for comic purposes the condition of old age and the occasions it presents for eccentric behavior. O'Connor is adept at comic caricature of all kinds and skillfully uses his sensitive ear for speech to exaggerate character and delineate the ridiculous and absurd in an otherwise apparently rational world.

O'Connor's novels may be conventional and may suffer the critical snobbery reserved for the entertaining and popular, but they provide a detailed, perceptive vision of Irish-Catholic life in America. At his best, O'Connor employs his imagination to reveal a dynamic, rather than static, ethnic experience, which shows Irish Americans coping with a variety of public and personal changes as their role in society evolves. Although O'Connor's sensibility is essentially tolerant and humane, it is conveyed with a typically Irish sense of humor, which recognizes but does not succumb to the uncertainties inherent in the human condition.

SELECTED BIBLIOGRAPHY

Works by O'Connor: *The Oracle*. Boston: Little, Brown & Co., 1951; *The Last Hurrah*. Boston: Little, Brown & Co., 1956; *Benjy: A Ferocious Fairy Tale*. Boston: Little, Brown & Co., 1957; *The Edge of Sadness*. Boston: Little, Brown & Co., 1961; *I Was Dancing*. Boston: Little, Brown & Co., 1964; *All in the Family*. Boston: Little, Brown & Co., 1966.

Works about O'Connor: Betts, Richard A. "The 'Blackness of Life': The Function of Edwin O'Connor's Comedy." *MELUS* 8 (Spring 1981), pp. 15–26; Dillon, David. "Priests and Politicians: The Fiction of Edwin O'Connor." *Critique* 16 (1974), pp. 108–20; Rank, Hugh. *Edwin O'Connor*. New York: Twayne, 1974; Schlesinger, Arthur, Jr., ed. *The Best and Last of Edwin O'Connor*. Boston: Little, Brown & Co., 1970. CA 93–96.

Richard A. Betts

FLANNERY O'CONNOR (1925–1964). Flannery O'Connor remarked in a letter of March 3, 1954: "Let me assure you that no one but a Catholic could have written *Wise Blood* even though it is a book about a kind of Protestant saint" (*The Habit of Being* 69). This comment about her first novel suggests the uniqueness of her brief career, lived mainly in the Protestant South, but managed under the shadow of the Roman Catholic Church. O'Connor often spoke of her fiction as belonging to the form labeled "romance" by Nathaniel Hawthorne. Her work is elegantly crafted and bears witness to an uncommon amount of revision; none of her thirty-one stories or two novels ever seems prematurely removed from the drawing board. A miniaturist, she shrinks the size of things with her untiring attention to detail. She is the most reliable recorder we have of grace working on a person unwilling to accept the action of grace. Now, more than two decades after her death, her place in the history of the American short story at least seems assured—probably next to her friend Katherine Anne Porter.*

Flannery O'Connor was born in Savannah, Georgia, on March 25, 1925. Her family moved to Milledgeville when she was twelve and this city, the capital of Georgia in the antebellum period, was to be the geographical nerve center of her career. She attended Peabody High School and Georgia State College for Women (now Georgia College) there, finally leaving for the University of Iowa, to earn a Master of Fine Arts degree in creative writing, in the fall of 1945. This began a five-year period away from her native Georgia, in the "interleckchul" North (as she later referred to it). After finishing at Iowa, she moved east and spent periods at Yaddo, in New York City, and at the Connecticut home of Robert and Sally Fitzgerald.

Ill health forced her return south in December 1950; after being hospitalized and treated for lupus erythematosus (which had killed her father ten years earlier), she and her mother retired to a farm outside Milledgeville, with the regal-sounding name "Andalusia." Here she spent the remainder of her lupus-shortened life, fine-tuning her stories and novels. This sedentary existence permitted occasional lecture tours and visits and even a trip to Lourdes and Rome in the spring of 1958. She spoke with grim finality in a letter of June 1, 1958, to the poet Elizabeth Bishop: "We went to Europe and I lived through it but my capacity for staying at home has now been perfected, sealed & is going to last me the rest of my life" (*The Habit of Being* 285). This rest of her life, six years, saw the completion of *The Violent Bear It Away* (1960) and her most finished work in the shorter form, like "Revelation," "Everything That Rises Must Converge," and "Judgement Day" (*Everything That Rises Must Converge*, 1956). "Judgement Day," interestingly, represents a career in miniature as it is the final product of a fictional gesture that began with Flannery O'Connor's first story, "The Geranium" (published in *Accent* in 1946 while she was still at Iowa) and passed through several stages of revision during the remainder of her writing life.

Two decades have passed since her death at the age of thirty-nine on August 3, 1964. The event was recorded at a symposium held in Sandbjerg, Denmark, in August 1984—an unlikely place for an O'Connor gathering, but testimony surely of her international recognition. David Farmer devotes a section of his *Flannery O'Connor: A Descriptive Bibliography* (1981) to translations of her work into Czech, Dutch, French, German, Greek, Hungarian, Italian, Japanese, Norwegian, Polish, Spanish, and Swedish. In the academic year 1975–1976 her *A Good Man Is Hard to Find and Other Stories* (1955) was added to the prestigious *agrégation* list, which meant that this first collection of her stories was required reading for all advanced graduate students in France who specialize in English and American literature. It joined an elite list of American classics, which included selected stories of Edgar Allan Poe, Sherwood Anderson's *Winesburg, Ohio*, and several novels of William Faulkner. Her position abroad is clearly as secure as it is in the United States.

The slender body of work she left behind includes two collections of stories, *A Good Man Is Hard to Find* and *Everything That Rises Must Converge* (1965), and two brief novels, *Wise Blood* (1952) and *The Violent Bear It Away*. To this fiction should be added the following posthumous collections: *Mystery and Manners: Occasional Prose* (1969), a gathering of essays and prose disjecta; *The Habit of Being: Letters of Flannery O'Connor* (1979), a generous sampling of her letters; and *The Presence of Grace and Other Book Reviews by Flannery O'Connor* (1983), a compilation of all her book reviews and some relevant correspondence. This oeuvre has an uncommon unity and sameness. It exudes an assurance about "the presence of grace" in the world despite the disruptive forces which attempt to undermine its impact.

The language of her fiction never markedly changes; it seems to derive as much from an oral as a written tradition. All her stories and her two novels use third-person discourse as unfailingly as Henry James used it. James was certainly one of two guides she had in respect to craft and technique—"I've read almost all of Henry James—from a sense of High Duty and because when I read James

I feel something is happening to me, in slow motion but happening nevertheless''
(*The Habit of Being* 99). The other guide was Gustave Flaubert. Her narrative
habit probably derived as much from Flaubert's *style indirect libre* as anything
else. Her sense of irony and understatement also has a Flaubertian ring.

One of the most knowing comments about her career was made by the writer,
Caroline Gordon,* who scrupulously examined all of O'Connor's fiction while
it was still on the drawing board: "At any rate, she is already a rare phenomenon:
a Catholic novelist with a real dramatic sense, one who relies more on her
technique than her piety." That "dramatic sense" kept her from writing lives
of saints and pushed her in the direction of flawed sensibilities who incidentally
had a capacity for redemption. The hero of her first novel, Hazel Motes, whom
she was later to call "a Christian *malgré lui*," sets the tone for the religiously
displaced types which haunt her fiction. These types preach strange gospels,
engage in rituals of drowning-baptism and "prayer healing" (burying morbid
newspaper stories), have visions near "hog pens" and before figures of artificial
Negroes, and have heads of Byzantine Christs tattooed on their backs. While
they all seem to be in "the presence of grace," they achieve this condition
through the most circuitous of means. There is always a forbiddingly dark,
Augustinian quality. Allen Tate* noted her Jansenist temperament. O'Connor's
is a world in which, as The Misfit remarked tellingly in "A Good Man is Hard
to Find," "Jesus thrown everything off balance."

Critics of O'Connor's work have mainly preferred her short stories to her
novels, as typified by Robert Drake's comment in his *Flannery O'Connor: A
Critical Essay*: "her real *forte* is the short story." The most serious objections
raised to her work are that she reversed the roles of heroes and villains, to the
point where she became "the pure poet of the Misfit"; that she constantly labored
under tonal difficulties; that she did not seriously enough consider reader response
or have a sure enough "sense of audience"; that she undermined the importance
of reason; and that she deprived the "secular world" of its "dignity and value."
Her considerable strengths, however, have turned the tide of critical commentary
very much in her favor. Her best fiction is intricately patterned and offers a nice
blend of the hieratic and the quotidian.

SELECTED BIBLIOGRAPHY

Works by O'Connor: *Wise Blood*. New York: Harcourt, Brace & Co., 1952; *A Good
Man Is Hard to Find and Other Stories*. New York: Harcourt, Brace & Co., 1955; *The
Violent Bear It Away*. New York: Farrar, Straus & Cudahy, 1960; *Everything That Rises
Must Converge*. New York: Farrar, Straus & Giroux, 1965; *Mystery and Manners:
Occasional Prose*, sel. and ed. Sally and Robert Fitzgerald. New York: Farrar, Straus
& Giroux, 1969; *The Complete Stories of Flannery O'Connor*. New York: Farrar, Straus
& Giroux, 1971; *The Habit of Being: Letters of Flannery O'Connor*, sel. and ed. Sally
Fitzgerald. New York: Farrar Straus & Giroux, 1979; The Presence of Grace and Other
Book Reviews by Flannery O'Connor, comp. Leo J. Zuber, ed. Carter W. Martin. Athens:
University of Georgia Press, 1983.

Works about O'Connor: Asals, Frederick. *Flannery O'Connor: The Imagination of
Extremity*. Athens: University of Georgia Press, 1982; Coles, Robert. *Flannery
O'Connor's South*. Baton Rouge: Louisiana State University Press, 1980; Friedman,
Melvin J., and Beverly Lyon Clark, eds. *Critical Essays on Flannery O'Connor*. Boston:

G. K. Hall, 1985. Friedman, Melvin J., and Lewis A. Lawson, eds. *The Added Dimension: The Art and Mind of Flannery O'Connor*. New York: Fordham University Press, 1966, 2d ed., 1977; Stephens, Martha. *The Question of Flannery O'Connor*. Baton Rouge: Louisiana State University Press, 1973. AW. AWW. CA1. CANR 3. DLB 2.

                                                                    Melvin J. Friedman

FRANK O'HARA (1926–1966). Frank O'Hara was a leader of the New York School of poets composed of writers who inspired and criticized each other's work and shared similar values. O'Hara's artistic manifesto was "personism" based on the idea that poetry was not dead on the page, but was as alive as words spoken between two people. While O'Hara contributed much to the New York art world at large (he was an accomplished art critic, museum curator, playwright, musician, and collaborator on paintings with such artists as Norman Bluhm, Larry Rivers, and Grace Hartigan), his fame arose primarily from his poetry. O'Hara's trademark was the transformation of mundane daily activities into elevated experiences. Walking down a busy city street with a new lover while eating french fries out of a paper cup was as worthy of comment, reflection, and appreciation to O'Hara as the fields above Tintern Abbey were to William Wordsworth. Through the artful and uncompromising use of colloquial language, O'Hara evoked images that turned the everyday into the exalted.

Frank O'Hara was born Francis Russell O'Hara on June 27, 1926, in Baltimore, Maryland. He grew up in Grafton, Massachusetts, and attended parochial schools in nearby Worcester. Ironically, the man who later wrote *Lunch Poems* (1964), a book banned in several school districts for its profanity, had a more formal and complete religious education than many of those who sought to expurgate his works from the library shelves. Born to strict, though loving, Irish-Catholic parents, O'Hara was weaned on the rigidity of the church. Later, O'Hara remembered his Catholic school days as exemplified by "cold windows and bleak desks." However, parochial schools did provide O'Hara the arena to acquire and develop a keen interest in literature. As the only male child in the extended O'Hara family for seven years, Frank was doted upon by older relatives who prompted and encouraged his early reading.

Whatever rigidity or severity O'Hara experienced at school was mirrored in his home. O'Hara was not allowed to get dirty or play like other children. He was never taught, as other children were, how to defend himself. The talents O'Hara was allowed to cultivate were music and literature. At the age of six, he began to play the piano, and by the age of sixteen, he was composing music and commuting to Boston to study at the New England Conservatory of Music.

Music became a release for O'Hara from the restrictions in childhood. Not until he was drafted into the U.S. Navy during World War II, however, did he begin to write. At sea, radio broadcasts of concerts were rare. Writing letters to his family provided him with a new creative outlet. It was at this time too that O'Hara made his first moves to break from the Church. Out of the clutches of his possessive mother and the overseeing religious eyes of his father, O'Hara began to assess the validity of the tenets of the Church in light of his observances of war.

Upon his discharge from the navy, O'Hara attended Harvard University where he further shaped and refined his writing. Inspired by his professors and encouraged by his peers, O'Hara began to experiment with poetry. Many of his early poems, published in the *Harvard Advocate*, resemble the works of his favorite writers Voltaire and Rimbaud. The friends O'Hara made while at Harvard introduced him to the vital underground culture of New York City which afforded him the opportunity to share ideas and works with older, more established members of the art world.

O'Hara received a bachelor's degree in English from Harvard in 1950. He then attended the University of Michigan where he obtained a Master of Arts degree in English and won the Hopwood Award for Creative Writing. This period in O'Hara's development as a poet was based more on imitation than innovation. The excitement of New York, which fueled his artistic energy, was not to be found in Ann Arbor, Michigan, and so O'Hara returned to New York after completing his master's degree.

During his years in New York, O'Hara worked for the Museum of Modern Art and was, at his death, assistant curator. Whether arranging an exhibit for the museum or having drinks and dinner with friends, O'Hara was constantly moving within the many circles of the New York art world. These activities and associations formed the basis for his poetry. Frank O'Hara was killed in an accident on Fire Island on July 27, 1966. *The Collected Poems of Frank O'Hara* (1971), edited by Donald Allen, won the National Book Award in 1972.

Content and language characterize O'Hara's poems which center on daily occurrences: a just-seen movie, the taste of a favorite food, a party, a walk— all transformed into emotionally direct words. O'Hara was often observed jotting poems down on napkins or on the backs of playbills; some poems were included in letters to friends.

The structure of the poems reflected O'Hara's pace; he used simple forms, relying on the sonnet and two-, three-, and four-line stanzas. What happened inside those strictures, however, was not traditional. Rarely depending on rhyme, O'Hara used everyday language to elevate activities and emotions. Each perception of daily life was important to the interpretation of the whole: walking along the Traversera de Gracia in Barcelona, describing an afternoon tea at a friend's house—her cat or her urn, the reflections of light on the upholstery— all illuminate the friend and their relationship.

It is interesting that O'Hara's pursuits in his life and poetry were so opposite those values that his parents and the Catholic Church tried to instill. The Church demanded restriction of sexual behaviors, but O'Hara was a practicing homosexual who drank heavily and revelled in activities the Church considered sinful. His poetry reflects the thrill of homosexual promiscuity or the enduring bonds of commitment, or the smells left after a raucous party. O'Hara once wrote in a letter that the "pontiff was a crutch for the spiritually lazy." Although O'Hara gave up the constraints of the Church in his adult life, he had not given up the underlying spirituality. His was not a devotion to a higher being, but the adoration of everyday life. While the Church taught the unimportance of the individual next to greater beings, O'Hara believed that there could be no significance higher than the substance of daily life.

SELECTED BIBLIOGRAPHY

Works by O'Hara: *A City Winter and Other Poems*. New York: Editions of the Tibor de Nagy Gallery, 1951, i.e., 1952; *Awake in Spain*. New York: American Theatre for Poets, 1960; *Lunch Poems*. Millwood, N.Y.: 1964, 1973; *Love Poems* (tentative title). New York: Tibor de Nagy Editions, 1965; *In Memory of My Feelings; A Selection of Poems*. New York: Museum of Modern Art, 1967; *The Collected Poems of Frank O'Hara*. New York: Knopf, 1971; *The Selected Poems of Frank O'Hara*. New York: Knopf, 1974; *Art Chronicles, 1954–1966*. New York: G. Braziller, 1975; *Standing Still and Walking in New York*. Bolinas, Calif.: Grey Fox Press, 1975; *Early Writing*. Bolinas, Calif.: Grey Fox Press, 1977; *Poems Retrieved*. Bolinas, Calif.: Grey Fox Press, 1977.

Works about O'Hara: Berkson, Bill. *Hymns of St. Bridget*. New York: Adventures in Poetry, 1974; Feldman, Alan. *Frank O'Hara*. Boston: Twayne Publishers, 1979; Perloff, Marjorie. *Frank O'Hara*. New York: G. Braziller, 1977; Smith, Alexander. *Frank O'Hara, A Comprehensive Bibliography*. New York: Garland Publishers, 1979. CA 9–10. DLB 5, 16.

Alison E. O'Hara

JOHN O'HARA (1905–1970). Regarded as a master of the modern American short story, O'Hara has been praised for his remarkable ability to capture the rhythms of American speech, for his superb rendering of social detail, and for his encyclopedic knowledge of the intricacies of the American class system. While he was always a reliable social historian, he most successfully integrated art and social observation in his shorter works: in his short novels, especially *Appointment in Samarra* (1934) and *Butterfield 8* (1935), in his novellas, and in his many short stories. In his longer social chronicles, the product of the second half of his career, the wealth of social detail often overwhelms the narrative. His best work is notable for its deft characterizations and marvelously timed revelations. O'Hara wrote in a letter to William Maxwell that his technique was to ''mesmerize'' the reader, and we read the best of his work almost instinctively, to an end which often startles us into a new awareness of the hidden patterns of love and violence that are woven into the mundane fabric of our lives.

O'Hara was born on January 31, 1905, in Pottsville, Pennsylvania, in the heart of the anthracite coal region. He was the oldest of eight children, the son of a successful Irish-Catholic physician, Dr. Patrick Henry O'Hara, and Katharine Delaney O'Hara. O'Hara attended Catholic grammar school and went on to a Jesuit prep school, Fordham Preparatory, in the Bronx. He was dismissed from Fordam and from his next two schools, Keystone State and Niagara Preparatory—from Niagara, on the morning he was slated to graduate as class valedictorian. He planned to attend Yale but could not afford college after the death of his father in 1925, and he worked instead as a reporter in Pennsylvania and New York. He became a *New Yorker* contributor in 1928. In 1931 he married Helen Petit, a Protestant, from whom he was divorced in 1933. In 1937 he married Belle Wylie, and their daughter Wylie was born in 1945. In 1949 the family moved to Princeton, New Jersey. A year after the death of Belle O'Hara in 1954, O'Hara married Katharine Barnes Bryan, and lived the remainder of his life in Princeton.

O'Hara published fiction in a variety of magazines including *Scribner's*, *Esquire*, *Collier's*, and *The Saturday Evening Post*, but he was primarily a *New Yorker* writer from 1928 to 1949. He published almost two hundred pieces in that magazine in those years, before breaking with it over its publication of an unfavorable review of his novel *A Rage to Live* (1949) and its unwillingness to pay him for his practice of giving the magazine first access to his new material. The rift lasted eleven years, years in which O'Hara did not write short fiction. His first novel, *Appointment in Samarra*, brought immediate recognition and critical acclaim. It was followed a year later by *Butterfield 8* and in 1938 by *Hope of Heaven*. In the 1930s and 1940s O'Hara worked in Hollywood and New York, writing screenplays and short stories, including the "Pal Joey" stories from which he formed the book for the 1940 Rogers and Hart musical *Pal Joey*. In 1949 he published his first novel in eleven years, *A Rage to Live*, which was the first in the series of lengthy chronicles of Pennsylvania life which included *Ten North Frederick* (1955), *From the Terrace* (1958), *Ourselves to Know* (1960), and *The Lockwood Concern* (1965). In 1960 he returned to writing short stories and to publication in *The New Yorker*, and he continued to write both novels and short stories until his death in 1970. His literary output was prodigious; before he died he published over thirty books, including seventeen novels and eleven collections of short stories.

While his sense of estrangement had been growing for some time, O'Hara seemed to mark his formal break with the Church from the time of his first marriage. He later wrote that his mother refused to meet his first wife until after their divorce. He was particularly scornful of institutional censorship and the Catholic habit of obedience that tolerated it, and he wrote disparagingly of "Professional Catholics." Yet he remained something of a cultural Catholic, and his work evidences a lasting fascination with the power of society to destroy by exclusion. O'Hara came to use the distinction between Catholics and Protestants as a kind of shorthand for all of the vague class enmity that belies the ostensible democracy of the American social scene. The Catholics in O'Hara's fiction belong to the country club but they are not included in the most fashionable parties; they are at the Catholic table in *Appointment in Samarra*, clannish, common, and curiously nonassimilable. That novel's protagonist is an attractive but flawed young man with all the right social credentials: Julian English is Protestant, wealthy, and charming; and ironically enough, his troubles begin when he throws a drink into the face of an Irish Catholic social climber named Harry Reilly. O'Hara's treatment of Catholics in the novel exhibits a deep ambivalence. While they are unattractive when viewed in the social context, the one formal representative of the Church, Monsignor Creedon, is the only person in the novel to offer Julian unconditional acceptance. O'Hara reworks the combinations in his 1947 story "The Last of Haley" (*Hellbox*, 1947), which also tells the story of a young man's suicide, but this time it is not the Protestant insider but rather the Catholic outsider who finds in the social web the impetus to self-destruction. Robert Haley realizes that he is in love with the Protestant wife of another Catholic club member, that she will never leave her husband, and that ultimately his personal situation will be as isolated as his social situation. His protest is expressed in his command to the waiter to bring a bottle of Scotch to the table when he finishes serving "those Protestants" at the next table. After a last dance with the girl, he leaves the club singing "McNamara's Band" and swims out to his death.

Common to both of these pieces is O'Hara's consistent sense of the dramatic interior life that lies buried in the trivial workings of the social machine. Like the traditional novelists of manners, O'Hara moves his fiction by the set pieces of social ritual—the dances, parties, weddings, and funerals—by which men order their lives. These can be "state occasions" of great formal significance, like the Fourth of July picnic which opens *A Rage to Live* or Joe Chapin's funeral in the first chapter of *Ten North Frederick*, or they can be scaled down to a suburban cocktail party or a country wedding, or even to a luncheon meeting between two men, as in "Graven Image," or couples meeting for drinks, as in "Are We Leaving Tomorrow?" Both of these stories push the limits of the convention of the social set piece, for these are encounters gone wrong, occasions where the uglier emotions are glimpsed beneath the polite facade. O'Hara's epiphanies occur in the social, rather than the spiritual, realm: revelation arrives through the device of the snub, the blunder, the faux pas.

Most often the slip is verbal. In "Are We Leaving Tomorrow?" an Ivy League type gets drunk and tells an obscene joke; in "Graven Image" a Racquet Club man ruins his chance at a New Deal post by a thoughtless social snub, a reference to his host's unfitness for membership in a Harvard club. O'Hara manages to convey, through minute shadings of diction, the inexplicable gulfs that separate us from each other. His gangsters and his debutantes are equally genuine, for his small details are always right. Such cultural totems as a Brooks Brothers suit or a Phi Beta Kappa key speak for their owners of the selves their owners have painstakingly constructed; that these constructs are always a complicated arrangement of heredity, environment, taste, and ambition is one of O'Hara's finer points.

In O'Hara's first novel, Julian English comes to realize that the world is a terrible place where no one can be trusted to return your love; love guarantees only a greater opportunity for betrayal. Julian's own disequilibrium, as he realizes that people like Froggy Ogden and his mother-in-law and his secretary and the Catholics—people whom he has taken for granted—may actively hate him, becomes the organizing principle of the book. The flat, affectless diction is well-suited to the material; we sense the increasing disorganization of Julian's thoughts, his inability, as the center falls part, to maintain an emotional order that depends by necessity on a social order. For the social order does seem to be disintegrating, and its failure to validate the lives of Julian and the people like him is a primary theme throughout O'Hara's novels. In *Butterfield 8* O'Hara travels to New York and explores the high life and the low life, the world of the Social Register and the world of the speakeasies, and he finds both corrupted from this loss of meaning, with the primary manifestation of the corruption the sexual immorality that links them. Sex is omnipresent in O'Hara's world because it is the only way his people can connect, to verify each other's existence. While the sex is hardly gratuitous, its frequent lack of emotional content was probably the reason O'Hara's novels were so often branded "obscene."

In his first three novels, the inhabitants of Gibbsville, New York, and Hollywood have no supportive framework of tradition; they must salvage a pseudo-order out of the wreckage of the old. The novels that date from the second period, 1949 to 1970, reflect O'Hara's growing conservatism and offer an ostensible return to tradition. O'Hara wrote that he conceived of these later novels as "old-fashioned morality novels," and he came to depend more and more upon such traditional methods of the social novel as narrative asides, time-distancing, and formulaic plotting. While some of the shorter novels of this period are still contemporaneous, like *Elizabeth Appleton* (1963), about a professor's wife, and *The Big Laugh* (1962), about a Hollywood actor, O'Hara's major effort was directed at writing the "big" novels of social history, the multi-generational epics that would create a living record of life in the first half of the twentieth century. While they contain a wealth of sociological data, these novels are less successful than the early novels and the short fiction, for they are less focused and less sure in their purpose; the indignation of the best of O'Hara's work has become mere petulance. Basic to the problem is the mismatch of form and content; the techniques of middle-ground fiction, the social fiction of organic change and orderly social evolution, were not meant to bear the material of disgust and despair, the sort of despair that leads almost every O'Hara protagonist to some form of self-destruction, be it the suicide of Julian English, the alcoholism of Joe Chapin in *Ten North Frederick*, or the promiscuity of Grace Tate in *A Rage to Live*, or the isolationism of George Lockwood in *The Lockwood Concern* and Alfred Eaton in *From the Terrace*. In the later years, it is only in the shorter works that O'Hara recognizes the possibility of reconciliation for his characters, and this often takes the form of an unlikely union of two social misfits who come together and find a separate peace in a private arrangement unsanctioned by the traditional order. "We'll Have Fun," about an alcoholic stable-groom and a Lesbian, is one of the best of these stories, and we can also see this pattern in the 1960 novella "Imagine Kissing Pete," about a married couple who, after years of abusive unhappiness, find transcendence in their mutual love of their child.

While O'Hara did not consider himself a Catholic and did not write extensively of Catholic material, it is possible to see in his fiction a very Catholic conscience. The punishments that his fictional characters receive for even minor transgressions seem disproportionately harsh—a slip of the tongue can end a man's effective life—and yet the logic that underlies that severity is that even small actions are tremendously significant when considered in the light of eternity. O'Hara possessed the essential quality of a novelist who would work within the confines of social realism, an extraordinary sense of the moral importance of the ordinary.

SELECTED BIBLIOGRAPHY

Works by O'Hara: *Appointment in Samarra*. New York: Harcourt, Brace & Co., 1934; *Butterfield 8*. New York: Harcourt, Brace & Co., 1935; *A Rage to Live*. New York: Random House, 1949; *Ten North Frederick*. New York: Random House, 1955; *Selected Short Stories of John O'Hara*. New York: Modern Library, 1956; *From the Terrace*. New York: Random House, 1958; *Ourselves to Know*. New York: Random House, 1960; *Sermons and Soda-Water*. (Three novellas in three volumes.) New York: Random House, 1960; *Elizabeth Appleton*. New York: Random House, 1963; *The Lockwood Concern*. New York: Random House, 1965; *"An Artist in His Own Fault": John O'Hara on Writers and Writing*. Ed. Matthew J. Bruccoli. Carbondale: Southern Illinois University Press, 1977; *Selected Letters of John O'Hara*. Ed. Matthew J. Bruccoli. New York: Random House, 1978; *Collected Stories of John O'Hara*. Ed. Frank MacShane. New York: Random House, 1984.

Works about O'Hara: Bruccoli, Matthew J. *The O'Hara Concern: A Biography of John O'Hara*. New York: Random House, 1975; Grebstein, Sheldon Norman. *John O'Hara*. New York: Twayne, 1966; Long, Robert Emmet, *John O'Hara*. New York: Ungar, 1983; MacShane, Frank. *The Life of John O'Hara*. New York: Dutton, 1980. AW. CA 5–6. DLB 9. TCA.

Ann Cramer

EUGENE O'NEILL (1888–1953). Eugene Gladstone O'Neill was born in New York on October 16, 1888, in a hotel on the corner of 43rd and Broadway, the future center of the theater district. When he wrote his first play he was only twenty-three, but his personal history was already dramatic enough to fill volumes. The son of the famous Irish-American actor James O'Neill and Ella Quinlan O'Neill (a morphine addict who blamed Eugene's difficult delivery for her demon), O'Neill was also sibling rival to James Jr. (Jaimie), who became a bitter, alcoholic actor. The playwright thus inevitably found the stuff of dramatic poetry all about him, both in his immediate family and in his own stormy marriages to Agnes Boulton and Carlotta Monterey. Added to this was a chaotic early life on the touring circuit with his father; a lonely stint in Catholic boarding schools (he told a classmate at St. Vincent's, "religion is so cold" and reacted angrily when a nun lectured him on the evil of the theater his good Catholic father represented); and a troubled adolescence. After a brief time at Princeton, he prospected for gold in Honduras and made several Atlantic voyages as a seaman. Bars and brothels became his hangouts; the nadir was reached in 1922 when he attempted suicide. He almost literally wrote his way out of the gutter while facing possible death in a tuberculosis sanitorium, by observing in play drafts what he had survived, thereby returning, paradoxically, to the theater world of his father. He developed his craft further as a member of Professor G. P. Baker's 47 Workshop at Harvard.

O'Neill's modernist, experimental plays eschewed the time-honored melo-dramatic traditions of the American stage that had made his father a star, while his appreciation of Henrik Ibsen, August Strindberg, and other European mod-ernists, coupled with his understanding of Sigmund Freud, brought a new so-phistication to the American theater. At the same time, his inherited Irish nationalism and love-hate relationship with the Church gave his work a strongly ethnic quality. O'Neill was to claim that "One thing that explains more than anything about me is the fact that I'm Irish." (Louis Shaeffer, *O'Neill: Son and Playwright*, Boston: Little, Brown, 1968, p. 10). He had a lifelong fascination with the sea and death, and frequently insisted he should have been born a "seagull or a fish. As it is, I will always be a stranger who never feels at home, who does not really want and is not really wanted, who can never belong, who must always be a little in love with death!"

Appropriately, O'Neill began to be taken seriously as a writer when he fell in with some theater people while visiting ocean-swept Provincetown with a drinking buddy. The group planned to open an experimental theater and asked O'Neill to read them his new play, *Bound East for Cardiff* (1916). "When the reading was finished," noted Susan Glaspell, " . . . we knew what we were for." The dramatist wrote a sequence of short plays set at sea (eventually titled the *S.S. Glencairn* series), which The Provincetown Players staged, along with many of O'Neill's other early plays, which frequently treated the sea, race, or marital relationships.

His life among the downtrodden was a strong influence on much of his work; O'Neill was the first white writer to write a play for an all black cast (*The Dreamy Kid*, 1919). He wrote starring black roles for two of his stronger plays, *The Emperor Jones* (1920), an impressionistic psychoanalytic treatment of a tyrant's fall from power on a Caribbean island, and *All God's Chillun Got Wings* (1924), which dramatized an interracial marriage.

His first Broadway play, *Beyond the Horizon* (1920), was a breakthrough for the American theater; set on a farm, it depicted the intertwined and thwarted destinies of two brothers who love the same woman. In swapping the roles they seem destined by life to play, they ruin their own lives and those of their family. This three-act drama marked the culmination of O'Neill's apprenticeship as a writer of one-act plays. Soon after, his characteristically fatalistic tone became more pronounced in the classically inspired *Desire under the Elms* (1924), a brooding retelling of the Phaedra story set in rural New England. This interest in translating the terms of Greek drama to America culminated in one of O'Neill's greatest works, an evening-long trilogy of plays entitled *Mourning Becomes Electra* (1931), a resetting of the *Oresteia* in post–Civil War New England. In earlier plays his God-defying stance had sometimes taken on pitying poses (in his one-acter, *The Web*, a tubercular streetwalker raised her arms and cries out "Gawd! Gawd! Why d'yuh hate me so?''); here, however, his self-flagellation and Catholic sense of penance can be seen in the ending, where Lavinia accepts the fate of self-punishing immolation in the Mannon house for the rest of her life.

During this same period, O'Neill took his place among the modernists, boldly experimenting with stream-of-consciousness techniques, symbolic expressionism, and masks, culminating in the tortured Freudianism of *Strange Interlude* (1928), another tale of frustrated desire revolving around the powerful Nina Leeds and the five men in her life. She revolts against patriarchal power, even to the point of addressing "God the Mother," but at the end of the play admits "our lives are merely strange dark interludes in the electrical display of God the Father!" Featuring spoken thought asides, and presented in nine acts punctuated by a dinner break, the play was unprecedented in Broadway history.

O'Neill's constant struggle with the spiritual found expression in several historical plays, such as *The Fountain* (1925), *Lazarus Laughed* (1928), and *Marco Millions* (1928). These and other plays profitted from his deep knowledge of the Bible (he once planned a dramatic adaptation of the Book of Revelation!). Many of his characters quote scripture, notably old Ephraim Cabot in *Desire Under the Elms*, who intones "God's hard, an' lonesome!" Indeed, when *Elms* opened, a critic complained, "These people unlike the people in everyday life! . . . talk freely of shameful things fit only to be printed in the Bible."

This historical cycle overlaps with what O'Neill called his "religious trilogy" (*Lazarus Laughed* (1927), *Dynamo* (1929), *Days Without End* (1934)), which was prompted by his continuing spiritual struggles. Like Herman Melville, O'Neill could neither believe nor be comfortable in his disbelief, even after Friedrich Nietzsche's gospel became his creed. ("The immortal Gods deliver me from Good and Evil! . . . To be true to one's self and one's highest hopes— that is Good!") The trilogy has been deemed a failure, even though O'Neill felt it was crucial "to get back, to the religious in the theater. The only way we can get religion back is through an exultance over the truth, though an exultant acceptance of life." He originally thought of titling the projected trilogy "God Is Dead! Long Live—What?" *Lazarus* was meant to explore "the death of the old God and the failure of science and materialism to give any satisfying new one for the surviving primitive religious instinct to find a meaning for life in, and to comfort its fears of death . . . " Nevertheless, the play also *affirms* God, in that the hero discovers there is no death. As O'Neill put it, the fear of death "is the root of all evil, the cause of all man's blundering unhappiness. Lazarus knows . . . there is only change. . . . Life itself is the self-affirmative joyous laughter of God." *Dynamo*, by contrast, suggests a future age of horror where God has been replaced by an electrical machine. In *Days Without End*, a central character seems to return to the Catholic Church for answers, but only after questioning a religion centered on a God of punishment who is seemingly "deaf and blind and merciless—a Deity Who returned hate for love and revenged Himself upon those who trusted Him!'' (These words refer to the crisis of faith O'Neill endured upon his discovery in 1903 of his mother's morphine addiction; his prayers to God for her cure went unrewarded and plunged him into lifelong rebellion against both God and the Church).

Paradoxically, O'Neill had said this better and more subtly in 1931; Christine Mannon in *Mourning Becomes Electra* voices his complaint: ''If I could only have stayed as I was then! Why can't all of us remain innocent and loving and trusting? But God won't leave us alone. He twists and wrings and tortures our lives with others' lives until—we poison each other to death!'' Sometimes the despair becomes too great to bear; once he drunkenly declared to his brother, ''I will tear down the curtain of Eternity that God has hung in the sky! Vomit all my poison up—on the bread and on the wine!''

In a completely different vein, *Ah, Wilderness* (1933), O'Neill's only comedy, punctuates his career at midpoint, and provides a charming coming-of-age story, using a Connecticut family, but with ominous undertones that look forward to *Long Day's Journey Into Night* (1956) and the other last plays; as O'Neill said, the piece provided a nostalgic view of what he wished his own youth had been.

O'Neill's last plays, in many ways his greatest, succeeded because of the maturation of his craft, but also because he based most of them to varying degree on personal and familial events; these include *A Moon for the Misbegotten* (1947), *A Touch of the Poet* (1957), *Hughie* (1958), *The Iceman Cometh* (1946), and *Long Day's Journey Into Night*. *Moon* is the tortured dramatic setting of Jaimie O'Neill's last days after his mother's death, focusing on his relationship with Josie, an Amazon-like farm woman. *Poet* examines the fall of a cocky nineteenth-century Irish-American braggart and his daughter's upcoming marriage into the local gentry. *Hughie*, by contrast, presents the desperate quest of the gambler, Erie Smith, to find a friend in the bored clerk of a seedy New York hotel.

Iceman and *Long Day's Journey* are among the greatest works of world drama. The former details the nature of illusion (''pipe dreams'') in the lives of the derelict habitues of Harry Hope's seedy bar. *Iceman* owes its title both to an obscene joke and a popular novel, *The Bridegroom Cometh*, but it also ironically comments on the failure of the Christian gospels to reach those who need it and the fact that most people do not really want to be saved. More than one critic has commented on the close parallels in the narrative structure and scenic grouping to Leonardo da Vinci's *The Last Supper*; the Bridegroom who does not come is Christ. Its derelicts, orchestrated by the salesman Hickey, mount a cacaphony of voices that ponder the conflict in man's heart between anarchic despair and religious hope, ending in Hickey's confession that he killed his wife, who unforgivably idealized him.

Long Day's Journey, O'Neill's most agonized and confessional play, lays bare his family's secrets, dreams, and terrors during an alcohol-fired evening they share in their Connecticut cottage in 1912 (significantly, the year O'Neill began to write), a night that marks the mother's return to her morphine addiction and thus the end of the family's hopes.

The pain of this "exorcising of old ghosts" eventually kept O'Neill from completing his ambitious multiplay cycle, *A Tale of Possessers, Self-Dispossessed*; he noted in his work diary that he had interwoven too many psychological and spiritual themes and motives. This seemed to be true in his own life as well. He once told Clifton Fadiman "I don't know a single final answer as a result of my own questioning, and I cannot believe in any of the answers that are faiths to others." Nevertheless, toward the close of his life, in pain, no longer able to write, O'Neill deplored the Catholic doctrine against suicide that continued to haunt him. Carlotta O'Neill reported that "He suffered horribly from his illness— in his soul . . . and though no longer Catholic, he still feared this Hell might continue after death, and was afraid to take his life." And yet he also told her,

When I'm dying, don't let a priest or Protestant minister or Salvation Army captain near me. Let me die in dignity. Keep it as simple and brief as possible. No fuss, no man of God there. If there is a God, I'll see Him and we'll talk things over.

He died, as he was born, in a hotel room, in 1953.

Extraordinary intensity often overpowers intellectual consistency in O'Neill's work. As a result, even though O'Neill is generally considered to be America's greatest playwright—and he is the only American dramatist to win the Nobel Prize (1936)—he has always been severely criticized by a minority of scholars for overblown rhetoric, posturing, lack of refinement, and an allegedly clumsy use of modernist techniques such as Freudianism and expressionism. During the past decades, however, revivals of his major plays (especially the late ones) have been well-received, and the British in particular have urged a reexamination of his work (the BBC presented *Strange Interlude* on public television in 1988 and plans to mount more O'Neill plays). For many, his depictions of man's mounting frustration, horror, and spiritual anguish as he simultaneously grasps for hope continue to echo powerfully and eloquently the conditions of modern life.

SELECTED BIBLIOGRAPHY

Works by O'Neill: SIGNIFICANT AND MAJOR PLAYS AND DATES OF PRODUCTION: *Bound East for Cardiff*. 1916; *The Emperor Jones*. 1920; *Beyond the Horizon.** 1920; *Anna Christie*. 1921; *The Hairy Ape*. 1922; *All God's Chillun Got Wings*. 1924; *Desire Under the* Elms. 1924; *Strange Interlude.** 1928; *Mourning Becomes Electra*. 1931; *Ah, Wilderness!* 1933; *Days without End*. 1934; *The Iceman Cometh*. 1946; *A Moon for the Misbegotten*. 1947; *Long Day's Journey Into Night.** 1956; *A Touch of the Poet*. 1957; *Hughie*. 1958. (*Awarded Pulitzer Prize.)

Works about O'Neill: Bogard, Travis. *Contour in Time; The Plays of Eugene O'Neill*, rev. ed. New York: Oxford University Press, 1987; Chothia, Jean. *Forging a Language; A Study of the Plays of Eugene O'Neill*. New York: Cambridge University Press, 1979; Gelb, Arthur, and Barbara Gelb. *O'Neill*. rev. ed. New York: Harper & Row, 1973; Martine, James J., ed. *Critical Essays on Eugene O'Neill*. Boston: G. K. Hall, 1984;

Sheaffer, Louis. *O'Neill: Son and Playwright*. Boston: Little, Brown, 1968; Sheaffer, Louis. *O'Neill: Son and Artist*. Boston: Little, Brown, 1973. AW. CA 77–80.

John Lowe

WILLIAM O'ROURKE (1945–). A novelist and social critic who commands both fictional and non-fictional forms, William O'Rourke is especially recognized for his ability to formulate incisive perceptions and surprising associations with Baconian aphoristic control. From a Midwestern, Catholic, liberal stance that is wholly private and nonpartisan, he translates directly into books, articles, and reviews the contemporary America he witnesses. His interest focuses particularly on the meaning of human behavior. Whether dealing with the matters controversial or benign, he writes stories and accounts that deal out the coherent present into episodes of significant activity. These he examines in minute detail, uncovering their meaning through reflection and a play of mind. While focusing human behavior under the illuminations of mythology, history, social custom, popular culture, and myriad other dimensions reachable through simile and metaphor, and while standing in the spotlight of his personal morality and sense of human decency, he fosters no public cause and imposes no ideology.

O'Rourke was born in Chicago on December 4, 1945, but he grew up in Kansas City, Missouri. He earned his B.A. in English at the City campus of the University of Missouri, then left for New York to earn a Master of Fine Arts in writing at Columbia University. While a Fellow at the Fine Arts Work Center, in Provincetown, Massachusetts, he covered the federal trial of Fathers Philip and Daniel Berrigan* and their Catholic, anti-Vietnam comrades. The publication in 1972 of *The Harrisburg 7 and the New Catholic Left*, still regarded as the best book on that episode, gave O'Rourke immediate recognition. He has since worked in the construction trades; taught at Rutgers, Mount Holyoke, and (currently) Notre Dame; and produced three novels, an anthology of short stories, and dozens of articles and reviews. He has won grants from the New York State Council on the Arts and from the National Endowment for the Arts. He was named the first James Thurber Writer in Residence, at the Thurber House in Columbus, Ohio.

While praised for his intellectual acuity and stylistic elegance, O'Rourke also deserves recognition for his originality and literary seriousness. He produced the best book on the New Catholic Left (*Harrisburg 7*), wrote the earliest novel depicting the Vietnam War's impact on the generation of draft-age boys at home (*The Meekness of Isaac*, 1974), edited the first anthology of short stories about work (*On the Job*, 1977)—and later wrote extensively about work (*Idle Hands*, 1981)—and treated sexual topics in fiction without subordinating them to violence, corruption, social problems, psychological theories, fantasy, or any other distorting perspective (*Idle Hands*). His gift for both figurative language and everyday speech, his eye for casting a scene from a striking angle and moving it toward a lucid effect, and the understanding out of which he creates highly individualized characters, both male and female, have advanced the mode of literary realism toward a purer realization. Together with his nonpartisan voice, his talent for both accurate depiction and telling perception make it possible to think of O'Rourke as a literary counterpart to neorealist painters.

SELECTED BIBLIOGRAPHY

Works by O'Rourke: FICTION: *The Meekness of Isaac*. New York: Thomas Y. Crowell, 1974; *On the Job: Fiction about Work by Contemporary American Writers*, ed. New York: Random House, 1977; *Idle Hands*. New York: Delacorte, 1981; *Criminal Tendencies*. New York: E. P. Dutton, 1987. NONFICTION: *The Harrisburg 7 and the New Catholic Left*. New York: Thomas Y. Crowell, 1972.

Works about O'Rourke: Review of *The Harrisburg 7 and the New Catholic Left*. *America* (7 October 1972), p. 268; Review of *Idle Hands*. *New York Times Book Review* (5 April 1981), p. 14; Review of *The Meekness of Isaac*. *New York Times Book Review* (22 December 1974), p. 6; Review of *On the Job*. *Prairie Schooner* 51 (1977), p. 318.

Edward Vasta

P

BREECE D'J PANCAKE (1952–1979). Breece David John Pancake's middle initials came by way of a printer's error, a minor oddity among the many mysteries of his brief life and career. For Pancake, with a promising future—accepted stories and job prospects—ended his career before it had well begun, a suicide in Charlottesville, Virginia, in 1979. Still, four years later there was a collection of stories which Joyce Carol Oates* described as prose poems and compared them favorably to Ernest Hemingway's first work.

Born in Milton, West Virginia, in 1952, Pancake studied at Marshall University and then taught at two Virginia military academies before entering the graduate writing program at the University of Virginia. One of his mentors there, John Casey, speaks of his "powerful *sense* of things" and of how his finished stories were "hard and brilliantly worn as train rails" ("Afterword," *Stories*, p. 172).

Both Casey and James Alan McPherson have tried to understand Pancake's suicide. He had converted to Catholicism sometime after his father and best friend had died and, Casey says, he "took on his faith with intensity" ("Afterword," p. 173). In one letter he even saw his faith as an obstacle to "getting a divorce from life" ("Afterword," p. 175). His mother's explanation was that he "saw too much dishonesty and evil" ("Foreword," p. 10). McPherson saw a tension between the West Virginia hills and life outside that kept Pancake from understanding "who or what he was" ("Foreword," p. 19). He also tells of a mysterious phone call and the immediate circumstances of Pancake's death: he had entered a friend's house when they were away and been mistaken for a burglar when they returned. He went home and shot himself.

Pancake's fictional world is a bleak one, physically and morally—sexist, lawless, violent, dehumanized. We are not too surprised to meet a narrator who feeds hitchhikers to his hogs. His characters are all alone, their feelings numbed by the harshness and cultural depravity of their lives. A sense of despair pervades the air: "Ain't nothin' goin' to change nohow," one says. It is possible to identify Pancake's overarching theme as the mystery of sin, but there are others as well: the betrayals and gifts of fathers, the power of sexual initiation, painful growth from childhood to adulthood and the overlapping of individual and human time.

There appears to be a consensus that his best stories are "Trilobites," Colley's reflection on the tyranny of land, the need for freedom, and his confusion; "The Mark," in which the pressures of life drive Neva mad; "Hollow," in which Buddy turns from the mine and a woman he abuses to slaughter a doe and eat the raw liver; "Fox Hunters," which follows Bo from his singular defense of Lucy's reputation to a drunken hunt during which he shoots at a dog and, afterward, thinks of escape in a rusting Impala; and "In the Dry," Ollie's haunting visit to the withered valley where Shiela's cousin Buster, badly crippled in an automobile accident with Ollie and now living for cigarettes, and his father, pumping Ollie for an explanation, prompt Ollie to flee by night, grinding the gears of his tractor truck, "an awful noise."

But in all there is the unmistakable precise detailing of a land that "lay brittle, open, and dead," of a world full of harsh images, most notably vehicles of escape that do not run. Pancake's eye and ear are accurate, his capture of his characters' desperation complete. What is lacking is hope, as they evade their guilt with acts of violence.

SELECTED BIBLIOGRAPHY

Works by Pancake: *The Stories of Breece D'J Pancake*, foreword by James Alan McPherson, afterword by John Casey. Boston: Little, Brown & Co., 1984, New York: Holt, 1984.

William H. Slavick

ANNE PELLOWSKI (1933–). Anne Pellowski is very possibly America's most cosmopolitan and best-known professional storyteller and author of children's literature. Having lectured, performed, and consulted in well over 100 countries, Pellowski has attracted, quite literally, a worldwide following; yet her children's literature is peculiarly American and establishes a model for the treatment of ethnicity in a pluralistic society.

Anne Pellowski was born on June 28, 1933, in Pine Creek, Wisconsin, where she grew up on the family farm. After completing local schools, Pellowski attended the College of St. Teresa in Winona, Minnesota, from which she graduated with honors in 1955. The next year she studied at the University of Munich on a Fulbright Fellowship, and in 1959 she earned a master's degree in library science from Columbia University. Following a year of teaching, Pellowski worked for the New York City Public Library as a storyteller, children's librarian, and group work specialist. In 1966 Pellowski founded the Information Center on Children's Culture, a section of UNICEF, which she directed until 1982. During this time, in addition to her official duties, Pellowski built a repertoire of stories and cross-referenced literature from around the world. In 1979 Pellowski was presented with the Grolier Award of the American Library

Association; and in 1980 she received the Constance Lindsay Skinner Award of the Women's National Books Association for "extraordinary contributions to the world of books and, through books, to society." Her citation reads:

Author, teacher, librarian, storyteller, and world traveler, she fosters understanding through folktale, and fable, fact and fiction. Using the magic of words and pictures, she educates adults and enchants children everywhere. With vitality, commitment and vision, Anne Pellowski transforms every year into the Year of the Book—every hour into the Children's Hour.

Since leaving UNICEF, Pellowski has spent her time writing and performing, in addition to lecturing and teaching at a wide variety of campuses including Columbia University and the Universities of Maryland, Wisconsin, and Pennsylvania.

In addition to her creative writing, Anne Pellowski has authored numerous books and dozens of articles and chapters on storytelling and children's literature; she has also recorded nine long-playing albums of folktales from a wide variety of countries for CMS Records. In these comments, however, it is Pellowski's Wisconsin farm tetralogy that is most relevant.

In 1981 and 1982 Pellowski published four books of children's literature— *First Farm in the Valley: Anna's Story* (1982); *Winding Valley Farm: Annie's Story* (1982); *Stairstep Farm: Anna Rose's Story* (1981); and *Willow Wind Farm: Betsy's Story* (1981)—which provide a chronicle for four generations of a Polish immigrant family settling the Latsch Valley of Tremplealeau County, Wisconsin. Based on the history of her own family, these books have established Pellowski as a creative writer of exceptional talent and special mission.

In the tetralogy Pellowski excels in all the literary skills demanded by narration in general and children's literature in particular. Action, characterization, and setting, for example, all contribute an extraordinarily vivid and realistic record of changes in social custom, farming, and living conditions covering a period from 1860 to the early 1980s. More importantly, however, Pellowski's art provides a clear vision into the world of childhood and the minds of children. In each book Pellowski manages the demanding task of supplying all the background necessary to a firm grasp of the narrative while essentially reporting the story from the point of view of a six-year-old child—a feat which sharpens the reader's vision of childhood without restricting one's overview of action and theme.

Another noteworthy feature of the tetralogy is Pellowski's promotion of a new kind of children's literature—"a literature which addresses children honestly." Here are no bowdlerized stories "which deal only with 'safe' topics, avoid unpleasantries, and . . . distort reality." By treating "sadness as well as joy, fear as well as courage, and death and pain as well as life and birth," Pellowski confronts children with real life which children know to be true and to which they can relate. Thus, Pellowski's work not only entertains children but "arouses their curiosity, and helps them to develop their intellects and to clarify their emotions."

Finally, Pellowski's tetralogy has helped to break new ground and serves as a model for the treatment of ethnicity in American literature. It is an observable fact that ethnicity is a central feature of identity for millions of Americans; yet American literature has generally not only failed to reflect this reality, it has obscured it. "Without apology or chauvinism Pellowski presents an identity different from that of White, Anglo-Saxon, Protestant Americans, establishes an appreciation for that identity, and manages to touch those universals which are the common bond of all humanity."

In all of this it is important to note that Anne Pellowski's religious background and her personal Catholic faith have significantly shaped her life and writings. In a recent interview, for example, she confirmed that much of the inspiration for her career and life as an independent professional woman came from aunts whose religious vocations as nuns fired her imagination. It also seems clear that a certain Catholic feminism has prompted Pellowski's commitment to the welfare and culture of children around the world and has influenced her selection of young girls as the central figures in her very successful tetralogy. In another literary consideration, readers delight at the manner in which Pellowski's vivid and accurate portrayal of Catholic customs and rites enhances the pleasure and verisimilitude of her writings.

In her treatment of immigrants and ethnics, Anne Pellowski has explored an almost uncharted area of the American experience and has exposed to all a vision of a global people; in so doing she promotes toleration and understanding.

SELECTED BIBLIOGRAPHY

Works by Pellowski: FICTION: *Willow Wind Farm: Betsy's Story*. New York: Philomel/Putnam, 1981; *Stairstep Farm: Anna Rose's Story*. New York: Philomel/Putnam, 1981; *Winding Valley Farm: Annie's Story*. New York: Philomel/Putnam, 1982; *First Farm in the Valley: Anna's Story*. New York: Philomel/Putnam, 1982; *Betsy's Up-and-Down Year*. New York: Philomel/Putnam, 1983. COLLECTIONS: *Have You Seen a Comet? Children's Art and Writing from around the World*. New York: John Day, 1971; *The Story Vine: A Source Book of Unusual and East-to-Tell Stories from around the World*. New York: Macmillan Co., 1984. SCHOLARLY STUDIES: *The World of Children's Literature*. New York: R. R. Bowker, 1968; *The World of Storytelling*. New York: R. R. Bowker, 1977. RECORDINGS: Nine Discs/Cassettes of Storytelling. New York: CMS Records, 1965–1970.

Works about Pellowski: Napierkowski, Thomas J. "Anne Pellowski: A Voice for Palonia." *Polish American Studies* 42, 2 (Autumn 1985), pp. 89–97. CA 23–24. CANR 9.

Thomas J. Napierkowski

WALKER PERCY (1916–). From his first novel, *The Moviegoer* (1961), which captured the 1962 National Book Award, Percy was a writer to whom reviewers and critics paid close attention. Each subsequent novel gained a larger and more appreciative audience. With each novel, the core of ideas that animated his writing achieved greater clarity and coherence. *The Moviegoer* suggested that Percy's chief intention was to write an existential novel. The second novel,

The Last Gentleman (1966), hinted that he really belonged to the Faulkner school. *Love in the Ruins* (1971), though, offered yet another departure, a satire against Utopianism. By then Percy's readers began to note that although each novel offered a different glimpse of the social scene, there was a markedly similar interior world haunting all of them. Both *Lancelot* (1977) and *The Second Coming* (1980) added information about the teller who inhabits his tales. An unfinished confession, Percy's fiction reveals man as *homo viator*, the wayfarer and pilgrim, the Church's image of man since the Middle Ages.

Born on May 28, 1916, in Birmingham, Alabama, Percy spent a comfortable childhood as a successful lawyer's son. After the suicide of his father in 1929 and the death of his mother in 1932, Walker and his two brothers were adopted by his father's Greenville, Mississippi, cousin, William Alexander Percy. "Uncle Will" was the embodiment of the concept of noblesse oblige. A poet by temperament and a lawyer by profession, he was an eloquent Southern advocate of both the examined and the public life. His autobiography, *Lanterns on the Levee* (1941), is the best entry to the Southern stoic mind. With his uncle's encouragement, Percy majored in chemistry at the University of North Carolina and then graduated from the College of Physicians and Surgeons of Columbia University (1941). But two events encumbered the physician's path. While in medical school, he had undergone three years of psychoanalysis, and soon after entering his career he contracted tuberculosis.

Deprived of an active life, Percy read for the first time books that explore spiritual existence: Fyodor Dostoyevski, Søren Kierkegaard, Martin Heidegger, Martin Buber, Jean-Paul Sartre, and Albert Camus. Later, he was ready for Augustine and Thomas Aquinas, even the Bible. Soon after his marriage to Mary Bernice Townsend in 1946, he and his wife became Catholics. Living on an inheritance, Percy settled in Covington, Louisiana, to search for a means of restoring modern man's sundered self.

From the beginning Walker Percy understood that the major problem for Western man is that he has grown hard of hearing. In essence, Percy began with John 1:1. Like the Patmos group, he recognized that man had been taught to depend so entirely on seeing that he could no longer build his primary world, which depends upon hearing. Thus living in a world thought to be nothing but things to be measured, man found himself unaccountably lonely. For, given his education in silence, he did not even know that he could speak and be spoken to, and by those acts learn to take the measure of himself. Percy thus began to write essays about speech, which by the agency of the symbol conveys meanings that transcend the world of isolated sight. Many of these essays were later incorporated into *The Message in the Bottle* (1975). A later examination of man as a symbol monger was *Lost in the Cosmos* (1983).

At the age of forty-five, after writing two unaccepted novels, Percy published *The Moviegoer*. In that first published novel, like a movie with its short scenes, fade-ins, and sharp cuts, Binx Bolling hides his bad faith by wearing disguises. To his Aunt Emily he is a rather frivolous young man, fallen away from the

aristocratic tradition. To his Uncle Jules he is a young businessman who successfully combines good breeding and making money. He thinks of himself as
a moviegoer, a person who has been taught to be a spectator of the movie of
life. But he is not engrossed by the movie; thus thinking of himself, he judges
himself, and finds himself to be guilty—until he participates in the welfare of
Kate Cutrer. By the end of the novel, after failure, their joined flesh is a manifestation of their joined words.

Will Barrett, a twenty-five-year-old displaced Southerner, chooses the telescope as his instrument of vision in *The Last Gentleman*. Using that Freudian
model, he thinks that he can engineer his life as if he were a ghost in a machine.
But the road he follows carries him back to the South and to his childhood,
neither of which he is ready to confront. So he lights out for the territory, there
to settle for a false father figure.

In *Love in the Ruins* Tom More has sufficient reason to become obsessed with
an instrument of visuality. His daughter has died of neuroblastoma, and Tom,
a despairing drunkard, invents a machine that will detect the onset of such a
condition. When he discovers that he can leap from neurological to psychological
diagnosis, he christens his invention the *lapsometer*, a measurer of the distance
that one has fallen away from aboriginal happiness. With the Devil's help, he
proposes to leap from diagnosis to therapy. The results are disastrous—until he
invokes the aid of his ancestor, Saint Thomas More.

Lance Lamar, in *Lancelot*, first uses a microscope to establish the polarities
that underlie any examination of the physical world. Then he uses closed-circuit
television to observe his wife as an object. At the end, finally mindful of the
pass that seeing has brought him to, he is ready to listen.

The Second Coming is Percy's happiest book, a story of the blissful consum-
mations available to God's children. Will Barrett, now a middle-aged widower,
has everything, but nothing. Allie Huger, a young abused woman, has very little
but potential. Each is a deprived consciousness, until together they look through
the glass of Allie's greenhouse, tinted as it is by a frame of stained glass. Will
has come from "bear it" to "have" it.

Percy's writing thus traces *homo viator*, on who "comes to himself," a
recurrent phrase in both his non-fiction and fiction. Man discovers that knowledge
based upon seeing alone has left him shipwrecked, needing "the message in the
bottle," from across the sea. Man also discovers—and this discovery is very
much a part of Percy's confession—that he is haunted by the loss of his father.
But, with each novel, Percy traces just a little more heavily his fundamental
story. Every man is like the young man in the Parable of the Prodigal Son—the
essential novel of Christianity. All he has to do is to come to himself and go
back home to the Father who will welcome him.

SELECTED BIBLIOGRAPHY

Works by Percy: NOVELS: *The Moviegoer*. New York: Alfred A. Knopf, 1961; *The
Last Gentleman*. New York: Farrar, Straus & Giroux, 1966; *Love in the Ruins*. New
York: Farrar, Straus & Giroux, 1971; *Lancelot*. New York: Farrar, Straus & Giroux,

1977; *The Second Coming*. New York: Farrar, Straus & Giroux, 1980. NON-FICTION: *The Message in the Bottle*. New York: Farrar, Straus & Giroux, 1975; *Lost in the Cosmos*. New York: Farrar, Straus & Giroux, 1983; *The Thanatos Syndrome*. New York: Farrar, Straus & Giroux, 1987.

Works about Percy: Broughton, Panthea Reid, ed. *The Art of Walker Percy*. Baton Rouge: Louisiana State University Press, 1979; Coles, Robert. *Walker Percy: An American Search*. Boston: Atlantic Monthly, 1978; Lawson, Lewis A., and Victor A. Kramer, eds. *Conversations with Walker Percy*. Jackson: University of Mississippi, 1985; Tharpe, Jac, ed. *Walker Percy: Art and Ethics*. Jackson: University of Mississippi, 1980. CA 3. CANR 1. CN. DLB 2.

Lewis A. Lawson

JOHN PIELMEIER (1949–). As a result of *Agnes of God* (1982), his long-running Broadway play and motion picture, John Pielmeier has become an important dramatist, his work overtly theatrical, emotionally powerful, and perceptive about Catholicism. His weakness is a tendency to overexplain; his characters may get bogged down in debates or narration which do little to advance the dramatic action. Born in Altoona, Pennsylvania, on February 23, 1949, Pielmeier graduated from Catholic University with a degree in Speech and Drama (1970). He then won a Shubert Fellowship to study playwriting at Pennsylvania State University. In 1978, as he was completing his M.F.A., he started writing *Agnes of God*. During the next four years he rewrote the play for two staged readings and eight regional productions. In 1980 he was cowinner of the Festival of New American Plays at the Actors' Theatre of Louisville, and in 1982 he was awarded a National Endowment for the Arts grant. His plays *Sleight of Hand* (1980) and *Jass* (1981) were runners-up at the Playbill Award Competition. In 1983 Pielmeier returned to Louisville with *Courage* (about J. M. Barrie, the author of *Peter Pan*). His play *The Boys of Winter* opened on Broadway in November 1985, and the film version of *Agnes of God*, for which he wrote the screenplay, opened shortly thereafter.

In writing *Agnes of God* Pielmeier began with the religious questions he kept asking himself: "Are there saints today? miracles? did these phenomena ever exist and, if so, have they or our perceptions of them changed?" At its simplest level the play presents Agnes as a contemporary saint with Mother Miriam as one who believes Agnes' life is miraculous and Dr. Livingstone as one who doubts it. Agnes, who is innocent and yet capable of killing her own child, is the fascinating character in the play. But the focus of the drama is really on the psychiatrist who, during her treatment of Agnes, receives the grace which effects in her a moral and intellectual conversion.

Pielmeier has a structural problem in the play; its two primary actions, Mother Miriams' and the doctor's struggle over Agnes and Dr. Livingstone's efforts toward self-discovery, are never fully integrated. The play is carried by its emotional fireworks, and its ideas, too often expressed in clumsy narration, may seem superfluous, even though Pielmeier is articulating the important theme of rational, modern man trying to justify faith.

The Boys of Winter is related to *Agnes of God* through what Pielmeier calls "the theme of innocence with blood on one's hands" (*New York Times*, November 24, 1985). The play concerns a Marine in Vietnam, Lt. Bonney, who (like the real-life Lt. William Calley) is accused of war crimes. However, the dramatic flow is interrupted as each soldier explains Bonney's behavior in an isolated monologue. Pielmeier is still trying to develop a style that will accommodate his philosophical and religious ideas without weakening the unity of his plays.

SELECTED BIBLIOGRAPHY

Works by John Pielmeier: PLAYS: *Agnes of God*. Garden City, N.Y.: Nelson Doubleday, 1982; *Haunted Lives: A Witch's Brew, A Ghost Story*, and *A Gothic Tale*. New York: Dramatists Play Service, 1984. UNPUBLISHED PLAYS: *Sleight of Hand*. 1980; *Jass*. 1981; *Courage*. 1983; *The Boys of Winter*. 1985. TELEPLAY: *Choices of the Heart*. 1983.

Willem O'Reilly

JOSEPH PINTAURO (1930–). Poet, playwright, and novelist, Joseph Pintauro has used his background and his times as a springboard to produce a personal body of work. His two novels, *Cold Hands* (1979) and *State of Grace* (1983), in which his protagonists decide to leave the priesthood, reflect the eight years he spent as a Roman Catholic priest. His poetry (*Trilogy of Belief*, 1968–1971), Pintauro's attempt to bridge old and new ways of seeing God, combined the ecstasy and the naiveté of the 1960s. And much of his work is regional, mirroring both New York City and the rural landscape of eastern Long Island— the two places Pintauro calls home.

While containing elements of his own life, the writing is not strictly autobiographical. The protagonist in *State of Grace*, for instance, is a Jesuit student in Rome; Pintauro never was. Nonetheless, his work has a strong religious base and grapples with concepts of grace.

In the early *Cold Hands*—singled out by *New York Times Book Review* as one of the best novels of the year—he handles a very different issue: the overwhelming, at times overtly sexual, love of two cousins. The book reflects Pintauro's talent for explosive urban dialogue, which comes center stage in his plays (*Cacciatore*, 1981; *Snow Orchid*, 1982; and *Short Plays for Small Stages*, 1985). In *Snow Orchid*, which was Pintauro's first full-length play, *New York Times'* Frank Rich noted the playwright's "talent for dramatizing . . . grand passions" and the "volcanic uproar of affection, obscenities and physical abuse worthy of (Scorsese's movie) *Raging Bull*." To some, however, this proved to be too much: Walter Kerr found the play "approximately 115 percent dramatic," adding that no group of characters could hope to survive that.

Pintauro makes deft use of metaphor, from the snow orchids that can survive neglect and cold, to the family recipe in *Pauline*, one of the *Short Plays*, that represents withdrawal and reconciliation. His vividly drawn characters run the gamut from battling Italian-American family members to a young punk star who takes sexual revenge on her callous father (*Dirty Talk*, also in *Short Plays*).

The basic theme of Pintauro's work is rejection: brother by brother, husband and wife by each other, children by parents. Yet Pintauro always returns to the question of forgiveness, to the seeking of expiation for a crime that has destroyed life, often beyond redemption.

SELECTED BIBLIOGRAPHY

Works by Pintauro: POEMS: *Trilogy of Belief*. New York: Harper & Row: vol. I, "To Believe in God," 1968, vol. II, "To Believe in Man," 1970, vol. III, "To Believe in Things," 1971; *One Circus, Three Rings, Forever and Ever Hooray!* New York: Harper, 1969; *The Rainbow Box: A Book for Each Season and a Peace Poster*. New York: Harper, 1970; *Kites at Empty Airports*. Perennial Education, 1972; *Earthmass*. New York: Harper, 1973. PLAYS: *Cacciatore* (three one-acts). New York: Dramatists Play Service, 1981; *Snow Orchid* (three-act), first produced at Circle Repertory Workshop in 1982; *The Hunt of the Unicorn*, first produced at Circle Repertory Workshop, no date; *Short Plays for Small Stages*, first produced at the Circle Repertory Workshop in 1985. NOVELS: *Cold Hands*. New York: Simon and Schuster, 1979; *State of Grace*. New York: Times Books, 1983.

Works about Pintauro: Kerr, Walter. "When the Stage Is Just a Prize-Ring." *New York Times* (2 March 1982), p. D3; Rich, Frank. "Drama: Joe Pintauro's *Snow Orchid*." *New York Times* (11 March 1982), p. C17. CA 81–84.

Patricia Glossop

DAVID PLANTE (1940–   ). Of the eleven novels David Plante has written to date, the Francoeur novels—*The Family* (1978), *The Country* (1981), and *The Woods* (1982)—investigate his French Canadian, Catholic heritage in an effort to come to terms with the loss of his father and to understand and express his love for his family. Essentially autobiographical, these works are traditional in their basic plot line and use of figurative language and imagery, unlike Plante's earlier works which were written in the mode of the French *nouveau roman*. His latest novels move from the concrete expression of the conventional memoir form to the abstract language of the timeless suggestions of emotional awareness. It is the Francoeur novels, however, that won him wide praise. *The Family* was nominated for the National Book Award in 1978.

Born on March 4, 1940, in Providence, Rhode Island, David Robert Plante received his primary and secondary education in Catholic schools. In 1957 he continued his Catholic education at Boston College. After attending the University of Louvain in Belgium from 1959 to 1960, Plante returned to Boston College and completed his B.A. in French in 1961. Plante was first employed as a teacher of English as a foreign language at the English School in Rome. From 1962 to 1964 he researched and wrote for Hart's Guide to New York. Employed as a teacher of French at St. John's Preparatory School in Danvers, Massachusetts, in 1965, Plante travelled to London in the summer of 1966 where he has resided ever since.

Plante's novels easily divide into two categories: the experimental and the traditional. *The Ghost of Henry James* (1970) and *Slides* (1971) in their allusion to Henry James and to Hawthorne's *Marble Faun* comprise a mixture of sensual realism and vague resolutions of emotional dilemmas. Fragmented dialogue, nameless characters and places, and sexual displacement approximate the nebulous world of human relationships. In both novels, established family relationships are tested by outsiders.

In *Relatives* (1972) and *The Darkness of the Body* (1974), Plante continues his experimentation. Intense moments of realism alternate with vaguely defined people and places. In *Figures in Bright Air* (1976) Plante demonstrates his affinity to the French nouveau roman by completely abandoning verisimilitude. Even though a relationship with a young boy ends in drowning, and a relationship with their parents ends in a break up, the emotional memory remains as a presence.

With the publication of the Francoeur novels, Plante departs from the experimental mode. His thematic concern is essentially the same: the delineation of emotional relationships between members of the family. Plante's own working-class, French Canadian, Catholic upbringing requires the traditional form of the autobiographical novel. In all three Francoeur novels there is a clear plot, realistically defined characters, and an extensive use of figurative language and imagery. In fact, all three novels explore Plante's family heritage and, in the end, enable the narrator to achieve a knowledge and an understanding of human relationships, absent in the more experimental fiction.

In *The Family*, the twelve-year-old narrator Daniel comes to terms with the problems of his family (mother, father, seven brothers) while maintaining an outside life for himself. Catholicism gives Daniel the faith necessary to hold together what are essentially fragile familial relationships. In *The Country* Plante continues his exploration of "the whole, ingrown, internally tangled family." Daniel returns from London to Providence, Rhode Island, to visit his parents, who are by this time old, and, finally, he returns to attend his father's funeral. The narrator's obsessive exploration of his American Indian heritage puts the loss of his father into context. *The Woods* focuses on Daniel's Boston College years. The emotional distance between self and other is again the emphasis. As in *The Family*, Daniel's Catholicism—in particular, the image of the mystical body of Christ—bridges the emotional gap in a human relationship.

On the surface the Francoeur novels seem a departure from his earlier, more abstract work. In all Plante's novels, however, the characters attempt to find a connection to each other and to establish relationships without sacrificing their emotional integrity. In the Francoeur novels, Plante finds in his Catholicism a faith that makes possible at least the attempt to love someone or to understand one's self better.

Plante's most recent work, *Difficult Women* (1982) and *The Foreigner* (1984) reflects his previous technical and thematic concerns. *Difficult Women* records Plante's perception of Jean Rhys, Sonia Orwell, and Germaine Greer in a nonfiction memoir. *The Foreigner* is experimental in the manner of Plante's first novels. Again, the emotional relationship of three characters overshadows any conventional concern for plot, character, or setting.

Plante's strength lies in his precise rendering of physical reality; his weakness is embedded in his strength. Although Plante's books have been described as "moving," they also have been described as self-defeating. That is, Plante records painful emotional experiences, the details of which, by their very nature, make the reading an emotionally difficult experience.

SELECTED BIBLIOGRAPHY

Works by Plante: NOVELS: *The Ghost of Henry James*. London: Macdonald & Co., 1970, Boston: Gambit, 1970; *Slides*. London: Macdonald & Co., 1971; Boston: Gambit, 1971; *Relatives*. London: Cape, 1972; New York: Avon, 1974; *The Darkness of the Body*. London: Cape, 1974; Harmondsworth, UK: Penguin, 1977; Paris: Gallimard, 1977, as *Le Nuit des Corps*; *Figures in Bright Air*. London: Gollancz, 1976; *The Family*. London: Gollancz, 1978; New York: Farrar, Straus & Giroux, 1978; *The Country*. London: Gollancz, 1981; New York: Atheneum, 1981; *The Woods*. London: Gollancz, 1982; New York: Atheneum, 1982; *Difficult Women*. London: Gollancz, 1982; New York: Atheneum, 1983; *The Foreigner*. New York: Atheneum, 1984; *The Catholic*. New York: Atheneum, 1986. TRANSLATION: Andreas Embiricos. *Two stories: Argo, or the Voyage of a Balloon*. Trans. David Plante and Nikos Stangos. London: A. Ross, 1967. SHORT STORIES: "The Fountain Tree" and "The Crack" in Penguin Modern Stories 1. Ed. Judith Burnley. Harmondsworth, UK: Penguin, 1969; Preface in *Beyond the Words: Eleven Writers in Search of a New Fiction*. Ed. Giles Gordon. London: Hutchinson, 1975; "Work" in *Prize Stories 1983*. The O. Henry Awards. Ed. William Abrahams. Garden City, N.Y.: Doubleday, 1983. "The Buried City." *Transatlantic Review* 24 (Spring 1967); pp. 78–85; "The Tangled Centre." *Modern Occasions* 1 (Spring 1971); pp. 356–60; "This Strange Country." *New Yorker* 55 (7 January 1980); pp. 32–40; "Mr. Bonito." *New Yorker* 56 (7 July 1980); pp. 30–34; "Work." *New Yorker* 57 (21 September 1981); pp. 41–48; "The Accident." *New Yorker* 58 (9 August 1982); pp. 29–38; "The State of Fiction. A Symposium." *New Review* 5 (Summer 1978); pp. 59–60; "Jean Rhys: A Remembrance." *Paris Review* 21 (1979); pp. 238–84; "A House of Women." *New Yorker* (28 April 1986); pp. 30–32; "The Virgin." *London Review of Books* (3 April 1986).

Works about Plante: Bixby, George, comp. "David Plante: A Bibliographical Checklist." *American Book Collector* 5 (1984), pp. 25–28; Review of *The Darkness of the Body*. *New Statesman* (1 February 1974), p. 159; Review of *Difficult Women*. *Time* (7 February 1983), p. 82; Review of *The Family*. *Newsweek* (24 July 1978), p. 82; Review of *The Woods*. *Time* (2 August 1982), p. 77. CA 37–40. CANR 12. CN.

John Marc Mucciolo

KATHERINE ANNE PORTER (1890–1980). Katherine Anne Porter's life has often proved as enigmatic as her fiction. Not until Porter's appointed biographer, Joan Givner, published her *Katherine Anne Porter: A Life* (1982) was the autobiographical fog created by Porter cleared away to reveal how much of her fiction grew out of her varied, exciting, although often difficult life. Psychological conflict and the conflict between men and women dominate both her life and her fiction, but her desperate quest for faith, hope and love colors all other struggles from her earliest work to her last. She wrote most of her fiction between 1922 and 1942, but her only novel, *Ship of Fools*, was not published until 1962, although she worked on it for twenty years and published it in parts as early as 1944. In 1965, she won a National Book Award and a Pulitzer Prize for *The Collected Stories of Katherine Anne Porter*, which contains the previously published short stories upon which her greatness rests.

Porter, named Callie Russell at birth, was born on May 15, 1890 in Indian Creek, Texas. Her mother died two months before Porter's second birthday; thus, her father, for whom she often expressed animosity, and her paternal grandmother, Aunt Cat (Catherine Anne), reared her. The Grandmother in "Old Mortality" and *The Old Order* suggests the importance of her grandmother in her life, as does Porter's legally changing her name to Katherine Anne in 1915. Under Aunt Cat's care, Porter experienced stern religious fundamentalism, against which she later rebelled, but she also learned strength and perseverance. Although Porter claimed to have been Catholic and educated in convents as a child, Givner proves that Porter converted from her family's Methodism to Catholicism in 1910, while married to her first husband, and that she received little formal education, presenting an aunt's experiences in a convent as her own (Givner 57). Much of her fiction, however, was drawn from her own experiences. From the poverty of her youth and her disastrous first marriage, she went on to work as a journalist, to travel extensively, to live in Mexico and throughout the United States, and finally, to achieve financial success and to win several literary awards, all the while living a personal life more turbulent than any of her fictional heroines and a spiritual life torn between her youthful encounter with her grandmother's faith and father's impiety and her own desire for faith and preference for Catholicism (Givner 68, 102).

In Porter's best work, the protagonist's struggle for faith, hope, or any type of charity or love usually ends in despair. The only stories ending with any hint of optimism are the Miranda stories, her most obviously autobiographical tales. The Miranda of "Pale Horse, Pale Rider" overcomes the death of Adam, serious illness, and loss of hope, to conclude with " 'I believe' " and with the final thought, "Now there would be time for everything." *The Old Order* ends with "The Grave," the magnificent story of Miranda's symbolic confrontation with sexuality and death that includes a Proustian recollection of the "dreadful vision" of an incident with her brother twenty years before. And finally, "Old Mortality," another story of growing up, ends with Miranda's looking to the future with hopefulness in defiance of the pessimism of the adults around her. Life for Miranda lies in front of her, but once Porter's protagonist reaches adulthood or old age, the outlook becomes less hopeful.

In "The Jilting of Granny Weatherall," a story from her first published collection, *The Leaning Tower and Other Stories* (New York: Harcourt, Brace & Co., 1944), Porter brings the struggle for faith together with hope and charity as nowhere else and creates a character who loses all. As Granny dies, she reaches in her memories to clean out thoughts of the jilting by George, recalls the pain with thoughts of hell, and admits that she has gotten everything back that George took, except for one thing, never identified directly, but implied in the conclusion of her story—her faith. The bridegroom George's desertion becomes the Bridegroom Christ's absence as she dies. Her devout life has been a lie, and peace never comes because she cannot forget the loss of George and cannot bring herself to confess her secret grief to anyone. Thus, without faith, hope, or even charity, Granny drops her rosary, cries for something alive, and dies totally alone.

Her most obviously despairing story, however, is "Noon Wine," from her second major collection. Whereas Granny Weatherall commits spiritual suicide, Mr. Thompson actually kills himself; Granny rejects the Church, but Thompson's church fails him. As a Protestant, and a half-hearted one at that, he cannot rid himself of his burden and as a selfish, prideful man, he has no place to turn but inward. The public confessions to which he drags his wife bring no relief, and he cannot find the "serenity and peace" of "unburdening" himself that the Church confessional provided Porter (Givner 508). Since for Mr. Thompson a man's religion is his own business, he carries his burden alone and, in his final hopelessness, dies without peace and without forgiveness.

Porter's "The Leaning Tower" and *Ship of Fools*, her last published fiction, present equally desperate characters. The stories, not as well written as her earlier fiction, lack the careful sense of coherence and realistic and penetrating characterization, but her depiction of the wasteland of modern society and of the emptiness of each character's life creates an uneasiness akin to that caused by the work of Porter's friend and sister Catholic writer, Flannery O'Connor.* Porter spent her own life searching for faith, hope, and love, and although most of her characters failed, she succeeded at least in part: she achieved success, filled her life with friends and lovers, and though unorthodox in the practice of her chosen religion throughout most of her life, turned to the Church in her last years, apparently finding more peace when she died than did Granny Weatherall (Givner 102).

SELECTED BIBLIOGRAPHY

Works by Porter: *Ship of Fools*. Boston: Little, Brown & Co., 1962. *The Collected Stories of Katherine Anne Porter*. New York: Harcourt, Brace & Co., 1965.

Works about Porter: Bloom, Harold, ed. *Katherine Anne Porter*. New York: Chelsea House, 1986; Brinkmeyer, Robert H., Jr. "Endless Remembering: The Artistic Vision of Katherine Anne Porter." *Mississippi Quarterly* 40 (1986–1987), pp. 5–19; DeMouary, Jane Krause. *Katherine Anne Porter's Women: The Eye of Her Fiction*. Austin: University of Texas Press, 1983; Givner, Joan. *Katherine Anne Porter: A Life*. New York: Simon and Schuster, 1982; Gretlund, Jan Nordby. "Katherine Anne Porter and the South: A Corrective." *Mississippi Quarterly* 34 (1981), pp. 435–44. AWW. CA 2. CANR 1. CN. DLB4, 9. TCA.

Deborah J. Barrett

CRAWFORD POWER (1909–). Crawford Power has never received the critical attention which his single work of fiction should have earned. Published first in 1951, issued again in 1965 and 1984 (Overlook Press), *The Encounter* dramatizes the contemporary crisis of spiritual value in conflict with materialism.

For Father Thomas Cawder, the hero of the novel, the pain of the struggle lacks the ameliorative power of love of God or humanity.

Born in 1909 in Baltimore, Maryland, Crawford Power was educated "first, by the nuns of Notre Dame," and later at the Gilman Country School. After a year at Georgetown, he transferred to Yale where he received a B.A. in 1931 and a B.F.A. in architecture in 1934. He held what he describes as "a couple of foolish" jobs in Washington before trying unsuccessfully during the middle of the depression to find architectural work in New York City. In 1938 he bought a farm in Virginia.

During World War II, Power worked for Civilian Defense and later served in the U.S. Navy as Specialist X, First Class in which capacity he "wrote answers to complaints from the Fleet in the Pacific."

In 1935, Power married Mary Cornelia Hunt with whom he had four children, three of whom survive. Mrs. Power died in 1978.

Crawford Power continues to live on his farm where he is preparing "a tentative Hebrew text of *Canticles*" and a book on the origins of stone architecture.

Power has said that *The Encounter* "started as an experiment in writing a novel (I wanted to see what writing a novel was like)," and is based on "a popular tale in the world of Byzantium . . . : a history of an austere monk famous for his sanctified life of penance and prayer." The monk asks an angel to show him another man who might be "equal in merit before God." The angel obliges by pointing out, "resting on the steps of the Church, a mountebank flute player, an iterant entertainer."

In Power's modernized version, the priest is Father Thomas Cawder, thin, all skin and bones" (p. 4), pastor of St. Gregory's Catholic Church in Lulworth, Pennsylvania, where parishioners "really have everything [they] need." (p. 3) Repulsed by "this cult of comfort" which, like the padded kneelers in modern churches, has nothing to do "with what is useful or desirable in a church" (p. 5), Father Cawder practices his own private forms of deprivation and austerity. To mortify himself, Cawder wears a heavy chain around his waist, but he discovers after four months that this "supererogatory pain could yield pleasure, a secret dandling conceit," and that a "crude penance for pride and egotism was in itself a goad to pride" (p. 236).

From his position of sanctified "metaphysical egomania" (p. 232), Father Cawder realizes and confronts the essential truth of his life: "the knowledge of being touched by nothing" (p. 272), especially love. The process of discovery develops through an encounter between his internal holy deprived self and the man who images Cawder's self living in the world.

In a dream, Cawder learns that he must search a visiting carnival to find "a lumpish grayish figure" of a man named Diamond, who, like the mountebank in the Byzantine fable, stands in equal merit with Cawder "in the eyes of God" (p. 34). While Diamond throws himself from great heights into a small pool of water because he likes the dive, Cawder dives into his quest as a proof of his unflappable faith.

Following his belief that Diamond's appearance in his life signifies the workings of God's grace in the world, Cawder commits himself to rescuing the child of Diamond's lover, Stella, from a brothel where she has lived since birth while Stella wanders the carnival circuit with Diamond. At first, it is difficult to say what motivates Cawder's action for he shows no real caring for Diamond, Stella, or Stella's lost child.

In fact, Cawder shows no love except a perverted vain love of self, "the core of faithful passion warming every man on earth except saints" (p. 152). Each of the characters whom he encounters serves to reveal Cawder's loathing not only of the human condition, but of individual human beings as well. He cruelly dismisses his well-intentioned housekeeper and he condescendingly tolerates Father Moran, his socially conscious young assistant as too much of the world. In the end, when Diamond murders Stella in a fit of jealousy and comes to Cawder seeking sanctuary, the dried up priest grants shelter to the murderer but shows no love or acceptance of Diamond's tortured humanity.

Ironically, Father Cawder discovers that he is very much like the killer Diamond who confuses love and possession: as Diamond must possess Stella in death, Father Cawder must possess God in a grip of cold spirituality. In killing the basic Christian tenet that God is love, Cawder in a sense kills God. Like Diamond who denies his crime of murder, Cawder has lied all his life about his love for God. Recognizing his similarity to Diamond means that Cawder must recognize his participation in the fallen mediocrity of all humanity and must accept that he is of equal merit with Diamond in the eyes of God; austerity alone does not make a saint.

If Father Cawder sees himself finally as a part of humanity, he remains apart from humanity. This realization brings home the essential terror of his loveless existence. When Cawder inspects Diamond's bloodied body outside Cawder's church, he realizes that were he himself to die, he would find no salvation with God because he has cut himself off from love.

But death would be no evil to those capable of love. . . . To rest suspended in that sun poorly named love . . . one remained oneself and one transmitted. . . . I am trivial and abominable, he pondered, I can envy the joy of those who love God, I who cannot love another man. (pp. 309–10)

Father Cawder's is the dilemma of a man who acts joylessly and dutifully on the basis of moral and religious abstractions: he can rescue Stella's daughter from the brothel not because he loves her or her mother, but because it is a proper act of charity. Similarly, he shelters Diamond out of conformity with the Church's medieval dictum to harbor the lost. Without love of God or human being, Cawder is left only with the cold comfort of belief in the existence of a distant Deity: " . . . in the face of the mystery which pervades all matter like consuming fire I can say only, Lord, I believe that You exist" (p. 309).

If there is faith but no love, if there is duty but no joy, if there is sacrifice but no compassion, can there be any hope for the miserable Father Cawder? The answer lies in Cawder's abiding sense of self-awareness: as Irving Howe has pointed out in his afterword to the 1983 edition of the novel, Father Cawder needs always to know where he stands in relationship with God. But awareness brings no relief from the torment of prideful self-deprivation. If there is hope for Father Cawder, it comes only from the possibility that, with the help of grace, self-awareness may eventually lead to change, to a warming of the heart. Ironically, Father Cawder is right about the presence of evil and decadence in the world, but his cold austerity provides little sustenance for his bloodless faith: "But it was of no benefit to oneself, it was not pleasing to God, to pretend to love when no such faculty was present." (p. 308).

Power's rendering of the presence (or absence) of grace and love in the world gains efficacy from the narrative structure which mirrors the encounter between a self-aware Joycean inner world and a materialistic outer world fully realized in naturalistic detail. We live in the dark dense world of Cawder's reflections and Diamond's carnival because we live in the conflict between the diction of abstraction and the diction of materiality.

Above all, Crawford Power's refusal to condemn the self-tortured Father Cawder sets *The Encounter* apart from works by writers like Flannery O'Connor* whose concerns with the mysterious workings of grace mirror those of Power, but whose human sympathies seem closer to those of Father Cawder. Perhaps this combination of compassion, intelligence, evocative language, and structure will raise *The Encounter* once again, as it has twice in the past, to remind readers of the truth at its center: love is the greatest of all virtues.

SELECTED BIBLIOGRAPHY

Works by Power: *The Encounter*. New York: W. Sloane, 1950; rpt. with Afterword by Irving Howe. Woodstock, N.Y.: The Overlook Press, 1983.

Works about Power: Review of *The Encounter*. *New York Times* (11 June 1950), p. 38; *Newsweek* (5 March 1984), p. 83.

Daniel J. Tynan

J(AMES) F(ARL) POWERS (1917–). J. F. Powers has said that he should not write junk because he is a Catholic writer. Beginning with his first story in 1942, writing slowly—often not more than a page or two a day—with painstaking craftsmanship, Powers has compiled three collections of stories and a novel, which won the National Book Award for 1962. Not impressive in quantity, his work receives the highest accolades from writers and critics alike. A consummate artist, a master of the short story, Powers writes in the comic mode, reflecting his vision of man as subject to the forces of both gravity and grace, and producing work of great richness of theme, tone, and ironic complexity.

One of the three children of James Ansbury and Zella (Routzong) Powers, James Earl Powers was born on July 8, 1917, in Jacksonville, Illinois, and grew up in economically comfortable conditions. He graduated from Quincy College

Academy in Quincy, Illinois, in 1935, where he was an average student but proficient in athletics, especially basketball. Although some of his closest friends entered the seminary, Powers never considered the priesthood for himself. Living with his parents, Powers sought work in Chicago in 1935. He was a clerk at Marshall Field's, sold insurance for the Fidelity Insurance Company, chauffeured a wealthy investor through the South, and served as an editor with the Chicago Historical Records Survey.

From 1938 to 1940, he attended classes at the Chicago branch of Northwestern University. While working as a clerk at Brentano's bookstore in 1942, he wrote his first story, "He Don't Plant Cotton." Meeting social rebels like the Catholic Workers, Negro jazz musicians, and political exiles from Europe helped shape Powers's attitude toward the war and American society. His strong religious convictions led to his becoming a pacifist in 1943, and to doing alternate service as a hospital orderly in a Chicago hospital. Also in 1943, Powers was the only layman to attend a priests' retreat in Collegeville, Minnesota. Following a one-man retreat at an orphanage in Oakmont, near Pittsburgh, where he read intensively, Powers wrote his first mature story, "Lions, Harts, Leaping Does." In 1945, Powers met Elizabeth Alice Wahl, also a writer, and they were married in 1946. They have three daughters and two sons.

In 1947, Powers lived at Yaddo to finish his first book of stories, *Prince of Darkness and Other Stories* (1947). Two of these stories won O. Henry citations and the critical success of his book gained him entrée to better-paying journals such as *Colliers*, *New Yorker*, *Partisan Review*, and *The Reporter*. He rarely completed more than one story a year.

Over the years Powers has taught briefly at various colleges and universities: Marquette University, 1949–1951; University of Michigan, 1956–1957; Smith College, 1965–1966; and at St. John's University in 1976. He spent another residency at Yaddo in 1951. In intervening years, Powers and his family lived in Ireland, at Greystones in 1951, and in Dalkey, 1957–1958, and again at Greystones, 1963–1965. Powers received a National Institute of Arts and Letters grant in 1948, a Guggenheim Fellowship in 1948, and Rockefeller Fellowships in 1954, 1957, and 1967. He is a member of the National Institute of Arts and Letters.

In large measure, J. F. Powers's reputation as a writer rests on his ironic and satiric treatment of priests, not in extreme circumstances, as in some of Graham Greene's novels, but in the everyday struggles of parish life. Even so, Powers's priests are men in tension between the ideal and the actual, the eternal and the temporal, the spiritual and the worldly. This conflict is also central to his non-clerical stories. In his first collection, *The Prince of Darkness and Other Stories*, "The Trouble," "The Eye," and "He Don't Plant Cotton" portray racial tensions and black-white violence. Three other stories, "Jamsie," "Renner," and "The Old Bird. A Love Story," reflect the broken dreams, prejudice, and disappointments symptomatic of fundamental moral and spiritual struggles besetting America as a whole. As a writer who is self-consciously Catholic, Powers explores throughout his work the burdens of Christian existence in a secular world.

Certainly on one level, Powers's clerical stories offer comic and satiric treatments of priestly venality, vain posturings, intense struggles over often petty or trivial matters. While a few churchly readers have taken umbrage at such portrayals, most of Powers's critics, within the Church as without, find his work a serious exploration of the human condition. For these readers, Powers's stories are not just about priests, but rather, and more importantly, about priests whose struggles mirror the moral and spiritual conflicts of us all, and offer a microcosm of the tensions between sin and virtue in our age. That his treatment is more often comic reflects Powers's profound compassion for his subjects, based on his conviction that humans are both fallen and redeemed.

The protagonist in Powers's story "Look How the Fish Live" (1975) declares that "all problems were at bottom theological," by which Powers does not mean doctrinal squabbles, but spiritual relevance. Stories of unworthy priests—as in "The Valiant Woman," "The Lord's Day," and "The Prince of Darkness"— make vivid the rift between the ideal and the actual. Moreover, Powers often leaves the resolution ambiguous, as in the clash between the old and young priests in "The Forks." Even the sad but well-deserved fate of Father Burner of "The Prince of Darkness" is not completely foreclosed; he may yet rediscover his vocation. Indeed, Powers comes back to Father Burner in his next collection, *The Presence of Grace* (1956). The stories "Defection of a Favorite" and "Death of a Favorite" show a man moving out of the spiritual wasteland he had made of his life. Father Didymus in "Lions, Harts, Leaping Does," also illustrates the internal struggle of a man caged by his own rationality who at last finds an incomprehensible peace through falling snow and the presence of saintly Brother Titus.

At stake in most of Powers's stories is not only the fate of an individual's soul, but also the nature of the Church and its position in the world. These issues are not mutually exclusive, and they are treated at length in Powers's award-winning novel *Morte D'Urban* (1962). The novel is a profound study of the spiritual paradoxes of success. Father Urban is "one of the Best," a real operator and go-getter, who gets sent to his order's Siberia for his efforts. While there Urban tries to make a humble retreat center into a country club, equating worldly success with spiritual progress, a view he forsakes through a series of temptations overcome and a blow on the head from the bishop's golf ball. The references to Thomas Malory and the weaving in of the Arthurian legend give additional resonance and complexity to the novel. Urban's "death" is the death of his prideful and egotistical self. Ascending to the provincial of his order, Urban makes few changes and seems in retreat, a mystery to those who knew him. What are the implications of this for the Church in the world? Does worldly success spell spiritual death?

Powers's third collection of stories, *Look How the Fish Live*, appeared in 1975 to mixed reviews. Some of the stories are an ambiguous treatment of the post–Vatican II Church and its misplaced or confused spirituality. One of the strongest stories is "Keystone," an exploration of the conflict between an aging bishop and his wheeling-and-dealing young chancellor, who has his way in the building of the new cathedral without keystones. Finally, the bishop notices cracks in all the arches, an ending suggesting ambiguities in the present course of the Church.

Powers continues to publish stories in such magazines as *New Yorker* and *Critic*.

SELECTED BIBLIOGRAPHY

Works by Powers: SHORT STORY COLLECTIONS: *Prince of Darkness and Other Stories*. New York: Doubleday, 1947, rep. New York: Random House, 1979, New York: Viking, 1982; *The Presence of Grace*. New York: Doubleday, 1956; *Look How the Fish Live*. New York: Knopf, 1975. NOVEL: *Morte D'Urban*. New York: Doubleday, 1962, rep. New York: Random House, 1979, New York: Viking, 1982. *Wheat That Springeth Green*. New York: Knopf, 1988.

Works about Powers: Evans, Fallon, ed. *J. F. Powers*. St. Louis: Herder, n.d.; Hagopian, John V. *J. F. Powers*. New York: Twayne, 1968; Kort, Wesley A. *Shriven Selves*. Philadelphia: Fortress Press, 1972; Preston, Thomas R. "Christian Folly in the Fiction of J. F. Powers." *Critique* 16, 2 (1974), pp. 91–107; Wynard, Eleanor B. "J. F. Powers: Comic Caricature and Christianity." *Cross Currents* 32 (1982), pp. 316–22. CA 3. CANR 2. Cat A (1952). CN. TCA.

John G. Parks

JESSICA POWERS (1905–   ). A member of the Carmel of the Mother of God in Pewaukee, Wisconsin, Jessica Powers, known as Sister Miriam of the Holy Spirit, has published over 240 poems in magazines in addition to two volumes of poetry. She was born in Mauston, Wisconsin, on February 7, 1905, the daughter of Scotch-Irish American parents. Following elementary and secondary schooling, she attended Marquette University in Milwaukee from 1922 to 1923, but returned to the family farm after the death of her parents. She went to New York in 1937. During her four years there she honed her writing skills with both poetry and short stories and became active in the Catholic Poetry Society of America. She also was introduced to the poetry of St. John of the Cross through friends in the religious life. Her first book of poems, *The Lantern Burns*, was published in 1939.

Even though her poetry was well received by readers and critics, poetry in itself was not sufficient to nourish the spiritual sensibility that more and more called her attention. In 1941 she returned to Wisconsin and entered the Carmel of the Mother of God; perpetual profession took place on May 8, 1946.

The dark, inner journey preoccupies her poetry; the touch of St. John of the Cross graces even early poems. The paradox that informs St. John's vision secures her poetry. The image of journey is also a mystical constant in her poems. It is difficult not to compare Jessica Powers to St. John of the Cross; in the dark journey elicited through simple, dense, paradoxical language, they are soul mates.

SELECTED BIBLIOGRAPHY

Works by Powers: POETRY: *The Lantern Burns*. New York: The Monastine Press, 1939; *The Place of Splendor*. New York: Cosmopolitan Science & Art Service, Inc., 1946. *Mountain Sparrow*. Carmel of Reno, n.d. Also in such magazines as *America*, *Commonweal*, *Catholic World*, *Sign*, *Spirit*, and *Poetry*, and in such newspapers as *Washington Post* and *New York Times*.

Works about Powers: Baldwin, S. M. Luke, SSND. "Burns the Great Lantern." *Catholic World* 168 (February 1949), pp. 354–61; Geigel, Winifred F. "A Comparative Study of the Poetry of Jessica Powers and St. John of the Cross." Unpublished thesis, St. John's University, 1960; Hopkins, J. G. E. "A Modern Poet with a Medieval Ideal." *America* 61, 21 (September 2, 1939); pp. 498–99; McDonnell, Thomas P. "The Nun as Poet." *Spirit* 26, 1 (March 1959); pp. 20–26; Schaeverling, Margaret. "Sister Miriam of the Holy Spirit." *Magnificat* 83, 4 (February 1949), pp. 168–72; Shufletavski, Dorothy. "Fosterling of Night." Clarke College *Labarum*. Dubuque, Iowa (1945), p. 252.

Mary E. Giles

MARIO PUZO (1920–). Confirmed in the subject of his latest book, *The Sicilian* (1984), Mario Puzo has been acclaimed a leading American writer whose works personify the contemporary widespread and organized violence in the nation. Puzo's various novels have received particular recognition because he deals aggressively with the areas of Italian Americans to which the mass media have given national notoriety. Readers are not always concerned with the possibility that criminality may be only a fractional aberration from the normal behavior of the members of a minority. Ironically, therefore, the protagonists command both respect and sympathy, stirring in the reader the wistful desire that genius be put to better use. Puzo portrays immigrants who, while battling among themselves, by their very nature obey the laws of the nation. This he does with fierce, intense, and compelling treatment of plot told in the most appropriate of language.

Mario Puzo has gathered his material from authentic personal sources. Born in New York City on October 15, 1920, he was educated at Columbia University and at the New School for Social Research. Once a civil service employee, and the former editor of *Male* magazine, he has been the literary reviewer for various periodicals. He lives with his wife and five children in Bayshore, Long Island. His major works include *The Dark Arena* (1953), *The Fortunate Pilgrim* (1964), *The Runaway Summer of Davie Shaw* (1966), *The Godfather* (1969), *Inside Las Vegas* (1977), *Fools Die* (1978), and *The Sicilian*. Having also written screenplays, he is continually busy writing fiction.

Puzo's basic theme is that material success in any area operates on the same dark principle. Hence, in *The Dark Arena* he writes about the occupation of Germany after World War II, exploring the extremes to which military occupation leads both the conquered and the conquerer. Dramatizing this exploration in the depiction of the problems of one soldier, the author creates a microscopic model of our national military machinery. With a masterful talent for precision and verisimilitude Puzo creates with inventiveness and evocation of mood and place.

His style is controlled and versatile, sounding the action of the situations, the intensities of emotional pressure, and the speech habits of the characters, especially Walter Mosca.

In his second novel, *The Fortunate Pilgrim*, Puzo lifts the story of one tenacious immigrant, Lucia Santa Angeluzzi-Corbo, to the broad American theme of the struggle of an ethnic minority to survive and achieve what social scientists call upward mobility. With survival as the basic theme personified in Lucia, Puzo examines the socioeconomic morality that he treats more extensively in *The Godfather*. The author tells a gripping story that is illuminated by recognizable people involved in dramatic episodes. In his precise portrayals, Puzo evidences no condescension, or reactive defensiveness. When he uses colloquial diction with ethnic overtones, it is to intensify the characters. In its legend, force, insight, language, authenticity, and persuasion, *The Fortunate Pilgrim* has been considered the classical Italian-American novel.

It was *The Godfather*—the fastest selling book in the history of American publishing—that placed Mario Puzo among the leading writers of America. With great sweep and hurtling pace, he constructs a unique story, setting in motion the plot and subplots that make the novel massive, turbulent, and vibrating with progressive tensions. In telling the story of Don Vito Corleone, Puzo is warning the nation of its sinister and powerful fraternities of crime free to operate only in a democracy whose law enforcement is corrupt. Thematically the book challenges America's racial categories, dynastic tendencies, and social prejudices. Structurally the book abounds with evil incident, debased sex, and primitive terror, realistically recording the solecisms and colloquialisms of the Italian-American characters. Puzo has written in *The Godfather* a powerful novel that confronts evils that must be checked.

In *Fools Die* Puzo deals with a composite national problem. He layers his action with a mixture of characters caught hopelessly in America's enchantment with chance and competition in the pursuit of power. The author states that when the power-mongers achieve success they feel no satisfaction; hence, the fools die. In the violent, green baize world of Las Vegas, and in the lionized literary figures of the age, Puzo has created a metaphor for contemporary American civilization—the gambling casino. He urges that "while we will not die as crooks, we must not die as fools.

Critics have noted that with his latest book, *The Sicilian*, Puzo has surpassed even *The Godfather*. In this account of Michael Corleone, who is charged with the mission of going to Sicily to return to America with Salvatore Guiliano, the action sets in motion a war with the Mafia. The author presents heroic action, deceit, and suspense—all in the intense dramatization of evil "on an epic scale," the momentum reaching heights by the magical terror of the "Friends of Friends." It is Puzo's brilliant talent that punctures the sinister reality of the story.

Mario Puzo has won acceptance for his books as both works of art and valid documents of American civilization. As one must know sin to save one's soul, so art distorts creation in order to recreate. Puzo has accepted the challenges of the distorted image of the Italian-American and has created contemporary heroes who confront both inadequacy and corruption. Michael Corleone joins the general family of America, but he keeps a wary eye on its humanity. In this way, the art of Puzo must be judged among the best of contemporary American fiction.

SELECTED BIBLIOGRAPHY:

Works by Puzo: *The Dark Arena*. New York: Random House, 1953; *The Fortunate Pilgrim*. New York: Atheneum, 1964; *The Godfather*. New York: Putnam's, 1969; *The Godfather Paper and Other Confessions*. New York: Putnam's, 1972; *Inside Las Vegas*. New York: Grosset and Dunlap, 1977; *Fools Die*. New York: Putnam's, 1978; *The Sicilian*. New York: Linden Press/Simon & Schuster, 1984. SCREENPLAYS: *The Godfather*. 1972; *The Godfather, Part II*. 1974; *Earthquake*. 1974; *Superman*. 1979; *Superman II*. 1980.

Works about Puzo: Chiampi, James Thomas. "Resurrecting *The Godfather*." *MELUS* 5 (1978), pp. 18–31; Di Pietro, Robert J. "Language, Culture and the Specialist in Ethnic Literature." *MELUS* 4 (1977), p. 2–6; McWilliams, Wilson Carey. "Natty Bumppo and the Godfather." In *The Artist and Political Vision*, ed. Benjamin R. Barber and Michael J. McGrath. New Brunswick, N.J.: Transaction Press, 1982; Minganti, Franco. "The Hero with a Thousand and Three Faces: Michele, Mike, Michael Corleone." *Rivista di Studi Anglo-Americano* 3 (1984–1985), pp. 257–68; Mulas, Francesco. "Prolepsis in Mario Puzo's *The Godfather*." *Rivista di Studi Anglo-Americano* 3 (1984–1985), pp. 353–63. CA 65–68. CANR 4. CN. DLB 6.

Rose Basile Green

Q

DAVID QUAMMEN (1948–). David Quammen's fiction displays a mastery of narrative structure, learned, Quammen tells us, from Robert Penn Warren, his mentor at Yale, and from the study of William Faulkner. Though readers may at times find character and action more fascinating than probable and may wish for a deeper probing of character and of the mystery of life, there are rich rewards in the swiftness of movement, the mastery of suspense, the witty prose, and the skillful and illuminating integration of fictional experience with historical events.

Quammen was born on February 24, 1948 in Cincinnati, Ohio, where he graduated from St. Xavier High School in 1966. He received his B.A. from Yale (1970) and a B. Litt. from Oxford (1970–1973) on a Rhodes Scholarship. In 1973, he moved to Montana to do some trout fishing, and ended up staying for the peacefulness of the woods and water. There he studied zoology at the University of Montana, began to write reviews and especially nature essays, and returned to the writing of fiction begun at Yale. He is a regular columnist for *Outside* magazine, and many of his nature essays have been collected under the title of his monthly column, *Natural Acts* (1985). When Quammen is not travelling on assignment, he resides in Bozeman, Montana, with his wife, Kristine Ellingsen.

In *To Walk the Line* (1970), John Patrick Scully, an idealistic college student, spends a frustrating but eye-opening summer on a social action project in a black Chicago ghetto in the turbulent 1960s. The project, headed by Jesuit seminarian Dan O'Brien, conducts a systematic campaign of harassment against the unscrupulous realtors who operate in the area. The novel focuses on the relationship between John and Tyrone Williams, an angry, young, streetwise black. Both John and Tyrone are brought to a painful awareness of how understanding, cooperation, and even loyalty can be limited by social, historical, and psychological dynamics. *To Walk the Line* is an insightful and unsentimental probing of American realities.

The Zolta Configuration (1983), set in contemporary California and New Mexico, is a hard-to-put-down spy thriller, in the background of which are the development of thermonuclear weapons and the Vietnam War. John North called it "a sweeping adventure told with staccato delivery and waspish wit." Mayberry, a Vietnam veteran and third-year medical student, is caught up in a complex intrigue when he unexpectedly comes into possession of an awesomely important document. The action is at times sensational but never pointless, and, if some of the characters verge on caricature, they are colorful and recognizable. The historical flashbacks are thought-provoking, and moral issues are implicit in the action. Mayberry, a shrewd but by no means idealized hero, handles problems within the framework of his own rugged situation ethics.

In 1987 Quammen published a third novel, *The Soul of Viktor Temkin*, and a collection of novellas, *Bloodline: Three Novellas*.

SELECTED BIBLIOGRAPHY

Works by Quammen: NOVELS: *To Walk the Line*. New York: Alfred A. Knopf, 1970; *The Zolta Configuration*. Garden City, N.Y.: Doubleday & Company, Inc., 1983. *The Soul of Victor Temkin*. New York: Doubleday, 1987. SHORT STORIES: "Walking Out." *TriQuarterly*. 1980 Spring; 48:175–202; "Nathan's Rime." 1982 Fall; 55:198–217. NOVELLAS: *Bloodline: Three Novellas*. St. Paul, Minn.: Graywolf Press, 1987. NON-FICTION: *Natural Acts*. New York: Nick Lyons Books, 1985.

Works about Quammen: Ellin, Stanley. "*The Zolta Configuration*." *The New York Times Book Review* (3 July 1983), 88:8. North, John. "*The Zolta Configuration*." *Library Journal* (1 June 1983), 108:1159.

Joseph H. Wessling

R

DAVID (WILLIAM) RABE (1940–). It will be some time yet before criticism can sketch a reliable portrait of the plays of David Rabe. For one thing, Rabe is a young writer whose work remains a curious mixture of unpolished potential and recognized accomplishment. For another, his plays have proven themselves controversial with respect to both style and substance. In 1985, for instance, *Hurlyburly* (1984)—Rabe's first major new play on Broadway since *Streamers* (1976)—was one of four finalists for that year's Tony Award. It eventually lost to Neil Simon's *Biloxi Blues*, but that did not deter its audience; as *Variety* (5 June 1985) pointed out, *Hurlyburly* was one of only four shows on Broadway to show a profit during the 1984–1985 season.

In a sense, the reception of *Hurlyburly*—which Rabe has referred to as his "guys' play" (*New York Times Magazine*, 26 May 1985), and which deals with four men who live in or around Hollywood and the women they use and misuse— might stand as a model for all the reaction Rabe has evoked so far. The play had an impressive audience response, and it drew largely favorable reviews from the critics. But in their end-of-season retrospectives, the critics seemed far less conclusive. Gerald Weales spoke of the play as a "disquieting" work that nonetheless contained scenes "so funny that I wanted to burst into tears," and he praised it as "clearly a contemporary play—discursive, ironic, inconclusive" (p. 620). Robert Leiter, on the other hand, found radical flaws in precisely the same locations where Neales had discovered central virtues; for him, *Hurlyburly* was "overly long, unconvincing, muddled in thought and filled with bombastic language masquerading as the height of realistic speech." "Ninety-eight percent of the play is hot air," he wrote, and noted that "it's a wonder that a contingent of feminists hasn't picketed the theater" (p. 297). And somewhere between these contradictory views comes the view of Rabe himself: "There are a lot of opinions about the women in *Hurlyburly* and accusations of misogyny that I don't think are particularly accurate. I find that the women are the forces for feeling in the play. In many ways, that's the most positive thing in it'' (*NYTM*).

Given only a thumbnail sketch of Rabe's life, one might expect a less raucous assessment of the merits of his work. He was born on March 10, 1940 in Dubuque, Iowa, and took his B.A. in English from Loras College in 1962. Thereafter he received an M.A. in theater from Villanova University (1968), and went on to a brief but successful stint with the *New Haven Register*, where his work for the *Sunday Pictorial Magazine* earned him an Associated Press award for feature writing. The early 1970s found him back at Villanova as an assistant professor in theater, and also marked the beginnings of his professional career as a dramatist. In 1967 he had received a Rockefeller grant for play-wrighting and had begun work on *The Basic Training of Pavlo Hummel*, which debuted at Joseph Papp's Public Theater in May 1971 and won an Obie Award. Its success was shortly thereafter surpassed by the reception of *Sticks and Bones* (1971), which won the Tony Award for Best Play on Broadway, a citation from the New York Drama Critics Circle, an Outer Circle Award, and an award from *Variety*. In 1974 *Sticks and Bones* and *Pavlo Hummel* were jointly honored by the American Academy of Arts and Letters; and in 1976 Rabe's *Streamers* won both the New York Drama Critics Circle Award for Best American Play and the Drama Desk Award for Outstanding New Play.

These three plays are generally referred to as a trilogy, and certainly they have their roots in the same dark corner of the garden. Drafted into the army in 1965, Rabe served until 1967; and both his tour of duty and the trilogy that followed in its wake centered on the experience of Vietnam.

The playwright wrote his own introduction to the volume that contains *Pavlo Hummel* and *Sticks and Bones*, and his remarks suggest that the writing of the trilogy was a necessary act of exorcism. He more than once speaks of his wartime experiences as an ''obsession,'' and he evokes nights after his return when his own writing ''amazed'' him as ''the feelings that most filled me then . . . were given a shape in language that made them ideas I understood instead of shifting phantoms possessing me.'' The depth of that possession is tellingly revealed in a line in which Rabe recalls a moment when he all at once ''sensed someone sitting down behind me and spun as if I might be ambushed.'' The setting for this event was not Vietnam, but the theater in which the 1971 production of *Pavlo Hummel* was in rehearsal; and the ''someone'' was Joseph Papp, who was by then play's principal backer.

Still, Rabe is also very much aware of the danger of being labelled as a singer who repeats one tune; he resists any description of himself as ''just this guy who got shook up by the war'' (*NYTM*), and has consistently rejected the claim that the Vietnam trilogy consists of antiwar plays. There is indeed evidence that Vietnam served Rabe not only as a deeply felt subject matter but as a backdrop against which he could work out other, more personal obsessions of his own, particularly his preoccupation with characters who begin their stage lives as outsiders and conclude as victims.

Streamers provides an apt case in point. Though it was the last play in the trilogy to be produced, it was "actually the first thing" Rabe began to write when he got out of the army (*NYTM*). He worked on the play intermittently for seven years, and his patience manifests itself in a tightly structured narrative that contrasts favorably with other of his more loosely packed plot lines. More to the point, the play centers on a homosexual and the troubled—and troubling—ways in which the soldiers around him react to his homosexuality; and it thereby sets the pattern for the classic Rabe protagonists, male and female misfits whose inability or refusal to blend into stereotypical social structures puts them at no small risk.

The full extent of those risks becomes clear in *Pavlo Hummel*, which catalogues the experiences of a young soldier in training camp and thereafter in Vietnam. The product of a broken home, Pavlo is a figure whose "basic training" for life has left him as unprepared for living as his basic training for war has left him unprepared for Vietnam. Never having known his father, he spends much of the play searching unsuccessfully for a surrogate, whether in the form of his drill sergeant or, more centrally, in his naive recollections of Jimmy Cagney's famous portrayal of the shell-shocked soldier who nonetheless ends up a hero.

Rabe clearly intended his audience to tease out the implications of the parallel between Pavlo and the Cagney figure. Both characters claim to be streetwise but are unmanned by the meaner streets of war; both lack guidance, and reject or dismiss the guidance they are given; both carve out a dangerously erratic path in a situation where conformity is literally the order of the day; both die in attempts to smother the impact of a hand grenade. But Pavlo's death owes nothing to Hollywood; the grenade that kills him is thrown by an American sergeant whom he has just beaten up after an argument about a prostitute. Here Rabe has consciously set out to subvert—more precisely, wreck—the myth of the heroic ending; and in this, as in much of his play's technique, he owes an evident debt to the thematic stance and technical innovations of Bertolt Brecht. While it would be stretching a point to compare Rabe's protagonist to the more complex protagonist of Brecht's *Mother Courage and Her Children*, a comparison of the two plays is not only appropriate but instructive. As with *Mother Courage*, *Pavlo Hummel* does an admirable job of demonstrating the Brechtian thesis that men and women in a wartime situation learn as little about the inner workings of war as the rabbit in the scientist's laboratory learn about biology. For "Pavlo," in short, read "Pavlov."

Sticks and Bones was begun late in 1968, shortly after the first draft of *Pavlo Hummel* was finished; and it followed its predecessor to the Public Theater in November 1971, less than six months after the earlier play had opened. Closely proximate in both conception and dates of production, the two plays are in fact twinned and complementary. *Pavlo Hummel* describes the grotesque journey out to Southeast Asia; *Sticks* diagnoses and equally grotesque return to what used to be home.

The framework for *Sticks* takes its cue from what was once one of America's most popular sitcoms. The parents in the play are named Ozzie and Harriet; they have a younger son named Ricky, who plays guitar and sings. They also have an older son named David, but Rabe's version of David has nothing to do with his television namesake. This time around, David has returned to the family home as a Vietnam veteran. He is neither homosexual (as in *Streamers*) nor unshaped (as in *Pavlo Hummel*), but he joins Rabe's other aliens in a different way: he is physically blind, profoundly embittered, and given to speaking the truth about essentials. Unable to cope with any of this, his parents and brother eventually seduce him into cutting his wrists in the hope that his death will restore life to the family.

This is not a pretty plot—none of Rabe's are—and it would be easy to criticize it on several counts. Most notably, only David and Ozzie come across as di-mensioned characters; Harriet is relegated to either small talk or an occasional minor insight, and Ricky is a caricature from start to finish. But in retrospect, it is equally easy to see that Rabe knew precisely which nerve endings he needed to touch to make his audience jump. *Sticks* is a more powerful play than *Pavlo Hummel*, largely because it takes a familiar setting—the living room of American dreamland—and renders it strange and deeply unsettling. The central figures in *Streamers* and *Pavlo Hummel* are outsiders in the army; but the figure of the outsider takes on a more deadly dimension when he is rejected by his own family and, implicitly, by us. In extending Pavlo's search for an absent father into an attack on the vacancy of American family life, *Sticks* performs a shrewd and accurate surgery on the way in which American sons were uncomprehendingly welcomed home as strangers, victimized by the welcome as they had been by the war.

Rabe's gallery of inner exiles includes female characters as well, most notably Chrissy, the self-described ''hunk a meat'' who works as a go-go dancer in *In the Boom Boom Room* (1973). But until *Hurlyburly*, none of Rabe's other plays had enjoyed anything like the acclaim that was visited on the trilogy; and he has produced few new plays since *Streamers*. It is clear that the production of *Streamers* marked the end of one phase of his career, less clear what might be coming next. Still, Rabe's very real abilities remain. Leiter rightly points out that the dialogue in a Rabe play can sometimes strike a dead note, but it is no less true that his style at its best shows an ear for local idiom that recalls works as notable as Arthur Miller's *Death of a Salesman*. He is also willing to tackle unpopular issues and, if need be, to stand by repellent conclusions. Perhaps most notable among the latter is his vision of fathers who are absent or ineffectual or (as in *Boom Boom Room*) monstrous. The motif of abandonment by the father is by no means new in modern drama; it runs from Henrik Ibsen through August Strindberg through Anton Chekhov and down to the present day. But Rabe is more explicit on the point than all but a few of his predecessors. In his hands, the betraying father becomes an emblem for the deity who fled the century and left us all outsiders. In the introduction to *Pavlo Hummel* and *Sticks and Bones*, he notes that the writing he did in college

was dominated by an urge to interpret the world to itself, to give the world a sermon that would bring it back to its truest self, for I thought then (and I did indeed believe it) that the history and exact nature of both mankind and the world were known, universal, and eternal.

Those Catholic sureties have long since been dismantled by Rabe's encounters with a universe of mute particulars, a world as little known and transient as his characters. Rabe's courage shows in his willingness to open doors into the dark; his predicament shows in his recent flawed attempts to translate his rage and disappointment into anything more resonant than rage and disappointment, his inability to set the darkness echoing.

SELECTED BIBLIOGRAPHY

Works by Rabe: *Sticks and Bones*. Produced in Villanova, Pa., 1969; New York, 1971; London, 1978; *The Basic Training of Pavlo Hummel*. Produced in New York, 1971; *The Basic Training of Pavlo Hummel and Sticks and Bones*. New York: Viking Press, 1973; *The Orphan*. Produced in New York, 1973. Published New York: French, 1975; *In the Boom Boom Room*. Produced as *Boom Boom Room* in New York, 1973; as *In the Boom Boom Room* (rev. version) in New York, 1974; London, 1976. Published New York: Knopf, 1975; *Burning*. Produced in New York, 1974; *Streamers*. Produced in New Haven, Conn., 1976; New York, 1976; London, 1978. Published New York: Knopf, 1977; *Goose and Tomtom*. Produced in New York, 1982; *Hurlyburly*. Produced at the Goodman Theater in Chicago, April 2, 1984.

Works about Rabe: "The Craft of the Playwright: A Conversation between Neil Simon and David Rabe." *New York Times Magazine* (26 May 1985), pp. 37 *passim*; Gottfried, Martin. "David Rabe." In *Contemporary Dramatists*, ed. James Vinson. London: St. James Press, 1977", pp. 651–53; Leiter, Robert. "Theater Chronicle." *The Hudson Review* 38 (1985–1986), pp. 297–99. Weales, Gerald. "American Theater Watch, 1984–1985." *The Georgia Review* 39 (1985), pp. 619–21. CA 85–88. CD. DLB 7.

Frank Kinahan

BROTHER JONATHAN RINGKAMP, O.S.F. (1929–1986). The most prolific dramatist/religious in America, Brother Jonathan was respected Off-Broadway, and well known in theatre circles in New York and London. Ringkamp's plays focus on passionate characters in crisis, especially fellow Franciscans trying to live in the modern world. His work is occasionally melodramatic, but it is always emotionally powerful. It originates from his deep understanding of Franciscan spirituality, which stresses ecclesiality, mysticism, and incarnationalism.

Born in Brooklyn, New York, on March 6, 1929, Brother Jonathan was professed in 1955. He studied painting at Pratt Institute (B.F.A. 1961, M.F.A. 1967) and was awarded a Fulbright Scholarship to attend the Accademmia di belli arti in Venice during 1961–1962. He changed careers permanently in 1967 when he cofounded (with Geraldine Fitzgerald) a street theatre company in his native Brooklyn. He subsequently had plays produced at top Off-Broadway theatres as well as at the Hampstead Theatre Club in London and the Milwaukee

Repertory Company. Brother Jonathan's most important works comprise a trilogy about Franciscan life: *The Dog Ran Away* (1975), *The Arbor* (1979), and *Bella Figura* (1982). Brother Jonathan was also a screenwriter, a theatre director, and a very influential acting and playwriting teacher at colleges and New York studios.

Brother Jonathan's work is psychological realism. His essential theme is the relationship of the alienated yet passionate individual to his community, to tradition, and ultimately, to God. For example, Brother William, the protagonist of *The Dog Ran Away*, was chosen by God through an ecstatic experience. But God has long seemed absent from his life, and William is enraged at being abandoned. His anger peaks when the senile Brother Joseph kills William's dog out of jealousy. William terrorizes the old man with threats of damnation until he finally recognizes his own cruelty. Only then, begging forgiveness on his knees, does Brother William rediscover a measure of spiritual peace.

The Arbor, set before the "sweeping changes" of Vatican II, seems at first to depict religious community life with nostalgia. But the brothers' virtuousness is threatened by hypocrisy and infighting and is, finally, overshadowed by a failure of compassion. They hound the bag lady McGuire to her death most unjustly: they learn too late that she and Brother Andy had been lovers as she claimed and that she was swindled out of her inheritance by the monastery.

The theme of sexual passion, which was important but off stage in the other two plays, is at the center of *Bella Figura*. Brother Jonathan, tracing his ideas back to St. Francis, believed that religious life requires passion. In this play the young monk Philip, frustrated in his spiritual development, first finds exhilaration in the attentions of Beatrice and then feels the pain of separation when she leaves him behind. Philip fails to find the ecstasy he seeks, but he has begun to understand the mysteries of love, an important step on his spiritual journey.

SELECTED BIBLIOGRAPHY

Works by Brother Jonathan: PLAYS: (unpublished, dates when first produced) *The Dog Ran Away*. 1975; *The Arbor*. 1979; *A Change of Mind*. 1979; *Bella Figura*. 1982; *Poisoner of the Wells*. 1983. SCREENPLAYS: *The Clairvoyant*. 1981; *Rapallo and Sons*. 1982. TELEPLAY: *You Can Run But You Can't Hide*. 1977.

Willem O'Reilly

CARYL RIVERS (1937–). Caryl Rivers describes the lives of successful "lace-curtain" suburban Irish Americans who remain aware that their culture and religion are significantly different from the majority society. In sketching family life during the 1950s, a turning point for Irish Catholics in America in a demographic as well as an intellectual sense, she implies that the mid-century witnessed a progressive decline in the traditionally high rates of fertility and permanent celibacy, replaced by patterns of family life, education, and marriage indistinguishable from the rest of American society. On the other hand, her characters' values indicate the persistence of distinct attitudes showing cultural and religious cohesion.

Rivers utilizes comic situations to show the absurd aspects of suburban society, parent-child relationships, the psychology of women, and the challenges in following strict religious rituals in an overwhelmingly secular, hedonistic society. She tells of the frailties and strengths of humans, growing in wise acceptance of their diverse personalities. Her tales serve a didactic purpose as she fuses elements of the tragic with the comic; by getting her protagonists into improbable situations, she shows the humorous aspects of their behavior as they seek to attain an ideal goal. Rivers uses exaggeration for heightened effect to depict human behavior. Her endings are occasionally improbable, but her purpose is to show characters struggling to behave in a humanitarian way, to examine the disparity between ridiculous behavior and reasonable justifications for actions. She is at her best when she writes about Irish-American life in the mid-century, about the use and abuse of power, and about the psychological needs of modern women.

Caryl Rivers, daughter of Hugh F. (a lawyer) and Helen (Huhn) Rivers, was born on December 19, 1937. She received a B.A. degree at Trinity College, Washington, D.C., 1959, and an M.S. degree at Columbia University, 1960. She is now associate professor of journalism at Boston University, and lives in Winthrop, Massachusetts, with *Boston Phoenix* columnist husband Alan Lupo and their two children.

Rivers was family editor, 1960–1962, for the *Middletown Record*, in Middletown, New York; Washington correspondent for *El Mundo* in San Juan, Puerto Rico, 1962–1966; and writer-in-residence for the *Washington Star*, 1976, contributing to the syndicated column, *One Woman's Voice*. She writes a guest column for Russell Baker in the *New York Times*. She has been a public affairs commentator for educational television, WGBH, in Boston, since 1968, and has appeared on *Hour Magazine*, *Today*, and *Good Morning America*.

A member of Women in Communication, Rivers received an award for "editing one of the best newspaper women's sections in the United States," in 1961, and was a finalist in the national competition for excellence in magazine journalism, in 1978, both from J. C. Penny–University of Missouri. She was cited for an article "The Girls of Summer," *Womensports*, 1979; honored as "best magazine writer," *New Times*, 1979, for "The Nightmare of Hugh Rivers, Jr." (a mental health system tragedy); and labeled as "best columnist" by the New England Women's Press Association, 1979, for columns appearing in *Boston Phoenix*.

Rivers' novel, *Virgins* (1984), relates the motley experiences of Peggy Morrison during the 1950s as a naive senior at Immaculate Heart School with its strict rules for Catholic girls and boys like seminary-bound Sean McCaffrey, whom Peggy loves. The young woman wants to be a prize-winning reporter, and Rivers develops some genuinely amusing scenes involving a beware-of-sex lecture and the creation of a fake St. Leon (Trotsky) for a newspaper's obligatory "Saints' Corner" column, and she includes some tragic events such as a classmate's suicide, the death of Peggy's father, and the brutality of a friend's parent.

Rivers' book is a bittersweet, wistful account of adolescent pangs, a recreation of high school memories. *Virgins* is an excellent primary source about growing up female and Catholic in mid-century America, and how life has changed from the time when a nun would get flustered just talking to a parish priest to the day a nun would challenge the Pope, championing more active Church leadership for women.

Instead of a novel, *Virgins* reads like a collection of short stories with a recurring theme, and each chapter is a capsule look at a particular event related to the attempts of Peggy and her friends to break the restrictive bonds of church, home, and innocent girlhood. Rivers skillfully describes school assemblies, the blue serge uniforms, "Marylike" dresses buttoned up to the neck of docile Catholic young ladies, collecting funds for pagan babies, and battling wits with the nuns.

Intimate Enemies (1987) shifts from the problems and satisfactions of Rivers' Catholic upbringing to the difficulties of enjoying intimacy in contemporary America. Its main characters are a liberal college provost named Jessie McGrath and a disabled Vietnam veteran named Mark Claymore. The central issue becomes whether an ex–1960s radical can overcome her politics and find true love with the psychically wounded, sexually attractive soldier. A reviewer in the *New York Times Book Review* (Sunday, January 17, 1988, pp. 24–25) found the novel redolent of young adult fiction and soap operas, lacking depth and seriousness.

During an interview published in *Contemporary Authors*, vol. 4, Rivers explained that since

my background is journalism . . . I am motivated by a curiosity about why things are the way they are and how they got to be that way. . . . I began to get restive with the traditional definitions of the important things a journalist was supposed to examine. I found the limits too confining. Too often, my fellow journalists and I were restricted to writing about the games men play—politics and sports. I started to move beyond these subjects to an area I now identify as social history: How do ordinary people live? What are the issues that affect their lives? What are the underlying forces that shape the times?

In particular, Rivers said she was interested in studying "the psychological forces that shape women's lives and how these forces can be countered, when they get in the way of the development of competence."

Rivers is effective in depicting the universal experiences and concerns of all women, not just Catholics. She has a knack for weaving together richly detailed remembrances of school and career happenings, wittily showing female effectiveness, achievement motivation, survival techniques for developing self-esteem, and strength.

SELECTED BIBLIOGRAPHY

Works by Rivers: *Aphrodite in Midcentury: Growing Up Female and Catholic in Postwar America.* New York: Doubleday, 1973; *Beyond Sugar and Spice: How Women Grow, Learn, and Thrive*, with Rosalind Barnett and Grace Baruch. New York: Putnam, 1979; *For Better! For Worse!, with Alan Lupo.* New York: Summit, 1981; *Lifeprints: New Patterns of Love and Work for Today's Women.* New York: McGraw-Hill, 1983;

Virgins. New York: St. Martin's/Marek, 1984; *Girls Forever Brave and True*. New York: St. Martin's, 1986; *Intimate Enemies*. New York: Dutton, 1987. Contributor to *World, Saturday Review, New York Times Magazine, Ms.*, among other newspapers and magazines.

Works about Rivers: Review of *Virgins. Kirkus Reviews* (1 July 1984), p. 594. CA 49–52. CANR 4.

Edith Blicksilver

BROTHER PATRICK RYAN (1943–). The contemplative, aesthetic, and intellectual fuse in this man who has been a member of the Cistercian Order since 1961. The second of six children, Brother Patrick was born on January 12, 1943, in the Bronx, New York. After attending Fordham University for one year, he entered Our Lady of the Genesee Abbey in Piffard, New York, of the Order of the Cistercians of the Strict Observance. He made solemn vows as a Cistercian monk at Genesee in 1969, and from 1964 to 1972 he studied philosophy and theology there. He also studied at the Medieval Institute, Western Michigan University, Kalamazoo in 1973–1974 and received a master of arts degree in medieval studies in 1977. He has given lectures on William of Saint Thierry, the subject of his master's thesis, at several American monasteries and convents and has published articles on monastic spirituality in various books and journals. Since 1970 he has taught Cistercian spirituality, church history, and philosophy at the monastery at Genesee.

Brother Patrick's is a movingly simple poetry, expressive of his deep commitment to love God through the little things of life. His short poems shine with the faith of the ''Pacific Monk'' who ''bends his head into his heart.'' Although his poetry has not yet been collected into a volume, his poems have appeared in several magazines. He is also known for his work on Thomas Merton.*

SELECTED BIBLIOGRAPHY

Works by Ryan: BOOKS: *Thomas Merton/Monk: A Monastic Tribute*, editor. New York: Sheed and Ward, 1974; *A Merton Concelebration*, editor with Deba Patnaik. Notre Dame, Ind.: Ave Maria, 1981. POETRY: In two collections: *Thomas Merton: Prophet in the Belly of a Paradox*, ed. Gerald Twomey. New York: Paulist Press, 1978; *Sing mir das Lied Meiner Erde: Bitten um den Geist*, ed. Drutmar Cremer. Würzburg, W. Germany; Echter, 1978. Also in such magazines as *America, The Bible Today, The Christian Century, Desert Call, Review for Religious, Sign, Sisters Today, Studia Mystica*.

Mary E. Giles

S

ERNEST SANDEEN (1908–). After fifty years of publication, this "tough old word artist" remains among the least visible of contemporary American poets. His quality has still to be assessed by reviewers or literary scholars or the many poets who know Sandeen and admire his work. Characteristically, Sandeen's poems are readable, vivid in their surprising and often bizarre images, intellectually challenging, and strikingly insightful. Appealing to eye, ear, heart, and mind, they illuminate life's immediate experiences and unveil its distant sources. Fellow poets call his works "universal" and they admire "the authenticity of his very humanity." Yet Sandeen's poems, though widely published in magazines and journals, have received small publication in collected editions and anthologies. Reviews of his four books are appreciative but brief, sometimes apologetic.

Born of a Swedish family in Galesburg, Illinois, home of Carl Sandburg, who was Sandeen's first literary influence (other principal influences are T. S. Eliot, Robert Frost, and W. H. Auden), Sandeen earned a B.A. at Knox College, a B. Litt. at Oxford, and a Ph.D. at the University of Iowa. Prior to undertaking doctoral studies he taught briefly at Knox College, where he married Eileen Bader; after doctoral studies he taught briefly at Iowa. From 1943 to 1946 he served in the U.S. Navy, then resumed his vocation as poet and teacher at the University of Notre Dame (he and his family converted to Catholicism in 1948). His long tenure in Notre Dame's English Department, from which he is now Emeritus, was interrupted only by visiting appointments to the University of Aarhus in Denmark, to the University of Minnesota, and to the English Institute in Hawaii.

Although Sandeen continues to write and publish, the main lines of his poetic development can be followed in *Collected Poems: 1953–1977* (1977), which contain poems written as early as 1938. Drawing their subjects from daily life, his poems constitute "an intimately personal record," he says, of "where I was in various times of my life and how it felt to be there.'' Readers may recognize these places, he continues, ''in their interior experience''—a telling phrase, for Sandeen's subject is ultimately the human spirit's condition as discernible in ordinary circumstances. He listens for ''the sea of the seasons'' and the ''toss and hum of night and day.'' Thus there is a preoccupation with time in Sandeen's poems as well as with personal history. Life comes into presence through a consciousness that extends to other times, other places, other persons, and to biological and spiritual realms that extend to humanity's origins and destinies. In effect, Sandeen writes not merely autobiographically but vatically, with the powers given to poets over and above, as he sees it, their redeemed humanity. It is this understanding that makes his poems strikingly universal and authentic.

Such a consciousness can only be realized in figurative and tropological language and in imaginative rhetorical strategies. Sandeen's early poetry proliferates, sometimes densely, with similes, metaphors, metonymies, synecdoches, paradoxes, oxymorons, and such figures as conflate multiple realms of time, reality, and meaning. In his later poetry, his language grows plainer, as rhetorical forms take on more of the burden of suggestiveness and ambiguity. Later poems make frequent use of personification and often push against parable, myth, and even allegory. Similarly, in his early poems versification is highly regular, although his skill in the rhythms of syntax and meaning disguise the disciplined control of meter, rhyme, and stanza form. His later verses are free, flexible, varied in form, and sometimes experimental in their prosody.

Throughout his work, subject and style are integral to the guise in which life opens itself to the mind. The truth about his personal life, and life itself, is revealed to Sandeen in its ironies, paradoxes, binary oppositions, antitheses, and the mystery of contradictions—how they exist despite logic, for good and for ill, once and for all. Such insights give his poems, whose titles are regularly humorous understatements of what they present, an intellectual vigor that is often difficult, at times almost impenetrable, but characteristically convincing and always surprising. His intellectualism, operating so well through imaginative forms and expressive language, gives many of his poems extraordinary emotional power.

Although Sandeen describes himself as a poet who, like Theodore Roethke, ''learns by going where I have to go,'' his appreciable number of works about poets and poetry allow one to infer a consistent, developing poetics. Early poems in this group equate poetry with story, song, prayer, thought: with the various forms in which reality, or the truth of things, comes to consciousness through words. Borrowing the title of his first book, one might characterize Sandeen's poems as ''antennas of silence,'' as verbal forms that give voice and consciousness to the poet, to humanity, and to life itself.

Later works use the word ''poem'' in two senses; the poem made of words seems to incarnate the creative foundation of life (suggesting, but never stating, that the poet's human words incarnate the Divine Word). ''Poem'' thus designates both the ''antenna of silence'' and the reality of life that the antenna receives and transmits. Poetic creativity cooperates with the force behind all creation, which in an interview Sandeen has suggested may have an aesthetic purpose. Conjoined with creativity's processes of birth and death, for example, the poet's poem constitutes a kind of unfleshing of the self even as the self lives.

This poetics reaches full development in Sandeen's most powerful poems, a series that opens the volume entitled *Like Any Road Anywhere* (1976). In these, the poem itself is metapoetically present as a personified character. "The poem has haunted most of my adult years," Sandeen wrote in a letter to a fellow poet, "The poem has always been there, troubling me, a kind of Platonic abstraction, I suppose, but always taking a concrete form." Now voiced and conscious, the poem is, in effect, reality witnessing itself being experienced. It observes and addresses the poet's persona, who gropes in the dark, struggling with his "story-thickened passions."

The poetics implied in Sandeen's work, of which only the gist is implied here, seems both traditional and original; it suggests affinities with ancient, medieval, modern, and post-modern theories, but distinctions from them as well. His poetics, in other words, seem all his own yet at the core of the theory and practice of poetry. In this sense also is his work universal and authentic.

Sandeen's poems have been collected in *Antennas of Silence* (1953) and in three books: *Children and Older Strangers* (1962), *Like Any Road Anywhere*, and *Collected Poems: 1953–1977*.

SELECTED BIBLIOGRAPHY

Works by Sandeen: *Antennas of Silence*. Baltimore: Contemporary Poetry, 1953; *Children and Older Strangers*. South Bend, Ind., University of Notre Dame Press, 1962; *Like Any Road Anywhere*. South Bend, Ind. University of Notre Dame Press, 1976; *Collected Poems: 1953–1977*. South Bend, Ind.: University of Notre Dame Press, 1977.

Works about Sandeen: Review of *Collected Poems*. *Hudson Review* 31 (1978), p. 540; Review of *Like Any Road Anywhere*. *Choice* 13 (1976), p. 1299. CA 45.

                                                                    Edward Vasta

RICHARD SHAW (1941–). With the publication of his first novel and two ecclesiastical biographies, Richard Shaw was acclaimed for his frank, vivid accounts of priests caught in the turmoil of history. *The Christmas Mary Had Twins* (1983) (first published as *Elegy of Innocence*) traces a priest's religious and personal struggles during the upheaval following Vatican II. Though episodic and occasionally reductive in characterization, the novel is a convincing portrait of a priest and a Church torn by dramatic changes.

Born in Brooklyn, New York, on October 9, 1941, Richard Shaw was graduated from Siena College in 1964, studied at St. Bonaventure's seminary, and was ordained a priest in 1968. He earned master's degrees in American history and criminal justice, and is working toward a doctorate in criminal justice at the State University of New York. Fr. Shaw has served the Albany diocese as a teacher and a parish priest, but since 1972 he has dedicated himself particularly to prison ministry.

The Christmas Mary Had Twins is a first-person narrative by Fr. Dennis Hogan, an idealistic, impulsive, and rather immature priest, whose characterization is the novel's greatest strength. Zealous in his desire to be a priest, once ordained Dennis becomes disillusioned by the bitter religious controversy following Vatican II. Alienated by the internecine conflict within the Church, he becomes sexually involved with a Jewish nurse. Only after leaving the priesthood and suffering the deaths of two beloved mentors does Dennis confront his own shortcomings and rededicate himself to his vocation.

Fr. Shaw's characterization of Dennis is unflinchingly honest: though a sympathetic character, Dennis betrays some of the same intolerance that he abominates in his parishioners and colleagues. In *The Christmas Mary Had Twins*, as in his biographies of Bishop John Dubois and Archbishop John Hughes, Richard Shaw speaks eloquently of the struggle between the Catholic Church's spiritual idealism and its human frailty.

SELECTED BIBLIOGRAPHY

Works by Shaw: FICTION: *Elegy of Innocence*. Huntington, Ind.: Our Sunday Visitor, 1979; *The Christmas Mary Had Twins*. Rev. ed. of *Elegy of Innocence*. New York: Stein and Day, 1983. "The Very, Very Last of the Old Breed." *Critic* 35 (1976), pp. 56–60; NON-FICTION: *Dagger John: The Unquiet Life and Times of Archbishop Hughes of New York*. New York: Paulist Press, 1977; *From Joques to JFK: Eleven Tales of Catholic Albany*. Albany, N.Y.: The Evangelist, 1986.

Works about Shaw: Review of *The Christmas Mary Had Twins*. *America* (24 March 1984), p. 222; Review of *Dagger John*. *America* (8 October 1977), p. 220; Review of *Elegy of Innocence*. *America* (16 June 1979), p. 499. CA 37–40.

Mary Kateri Fitzgerald

WILFRID (JOHN JOSEPH) SHEED (1930–). Widely known as a critic, an editor, and a biographer, Wilfrid Sheed has also written eight novels and a long story which are characterized by the same wit, humor, and insight that mark his non-fiction. Sheed's first three novels received mixed critical reaction, but he is generally agreed to have hit stride with his fourth, *Office Politics* (1966); both both this novel and the later *Max Jamison* (1970) were nominated for the National Book Award. The most frequent criticism of Sheed's fiction concerns a static quality which typifies each work as a whole despite the brilliance of many particular passages.

Wilfrid Sheed was born in London, England, on December 27, 1930, to Frank Joseph Sheed and Maisie Ward Sheed, the founders of the Roman Catholic publishing house, Sheed and Ward. The family moved to America in 1940 when Sheed and Ward opened a branch in New York. Wilfrid was educated in Pennsylvania until, after World War II, he attended the Benedictine preparatory school, Downside, in England. He took his B.A. (1954) and his M.A. (1957) from Lincoln College, Oxford. Sheed's serious adult writing began after graduation during a year spent in Australia with members of his father's family. His fiction writing, as well as his editing and writing of book-length non-fiction, has been intertwined with assignments to various periodicals: associate editor, *Ju-*

bilee, 1959–1966; film critic, *Jubilee*, 1959–1961; drama critic and book review editor, *Commonweal*, 1964–1971; movie critic, *Esquire*, 1967–1969; and essayist, *New York Times Book Review* and other publications, 1971–present. Sheed has campaigned for Senator McCarthy (1968), taught at Princeton University as creative arts lecturer (1970–1971), and served as a judge for the Book of the Month Club (1972).

At least superficially, the subjects and situations of Sheed's fiction have been drawn directly from the events of his own life. Sheed's changes of residence between England and America estranged him from both cultures rather than making him feel at home in either. He approached this problem in his early fiction, *The Blacking Factory* (1964) and *A Middle Class Education* (1960), as well as in *Transatlantic Blues* (1978). The American part of his childhood furnished the setting for *Pennsylvania Gothic* (1969). His knowledge of magazine publishing, as contributor and editor, emerged in *The Hack* (1963), *Office Politics*, and *Max Jamison*. *Square's Progress* (1965) concerns marital adjustment and fidelity in suburban America. Sheed's bout with polio at the age of fourteen and his presidential campaign experience structure *People Will Always Be Kind* (1973). Concern with Catholic training, especially as impinging on self-image, adolescent development, and later-life styles, underlies all of the novels.

Sheed is honest and realistic in presenting complex and contradictory aspects of human experience. He dramatizes the careless ease with which we sometimes walk out on our most binding commitments. He shows the sometimes seamy, sometimes visionary struggles of the male adolescent mind and spirit. He reminds us of the fine line separating confident achievement from despair and even madness. He laments both the loss of the pre–Vatican II Church and the moral and social consequences affecting those who have taken it seriously. He explores the private and public personas of political life. He sees the limitations of provincialism and uprootedness of ways of life. In depicting such situations, Sheed rightly resists pat solutions and premature resolutions.

Sheed uses language with facility and enjoyment. His gifts of expression, combined with such rich material, make the beginning Sheed reader expect a great fictional experience. That these hopes are frequently disappointed seems primarily due to the author's stance toward his material. While willing to depict real people and real problems, Sheed seems reluctant to commit himself—to his characters, to any particular way of understanding or resolving a problem, or even to his art, which if served well, would at least give his fiction shape and direction—as though Sheed, expatriate as a child, now holds himself aloof from worlds as an adult.

SELECTED BIBLIOGRAPHY

Works by Sheed: FICTION: *A Middle Class Education: A Novel*. Boston: Houghton Mifflin Co., 1960, London: Cassell, 1961; *The Hack*. New York: Macmillan Co., 1963, London: Cassell, 1963; *Square's Progress: A Novel*. New York: Farrar, Straus, 1965, London: Cassell, 1965; *Office Politics: A Novel*. New York: Farrar, Straus, 1966, London: Cassell, 1967; *The Blacking Factory and Pennsylvania Gothic: A Short Novel and a Long*

Story. New York: Farrar, Straus, London: Weidenfeld and Nicholson, 1969; *Max Jamison: A Novel*. New York: Farrar, Straus, 1970, as *The Critic: A Novel*. London: Weidenfeld and Nicholson, 1970; *People Will Always Be Kind*. New York: Farrar, Straus, 1973, London: Weidenfeld and Nicholson, 1974; *Transatlantic Blues*. New York: Dutton, 1978; *The Boys of Winter*. New York: Knopf, 1987. ESSAYS: *The Morning After: Selected Essays and Reviews*. New York: Farrar, Straus, 1971; *The Good Word and Other Words*. New York: Dutton, 1978.

Works about Sheed: *Time* 92 (20 September 1968), pp. 108–9. CA 65–68. CN. DLB 6.

Linda Schlafer

BETTY SMITH (1896?–1972). "One night," wrote Betty Smith, . . . I, an obscure writer living quietly and on modest means in a small, Southern town, went to bed as usual. I woke up the next morning to be informed that I had become a celebrity. My first novel . . . had been published." This novel, *A Tree Grows in Brooklyn* (1943), the story of a poor but determined Irish-American, Catholic girl, Francie Nolan, was to sell nearly three million copies. An immediate best-seller in 1943, it was chosen as a book club selection. Amazingly, this first novel about the misery, deprivation and poverty of life in the slums was to be translated into sixteen languages, made into a motion picture and a Broadway musical, and included on Harper's list of its best-selling novels along with *Ben Hur* and *Love Story*.

To some degree *A Tree Grows in Brooklyn* is autobiographical since Betty Smith was herself born in the Williamsburg section of Brooklyn, the granddaughter of Irish-Catholic immigrants on her father's side and of German-Catholic immigrants on her mother's. She attended P.S. 23 in Greenpoint, but much of her education took place in the neighborhood public library and at the Jackson Street Settlement House where she learned to cook and to sew. Smith wrote over seventy plays, many of them unpublished, and edited several texts and collections for drama classes. This interest, too, probably dates from her childhood afternoons at the Williamsburg YMCA where she acted in several amateur plays. In any case, both her formal education and any youthful respite from the constant struggle for survival ended after eighth grade. At the age of fourteen the author became part of the workforce in a succession of New York and Brooklyn factories, offices, and stores.

In 1924 Betty Wehner married George A. E. Smith, a Brooklyn law student at the University of Michigan from whom she was divorced in 1938; this marriage produced two daughters who were born a year apart. When her daughters entered kindergarten Smith petitioned the university for permission to audit several English courses, since she had not graduated from high school and could not enroll in regular undergraduate courses. She was allowed to audit classes for five hours per week. During this three-year period (1927–1930) she won the Avery Hopwood award for playwriting and began to have her one-act plays published. While in Michigan Betty Smith also became a feature writer for the *Detroit Free Press* and NEA, a newspaper syndicate. This pattern, a kind of insatiable reaching out for knowledge, coupled with an enviable level of accomplishment, was to define her life.

From 1930 to 1934 Smith attended the Yale Drama School and studied with George P. Baker. She was also a member of the Federal Theatre Project and through that involvement met the dramatist, Paul Green, who suggested that she move to North Carolina. The University of North Carolina awarded her a Rockefeller Fellowship. This enabled her to write seventy-five one-act and five full-length plays and to begin work on *A Tree Grows in Brooklyn* which she wrote, at a page a day, for three years. She sent her 1,000-page manuscript (later trimmed to 400 pages) off to Harper on December 31, 1942. From 1943 to 1951 she was married to Joseph Piper Jones, the assistant editor of the *Chapel Hill Weekly* with whom she lived in a brick and frame house on Rosemary Street where she planted an ailanthus, "a tree that liked poor people," to remind her of the trees which defied the odds, as she had, in the slums of Williamsburg. "Some people," she wrote, "called it the Tree of Heaven. No matter where its seed fell, it made a tree which struggled to reach the sky. It grew in boarded-up lots and out of neglected rubbish heaps and it was the only tree that grew out of cement." This marriage was dissolved in 1951. She married Robert Finch, with whom she collaborated on several plays, in 1957; he died in 1959.

Orville Prescott, who included *Tree* in "Outstanding Novels" (*The Yale Review of 1943*) said that "Miss Smith spares nothing" in her depiction of the life of Francie Nolan, from her first year to age nineteen, and that of her alcoholic father, the sometimes singing waiter, and her occasionally joyous, archetypal, long-suffering mother. But it is Francie, assertive, eager, knowledge-thirsty, and resilient, who dominates the novel and who is Smith's most memorable character. In fact, as Smith herself noted, "one-fifth of my letters start out, 'Dear Francie'." She remains interesting to the contemporary reader because without role models, in a provincial environment, she typifies the potential victim—almost trapped by poverty (stale bread and soup bones), ignorance ("if normal sex was a great mystery in the neighborhood, criminal sex was an open book"), stupidity (a father who rubs carbolic acid on her leg where a failed rapist's genitals had touched her), and the school-day humiliations familiar to all poor students in immigrant neighborhoods. However, more than poverty was presented in *Tree* and *Tomorrow Will Be Better* (1948), her second book, "but a group of aching, breathing enduring human beings . . . who must daily feel, in the long passage of their lives, that happiness is due on the next delivery." *Joy in the Morning* (1963), particularly, does not pretend to answer difficult questions or solve problems; it is simply a touching picture of experience. It is just that quality— an almost naturalistic depiction of experience, without the pessimistic assumptions of inescapability—which accounts for *Tree*'s readability today. Poverty and the immigrant experience have certain common denominators, but it is not enough for characters to be typical, and as Walter Harrighurst has noted, to "embody the hurts of childhood, the hopes of youth, and the regrets that follow" [*The Saturday Review of Literature* 34 (21 August 1948)]. That was the failure of Betty Smith's second novel, *Tomorrow Will Be Better*, the story of another Brooklyn girl, Margy Shannon, which is less joyous in its suffering, less hopeful, and more studied and deliberate.

Maggie-Now (1958), her third book with a Brooklyn setting, was written during Smith's recovery from a 1952 automobile accident, and although it is less successful than *Tree*, its somber tone and sense of the amorphous and even uncontrollable direction of a conventional life in an unremarkable setting is somehow modern and memorable. *Maggie-Now* is a character caught in time, ostensibly the present. Her mother says, "Hush, Maggie, now." And later: "Maggie, now give me those scissors. . . . Maggie, now mind your father." She grows up but not away and remains the dutiful female appendage to other people's supposedly more important lives. Ironically, she is as locked in the past as any Faulknerian sufferer in Yoknapatapha County; she is trapped by her own memory and the unfulfilled dreams of her husband and father.

Betty Smith was an author who noticed the details, the "eggshell-thin . . . crust [of the bread that] collapsed into flakes with a sound like a small sigh." And she understood that the failed desires and disappointed dreams of ordinary people to some degree replicate and explain the inner lives of all of us. She said, "I loved the people I was writing about," and it is this intensity and this commitment which the reader, through Smith, experiences.

SELECTED BIBLIOGRAPHY

Works by Smith: NOVELS: *A Tree Grows in Brooklyn*. New York: Harper, 1943; *Tomorrow Will Be Better*. New York: Harper, 1948; *Maggie-Now*. New York: Harper, 1958; *Joy in the Morning*. New York: Harper, 1963. PLAYS: *Folk Stuff* (one act), with Jay G. Sigmund. New York: French, 1935; *His Last Skirmish* (one act), with Robert Finch. New York: French, 1937; *Naked Angel* (one-act comedy), with Robert Finch. New York: French, 1937; *Plays for Schools and Little Theatres: A New Descriptive List*, with Robert Finch and Fredrick Henry Koch. Chapel Hill, N.C.: University of North Carolina Extension Division, 1937; *Popecastle Inn* (one-act comedy), with Robert Finch. New York: French, 1937; *Saints Get Together* (one act), with Jay G. Sigmund. Minneapolis, Minn.: Denison, 1937; *Trees of His Father* (one act), with Jay G. Sigmund. New York: French, 1937; *Vine Leaves* (one-act comedy), with Jay G. Sigmund. New York: French, 1937; *The Professor Roars* (one-act comedy), with Robert Finch. New York: Dramatic Publishing, 1938; *Western Night* (one act), with Robert Finch. New York: Dramatists Play Service, 1938; *Darkness at the Window* (one act), with Jay G. Sigmund. New York: Dramatic Publishing, 1938; *Murder in the Snow* (one act), with Robert Finch. New York: French, 1938; *Silvered Rope* (one-act Biblical), with Jay G. Sigmund. Minneapolis, Minn.: Denison, 1938; *Youth Takes Over; or, When A Man's Sixteen* (three-act comedy), with Robert Finch. New York: French, 1939; *Lawyer Lincoln* (one-act comedy), with Chase Webb. New York: Dramatists Play Service, 1939; *Mannequins' Maid* (one act), Minneapolis, Minn.: Denison, 1939; *They Released Barabbas* (one act), with Jay G. Sigmund. New York: Eldridge, 1939; *A Night in the Country* (one act), with Robert Finch. Evanston, Ill.; Row Peterson, 1939; *Near Closing Time* (one-act comedy), with Robert Finch. Minneapolis, Minn.: Denison, 1939; *Package for Ponsonby* (one-act comedy), with Robert Finch. *Western Ghost Town*, with Robert Finch. Minneapolis, Minn.: Denison, 1939; *Bayou Harlequinade*, with Clemon White. New York: French, 1940; *Fun after Supper*. New York: French, 1940; *Heroes Just Happen* (three-act comedy), with Robert Finch. New York: French, 1940; *Room for a King* (one-act Christmas play). New York: Eldridge, 1940; *Summer Comes to the Diamond O* (one-act comedy) with Robert Finch. New York: Dramatists Play Service, 1940; *To Jenny with Love* (one act) with Robert Finch. New York: Eldridge, 1941; compiler 25 non-royalty one-act plays for all-girl casts, Sykesville, Md.: Greenberg, 1942; *20 Prize-Winning Non-Royalty One-Act Plays.* Sykesville, Md.: Greenberg, 1943; *Boy Abe.* W. H. Baker, 1944; *Young Lincoln.* New York: Dramatists Play Service; *A Tree Grows in Brooklyn* (musical), with George Abbott. New York: Harper, 1951; *A Treasury of Non-Royalty One-Act Plays* editor, with others. New York: Garden City Books, 1958; *Durham Station* (one act), North Carolina Centennial Commission, 1961. Has published or produced many other plays.

Works about Smith: Havighurst, Walter. "City of Failure and Loneliness." *The Saturday Review of Literature* (21 August 1948), p. 9; Prescott, Orville. "Outstanding Novels." *The Yale Review* 33, 1 (1943), pp. vi–xii; Trilling, Diana. "Fiction in Review: *A Tree Grows in Brooklyn. The Nation* (4 September 1943), p. 274; "On Looking Back." In *Michigan,* ed. Erich A. Walter. Ann Arbor: University of Michigan Press, 1966, pp. 78–80. PAPERS: The Betty Smith Papers, along with numerous plays by Betty Smith and articles by and about the author, are in the Southern Historical Collection, University of North Carolina Library, Chapel Hill. CA 5–6. TCA.

Mickey Pearlman

SR. MARIS STELLA, C.S.J. (1899–). A native of Iowa, Sister Maris Stella attended public schools until she went to college, when she studied at the College of St. Catherine in St. Paul, Minnesota, from 1918 to 1920. She became a Sister of St. Joseph and after studying at Oxford in England, she joined the faculty of St. Catherine's College as a professor of English. From 1940 to 1953, she attended workshops at the University of Chicago, the University of Notre Dame, Loretta Heights College, and St. Mary's in Los Angeles, and she travelled both in the United States and abroad.

Sister Stella's poetry includes two volumes, *Here Only a Dove* (1939) and *Frost for St. Brigid* (1949), and poems in *America, The Sign, Spirit, Literary Digest,* as well as in various poetry anthologies.

Sister Stella favors the sonnet form in reflecting on a variety of religious themes as well as on the seasons of nature. The poems are quiet, effortless, and simple. Even when writing about childhood and youth, she avoids sentimentality while retaining a stylish fluidity.

After Vatican II, Sister Stella reclaimed her baptismal name and became Sister Alice Smith.

SELECTED BIBLIOGRAPHY

Works by Stella: *Here Only a Dove.* Cincinnati, Ohio: St. Anthony's Guild, 1939; *Frost for St. Brigid.* New York: Sheed and Ward, 1949.

Sister Ann Edward Bennis

MICHAEL GREGORY STEPHENS (1946–). More than other writers of his generation, Michael Stephens conveys his ideas through a peculiarly intimate involvement with language. His poetry, prose, and drama are written in a lean narrative style; but a form of lyricism threatens to take over events, settings, and character studies embodied in this style. Happily, Stephens' lyrical thread is his clear and intelligent voice of poetic or prosaic form assuming the very thought it contains. Noted by critics for laboring in the spirit and tradition of Samuel Beckett and James Joyce, Stephens frequently eschews fixed literary shapes. Moreover, although he is a first-rank black humorist, Stephens' stories are comic attacks on a world involved in a spiritual life-and-death struggle.

Stephens grew up in and around New York City but left home in his mid-teens. He studied literature and the other arts, and his lyricism is in part due to a love for jazz, particularly the music of Thelonious Monk. After dropping out of college, Stephens finally returned to academia; he received an M.A. in English from The City College of New York and an M.F.A. in drama from Yale University. He lives in New York City with his wife and daughter, and recently stopped teaching at Columbia and Fordham Universities in order to devote his time to writing plays. Like his fiction, his plays—particularly *Our Father* (1980)—achieve lyrical vitality through musical dialogue and textured imagery.

More than his poetry, Stephens' drama and especially his fiction delineate the particularities of both a physical and a psychic terrain while juxtaposing the incongruous aspects of civilization with its untamed natural universe. Stephens writes of the sea with a painter's acuity, as in the novella *Shipping Out* (1979), drawn from Stephens' own early experiences after leaving home to become a merchant sailor. Stephens sees crossings of latitude and longitude as concomitant with the similar crossing of cultures, as well as a penetration of nature by man and machine.

Stephens' initiation into manhood on an often unruly sea allows him a range of description in which to treat heroism in a context of material and ideological conflict. From the point of view of a contemporary Ulysses, Stephens looks at civilization but cherishes an adjacent primeval world quite out of reach of all but his senses. Yet he participates, like the ship itself, in a journey of heart and mind.

Unlike the stolid verities in *Shipping Out*, however, Stephens' surrealistic fictionalized account of his family and upbringing in *Season at Coole* (1972), addresses the problems of mankind in and out of harmony with his environment. A terrible conflict with poverty in an unyielding society of steel and concrete produces only hypocrisy. Devastating portraits, like that of Stephens' mother Rose, reveal the spiritual and religious malady of an unsustaining Irish-American ethos.

Rather than a studied, psychological account of multiple or schizophrenic personalities in his family, Stephens creates through language and a diaphanous plot structure a "hysteria" that becomes increasingly credible. Jerome Klinkowitz in *The Life of Fiction* sees in Stephens' work an "inebriety with physical things, . . . associations so rampant that there is no abstract place for [Stephens'] feelings to hide, no preordained form to be imposed on his writing." Readers have a hard time finding sanctuary from Stephens' often brutal clarity. Even when he is at times drunkenly in love with the world, Stephens is finally convinced by his darkening landscapes.

Stephens does not have an explicit, unifying vision, but he has a compassionate care for details. These suggest his ongoing and trenchant meditation: ultimately, Stephens does hold out hope that the world will, indeed, survive its own madness. His writing style—always a focus on the people and things of the world, as opposed to a preoccupation with a philosophy—is not suited to overt statements but, on the other hand, reflects accurately, authentically, this world's disorder.

SELECTED BIBLIOGRAPHY

Works by Stephens: NOVEL: *Season at Coole*. New York: E. P. Dutton, 1972, Chicago: Dalkey Archive Press/Review of Contemporary Fiction, 1984, Krakow, Poland: Literarckie Wydawnictwo, a forthcoming translation. SHORT STORIES: *Paragraphs*. Amherst and New York: Mulch Press, 1974. NOVELLAS: *Still Life*. New York: Kroesen Books, 1978; *Shipping Out*. Cambridge, Mass.: Apple-wood Brooks, 1979. POETRY: *Alcohol Poems*. Binghamton, N.Y.: Loose Change Press, 1973; *Tangun Legend*. Iowa City: Seamark Press, 1977; *Circles End*. New York: Spuyten Duyvil, 1982, dramatized at the Agassiz Theatre, Radcliffe College, 1985. DRAMA: *A Splendid Occasion in Spring*. 1974; *Off-Season Rates*. Yale Playwrights Projects, 1978; *Cloud Dream*. Yale Playwrights Projects, 1979; *Our Father*. Produced by Private Theatre Corp., Colonnades, N.Y., 1980; *Horse*. Staged reading at Harvard's American Repertory Theatre, 1984. TRANSLATION: *Translations* (of Korean Poetry). New York: Red Hanrahan Books, 1984. CRITICISM: *The Dramaturgy of Style: Voice in Short Fiction*. Carbondale, Ill.: Southern Illinois University Press (forthcoming). OTHER WRITINGS: Have appeared in over 100 magazines and journals including *American Book Review, Paris Review, North American Review, Pequod, Rolling Stone, Village Voice, Baltimore Sun, The Nation, New Letters, Tri-Quarterly, Evergreen Review, American Pen, Boston Phoenix, Strange Faces*, and *Galley Sail Review*.

Works about Stephens: Klinkowitz, Jerome. *The Life of Fiction*, Champagne, Ill.: University of Illinois Press, 1977; Klinkowitz, Jerome. *Literary Disruptions*. Champagne, Ill.: University of Illinois Press, 1980; Levin, Martin. Review of *Season at Coole*. *New York Times* (16 July 1972), VII, p. 30; *Rolling Stone* (3 August 1972); *Hampstead and Highgate Express* (Great Britain) (6 September 1985).

Burt J. Kimmelman

ROBERT STONE (1937–). After four novels, the first of which, *A Hall of Mirrors* (1967), won the William Faulkner Foundation Award for "notable first novel" in 1968, Robert Stone has secured his place as one of the finest writers in America today. While his vision of contemporary life is harsh and pessimistic, Stone's novels have ambitious aims—to show ideas and morality in action in darkly extreme circumstances; to probe the spiritual depths of the American experience. Criticized for the unrelieved harshness of his portrayal of the human condition, Stone nevertheless earns praise for his uncompromising honesty and artistic integrity.

The only son of C. Homer and Gladys Catherine (Grant) Stone, Robert Anthony Stone was born in New York City on August 21, 1937, and grew up in economically difficult circumstances. He left high school before graduation and served in the U.S. Navy from 1955 to 1958. He attended New York University from 1958 to 1959. He was an editorial assistant for the New York *Daily News* from 1958 to 1960. He married Janice G. Burr on December 11, 1959; they have two children. In 1962 he was a Stegner Fellow at Stanford University, where he met Ken Kesey and became involved with the "Merry Pranksters" and the counterculture. In addition to his four novels, *A Hall of Mirrors*, *Dog Soldiers* (1974), which won the National Book Award in 1975, *A Flag for Sunrise* (1981), and *Children of Light* (1986), Stone has written a number of short stories, reviews, and essays in such journals as *Esquire* and *Atlantic*. He has taught writing courses at a number of American colleges, including Princeton, Amherst, Stanford, University of Hawaii-Manoa, Harvard, University of California at Irvine, and New York University.

In addition to the Faulkner Award and the National Book Award, Stone was awarded the John Dos Passos prize for literature and the American Academy and Institute of Arts and Letters award for 1982. He was a Guggenheim Fellow in 1971, and an NEH fellow in 1983. He is a member of PEN. He lives in a small town on the Connecticut coast.

Although Robert Stone attended Catholic schools, and attributes a good deal of influence to that experience, he does not formally practice Catholicism. Even so, he claims to be "some kind of Catholic," a "fellow traveler of Christianity." His religious and moral concerns pervade his work. In an interview Stone says: "In a sense, I'm a theologian" (Woods, p. 44). "I feel a very deep connection to the existentialist tradition of God as an absence—not a meaningless void, but a negative presence we live in terms of" (Woods, p. 48). Moreover, his work probes the moral discrepancies between America's idealistic protestations and its actual behavior. Accordingly, he tries to portray individuals against the background of social forces. He sees American society as fractured and lacking a moral center. Stone's fiction tries to answer fundamental questions: who do we think we are and what do we think we are doing?

Each of Stone's novels depicts an embattled society. *A Hall of Mirrors* brings together three deracinated and deeply wounded individuals in a New Orleans rife with racial tensions and right-wing conspiracies. Here is an America coming apart. Rheinhart, once a talented musician and composer, a man of high sensibilities, now deflects personal responsibility through constant drinking, and takes a job as an announcer for a right-wing radio station, which spews forth racism and white supremacy—but for Rheinhart nothing really matters anymore. Morgan Rainy represents liberalism and a conscience gone to seed and rendered ineffectual against the enormities about him. Even more vulnerable is Geraldine, who comes to New Orleans scarred but hopeful of a new start. Her decency, her capacity to love and to care are no match for the forces swirling about her, and she is crushed by them. Here is a "California of the mind," a world out of margins, a new moral Ice Age. Rheinhart survives the chaos and violence of the big rally at the end of the novel, a scene reminiscent of Nathanael West's *The Day of the Locust*. But at what price does survival come?

In *Dog Soldiers* Stone brings the Vietnam War home in the form of three kilograms of pure heroin, a symbol of the corruption tainting and imprisoning everyone. A naive journalist in Vietnam, John Converse sees a world where literally anything can happen and often does. To Converse, Vietnam is "the place where everybody finds out who they are." To rationalize smuggling drugs, Converse says that in a world like this "people are just naturally going to want to get high." Converse persuades his friend Hicks, a Nietzsche-reading samurai figure, to smuggle the drugs to Converse's wife, Marge, in California. Marge, who looks like a school teacher but works as a cashier in a porno theatre, is already strung-out on pills. Their get-rich-quick scheme is shattered when corrupt government drug agents and their thugs move in for a quick score of their own. Thus ensues a flight and a chase through some of California's seamy landscapes and encounters with burntout cases—a land of lost dreams and paranoia. Hicks digs in and attempts to take charge of events, but his confused loyalty kills him, even though he imagines himself in his death as the bearer of pain, a kind of Christ figure. Converse and his wife survive, and the drugs are left for the rapacious agents. The moral displacement is complete. Converse tells his wife: "I don't know what I'm doing or why I do it or what it's like. . . . Nobody knows. . . . That's the principle we were defending over there. That's why we fought the war." Unlike Ernest Hemingway, who replaced worn-out creeds and ideals with a code of individual courage and dignity, here is a generation truly "lost" and morally bankrupt.

The memory of Vietnam lingers and haunts the characters of *A Flag for Sunrise*. The moral combat zone now is Central America, where burn-outs of old wars converge for revolution, perhaps even for revelation. Frank Holliwell, a Vietnam veteran, who once did favors for the CIA, cynical and world-weary, drinking his way through each day, is an anthropologist (a fitting profession) who comes to Central America to give a lecture. Even though he refuses an invitation to spy for the CIA in Tecan (Stone's fictional country), he goes there anyway out of curiosity.

Paralleling Holliwell's journey south, but from much seedier settings, is that of Pablo Tabor, a half-breed American, a Coast Guard deserter, whose constant pill-popping feeds his paranoia, his fear that people are always trying to "turn him around." Despite his murderous character, Pablo is a man desperately searching for clarity, for coherence, for a sense of the scheme of things and for his place in it. Pablo falls in with some American gunrunners contracted to deliver weapons to the revolutionaries in Tecan.

At the center of Tecan is a failing Catholic mission presided over by the alcoholic Father Egan who preaches a kind of gnosticism to youthful drifters camping among Mayan ruins. Assisting him is Sister Justin Feeney—the true moral center of the novel—who struggles to find her vocation, to translate her faith into action. She wants desperately to be useful in a just cause. Instead, she is used, exploited—her decency, her love ineffectual against the murderous plots and betrayals of power politics. She joins the revolutionaries, and when the coup fails, she is captured by the sadistic Lieutenant Campos who tortures and kills her. While her last words—"Behold the hand-maid of the Lord"—suggest a moral victory, it is one that is lost on most of the combatants. As Holliwell says at one point: "There's always a place for God. . . . There is some question as to whether He's in it."

To trust anyone in this world is fatal. At the end Tabor and Holliwell escape on a small boat and engage in what Stone calls the "final communication." Holliwell murders Tabor, throws him overboard, and awaits rescue, another one of Stone's undeserving survivors. Holliwell is convinced that he knows how things are, how things work—the world holds no more mysteries for him. "A man has nothing to fear, he thought to himself, who understands history." Thus ends a novel, reminiscent of Joseph Conrad and Graham Greene, not so much about the next war but the one that is ongoing. The title of the novel invokes lines from Emily Dickinson. Characters wait to see what the sunrise will bring; for most, it is nothing.

Stone's first two novels were made into disappointing films. *A Hall of Mirrors* became *WUSA*, starring Paul Newman and Joanne Woodward; it received rather negative reviews. *Dog Soldiers*, released under the title *Who'll Stop the Rain*, was dropped by its distributor. Stone collaborated on the screenplays for the films and was not altogether satisfied with the results. Stone uses some of his Hollywood experiences in his fourth novel *Children of Light*, which has met with mixed reviews. It is a novel which explores some of the same spiritual terrain as that of Nathanael West and Joan Didion. The title recalls Robert Lowell's poem "Children of Light," a line from which Stone used for the title of his first novel. But the title also suggests Biblical references (to I Thessalonians), and light and dark images pervade the book.

In Stone's first three novels, weak and fallen individuals were tested and found wanting against the backdrop of powerful social and historical forces. In *Children of Light* these larger social forces are not as prominent. Instead, Stone casts beleaguered selves into the artificial realities of the Hollywood "dream factories." The characters are talented artists, privileged people who, incomprehensibly, seem determined to destroy themselves. At times it is hard to care about people so self-indulgent, so self-destructive. Gordon Walker, a screenwriter and sometime actor, coming off a successful portrayal of Lear in a Seattle production, sustaining himself with booze and cocaine, sees "a vision of his life as trash," he is a man desperately needing a dream. He drives down to the Mexican set where his screenplay of Chopin's *The Awakening* is being filmed starring his former lover Lu Anne Bourgeois as Edna.

Before Walker arrives, Lu Anne goes off the drug which controls her schizophrenia, her hallucinating of what she calls the "Long Friends," because she believes that the drug inhibits her acting. Fearing her madness, her psychiatrist husband leaves her. Surrounded by predatory failed writers and cynical directors whose major concern is their own aggrandisement and the bottom line, Lu Anne is vulnerable to a disaster. Walker's presence is the catalyst for Lu Anne to follow her perceptions to their fatal ends. Like Edna, Lu Anne walks into the sea; Walker is unable to save her. At the end, Walker, chastened by the experience, is sober and beginning a new life in the East. In this world art is sacrificed to technique and offers no solace to rootless souls. Lacking a moral center, the self knows no limits, and, as so often in the American tradition when that is the case, the consequences are disastrous.

Robert Stone is a naturalist of the moral life. The inevitability of his characters' fates is a moral inevitability—things could have gone differently; nevertheless, we are responsible for the consequences. In many respects, Stone explores the implications for our time of Yeats' lines from "The Second Coming": "The best lack all conviction, while the worst/Are full of passionate intensity." While his vision is harsh, often violent, Stone's art is not gratuitous. He says: "I deal with much that is negative and gruesome, but I don't write to dispirit people. I write to give them courage, to make them confront things as they are in a more courageous way" (Woods, p. 50).

SELECTED BIBLIOGRAPHY

Works by Stone: NOVELS: *A Hall of Mirrors*. Boston: Houghton Mifflin, 1967; *Dog Soldiers*. Boston: Houghton Mifflin, 1974; *A Flag for Sunrise*. New York: Knopf, 1981; *Children of Light*. New York: Knopf, 1986. STORIES: "Porque No Tiene, Porque Le Falte." *New American Review* 6 (1970), pp. 198–226. "Aquarius Obscured." *American Review* 22 (1975); "War Stores." *Harper's Magazine* (May 1977), pp. 63–66. "The Human Factor." *Harper's Magazine* (April 1978), pp. 78–93.

Works about Stone: Epstein, Joseph. "American Nightmares." *Commentary* (March 1982), pp. 42–45; Karagueuzian, Maureen. "Irony in Robert Stone's *Dog Soldiers*." *Critique* 24, 2 (1983), pp. 65–73; Moore, L. Hugh. "The Undersea World of Robert Stone." *Critique* XI, 3 (1969), pp. 43–56; Shelton, Frank W. "Robert Stone's *Dog Soldiers*: Vietnam Comes Home to America." *Critique* 24, 2 (1983), pp. 74–81. Woods, W. C. "Interview with Robert Stone." *The Paris Review* 27 (Winter 1985), pp. 25–57. CA 85–88.

John G. Parks

RICHARD SULLIVAN (1908–1981). As a teacher, novelist, historian, dramatist, reviewer, and writer of short stories, Richard Sullivan was for forty years a presence in Catholic American letters.

Born on November 29, 1908, in Kenosha, Wisconsin, of Irish-German parents, Sullivan studied at the Art Institute of Chicago, the Goodman School of Drama, and the University of Notre Dame, graduating in 1930. After six years of freelance writing, he returned to Notre Dame where he taught until his retirement in 1976, one of many teacher-writers (among them John Logan,* John Frederick Nims* and Ernest Sandeen*) who enriched the academic climate of that institution. Married to Mabel Constance Priddis in 1932 and father of two children, he died on September 13, 1981, in South Bend, Indiana.

A concerned, inspirational teacher and a stern, disciplined critic, Sullivan opposed American literary naturalism as a biased and incomplete philosophy. He consistently pointed out its limitations: its determinism, biological or environmental, its neglect of man's potential for personal change; its harsh, negative portrayal of the human condition; and its emphasis on coarse sexuality and violence as dominant in human life. As an alternative, he posed Catholic fiction, but he did not understand "Catholic" to be narrowly sectarian and doctrinaire. He rejected the demand—strong in the 1940s and 1950s—that Catholic writers should produce pious tracts or inspirational homilies; this, he believed, was restrictive and demanded the artist's vocation. Sullivan saw Catholic literature as religious, presenting an arena in which moral and spiritual concerns were central, life was seen as a journey to a goal, and man was understood as a creature of soul and body, touched by God, spoiled by sin, but capable of free choice.

His fiction exemplifies this view. Nature may be harsh and often destructive, but it is not hostile or indifferent and is understandable in terms of a regularity and renewal reflective of order in the universe. Society and all human institutions are flawed, but they are made and modified by human beings not governed solely by greed and self-interest. People are imperfect; but they are not depraved: they struggle toward new awareness, adapt to change, help themselves and others. Sullivan's characters are fortified by or progress toward a knowledge of continuity in human experience and a sense of mystery. Man is not alone; he inhabits God's world.

These are the themes of great literature, but Sullivan was not a master of the craft of fiction. His plots are not sustained, extended narratives: his short stories are sketches, his novels essentially short stories held together by locale or the presence of a protagonist. His characterizations suffer from a thinness, a tendency to stereotype, and predictability. His execution, though careful and competent, is not original or innovative. Sullivan's work offers a sturdy, honest rendering of the familiar, but not a bold, imaginative creation of the new.

As a significant Catholic literary tradition develops in the United States, Sullivan will be seen standing at its beginnings—a minor writer whose presence, exceeding his achievement, was an important contribution.

SELECTED BIBLIOGRAPHY

Works by Sullivan: NOVELS: *Summer after Summer*. New York: Doubleday and Co., 1942; *The Dark Continent*. New York: Doubleday and Co., 1943; *The World of Idella May*. New York: Doubleday and Co., 1946; *First Citizen*. New York: Henry Holt and Co., 1948; *311 Congress Court*. New York: Henry Holt and Co., 1953; *Three Kings*. New York: Harcourt, Brace and Co., 1956. SHORT STORIES: *The Fresh and Open Sky*. New York: Henry Holt and Co., 1950. DRAMA: *Our Lady's Tumbler*. Chicago: Dramatic Publishing Co., 1940. History: *Notre Dame: The Story of a Great University*. New York: Henry Holt and Co., 1951.

Works about Sullivan: Warfel, H. R. *American Novelists of Today*. New York: American Book Co., 1951. CA 77–80. Cat A (1947). TCA.

James L. McDonald

WALTER SULLIVAN (1924–). A convert from the Episcopal church in the 1970s, after the Book of Common Prayer revision controversy, Walter Sullivan is better known as a professor of English at Vanderbilt University, and the author of two studies of modern Southern writing. But he is also the author of two well-received novels and several short stories, and he has returned to fiction with the publication of three stories in the 1970s, including "Elizabeth" (*Sewanee Review*, Summer 1979), an O. Henry Award story in 1980. He is currently working on a novel, *Ten Thousand Places*.

Born on January 4, 1924, in Nashville, Tennessee, he married Jane Harrison in 1947 after serving three years in the Marines. They have three children. Sullivan took a B.A. from Vanderbilt in 1947 and an M.F.A. from Iowa in 1949, then he began teaching at Vanderbilt.

His story, "The Blue Eyed Boy" (*Western Review*, Summer 1950), is a boy's account of his stubborn father's resistance to sending a black servant to veterinary school. Josh/Ezekiel warns Ben that his prize race horse might lose a match race but Ben, with the fatalism of one of Faulkner's outwitted aristocrats, invites defeat at the shrewd black's hands. Another story, "Fowling Piece," appeared in the *Georgia Review* in 1951.

Sojourn of a Stranger, published in 1957, is a Civil War period novel of the baronial pride of Southern aristocracy in tension with miscegenation richly realized in the characters of Marcus Hendrick, pursuing honor and justice; Lucy, setting her son in the right direction; and the mulatto son Allen, bent upon winning Kathleen Rutledge. The evil of the war consumes Kate's brother, Percy, and threatens Allen with "the destructive quality of revenge." Only great strength, moral wisdom, love, and forgiveness lead to hope for the peace the stranger's cry asks for in Psalm 39. Meanwhile, Allen is humbled in realizing how so many have helped him on the way and how selfish has been his impatience for justice.

The Long, Long Love (1959) focuses on Horatio Adams, orphaned by the sinking of the Titanic, who early knows the doom of time and is eventually fixated on his Confederate general grandfather's grave as a vehicle for convincing himself of immorality ("something that we can all be proud of"). Told skillfully in several voices, the story turns into a mystery—and doom for two marriages in which beauty and love are defeated by failure of humanity. Very late, loneliness yields to wisdom. Ironically, the ancestor had chosen beauty over doom.

Sullivan's later stories evoke the power of love ("The Penalty of Love," *Sewanee Review*, Winter 1971), the slavery of art ("The Brief Detention of Charles Weems," *Southern Review*, Autumn 1978), and the transforming power of simple faith in "Elizabeth," in which Lucky's violent abuse occasions her journey from love to the cross to the empty tomb and to resurrection.

Sullivan's earlier fiction merits praise for the rich social fabric of history he provides and the moral richness of his themes. One suspects that the reservations of reviewers rose from his understated style, which builds deftly upon the manners of Middle Tennessee. His later work forecloses such criticism.

SELECTED BIBLIOGRAPHY

Works by Sullivan: *Sojourn of a Stranger*. New York: Holt, 1957; *The Long, Long Love*. New York: Holt, 1959, New York: New American Library, 1960.

Works about Sullivan: Review of *The Long, Long Love. Chicago Sunday Tribune* (10 May 1959), p. 17; Review of *Sojourn of a Stranger. New York Times* (11 August 1957), p. 18. CA 15–16.

Walter H. Slavick

HARRY SYLVESTER (1908–). Journalist, short-story writer and novelist, Harry Sylvester speaks strongly about the influence of Roman Catholicism on his life: "I cannot write of myself as a writer without making clear my relation to the [Catholic] Church, past and present" (*Twentieth Century Authors: First Supplement*, p. 977). This statement, made in 1954, does not mean that Sylvester is a Catholic writer in any traditional sense, because after writing three serious novels about the Church, Harry Sylvester underwent what he calls a "disconversion" in March 1949 and left Catholicism "permanently and irrevocably" (p. 977). However, through bitterness and commitment the struggle with his faith produced Sylvester's greatest fiction.

Born on January 19, 1908, in Brooklyn, New York, Harry Sylvester graduated in 1930 from the University of Notre Dame with a B.A. in journalism. After writing for the New York *Herald Tribune*, the New York *Post*, and the Brooklyn *Daily Eagle*, Sylvester gave up newspaper work in 1933 and became a free-lance writer. His short stories have appeared in *Commonweal*, *Esquire*, *Story*, and many other magazines, and several have achieved recognition in *The Best Short Stories* for the years 1935, 1939, and 1940; fourteen were collected in *All Your Idols* (1948). His four novels were published between 1942 and 1950; "There might have been more books," he wrote in 1954, "if there had not been an almost constant financial pressure requiring me to sell over the years about 150 short stories" (p. 977). Since 1954, Sylvester has published little except book reviews, political comment, and letters. He has become a Quaker (as is his present wife), "raised four children, for a time on my own . . . worked for various government agencies including the State Department" (Letter, August 20, 1986) where he served as a briefing officer for Cuban affairs. Now retired, Sylvester has completed what he calls his "best novel," a " 'moral tale' of the sort the late John Gardner might have approved"; it is not concerned with the Catholic Church.

His best short stories deal with subjects as far ranging as boxing, labor disputes, hunting, the nature of faith and miracle, and bullfighting. Many of the stories reflect not only Sylvester's Catholicism and his life-long interest in Mexico and Latin America, but also the early influence of Ernest Hemingway. The presence of guns, the effects of war on men, the crisis at the moment of defeat, the intensity of life when its dreams collapse—all these reflect Hemingway's need to show men responding with or without grace under fire when circumstances get beyond a man. Sylvester's prose, too, rings of Hemingway's spare syntax and colloquial diction: " 'That's how you could be sure to die. Just be good or brave or a fine athlete or a good poet and you could be sure you'd go out early' " ("The Evening Hawk," *All Your Idols* 33).

In his three religious novels Sylvester leaves Hemingway behind and finds his own voice. The novels concern mainly the crisis of faith arising from a recognition of hyprocrisy in the Church, but the tone varies from the skepticism of *Dearly Beloved* (1942) to the gentler acceptance of grace in *Dayspring* (1945) to the embittered rejection in *Moon Gaffney* (1947). But always Sylvester confronts the enormous presence of Catholicism in his world.

Dearly Beloved dramatizes the gap between Christian principles of brotherhood and the racist, selfish and anti-Semitic actions of ordinary Catholics and, more especially, priests and bishops. Sylvester pulls no punches; he gets right to the heart of a tough moral issue: how can it be right for the Church to perpetuate the institution of slavery? And yet, Father Kane, the central character in the novel, worries that the timeless principles of the Church must change to meet the demands of history; after all, the Jesuits once owned slaves but do not anymore.

Perhaps reflecting Sylvester's own concerns at the time, Kane thinks about many ecclesiastical problems, ''of the difference between the Church as a radical idea and the Church as a conservative organization; of the Church immature in America and now coming of age; and of how a man might be ground between the millstones of the idea and the organization'' (p. 58). These issues take many forms in the novel including the fight between the animal and the spiritual in human beings.

In the end, some people can return to the true principles of the Church in spite of institutional corruption, even though most Catholics—including priests— violate most offensively the tenets of Christianity.

In *Dayspring*, Sylvester explores another aspect of faith: the conflict between intellectual detachment of Christian commitment, and the place of grace in the process of conversion. A University of Chicago anthropologist named Bain goes to Mexico to study the Penitentes. Bain converts to Catholicism in order to observe the Good Friday rituals of the Brotherhood from the inside. Although he believes intellectual curiosity motivates his conversion, he finds, ironically, ''that his conversion had been sincere'' (p. 56). Dragging the *carrete de muerte* in the Good Friday procession, Bain insists that his involvement springs from intellectual commitment, even though he cannot explain the feeling of peace which pervades his soul. Finally, he comes to accept that his performance constitutes penance for past sins; reluctantly, he embraces Roman Catholicism.

Sylvester is not content, however, to leave Bain in a peaceful moment of confident faith. Rather, he traces Bain's movement into pride and fear (that he will need to stand up for what he believes), to denial of his faith before the temptations of sex and power, and finally, to a rejection of his intellectual pride in favor of a quiet faith. Sylvester shows that belief demands courage and rejection of the worldly, but he also shows that fanaticism in the name of the world or in the name of Christ can lead to self-destruction. Even more profoundly, the novel explores the work of grace in Bain's final acceptance that ''it's the heart and not the mind that really informed a man's actions.'' (p. 237). Like

Dearly Beloved and *Moon Gaffney*, *Dayspring* condemns the Church's obsession with humanity's sexuality, but it affirms in gentler tones—and apparently for the last time in Sylvester's career—the power of grace to effect conversion and infuse peace in the faithful.

In *Moon Gaffney*, Sylvester links the power of the Church with the power of politics. Catholic sentimentality, a morose preoccupation with sexual sins, hypocrisy, a need to preserve its order and authority at the expense of human needs—all combine to drive Moon Gaffney away from Catholicism. Most significantly though, the worldly condition of the modern Church—what Moon calls "the vague perversion of a noble thing" (p. 220), "the Church, seeking order and the fulfillment of the word of God, had bade them in charity endure one another, and in time they could and did endure anything, but almost always for the wrong reasons" (p. 232). Moon weeps for his shaken faith (p. 220).

Important scenes occur in bars, in parish meeting halls, in the chancery, at wakes, and in the home, suggesting that Moon's separation combines public actions and private reflections just as the political and social powers of the Church betray its internal spiritual principles. When Moon discovers that the Church will sell off the houses of poor Italian immigrants in order to increase its capital liquidity, he challenges the authority of the Church and thus loses the Church's backing for his political advancement.

Although strongly anti-clerical, the novel avoids simplistic anti-Catholicism. In the end, Moon gives up his chance for political office in order to concentrate his legal skills in the defense of poor immigrants, Communists, and blacks. In this bleak story of the Church's betrayal of its own principles, this ending seems almost optimistic because Moon has not, like other characters, surrendered his faith to despair—the ultimate mortal sin. Rather, he will redefine his Catholicism as social action—even though there is little hope that Church authority will ever condone his actions or the principles on which they are based.

Living in relative obscurity, Sylvester is another author whose works deserve reexamination if not for their inspirational prose or formal experimentation, then for their realistic portrayal of the process of gaining and losing faith in a Church which, in its fervor, too often perverts the values on which it was founded.

SELECTED BIBLIOGRAPHY

Works by Sylvester: *Dearly Beloved*. New York: Duell, Sloan and Pearce, 1942; *Dayspring*. New York: Appleton-Century, Co., 1945; *Moon Gaffney*. New York: Henry Holt, 1947; *All Your Idols*. New York: Henry Holt, 1948; *A Golden Girl*. New York: Harcourt, Brace & Co., 1950.

Works about Sylvester: Review of *Dayspring*. *Book Week* (8 April 1945), p. 4. Cat A (1947). TCA.

Daniel J. Tynan

T

ALLEN TATE (1899–1979). Few twentieth-century American writers have shared Allen Tate's concern for the plight of man in a pragmatic, materialistic society. One of the most original poets and among the most influential critics of his time, he was always searching for a belief that would "unify religion, morality, and art." Although he was strongly attracted to the Catholic Church as a young man and haunted by the profound need for a deep religious sense throughout his career, he did not officially join the Church until 1950. Despite his conviction that he must avoid any affiliation that would restrict the range of his art, one can detect throughout his career the influence of Catholicism, and his attempts to come to grips with it.

His earliest poetry reveals his insatiable desire for a force that would give aim, purpose, and direction to his life and art. In "Mr. Pope" he argues that "Pope's use of traditional rhyme and meter" gave a form and order to his life and work that the modern poet, with his preference for free verse and eccentric design, cannot share. The carefully controlled work of art is important; not the imperfect, helplessly deformed creature who created it.

Tate's best-known poem, "Ode to the Confederate Dead," describes a world without a sense of purpose, one in which religious principle has become confused with social concern. Unlike Keats, who can join the nightingale "on the wings of poesy," Tate's protagonist cannot know the valor of those "who gave their life for a sacred cause because he has lost his sense of tradition." How significant this loss is, Tate explains in "What Is a Traditional Society?"

It means that in ages which suffer the decay of manners, religion, morals, codes, our indestructible vitality demands expression in violence and chaos; it means that men who have lost both the higher myth of religion and the lower myth of historical dramatization have lost the forms of human action. (*Essays of Four Decades*, 554)

Man is like the blind crab: he has movement but no direction; energy but no purposeful world in which to use it.

All of his life Tate searched for a resolution to the conflict between naturalism and mysticism, looking first to art and then to the tradition of the Old South. In the poems and the essays of the 1920s and early 1930s—particularly the "Ode"— this tension is obvious. Nevertheless, Catholicism, apparently, has little to offer his character Lacy in *The Fathers* (1938), even though that novel, like his essays and poems of what he called his period of "believing unbelief," reiterates the conviction that the problems of sin and evil cannot be explained by social and economic theories. Modern society, in Tate's view, is based on the hope of man's perfectibility through education and social reform, demanding that he surrender his essential being to gnosticism, and to the hope of gaining superior material satisfaction in the future.

Despite Tate's dissatisfaction with the modern world, Catholicism still was not the answer. Catholicism in the novel is presented primarily through Jarman Posey, a character who has withdrawn completely from life. He has shut himself in his dormer room and comes downstairs only once a year. He has "had so long an assured living that he no longer knew it had a natural source in human activity." Living for him is merely a succession of absolute abstractions.

From the French writer, Maritain, whom he began reading seriously before World War II, Tate learned that being a Catholic need not in itself cut him off from the natural world. Although Jacques Maritain, like Augustine, emphasized the importance of the earthly realm (the here and now), both of these great religious thinkers emphasized the need to strive for the Heavenly. The sensible, dedicated man must seek a medium between the two. The earthly realm is merely a means of knowing the Heavenly.

The artist who most influenced Tate, perhaps, was Dante. From the great medievalist he received not only the inspiration for some of his best poetry, but also convincing evidence that religion did not destroy art. In two of his most evocative essays ("The Angelic Imagination" and "The Symbolic Imagination" *The Man of Letters in the Modern World*), Tate contrasts Edgar Allan Poe's use of analogy with Dante's. Dante tried to transcend the natural world so that he might know the presence of God; Poe endeavored to put himself in the seat of God by circumventing the natural world. From Dante, Tate learned that there is nothing in the intellect that does not come from the senses, and so the vision of God, too, must come from the senses. Dante showed Tate how to remain a part of the natural world while experiencing metaphysical reality. His latest works, and some say his best, embody this knowledge. "The Maimed Man" (1952), "The Swimmers" (1953), and "Buried Lake" (1953) are all deeply religious poems which examine Tate's life as it has been transformed by this new-found faith.

"The Maimed Man" examines an early confrontation with the spirit of Christ. The poet is reluctant to accept the headless man he sees as the body of Christ because to do so would alienate him from the ordered world he knows. In other words, he is struggling with the same problem that has obsessed him for years: religious faith might disassociate him from the natural world. In "The Swimmers" the poet sees Christ in the form of a black man who has just been lynched by a mob.

The influence of Dante on "The Seasons of the Soul," generally considered Tate's masterpiece, is undeniable, and Tate himself has admitted that the poem is linked to James Thompson's *The Seasons*. But the seasonable framework is about all of Thompson's poem that one can see in Tate's. Each of the four sections of "The Seasons of the Soul" contains six stanzas of sixty lines, and the pervasive concern in each section is sin and salvation. In "Summer," one detects immediately Tate's obsession with the necessity of a balance between the heart and intellect, between reason and faith. He searches for a childhood scene that will allow him to move by analogy from the natural world to the spiritual realm. Despite calling up and examining many incidents in detail, his labor goes unrewarded. In the "Autumn" section, he descends "down in the dark well," echoing exactly Dante's phrase for the descent into hell. Struggle as he may, he cannot escape; he merely returns to where he began. He sees his father briefly but he disappears. Then "From one room to another," he watched familiar old men and women, boys and girls "come and go," even his "downcast mother. Clad in her street clothes," but he can attract no one's attention. The separation of the self is complete. This is one journey he must make alone. The third section, "Winter," makes it obvious that the poem was written during World War II because only in a world from which God has disappeared can such senseless human slaughter occur. The war has widened the fissure between heart and head. The concluding section, "Spring," is centered on an old mother, associated with Saint Monica, the mother of Saint Augustine. Tate refers to the passage in the *Confessions* where the old lady is dying. She goes to the window to look out, and she and her son communicate without words. Tate has found a means of suggesting the process by which the natural and spiritual realms may be joined—by faith. Tate does not say that men who are strained between physical and spiritual desire can know metaphysical reality through analogical vision, but he does believe that man can perform this miraculous feat by no other means.

SELECTED BIBLIOGRAPHY

Works by Tate: CRITICISM: *Reactionary Essays on Poetry and Ideas*. New York: Scribner's, 1936; *Reason in Madness: Critical Essays*. New York: Putnam's, 1938; *Essays of Four Decades*. Chicago: Swallow, 1968. NOVEL: *The Fathers*. New York: Putnam's, 1938; rev. ed. *The Fathers and Other Fiction*. Baton Rouge: Louisiana State University Press, 1968. POETRY: *Mr. Pope and Other Poems*. New York: Minton, Balsh, 1928; *Poems: 1928–1931*. New York: Scribner's, 1932; *The Mediterranean and Other Poems*. New York: Alcestis, 1936; *Selected Poems*. New York: Scribner's, 1937; *Poems, 1920–1945: A Selection*. London: Eyre and Spottswood, 1947; *Collected Poems, 1919–1976*. New York: Farrar, Straus & Giroux, 1977.

Works about Tate: Brinkmeyer, Robert H. *Three Catholic Writers of the Modern South*. Jackson: University Press of Mississippi, 1985; Brown, Ashley, and Frances Neel Cheney. *The Poetry Reviews of Allan Tate*. Baton Rouge: Louisiana State University

Press, 1983; Dupree, Robert S. *Allen Tate and the Augustine Imagination*. Baton Rouge, Louisiana State University Press, 1983; Squires, Radcliffe. *Allen Tate: A Literary Biography*. New York: Pegasus, 1971; Squires, Radcliffe, ed. *Allen Tate and His Work*. Minneapolis: University of Minnesota Press, 1972. AW. CA 5–6. Cat A (1952). CN. DLB 4, 45. TCA.

Thomas Daniel Young

ALEXANDER LOUIS THEROUX (1939–). Theroux's novel, *Darconville's CAT* (1981) has been hailed as "the strongest work of fiction published in the United States since *Gravity's Rainbow*." It has also been condemned as "a 700-page attack of logorrhea." The "length and copiousness" of the novel have been praised as its strongest points and damned as "inflation . . . out of control." His first novel, *Three Wogs* (1972), met less critical opposition, even though, for this work also, his love of words (and non-words) received mixed reviews.

A member of the literary Theroux family, Alexander was born in Medford, Massachusetts. He attended St. Francis College in Maine and did graduate work at the University of Virginia. He has taught at Longwood College in Virginia, at Harvard University, and at Phillips Academy. Like the protagonist of *Darconville's Cat*, he once spent two years in a Trappist monastery, then became a novice in a Franciscan seminary. He has received Fulbright and Guggenheim fellowships. In addition to his two novels, Theroux has published three fables (usually inappropriately called children's books): *The Great Wheadle Tragedy* (1975), *The Schinocephalic Waif* (1975), and *Master Snickup's Cloak* (1979). He has also contributed articles to periodicals, including *Esquire* and *National Review*.

Religion is not the dominant theme in Theroux's books. *Three Wogs* consists of three novellas about English opposition to minorities—blacks of all origins, Orientals, Irishmen, and Italians. "Wogs" is the English derogatory term for anyone who is "not one of us." *The Great Wheadle Tragedy* parodies sentimental, melodramatic circus stories; *The Schinocephalic Waif* parodies both sentimental children's stories about orphans and folktales about origin. *Darconville's Cat* is a boy-meets-girl story about the opposition between life and art.

Yet Theroux's religious education plays a role in all of these works, not only in the omnipresent Latin (even in the fables), but also in the frequent references to saints, real or imagined, and in logic of all kinds, from casual syllogisms to the elaborate *Oratio Contra Feminas* of Dr. Crucifer in *Darconville's Cat*. Scholastic delight in unanswerable questions predominates. The innocent little trapeze artist of *The Great Wheadle Tragedy*, pondering the possibility that her uncle murdered her twin, asks: "Does *ought* imply *is*?" The homosexual Anglican priest of *Three Wogs* asks a series of questions beginning with: "When Mass is being said at two ends of a church, where precisely is the Holy Ghost?" Often the questions are followed by long expositions, as when Darconville wonders why he wants to write a book:

I? Perhaps, he thought, there isn't an I at all and we're simply the means of expressions of something else. *Wonder*? What is wonder but the imagination seeking what it hasn't. *Shy*? Y: the past tense of antique verbs resurrected to predicate present behavior. (p. 595).

Religion, like everything else, is a target of Theroux's satire, but the religious practices he satirizes are not his own, but other people's. In *Three Wogs* it is an Anglican priest who draws Theroux's fire. In *Darconville's Cat*, it is the Southern Baptists. The Anglican priest (named the Rev. Which Therefore) may have a vision of God as "an inflexible, fault-finding precisian, as warty as Cromwell" who sports with human creatures, "humiliatingly dunked into ponds in ducking stools," and the members of the Wyanoid Baptist Church may belt out hymns with names like "The Flame on My Wick Is Bright Tonight," but at St. Teresa's, the small Catholic church in Quinsyburg, Darconville could always find peace. For Theroux, not God but humanity is to be blamed.

Several critics have lamented that Theroux's second novel had not fulfilled the promise of the first. I disagree. For better or for worse, *Darconville's Cat* exceeds the promise of *Three Wogs*. With misanthropy exceeded only by misogyny, Theroux moves even farther in the direction already established: the satire is more brutal; the characters are more limited; the plot is less consequential. There are far more words.

SELECTED BIBLIOGRAPHY

Works by Theroux: NOVELS: *Three Wogs*. Boston: Gambit, 1972; *Darconville's Cat*. Garden City, N.Y.: Doubleday, 1981; *An Adultery*. New York: Simon and Shuster, 1987. FABLES: *The Schinocephalic Waif*, ill. Stan Washburn. Boston: Godine, 1975; *The Great Wheadle Tragedy*, ill. Stan Washburn. Boston: Godine, 1975; *Master Snickup's Cloak*, ill. Brian Froud. New York: Harper, 1979.

Works about Theroux: REVIEWS: Beatty, Jack. "Logorrhea!" *The New Republic* 184, 14 (4 April 1981), pp. 38–40; DeMott, Benjamin. "Awash with Lists and Catalogues." *New York Times Book Review* (3 May 1981), pp. 9, 30–31; Donald, Miles. "Shaker Country." *New Statesman* 86, 2209 (20 July 1973), p. 95; Johnson, Diane. "Wog Good, Us Bad." "Book World," *Chicago Tribune* VI, 7 (13 February 1972), p. 8; Leonard, John. " 'Darconville's Cat'." *New York Times* (28 May 1981), p. 367–69; Ottenberg, Eve. " 'Also But Not Yet the Wombat Cries . . .' " *The Village Voice* XXVI, 16 (15–21 April 1981), p. 46; Tate, J. O. "Bedtime for Boethius." *National Review* XXXIII, 10 (29 May 1981), pp. 620–21. CA 85–88. CANR 20.

Ruth Barton

PAUL THEROUX (1941–). Paul Theroux's writing has provided a marvelous range of situations and characters, from the thirteen-year-old narrator of *The Mosquito Coast* (1982) to the seventy-year-old woman who narrates *Picture Palace* (1978). His non-fiction, which gained him his first best-seller with *The Great Railway Bazaar* (1975), also ranges widely, from the railways of the Raj to the subways of New York City. Paul Theroux's work consistently pursues themes of the exotic and the picaresque. His characters are almost always exiles of one kind or another, as he himself has been for much of his life. But the exiles are always presented as members of families, and the importance of family (whether natural or by extension) is another prominent theme in his work. Catholicism, however—while important in Theroux's upbringing—has little direct influence on his work. Indirectly, the problem of evil and conflicts between spirituality and materialism may find their roots in Theroux's Catholic sensibility.

Paul Edward Theroux was born on April 10, 1941, in Medford, Massachusetts, of French-Canadian and Italian parents, one of seven children (two of his brothers, Alexander and Joseph, are also published novelists). Theroux was educated in the public schools of Medford before attending the University of Maine. He graduated from the University of Massachusetts at Amherst in 1963 and studied briefly at Syracuse University before joining the Peace Corps later that year. The Peace Corps sent him as a lecturer in English to the East African nation of Malawi, where he spent the next two years until he was expelled on charges of plotting against the government. From 1965 to 1968, he was a lecturer in English at a university in Uganda where he met V. S. Naipaul, a writer who was to influence and encourage him. It was also in Uganda that he met and married Anne Castle. Between 1968 and 1971 he taught at the University of Singapore; in 1971 he decided to move to London and devote his full time to professional writing. Now the father of two sons, he divides his time between London and another home on Cape Cod, so that after many years of travel, Paul Theroux spends at least part of every year in the United States. His fiction has earned numerous awards; he is a fellow of the Royal Society of Literature and a member of the American Academy of Arts and Letters.

Paul Theroux's output has been truly remarkable, and it is possible to touch on only some of the highpoints of his achievement. His fifth novel, *Jungle Lovers* (1971), contains promise of what is to come; the central character is an American trying to sell insurance to the people of Malawi. The only character as ridiculous as Calvin Mullett is a revolutionary, also a white man, who tries to stir the people to rebel against their dictatorial ruler. Both the revolutionary and Mullett are living in worlds that have little to do with the actual life of the people in Malawi. Calvin Mullett is predictably unhappy. He spends a good deal of his time writing a book with an African narrator; called *The Uninsured*, is is supposedly written by A. Jigololo. Before very long, the book falls into the wrong hands and is transformed, as *Unite Brothers*, into a piece of anti-government propaganda. Marais, the revolutionary, is also a writer, who keeps extensive journals. Both Cal and Marais are idealists who come to realize that Malawi is not really a country at all but, as Cal says, a "parish," and neither he nor Marais really belongs. The Africans are more interested in life than in politics or money, so Cal forgets insurance and Marais abandons revolution. Cal finds family in a liaison with a black girl, and they live in a hotel that is really a brothel.

The pointlessness of idealism is a theme to which Theroux returns. In his first major novel, *Saint Jack* (1973), Jack Flowers (Fiori) is another American in a strange environment, in Singapore on the run from a trivial drug charge in the United States. A man with high ideals, he fantasizes himself as a writer, sainted for his great gifts. In reality, he is a fifty-three-year-old pimp who has never amounted to very much; he relies on his girls and on his chums at the Bandung Club to provide family support. The past haunts him in his experience of Mr. Leigh, who appears long enough only to ask some pointed questions before he dies of a heart attack: "How do you stand it? How do you manage?" Jack tries to pray about his despair over the death of Mr. Leigh, but all he can manage is to raise still another question, "Is this all?" The novel portrays a man whose life has been aimless and yet who in the end is able to perform one act that saves him from complete corruption.

In *The Family Arsenal* (1976), Theroux strengthens his place as one of America's finest young writers. Again he focuses on an American, Valentine Hood, who is fired from his job as an American consul in Vietnam after he strikes a local government official. He has taken up residence with a trio of IRA terrorists in South London. Seeing no particular meaning in life, Hood chooses to help these people, and they develop a kind of family relationship. As so often in his work, Paul Theroux consciously pays homage to writers whom he admires, in this case to Joseph Conrad, whose *Secret Agent* lies behind *The Family Arsenal.*

Picture Palace, an award-winning novel published in 1978, focuses on a first-person narrator, Maude Coffin Pratt. This seventy-year-old photographer's whole life, recaptured through a retrospective of her pictures, has revolved around an obsession with her brother. In this novel Theroux risks introducing historical characters and for the most part succeeds in making Graham Greene, Alfred Stieglitz, T. S. Eliot, and others live on the page. Like most of his earlier novels, *Picture Palace* received mixed reviews, either for its pretentiousness on the one hand, or its profoundly contemplative spirit. Theroux's fascination with light is evident here and elsewhere.

The Mosquito Coast studies an eccentric inventor, Allie Fox, who has decided that America is falling apart and will soon go to war. He is "the last man" and he must therefore escape before the whole structure collapses. Moving his family to the Mosquito Coast of Honduras, he subjects them to extraordinary adventures and privations, viewed from the perspective of Allie's thirteen-year-old son, Charlie Fox. *The Mosquito Coast* is Theroux's most ambitious and successful novel and the one that comes closest to escaping the landscape of pointlessness he is so fond of drawing. It displays Theroux's control of narrative and character, and his gift for names and language. Allie is, indeed, "crazy like a fox," the ship that carries the family south is aptly named the *Unicorn*, and Allie's jungle city is, appropriately, Jeronimo. The novel operates well on many levels; it is an allegory of the conflict between science and religion, a consideration of complex family relationships, a mediation on the meaning of civilization. Building a giant ice plant in the jungle, Allie has the temerity to echo scripture (which he knows well), "This is why I'm here. This is why I came." But the idealist cannot escape reality, as his children demonstrate in their secret, rival settlement, the Acre, with its allusions to *Lord of the Flies*. Allie's dream perishes in his extremism, which leads him to betray his own family, whose welfare was the presumed purpose of the jungle exile. Allie's story is bleak; the hope in the novel lies in Charlie, sensitive and perceptive, who can observe: "The days were long and unbroken like a sentence with no commas and we felt lost like this."

Theroux's greatest weakness is the undifferentiated voice of his narrators, whether omniscient or first person. The narrative tone is wonderful, but it does not change to suit different speakers. Yet he has a good ear for distinctive voices in conversations. And his gifts for plot and characterization are enhanced by his skill with language, in the imagery of the painting in *The Family Arsenal*, of photography in *Picture Palace*, of the city in *The Mosquito Coast*. In much of his best work, Theroux conjoins imagery with his favorite themes of exile and family.

His pervasively bleak and sometimes shocking portrayal of the evil that is within yields finally to a thin note of optimism: *Jungle Lovers* ends with a birth; in the last chapter of *The Family Arsenal*, Valentine Hood sets off, with a "family" reorganized by murder and treachery, for Guatemala; Maude Pratt comes to a self-accepting if bitter peace through understanding; young Charlie Fox sees glory in the shabbiness of everyday normalcy after his "Heart of Darkness" experience. But whether Paul Theroux's proves ultimately a voice of hope in a tragic world remains for this prolific writer's future work to show.

SELECTED BIBLIOGRAPHY

Works by Theroux: *Waldo*. Boston: Houghton Mifflin, 1967; *Fong and the Indians*. Boston: Houghton Mifflin, 1968; *Girls at Play*. Boston: Houghton Mifflin, 1969; *Murder in Mount Holly*. London: Alan Ross, 1969; *Jungle Lovers*. Boston: Houghton Mifflin, 1971; *Sinning with Annie, and Other Stories*. Boston: Houghton Mifflin, 1972; *Saint Jack*. Boston: Houghton Mifflin, 1973; *The Black House*. Boston: Houghton Mifflin, 1974; *The Family Arsenal*. Boston: Houghton Mifflin, 1976; *The Consul's File*. Boston: Houghton Mifflin, 1977; *Picture Palace*. Boston: Houghton Mifflin, 1978; *A Christmas Card*. Boston: Houghton Mifflin, 1978; *London Snow*. Boston: Houghton Mifflin, 1980; *World's End and Other Stories*. Boston: Houghton Mifflin, 1980; *The Mosquito Coast*. Boston: Houghton Mifflin, 1982; *The London Embassy*. Boston: Houghton Mifflin, 1983; *Half Moon Street*. Boston: Houghton Mifflin, 1984; *O-Zone*. New York: Putnam's, 1986. NONFICTION: *V. S. Naipaul*. New York: Africana Publishing, 1972; *The Great Railway Bazaar*. Boston: Houghton Mifflin, 1975; *The Old Patagonian Express*. Boston: Houghton Mifflin, 1979; *The Kingdom by the Sea*. Boston: Houghton Mifflin, 1983; *Sailing through China*. Boston: Houghton Mifflin, 1983; editor, *What Maisie Knew*, by Henry James. New York: Penguin Classics, 1984; *Sunrise with Seamonsters*. Boston: Houghton Mifflin, 1985; *The Imperial Way*, with Steve McCurry. Boston: Houghton Mifflin, 1985; *Patagonia Revisited*, with Bruce Chatwin. Boston: Houghton Mifflin, 1986.

Works about Theroux: Bell, Robert F. "Metamorphoses and Missing Halves: Allusions in Paul Theroux's *Picture Palace*." *Critique* 3 (1981), pp. 17–30; Chaney, Bev, comp. "Paul Theroux: A Bibliographical Checklist." *American Book Collector* 4 (1983), pp. 30–37; Coale, Samuel. "A Quality of Light: The Fiction of Paul Theroux." *Critique* 3 (1981), pp. 5–16. CA 33–36. CANR 20. CN. DLB 2.

John W. Mahon

JOHN KENNEDY TOOLE (1937–1969). Hailed as "one of the funniest books ever written," "a masterwork of comedy," and "a great rumbling farce," John Kennedy Toole's *A Confederacy of Dunces* (1980) has met with almost unanimous praise and won the Pulitzer Prize for fiction in 1981. Likened to a modern *Don Quixote*, and reminiscent of Jonathan Swift, the novel's intricate plot and rich characterizations combine in a hilarious double-edged satire of the modern age.

Born in 1937 in New Orleans, Louisiana, the son of John and Thelma Toole, a car salesman and a teacher, John Kennedy Toole spent much of his life in New Orleans, the city he captures so well in his novel. A bright and imaginative child, he skipped the first and fourth grades and graduated from high school early. At sixteen he entered Tulane University, having already written his first novel entitled "Neon Bible," still unpublished and embroiled in a legal controversy over publication rights. After graduating from Tulane in 1958, he left New Orleans for New York's Columbia University, where he earned his master's degree in English in 1959. He then taught for a year at the University of Southwestern Louisiana, where he purportedly got the idea for the character of Ignatius J. Reilly, possibly modeled on a friend and colleague in the English department. Toole wrote *A Confederacy of Dunces* while he was serving in the army in Puerto Rico from 1962–1963. Following his discharge, he returned to New Orleans, where he lived with his parents, taught at Saint Mary's Dominican College, and began work on a Ph.D. at Tulane University. For three years Toole negotiated with Simon and Schuster for publication of his novel, which was finally rejected in 1966. After resigning his job in December 1968, Toole traveled around the country for several months. On March 26, 1969, Toole was found dead in his car in Biloxi, Mississippi, a suicide by carbon-monoxide poisoning.

A Confederacy of Dunces would have remained unpublished were it not for the persistent efforts of Thelma Toole, who over the next seven years sent a single carbon copy of the novel to eight publishers, all of whom rejected it. In 1976, after great importunity, Thelma got Walker Percy* to read the manuscript. His reluctance soon turned to enthusiasm, and Percy sought to get the novel published, first by his own publisher, Farrar, Straus and Giroux, which rejected it. Finally, Louisiana State University Press published the novel in May 1980 to rave reviews. The Book-of-the-Month Club offered it as an alternative selection, Grove Press bought the paperback rights, and Twentieth Century-Fox obtained the rights to a film version. Over 40,000 hardcover copies were sold in less than a year, and in April 1981 the novel received the Pulitzer Prize.

The true-life fate of Toole's novel offers an ironic parallel to one of the major themes in *A Confederacy of Dunces*—the control of human destiny in a world apparently bereft of order and control, a theme appropriate to the comic mode. For Toole, as for Mark Twain, laughter is our best weapon against the vice and folly of our age, the defeat and despair of human history. Presiding over Toole's novel is one of the finest comic creations in contemporary fiction—Ignatius J. Reilly, a gargantuan, chronically unemployed, thirty-year-old mother's boy, dressed in baggy tweed trousers and a green hunting cap with ear flaps, and condemning a world in which he is fated to live, a world lacking "theological and geometrical standards," a world so given to excess and perversity that it causes Ignatius' pyloric valve to shut at the slightest provocation.

The grotesque and ironically named Ignatius is a practitioner of several of the Seven Deadly Sins, most notably Sloth and Gluttony, and he spends his time in his room writing diatribes against the twentieth century on Big Chief writing tablets, indulging in onanism, and pondering his favorite book, Boethius' *The Consolation of Philosophy*. Like Henry Adams, Ignatius feels out of place in this century and yearns for the return of the early middle ages. Ignatius declares: "With the breakdown of the Medieval system, the gods of Chaos, Lunacy, and Bad Taste gained ascendency," and "What had once been dedicated to the soul was dedicated to the sale." An accident forces him out of his self-preoccupation and into the world to seek a job. This unleashes an intricate series of overlapping events involving one of the strangest casts of characters ever assembled in one novel. It is a strength of Toole's work that his many characters are so finely realized and his seemingly diverse subplots unify so well at the end.

Such condemnation from so grotesque a hero suggests the double-edged nature of Toole's satire. Ignatius is both the *eiron* and the *alazon*, the self-deprecating wit and the boastful fool; he embodies what he rejects. This self-deceiving and hypocritical buffoon botches everything he attempts. But all the characters are subject to the capricious shifts of Lady Fortuna, who rules this comedy. In a real sense, the fate of the characters is connected to the fate of Ignatius' copy of Boethius' *The Consolation of Philosophy*, for the book gets passed around several times, even becoming a prop in a pornographic postcard. Ignatius is always urging people to read Boethius, but he himself neglects to take Boethius' teaching to heart—he is so concerned about Lady Fortuna's cycles that he forgets the consolations which Lady Philosophy can bring to a world in desperate straights. Perhaps what his mother says of him is right: "You learnt everything, Ignatius, except how to be a human being." If Ignatius is a genius—as Toole's epigraph from Jonathan Swift would imply—he is also the chief of the dunces. Yet Toole is kind here, allowing the good dunces to fare better than the bad ones. Ignatius himself is saved in the nick of time from committal to a psychiatric ward by the fortunate appearance of his old girlfriend Myrna Minkoff who carries him out of New Orleans. Thus ends a novel which, at least implicitly, offers standards by which to judge a world too highly committed to sensuality and materialism, while at the same time, pointing up the limitations of would-be reformers and critics.

SELECTED BIBLIOGRAPHY

Works by Toole: *A Confederacy of Dunces*. Baton Rouge: Louisiana State University Press, 1980; "Neon Bible," unpublished.

Works about Toole: Daigrepont, Lloyd M. "Ignatius Reilly and The Confederacy of Dunces." *New Orleans Review* 9 (1982), pp. 74–80; McNeil, David. "*A Confederacy of Dunces* as Reverse Satire: The American Subgenre." *Mississippi Quarterly* 38 (1984–1985), pp. 33–47; Miller, Keith D. "The Conservative Vision of John Kennedy Toole." *CCTE Proceedings* 4 (1983), pp. 30–34; Nelson, William. "The Comic Grotesque in Recent Fiction." *Thalia* 5 (1982–1983), pp. 36–40; Patteson, Richard F., and Thomas Souret. "The Consolation of Illusion: John Kennedy Toole's *A Confederacy of Dunces*." *The Texas Review* 4 (1983), pp. 77–87. CA 104.

John G. Parks

W

TENNESSEE WILLIAMS (1911 or 1914–1983). With Eugene O'Neill* and Arthur Miller, Tennessee Williams (Thomas Lanier Williams) stands foremost among American playwrights—in his realization of the inner worlds of his vivid characters and his successful utilization of expressionistic technique, colorful imagery, and poetry to explore modern man's alienation, the frustration and anxiety of lost souls, the mystery and pain of sex, the burden of guilt, the reality of death, and the need for community and love.

Williams' great work was behind him and he was entering what Reynolds Price calls the "drugged dementia" of his last twenty years when he became a Catholic in 1968. Five years later, he told Virginia Spencer Carr, "I liked the trappings of Catholicism, but its deeper meanings escaped me." Still, he told one interviewer that in times of distress he prayed, though he didn't think of God listening to individual appeals. (A later character observed of a death, "If I should say that the circle of light is the approving look of God, it would be romantic, which I refuse to be.") And his characters, Delma Eugene Presley has argued, reach out in their loneliness for community, for a savior—for the community that opens to faith, for the "little act of grace" that frees the iguana. What they often find is the "speechlessness of God that explains our lost world," leaving them seeking an answer to what he called "the affliction of loneliness that follows me like a shadow." Unfortunately, when his concern with religious themes is more overt, in the later plays, they tend to abandon the complexities of life that enrich his best work.

Williams' birth—in Columbus, Mississippi, on March 26, 1911 (some accounts give 1914)—into an old Southern family contributed to his work a dream of aristocratic elegance and sensitivity. It also contributed the polarities of conflict between what he called the Puritan and Cavalier—the callous, wandering father, a shoe salesman whose thirst for life echoes in Williams' crude Creole and Latin characters, and the genteel, hypochondriac mother, an Episcopalian rector's daughter, whose possessiveness appears to have scarred Williams for life. His family moved often; Williams himself became a lifelong wanderer. He rebelled against puritanism and found guilt. His sister Rose's schizophrenia gave him dramatic sympathy for the vulnerable and his failure to prevent Rose's prefrontal lobotomy doubled his guilt and burden.

His adolescent years in the urban ugliness of St. Louis apparently gave rise to the first of Williams' neuroses. After three years at the University of Missouri, where he began writing, he worked as a shoe salesman for two Depression years; hypochondria resulted. He continued writing plays at Washington University and Iowa where he took a B.A. With a publication in *Story* in 1939, he abandoned the names Thomas Lanier: Tennessee Indian fighters were among his ancestors and he had lived with his grandfather in Memphis.

From 1938 to 1944 he wandered south and west, working at odd jobs, writing plays, stories, poetry, and for the screen. *Battle Angels*, later reworked as *Orpheus Descending*, failed in Boston in 1940, but in 1944 *The Glass Menagerie* launched his career, first in Chicago, then with 561 performances in New York City, followed by *A Streetcar Named Desire* in 1947, which was even more successful and won the Pulitzer Prize. At least eight further successes and another Pulitzer Prize followed in the next fifteen years. Meanwhile, he published his first novel and a collection of shorter plays.

Long driven by success and worry about his family and friends, after the death of his closest companion, Frank Merlo, in 1962, Williams became a chronic hypochondriac and between drugs and alcohol, hospitalization and a death wish, his work was seriously compromised. Yet, while he "slept through the sixties," as he put it, he wrote on and on, his one way of sustaining dignity. He himself pointed to a long speech by Quentin, in *Small Craft Warnings* (1972), as his chief wisdom of that period, a confession of the "deadening coarseness" in the experience of most homosexuals so that "their act of love is like a jabbing of a hyperdermic needle to which they're addicted but which is more and more empty of real interest and surprise." The "startled" sense of "being myself, living" has passed; astonishment at life has given way to "Oh, well."

Williams choked to death during the night of February 24–25, 1983.

Tennessee Williams' plays and stories arise from the conflicts of his haunted experience. Frequently in his plays, it is the conflict between sexual passion and virility and sickness related to repression. He offers loss, helplessness close to psychological determinism, and loneliness enough for all. Few of his broken spirits are sufficiently heroic to be tragic; Nancy Tischler notes their slip from romantic to the disillusioned. Williams' sympathy is with the sensitive and passionate. Passion thwarted produces disease. As John MacNicholas observes, the gentleman caller and artist-poet bring hope as soul physicians. The sacramental Williams finds is in humanity itself, not God, this worldly—"the kindness of strangers" his protagonists seek. In despair, they look for community and learn to survive.

A *Glass Menagerie* offers Tom Wingfield's reflections on life in St. Louis with his mother, a faded aristocrat, and his crippled sister Laura who has retreated into a world of glass animals, particularly on an evening when he brings home a potential suitor who, it turns out, is already engaged, the evening when he fled his mother's possessive love—only to be burdened ever after by his guilt at abandoning Laura.

In *A Streetcar Named Desire*, the still sensitive if pretentious Blanche, strong in her quest for community and weak in guilt regarded her homosexual husband's suicide, clashes fatally with the brutal Stanley Kowalski who destroys her to save his marriage with her sister.

In *Summer and Smoke* (1948), the central characters pass in the night, the wayward John becoming responsible just as his puritanical wife becomes licentious. After *The Rose Tattoo* (1951), a celebration of D. H. Lawrence sexuality, and a glorification of sex in *Baby Doll* (1956), he experimented with fantasy in *Camino Real* (1953). In *Cat on a Hot Tin Roof* (1955), the senility of Big Daddy is joined with greed and sexual failure.

As Philip Armato has noticed, the major plays surrounding the year of Williams' conversion all address the problem of death. Sebastian Venable's encounter with the cannibalism of nature in *Suddenly Last Summer* (1960) leads to his despair of the human condition and he dies, deliberately, in despair. But throughout Venable is shadowed by allusions to St. Sebastian whose life and death in significant ways parallel his but lead to redemption. Shannon, angry with mother and God and in love with death in *The Night of the Iguana* (1962), is likewise matched—by Hannah who responds with love and courage and her grandfather's poem-prayer for the courage to cherish life. And in *The Milk Train Doesn't Stop Here Anymore* (1964), Sissy Goforth's fear of death is answered by an artist who teaches her to revere death. If Williams' characters lack religious faith, several of them practice love of neighbor.

Williams' stories, like his shorter plays, often prefigure his full-length plays; "Three Players in a Summer Game" is arguably superior to *Cat on a Hot Tin Roof*. Several build successfully on his youthful experience, developing themes found in his plays; others display experimentation with magic realism, such as "Desire and the Black Masseur." Here, too, his best work, lyrical and rich in characters, preceded the 1960s; afterward, something falls apart in his life and his rage obscures meaning.

The Roman Spring of Mrs. Stone (1948), the first of his two novels, is another story of decadence, of disintegration, this time transported to Rome, in which time is antagonist as in several of his plays.

His 1936 collection of poems, a modest volume, reflects the influences of Charles Baudelaire and Hart Crane, and, often explicitly, sexual and mental ills.

Williams rejected traditional realism for romance, but his objectivity and use of expressionist techniques, strong imagery, and poetry make his style singular. His work is often criticized for the preponderance of sick or violent characters, and he has far more failures than successes. But his explosive poetic style and power of characterization, particularly of women, and his portraits of modern alienation are more than balancing strengths.

SELECTED BIBLIOGRAPHY

Works by Williams: PLAYS: *The Glass Menagerie*. New York: Random House, 1945; *27 Wagons Full of Cotton and Other One-Act Plays*. Norfolk, Conn.: New Directions, 1946; *A Streetcar Named Desire*. New York: New Directions, 1947; *The Eccentricities of a Nightingale and Summer and Smoke*. New York: New Directions, 1948; *The Rose Tattoo*. New York: New Directions, 1951; *Camino Real*. Norfolk, Conn.: New Directions, 1953; *Cat on a Hot Tin Roof*. New York: New Directions, 1955; *Baby Doll*. New York: New Directions, 1956; *In the Winter of Cities*. Norfolk, Conn.: New Directions, 1956; *Orpheus Descending with Battle of Angels*. New York: New Directions, 1958; *Suddenly Last Summer*. New York: New Directions, 1960; *Period of Adjustment*. New York: New Directions, 1962; *The Night of the Iguana*. New York: New Directions, 1962; *The Milk Train Doesn't Stop Here Anymore*. New York: New Directions, 1964; *Kingdom of the Earth*. New York: New Directions, 1967; *Dragon Country*. New York: New Directions, 1970; *Small Craft Warnings*. New York: New Directions, 1972, London: Secker and Warburg, 1973. NOVELS: *The Roman Spring of Mrs. Stone*. New York: New Directions, 1948; *Moise and the World of Reason*. New York: Simon and Schuster, 1975, London: Allen, 1976. NON-FICTION: *Memoirs*. Garden City, N.Y.: Doubleday, 1975; *Where I Live: Selected Essays*. New York: New Directions, 1978.

Works about Williams: Falk, Signi Lenea. *Tennessee Williams*. New York: Twayne Publishers, 1961; Jackson, Esther. *The Broken World of Tennessee Williams*. Madison: University of Wisconsin Press, 1965; Nelson, Benjamin. *Tennessee Williams: The Man and His Work*. New York: Ivan Obolensky, 1961; Tischler, Nancy. *Tennessee Williams: Rebellious Puritan*. New York: Citadel, 1961; Williams, Edward Dakin. *Remember Me to Tom*. New York: Putnam's, 1963. AW. CA 7–8. CD. CN. DLB 7. TCA.

William H. Slavick

Z

JOHN RESTER ZODROW (1944–). John Zodrow questions the nature of man, of "sin," of reality; investigates man's relationship to his environment and to his fellows; and considers the savage behind the civilized facade—man at his most primitive, man at his most self-sacrificing. His books engage in an interesting counterpoint—the cynical to the idealistic. He depicts violence and cruelty alongside heroism and love; he exposes the greed and corruption of the Church, and yet demonstrates the good and the true that endure. A sense of contradiction, of duality dominates his works: civilized men who torture and rape; savages who love and sacrifice themselves for others; a truly good man who seeks to do right but who is really the anti-Christ; a Church built on spiritual truths but controlled by financial, economic, and political machinations. His novels give a highly detailed sense of place and character; they provide fast-paced, gripping entertainment with multilevel action and plotting, and yet they have a strong, underlying moral base.

Born on the Colby Ranch in northwest Kansas on October 20, 1944, John Zodrow grew up on a sheep farm near the Solomon River. He attended Loyola of Los Angeles, where he received a B.A. in 1969 and an M.A. in 1971. After spending nine years as a seminarian in a California monastery, he left to pursue a career as a radio producer, filmmaker, teacher, and writer. At present he divides his time between Los Angeles, where he teaches writing at Loyola University, the mountains of Ketchum, Idaho, and a cattle ranch in the Arkansas Ozarks. When he is not teaching or writing (novels and screenplays for films and television), he is hunting, ranching, or socializing with the residents of Little Flint Hollows, Arkansas. Of his own works Zodrow remarks that he prefers stories in which characters "are tried by extreme circumstances" and "a complex, psychological insight" results.

His first novel, *Bright Green Hell* (1978), researched in the Amazon jungles of Peru, reflects an interest not merely in the flora and fauna of that primitive region, but also in tribal peoples, their customs and survival techniques, their interaction within the tribe, between tribes, and with "modern," "civilized" man. Zodrow suggests that beneath a veneer of culture, civilized or primitive, all men are basically the same, with natural drives and instincts and a need to belong. The story focuses on a twelve-year-old Peruvian, Alissa, the pampered daughter of a millionaire, who, together with her mother and a Vietnam veteran, are the sole survivors of a plane crash in the Amazon. The mother, constantly protesting that they are *not* savages, soon commits suicide, but the veteran, an eccentric backwoodsman, knowledgeable about survival in the wild but malad-justed to "civilized" life, teaches the daughter to survive by reverting to "sav-age" patterns, becoming a part of the terror which threatens them, and learning to see with jungle eyes, to strike out with violence and brutality when necessary, to take pleasure in the comfort of the moment. When he dies, mauled by a jaguar, the young girl must continue on her own until rescued from quicksand and taken to wife by the chieftain of a fierce, unconquered local tribe.

In the Name of the Father (1980), a tale of demonic influence and the coming of the anti-Pope, demonstrates how evil could come of seeming good. It questions motives and methods as it portrays an ambitious cardinal, who has longed to be pope, carefully grooming his resistant, adopted son for that position.This book provides a close-up look at the political maneuverings and strategies involved in progression up the Vatican hierarchy, and the non-religious motives behind Church assistance worldwide. It also traces the prophecies concerning the anti-Pope of *Revelations* and speculates that democracy is the one thing that could destroy the Church, for it would breed factions that would subvert a "spiritual world . . . into a temporal, military power" (p. 304). Its central concept is that of evil deriving from blinded men who only want to do good.

Vatican Gold (1983) contrasts the charity of Catholics who donated millions to save Jewish survivors of the death camps with the stinginess and greed that Zodrow feels characterized the Vatican under Pope Pius XII. It forcefully attacks the Vatican for its "neutrality" during World War II, its quiescent acceptance of the massacre of the Jews, its heavily Germanic post-war political superstruc-ture, its protection of rich war criminals, its obsession with amassing wealth by taking advantage of the end-of-the-war depression, its isolation from its fellow Catholics, its injurious and cruel stand on divorce, its system of giving dispen-sations to the wealthy before the poor, and its lack of charity toward the oppressed and the persecuted. Despite so negative a portrait of the Vatican, Zodrow finds hope in the election of a new pope who clearly seeks to rectify the wrongs of his predecessor.

Though exciting entertainment, with intriguing plots and perilous encounters, Zodrow's novels are tough-minded analyses of the dual nature of man: selfish-ness, greed, cruelty, and lust; also heroism, humanity, self-sacrifice, and love. They demonstrate the reality behind the facade—for good or for evil.

SELECTED BIBLIOGRAPHY

Works by Zodrow: NOVELS: *Bright Green Hell*. New York: Dell Publishing, 1978; *In the Name of the Father*. New York: Dell Publishing, 1980; trans. into Spanish and published as *En el nombre del Padre*. Planeta, 1982; *Vatican Gold*. New York: Dell Publishing, 1983. PLAYS: *All Out*. Dramatic Publishing, 1981; "Raisin' Wine," unpublished. SCRIPTS: *The Ultimate Thrill*. Centaur Films, 1975; *Kate Bliss and the Tickertape Kid*. ABC, 1978; *The Hunter*. Paramount, 1979; *Insight*. 1970's television series.

    Works about Zodrow: Review of *Bright Green Hell*. *Publishers Weekly* (23 May 1977), p. 245.

Gina Macdonald

BIBLIOGRAPHICAL NOTE

The fecund field of contemporary Catholic American writing has attracted surprisingly little scholarship. Biographical dictionaries of Catholic writers have become outdated. Matthew Hoehn edited *Catholic Authors: Contemporary Biographical Sketches, 1930–1947* (New York: J. J. Little and Ives, 1948; rep. Detroit: Gale Research, 1981). *The Book of Catholic Authors*, edited by Walter Romig (Milwaukee: Romig and Company, 1942–1963) includes American writers, but the bulk of the series is given over to English and European writers. *Stories of Our Century by Catholic Authors*, edited by John Gilland Brunini and Francis X. Connolly (Philadelphia and New York: Lippincott Co., 1949) contains brief biographical sketches of twenty-four twentieth-century Catholic authors, only ten of whom are American and almost all of whom were published primarily before 1945.

Interest in contemporary Catholicism has produced little criticism of Catholicism in works by contemporary Catholic American authors. Sister M. Regis, I.H.M., editor, considers the problem of defining Catholic literature generally in *The Catholic Bookman's Guide: A Critical Evaluation of Catholic Literature* (New York: Hawthorn Books, Inc., 1962). *The Vision Obscured: Perceptions of Some Twentieth-Century Catholic Novelists*, edited by Melvin J. Friedman (New York: Fordham University Press, 1970), concentrates on English and European writers, but includes essays on J. F. Powers and Flannery O'Connor. Like Friedman, Albert Sonnenfeld prefers non-American writers, mentioning only briefly Mary Gordon in his *Crossroads: Essays on the Catholic Novelists* (York, S.C.: French Literature Publications Co., 1982). Robert H. Brinkmeyer, *Three Catholic Writers of the Modern South* (Oxford, Miss.: University Press of Mississippi, 1985) studies the writings of Allen Tate, Caroline Gordon, and Walker Percy. Gene Kellogg's *The Vital Tradition: The Catholic Novel in a Period of Convergence* (Chicago: Loyola University Press, 1970), like Sonnenfeld's *Crossroads*, articulates clearly the narrow definition of the Catholic novel as springing from the mainstream of Catholic thinking. Kellogg examines the convergence of the Catholic novel with the secular world in Revolutionary France, Protestant England, and twentieth-century America. Arguing that Catholic novelists find their creative inspiration in the abrasiveness between Catholicism and secular society or between Catholic interpretations of Catholic dogma within the Church itself, Kellogg believes that Catholicism has become so confluent with the values of a secular society that it is now impossible to discern a distinctly Catholic novel. Hence, the American writers J. F. Powers and Flannery O'Connor have written the last words of truly Catholic fiction, according to Kellogg's definition. However, Kellogg's criticism, published in 1970, could not have taken into account Walker Percy, for example, whose works sustain the abrasive tone of self-examination which generates intense creative energy.

Like book-length studies, few scholarly articles explore more generally the question of American Catholic literature, even though it would be less difficult to find articles on individual authors. Aside from the academic concerns, journalistic interest continues high in contemporary Catholic writing. Two examples are Andrew Greeley's "Fiction and the Religious Imagination" (*America*, April 6, 1985, pp. 274–77), which considers the cross-fertilization powers of the religious imagination and the process of storytelling. In "Catholics Coming of Age: The Literary Consequences" (*New Catholic World*, July/August, 1985, pp. 148–52), William O'Rourke examines the reasons behind the popularity of writers like Greeley, James Carroll, and Mary Gordon.

INDEX

Note: page numbers in italics indicate main entries.

ABOUT THE CONTRIBUTORS

LINDA BANNISTER, director of University Writing Programs and assistant professor of English at Loyola Marymount University in Los Angeles, is the author of articles on the composing process and writing across the curriculum. She is working on rhetorical theory text linking creativity, metaphor making, and writing across the curriculum.

DEBORAH J. BARRETT, assistant professor of English and director of the Writing Specialization at Houston Baptist University, has published on Sir Walter Scott, Walt Whitman, and Walker Percy. She has just finished an article entitled "Katherine Anne Porter's Search for Belief," which is part of her planned book on the influence of Porter's religious beliefs on her fiction.

RUTH BARTON, who teaches English at Colorado College, has published essays on modern poetry. She is currently working on research on children's literature set in Great Britain.

SISTER ANN EDWARD BENNIS, S.S.J., professor of English at Chestnut Hill College, teaches courses on the age of Chaucer and Milton. She served for five years on the editorial and contributors' boards of the British bibliography of English and American literature.

ANTHONY J. BERRET, a Jesuit priest and assistant professor of English at St. Joseph's University in Philadelphia, teaches American Literature and has published articles on Mark Twain in *American Literary Realism* and *American Studies*.

RICHARD A. BETTS, assistant professor of English at Pennsylvania State University, Delaware County Campus, has published articles on John Barth, Thomas Berger, and William Styron and is presently engaged in research on the contemporary American historical novel.

EDITH BLICKSILVER, associate professor of literature at Georgia Institute of Technology, Atlanta, helped organize MELUS (The Society for the Study of the Multi-Ethnic Literature of the United States) and served as the first secretary. She is first vice president of the College English Association, and edited *The Ethnic American Woman: Problems, Protests, Lifestyle*, cited as the Best Non-Fiction Book of the Year by the Dixie Council of Authors and Journalists. She is currently completing the compilation of how ethnic American women cope creatively with their lives.

ROBERT H. BRINKMEYER, JR., assistant professor of English at Tulane University, has written extensively on Southern literature and is the author of *Three Catholic Writers of the Modern South*, a study of Allen Tate, Caroline Gordon, and Walker Percy. He is currently working on a book about Flannery O'Connor.

MARY LYNN BROE, Louise R. Noun Professor of women's studies and English at Grinnell College, is author of *Protean Poetic: The Poetry of Sylvia Plath*, the forthcoming *Silence and Power: A Reevaluation of Djuna Barnes* (Southern Illinois) and co-editor of *Alien and Critical: Women Writers in Exile, Volumes I and II* (North Carolina). Her work on women writers and feminist theory has been widely published.

ANN CRAMER has recently earned her Ph.D. from the University of Chicago where she wrote her dissertation on John O'Hara.

JOHN R. DUNLAP holds a joint appointment as lecturer in English and classics at Santa Clara University, where he teaches English, Latin, and Greek. He is currently at work on a textbook in argumentation.

JANET EGLESON DUNLEAVY is professor of English at the University of Wisconsin-Milwaukee. A former Guggenheim Fellow and Fulbright Scholar, she is the author of books and articles on Mary Lavin, George Moore, Elizabeth Bowen, James Joyce, Flannery O'Connor, Anthony Trollope, and other major writers of novels and short fiction, as well as the cultural history that is the matrix of their work. She is currently completing a study of the art of Mary Lavin and, with Gareth W. Dunleavy, a definitive biography of Douglas Hyde.

JOSEPH J. FEENEY, SJ, professor of English at St. Joseph's University, has written about Gerard Manley Hopkins in *Victorian Studies, The Hopkins Quarterly,* the *Victorians Institute Journal,* and two forthcoming collections of essays. He has also published studies on American and modern British writers, and is currently working on Hopkins and on the religious imagination in contemporary America.

LARAINE R. FERGENSON, professor of English at Bronx Community College, City University of New York, holds a doctorate form Columbia University and has published articles on English and American literature. She is a contributing editor to the forthcoming *Health Anthology of American Literature* and author of *A Stylistic Approach to Composition,* to be published by Holt, Rinehart, and Winston.

MARY KATERI FITZGERALD is assistant professor of English at Siena College. She is currently engaged in editing *Mark Twain: Ritual Clown,* a collection of critical essays.

MELVIN J. FRIEDMAN, professor of comparative literature and English at the University of Wisconsin-Milwaukee, is the author or editor of a dozen books; his most recent title is *Critical Essays on Flannery O'Connor* (1985). He serves on the editorial boards of a number of journals, including *Contemporary Literature, Studies in American Fiction, Studies in the Novel, Journal of Beckett Studies, Yiddish, Journal of American Culture,* and *International Fiction Review.*

MARY E. GILES, professor of humanities and religious studies at California State University, Sacramento, publishes in the areas of Spanish mysticism and women's spirituality. She is the founding editor of *Studia Mystica,* a quarterly journal on mysticism and the arts. Her books include *The Feminist Mystic, When Each Leaf Shines, The Poetics of Love: Meditations with John of the Cross,* and the translation from Spanish, with critical introduction, of Francisco de Osuna's *Third Spiritual Alphabet.*

PATRICIA GLOSSOP has an M.A. in comparative literature from the Graduate School, City University of New York, and is currently in the Ph.D. program there. The author of a number of articles about broadcasting and the arts, she is on the staff of *Newsweek.*

ROSE BASILE GREEN, professor of English, chaired the Department of English at the University of Tampa prior to being a professor at Temple University, Philadelphia, and ultimately chaired the Department of English at Cabrini College, Radnor, Pennsylvania. Socially and civically involved on numerous boards of directors, she is recognized chiefly as a critic and a contemporary poet. Her published works include *The Italian-American Novel—A Document of the Interaction of Two Cultures*, *The Cabrinian Philosophy of Education*, a translation of *The Life of St. Frances Cabrini*, and volumes of poetry including *The Violet and the Flame, To Reason Why, Primo Vino, Seventy-Six for Philadelphia, Woman the Second Coming, Songs of Ourselves, The Pennsylvania People, Challenger Count Down*, and *Day by Day*. She is currently working on a long epic related to the five centuries of American history.

VICTOR GRETO is a poet and a short story writer.

LOUIS HASLEY was professor emeritus of English at Notre Dame University until his death in 1985.

JAMES CRAIG HOLTE, associate professor of English at East Carolina University, has published in the fields of American literature, film, ethnic studies, and popular culture. He is currently completing a study of ethnic American autobiographies.

RICHARD L. HOMAN is assistant professor in fine arts at Rider College, Lawrenceville, New Jersey. He has published studies of modern American and British drama, and of medieval English drama and theatre.

TIM HUNT, dean of Deep Springs College, is the author of *Kerouac's Crooked Road: Development of a Fiction* and *Lake County Diamond*, a collection of poems. He is currently completing a collected edition of the poetry of Robinson Jeffers.

LEO E. KEENAN, JR., professor of English, is chairman of the English Department at St. Bonaventure University. His special interest is in American literature of the second half of the nineteenth century.

EILEEN KENNEDY, professor of English at Kean College of New Jersey, Union, directs the M.A. in liberal studies. Her scholarly articles have appeared in journals like the *James Joyce Quarterly, English Literature in Transition, Eire-Ireland, The Irish Literary Supplement*, and *The Hopkins Journal* as well as in collections such as *Modern Irish Literature* and *Contemporary Irish Writing*.

BURT J. KIMMELMAN, Ph.D. candidate in English literature at the City University of New York Graduate Center, is a poet and co-editor of *Poetry New York*, a journal of poetry and translations; his essay on William Bronk and Wallace Stevens will appear in a forthcoming issue of *Credences: A Journal of Twentieth Century Poetry and Poetics*. He is also a co-editor of a forthcoming new edition of Thomas Hoccleve's *Regiment of Princes*.

FRANK KINAHAN is associate professor of English and general studies at the University of Chicago, where he teaches Anglo-Irish literature and modern drama and directs the university theater. His *Texts in Context: Folklore, Occultism, and the Early Work and Thought of William Butler Yeats* is forthcoming from Allen & Unwin.

DAVID KIRBY, professor of English at Florida State University in Tallahassee, is the author or editor of ten volumes, including reference books, cultural and literary criticism, and poetry. His *Saving the Young Men of Vienna* won the University of Wisconsin's Brittingham Prize in Poetry, and among his other awards is a writing fellowship from the National Endowment for the Arts.

VICTOR A. KRAMER is professor of English at Georgia State University in Atlanta. He has published books on James Agee and Thomas Merton. He co-authored a reference guide on Andrew Lytle, Walker Percy, and Peter Taylor. He has edited books on Frederick Law Olmsted, literary theory, and Walker Percy. Books on Merton and Agee are forthcoming from Cistercian Publications and the University of Tennessee Press.

LEWIS A. LAWSON is professor of English at the University of Maryland, College Park. He is the author of *Another Generation* and *Following Percy* and coeditor of *Conversations with Walker Percy*.

DAVID LLOYD, assistant professor of English at Le Moyne College, has published articles and reviews on Emily Dickinson, Seamus Heaney, and David Jones, and on other British and American poets. His poetry and fiction have appeared in numerous magazines in the United States and the United Kingdom.

JOHN LOWE, associate professor of English at Louisiana State University, Baton Rouge, also teaches English and Afro-American studies courses at Harvard University each summer. He has published essays on William Faulkner, Afro-American and native American literatures, theories of ethnic humor, and various other topics in journals such as *American Quarterly*, *Appalachian Journal*, and *Studies in American Indian Literatures*. He has just completed a book on Faulkner and religion and is now writing *The Americanization of Ethnic Humor*.

ANDREW F. MACDONALD, assistant professor of English at Loyola University of New Orleans, has published articles about William Shakespeare, applied linguistics, and detective fiction. He is currently working on a study of the conventions of crime fiction.

GINA MACDONALD is an assistant professor at Loyola and Tulane universities in New Orleans. She has published articles on Robert Greene, William

Shakespeare, and detective fiction. She is currently working on a major study of the conventions of crime fiction.

JOHN W. MAHON, associate professor of English at Iona College in New Rochelle, New York, has published on William Shakespeare and Evelyn Waugh and is preparing studies of Mary Gordon, Brian Moore, and Piers Paul Read.

DAVID MASON has taught English at the University of Rochester and at Colorado College. He has published essays, reviews, translations, stories, and poems in such journals as *The Literary Review*, *The New Orleans Review*, and *Translation*.

ANNE KEELER McBRIDE, an English teacher at Camden Catholic High School, Cherry Hill, New Jersey, formerly taught writing, research, and literature courses at Georgia State, Rutgers-Camden, and Temple universities. She has also published in *The Southern Literary Journal*.

JAMES L. McDONALD, professor of English at the University of Detroit, has published essays on James Joyce, Theodore Dreiser, Vladimir Nabokov, Ernest Hemingway, Graham Greene, John Barth, Saul Bellow, Joseph Heller, John Knowles, and the Southern agrarians.

A. J. MONTESI is a professor of English at Saint Louis University, St. Louis, Missouri, where he teaches modern literature and creative writing. He is the author of five books of poetry: *Micrograms*, *Windows and Mirrors*, *Robots and Gardens*, *Five Dinners to Quick Lunch* with Richard Hill, and *Al and Richard, Indeed*; one critical study *Radical Conservatism: The Southern Review* (1935–1942); one children's book, *Peter Bently: the Super-Sleuth Cat*; and four plays.

JOHN MARC MUCCIOLO is a graduate student at The City University of New York.

THOMAS J. NAPIERKOWSKI, professor of English at the University of Colorado in Colorado Springs, has written widely on ethnic American literature with special attention to the works of Polish-American authors.

LEO F. O'CONNOR, professor and director of American studies at Fairfield University, is the author of *Religion in the American Novel: The Search for Belief*. He is currently completing work titled *The Protestant Novel in American literature: A Selective Annotated Bibliography*, to be published by Garland Publishing Company.

ALISON E. O'HARA, a law student at the University of Colorado, is the niece of poet Frank O'Hara.

ALEXANDRA HENNESSEY OLSEN is associate professor of English at the University of Denver. Her published work includes *Guthlac of Croyland: A Study of Heroic Hagiography and Speech, Song*, and *Poetic Craft: The Artistry of the Cynewulf Canon*. She has recently completed *"Between Ernest and Game" : The Literary Artistry of the "Confessio Amantis"* and is working on a study entitled *The Influence of Old English Poetry on Anglo-Latin Hagiography*.

WILLEM O'REILLY is currently writing a book on contemporary American Catholic playwrights. He is an administrator in the Office of Program Development at Rutgers University.

GENARO M. PADILLA, assistant professor of English at the University of California, Berkeley, has recently edited *The Short Stories of Fray Angelico Chavez* for the University of New Mexico Press. He is currently preparing a study of the emergence of Chicano autobiography.

LOUIS J. PARASCANDOLA, adjunct assistant professor of English at Long Island University, has had articles accepted for *British Women Writers*. He is currently completing his dissertation on Captain Marryat for the CUNY/Graduate Center. He also has a master's degree in library science and works for the New York Public Library.

JOHN G. PARKS is associate professor of English at Miami University in Oxford, Ohio, where he specializes in twentieth-century American literature, especially fiction since World War II. He has published essays and reviews in a number of scholarly journals.

MICKEY PEARLMAN, assistant professor of English at Iona College, is the author of "Re-Inventing Reality: Patterns and Characters in the Novels of Muriel Spark," essays on Rumer Godden, Margery Sharp, Jan Struther, Honor Tracy, Irini Spanidou, and Francesca Duranti, and is working on a book about Tillie Olsen and on two collections of articles on contemporary American women writers.

NEALE R. REINITZ is a professor of English at the Colorado College and a faculty fellow of the Newberry Library.

ROBERT A. RUSS is instructor in English at West Georgia College in Carrollton. He is currently engaged in work on Claude McKay and is writing a screenplay.

CAROLANN RUSSELL, assistant professor of English and chair of the creative writing program at Southern Connecticut State University, is the author of *The Red Envelope*, a collection of poetry. She is a former poetry editor of *Cutbank* magazine and a former co-editor, with Madeline DeFrees, of *GiltEdge, New Series*. She has completed two more books, for which she is seeking publication.

FRANK L. RYAN is professor of English at Stonehill College.

BARRY SARCHETT, assistant professor of English at Incarnate Word College in San Antonio, Texas, has published on modern and contemporary American fiction. He is currently working on a study of Lionel Trilling and the nature of ideology.

LINDA SCHLAFER, assistant professor and assistant to the chairman of the English Department, at Marquette University, has published work on Flannery O'Connor and is particularly interested in aesthetics and creative writing.

ROBERT M. SEBASTIAN is an attorney and retired Petroleum Company executive. He is a former vice-president of the Philadelphia Board of Public Education, and the author of *Memoirs of a Paid Mourner*.

JOHN SHERIDAN, head librarian at the Colorado College, dates his disenchantment with literary criticism from the fine grade he got for a terrible paper he wrote on Studs Lonigan and Stephen Dedalus.

JOHN L. SIMONS, professor of English at the Colorado College, has published in the fields of American literature and American film, including articles on John Berryman, Nathanael West, William Carlos Williams, Philip K. Dick, and Sam Peckinpah.

WILLIAM H. SLAVICK, professor of English at the University of Southern Maine, is the author of *DuBose Heyward* and the editor of Elizabeth Madox Robert's *I Touched White Clover*. He is editing a volume of papers of the Downeast Southern Renascence Conference and Elizabeth Madox Roberts' letters and papers and writing a study of economic motifs in William Faulkner's fiction.

JOHN R. THELIN is a free-lance writer and poet.

CHARLES TRAINOR is assistant professor of English at Siena College in Loudonville, New York. In addition to work in eighteenth-century British literature, he has published on several twentieth-century authors including P. G. Wodehouse and Edward Hoagland.

DANIEL J. TYNAN is professor English at the Colorado College. He has written on John Gregory Dunne and Mary Gordon, as well as on Herman Melville and Edgar Allan Poe.

EDWARD VASTA, professor of English at the University of Notre Dame, speciaizes in Middle English literature. He teaches courses in humanities and writing, as well as in English literature. His publications include *The Spiritual Basis of Piers Plowman, Middle English Survey: Critical Essays, Interpretations of Piers Plowman*, and *Chaucerian Problems and Perspectives*.

JOSEPH H. WESSLING is associate professor of English at Xavier University in Cincinnati, Ohio. His poems and occasional prose pieces have appeared in various publications.

LAMAR YORK, associate professor of English at DeKalb College, the University System of Georgia, is editor of *The Chattahoochee Review*, a literary quarterly. His published work concerns Old English elegiac poetry, contemporary Southern fiction, pedagogy, and the Middle East.

THOMAS DANIEL YOUNG, Gertrude Conaway Vanderbilt Professor of English Emeritus at Vanderbilt University, has written or edited twenty-five books, including *Gentleman in Dustcoat*, the authorized biography of John Crowe Ranson, *The Past in the Present*, and *The Literary Correspondence of Allen Tate and Donald Davidson*. He is currently working on *The Correspondences of Allen Tate and Andrew Lytle*.